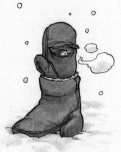

This is just how I feel personally, but the most
exciting part of any superhero movie or comic
is the process of becoming a hero. And I mean
"exciting," which goes a level beyond "interesting"
in how it creates a sense of anticipation.

So I set out to make a story about becoming the
greatest hero there ever was that would perfectly
capture that excitement, even for myself as the author.

The stage for that was set way earlier than
I expected, but I've still got a ton of story in
me, so I'm going ahead at full throttle.

KOHEI HORIKOSHI

MY HERO ACADEMIA

7

SHONEN JUMP Manga Edition

STORY & ART **KOHEI HORIKOSHI**

TRANSLATION & ENGLISH ADAPTATION **Caleb Cook**
TOUCH-UP ART & LETTERING **John Hunt**
DESIGNER **Shawn Carrico**
SHONEN JUMP SERIES EDITOR **John Bae**
GRAPHIC NOVEL EDITOR **Mike Montesa**

Printed in the U.S.A.

Published by VIZ Media, LLC
P.O. Box 77010
San Francisco, CA 94107

10 9 8 7 6 5 4 3 2 1
First printing, February 2017

www.viz.com

PARENTAL ADVISORY
MY HERO ACADEMIA is rated T for Teen and is recommended for ages 13 and up. This volume contains fantasy violence.
ratings.viz.com

www.shonenjump.com

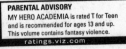

MY HERO ACADEMIA

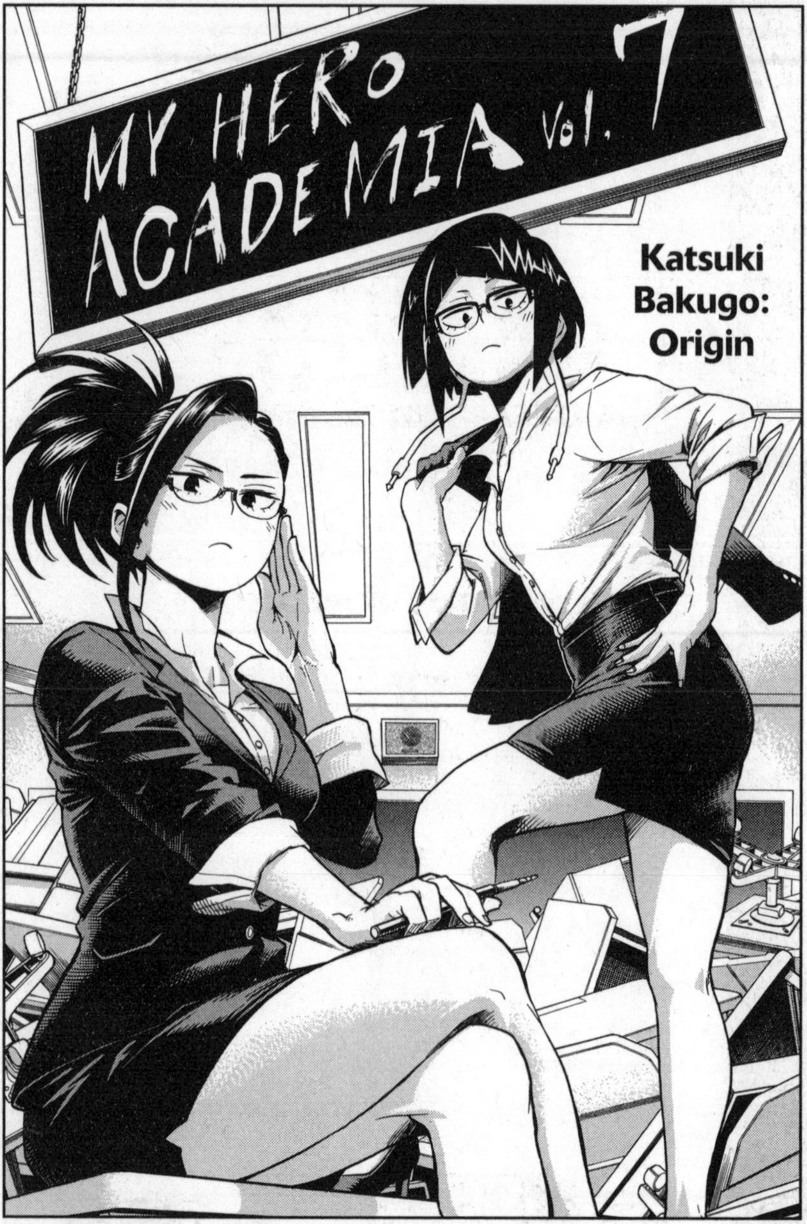
MY HERO ACADEMIA Vol. 7

Katsuki Bakugo: Origin

KOHEI HORIKOSHI

SHONEN JUMP MANGA

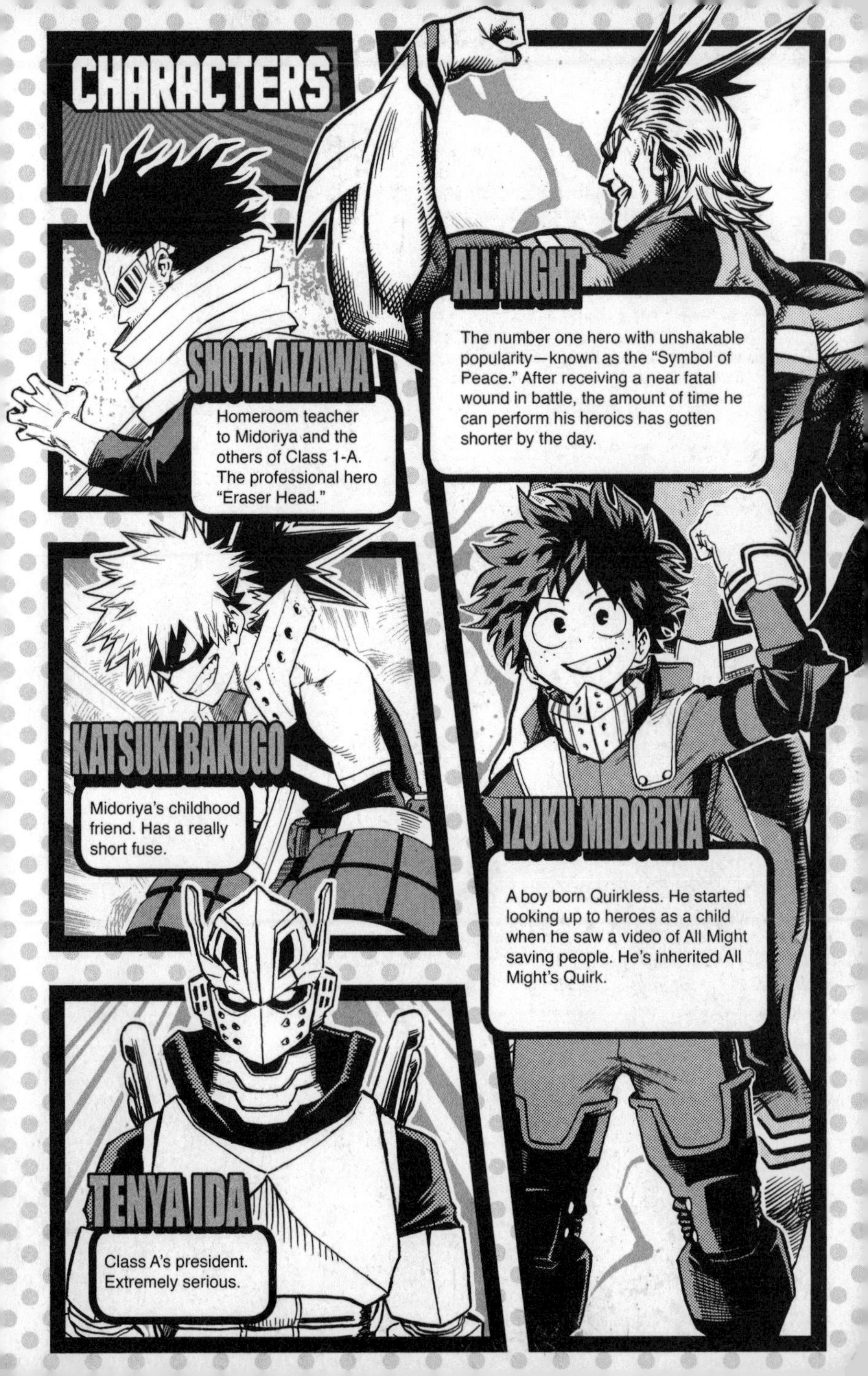
CHARACTERS
ALL MIGHT
The number one hero with unshakable popularity—known as the "Symbol of Peace." After receiving a near fatal wound in battle, the amount of time he can perform his heroics has gotten shorter by the day.
IZUKU MIDORIYA
A boy born Quirkless. He started looking up to heroes as a child when he saw a video of All Might saving people. He's inherited All Might's Quirk.
SHOTA AIZAWA
Homeroom teacher to Midoriya and the others of Class 1-A. The professional hero "Eraser Head."
KATSUKI BAKUGO
Midoriya's childhood friend. Has a really short fuse.
TENYA IDA
Class A's president. Extremely serious.

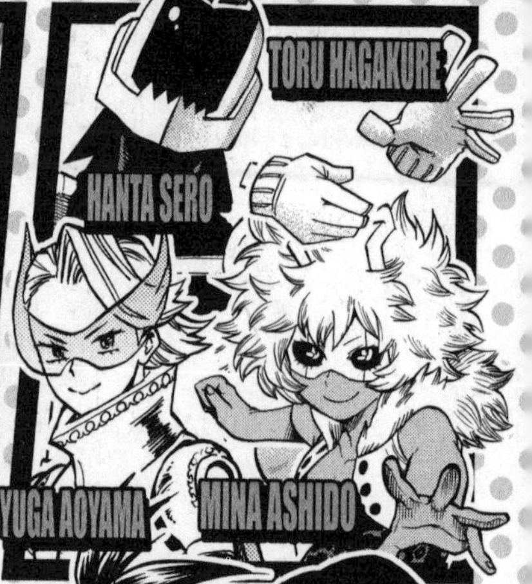
TORU HAGAKURE
HANTA SERO
MINA ASHIDO
YUGA AOYAMA

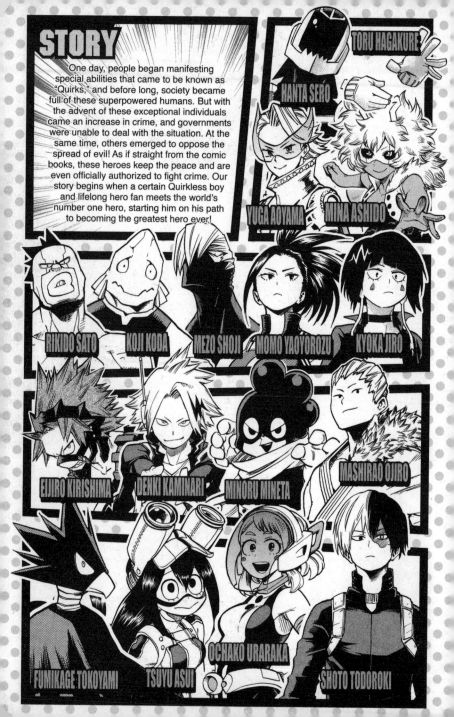

STORY

One day, people began manifesting special abilities that came to be known as "Quirks," and before long, society became full of these superpowered humans. But with the advent of these exceptional individuals came an increase in crime, and governments were unable to deal with the situation. At the same time, others emerged to oppose the spread of evil! As if straight from the comic books, these heroes keep the peace and are even officially authorized to fight crime. Our story begins when a certain Quirkless boy and lifelong hero fan meets the world's number one hero, starting him on his path to becoming the greatest hero ever!

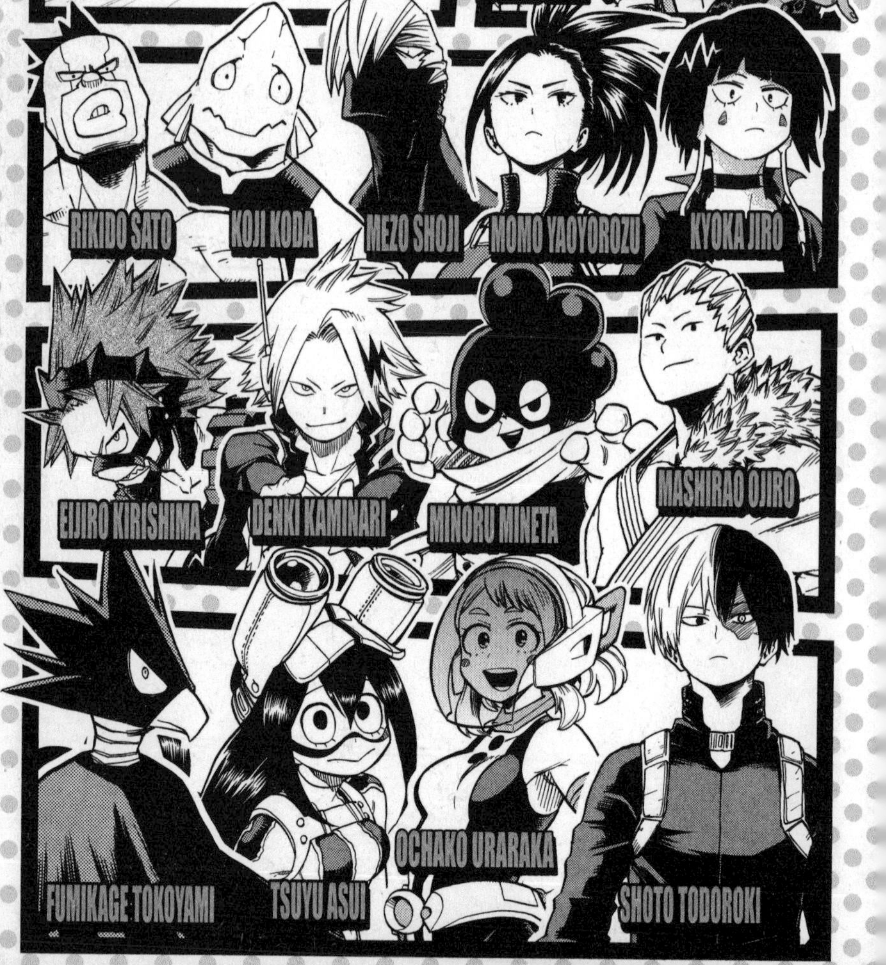
KYOKA JIRO
MOMO YAOYOROZU
MEZO SHOJI
KOJI KODA
RIKIDO SATO
MASHIRAO OJIRO
MINORU MINETA
DENKI KAMINARI
EIJIRO KIRISHIMA
SHOTO TODOROKI
OCHAKO URARAKA
TSUYU ASUI
FUMIKAGE TOKOYAMI

MY HERO ACADEMIA

Vol. 7

CONTENTS

Katsuki Bakugo: Origin

RECOVERY GIRL'S
FIELD MEDICAL STATION
OPEN

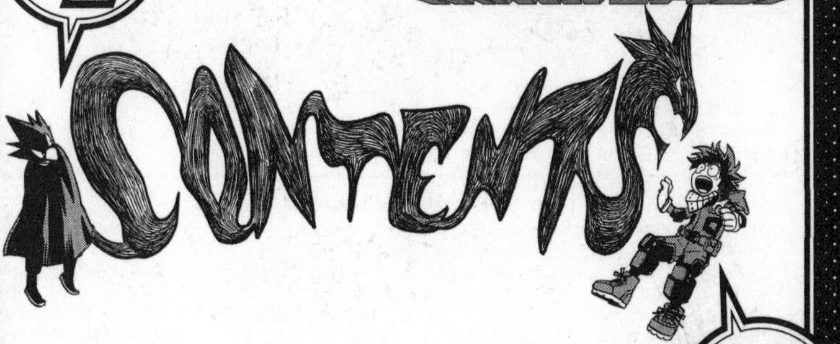

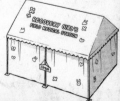

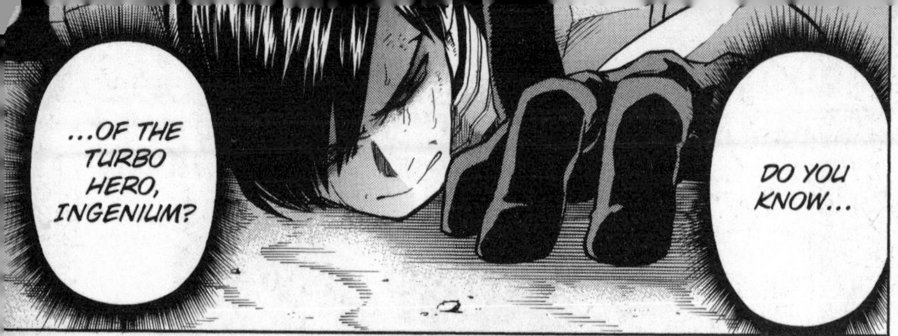
DO YOU KNOW...
...OF THE TURBO HERO, INGENIUM?

NO. 54 - RE: INGENIUM

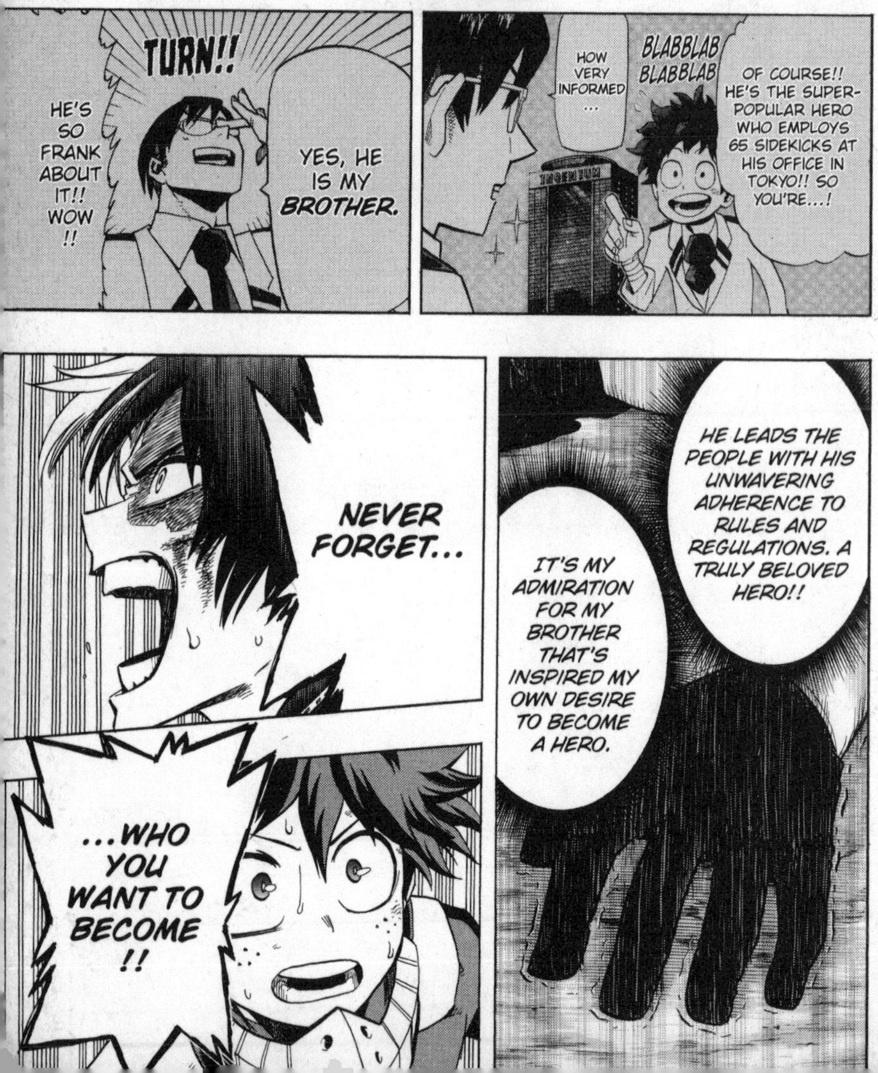
OF COURSE!! HE'S THE SUPER-POPULAR HERO WHO EMPLOYS 65 SIDEKICKS AT HIS OFFICE IN TOKYO!! SO YOU'RE...!
BLABBLAB BLABBLAB
HOW VERY INFORMED ...
INGENIUM
YES, HE IS MY BROTHER.
TURN!!
HE'S SO FRANK ABOUT IT!! WOW !!
HE LEADS THE PEOPLE WITH HIS UNWAVERING ADHERENCE TO RULES AND REGULATIONS. A TRULY BELOVED HERO!!
IT'S MY ADMIRATION FOR MY BROTHER THAT'S INSPIRED MY OWN DESIRE TO BECOME A HERO.
NEVER FORGET...
...WHO YOU WANT TO BECOME !!

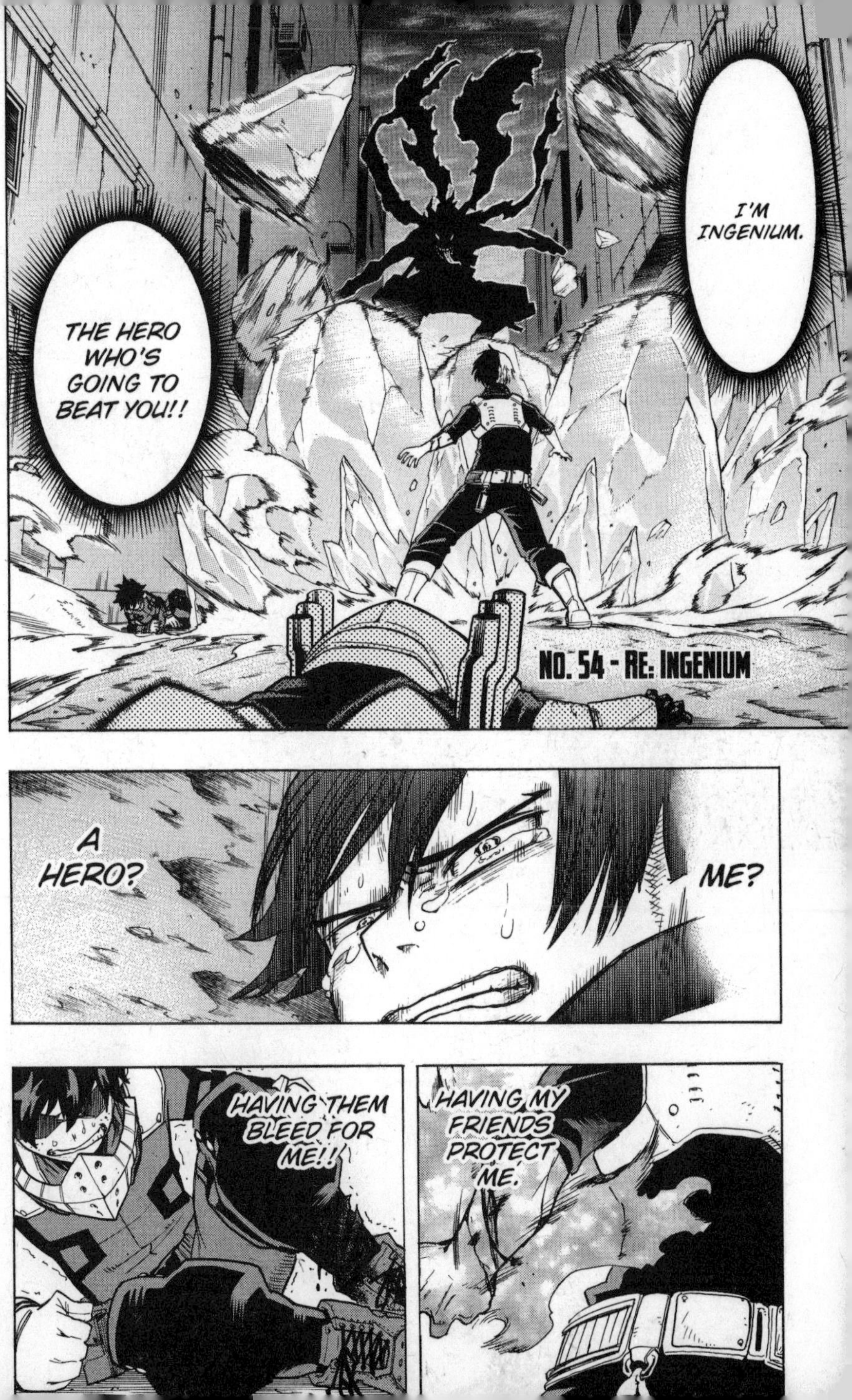
I'M INGENIUM.
THE HERO WHO'S GOING TO BEAT YOU!!
NO. 54 - RE: INGENIUM
ME?
A HERO?
HAVING MY FRIENDS PROTECT ME.
HAVING THEM BLEED FOR ME!!

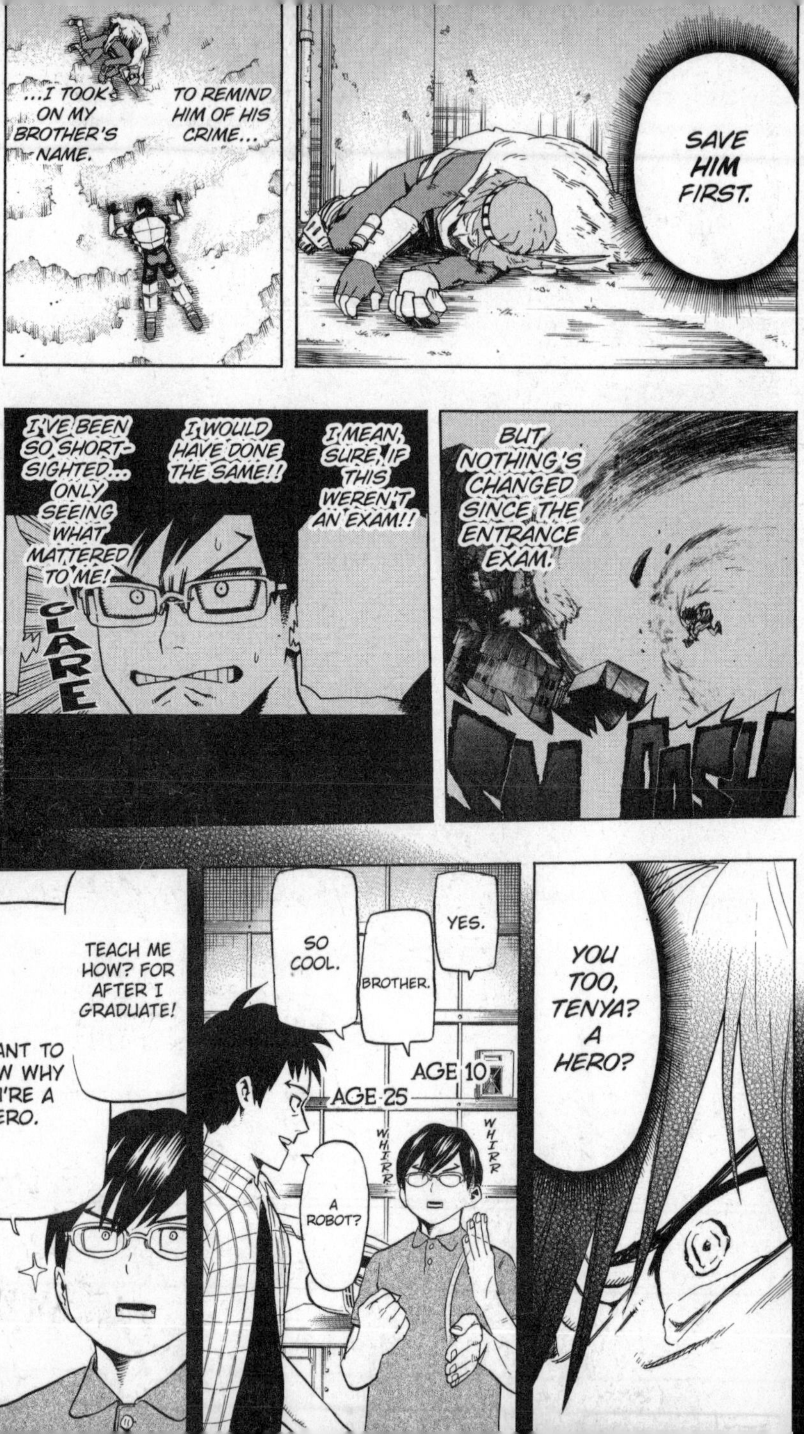
SAVE HIM FIRST.
TO REMIND HIM OF HIS CRIME...
...I TOOK ON MY BROTHER'S NAME.
BUT NOTHING'S CHANGED SINCE THE ENTRANCE EXAM.
I MEAN, SURE, IF THIS WEREN'T AN EXAM!!
I WOULD HAVE DONE THE SAME!!
I'VE BEEN SO SHORT-SIGHTED... ONLY SEEING WHAT MATTERED TO ME!
GLARE
YOU TOO, TENYA? A HERO?
YES.
BROTHER.
SO COOL.
AGE 10
AGE 25
WHIRR
WHIRR
A ROBOT?
TEACH ME HOW? FOR AFTER I GRADUATE!
I WANT TO KNOW WHY YOU'RE A HERO.

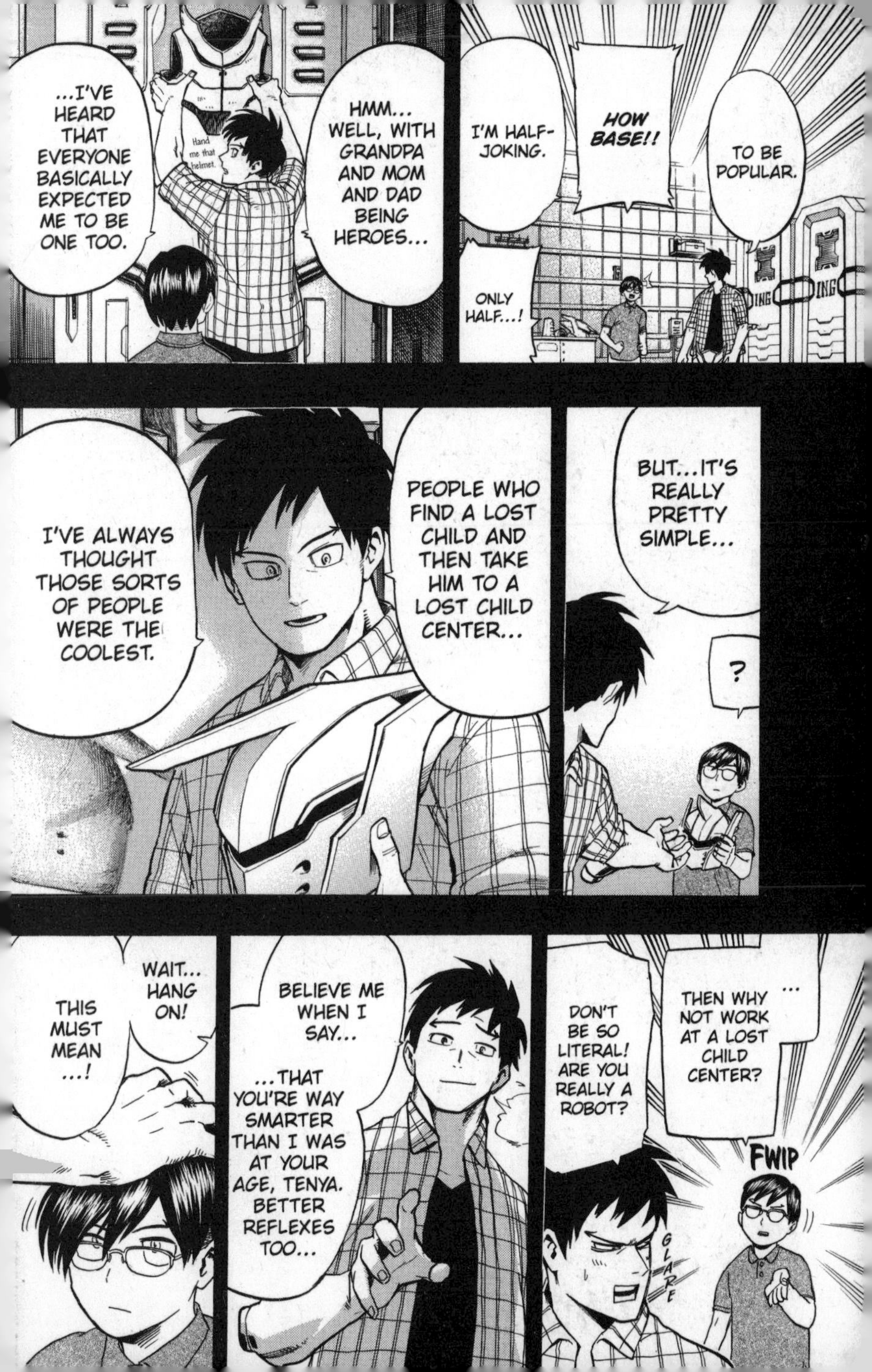
TO BE POPULAR.
HOW BASE!!
I'M HALF-JOKING.
ONLY HALF...!
HMM... WELL, WITH GRANDPA AND MOM AND DAD BEING HEROES...
Hand me that helmet.
...I'VE HEARD THAT EVERYONE BASICALLY EXPECTED ME TO BE ONE TOO.
BUT...IT'S REALLY PRETTY SIMPLE...
?
PEOPLE WHO FIND A LOST CHILD AND THEN TAKE HIM TO A LOST CHILD CENTER...
I'VE ALWAYS THOUGHT THOSE SORTS OF PEOPLE WERE THE COOLEST.
...
THEN WHY NOT WORK AT A LOST CHILD CENTER?
FWIP
DON'T BE SO LITERAL! ARE YOU REALLY A ROBOT?
GLARE
BELIEVE ME WHEN I SAY...
...THAT YOU'RE WAY SMARTER THAN I WAS AT YOUR AGE, TENYA. BETTER REFLEXES TOO...
WAIT... HANG ON!
THIS MUST MEAN ...!

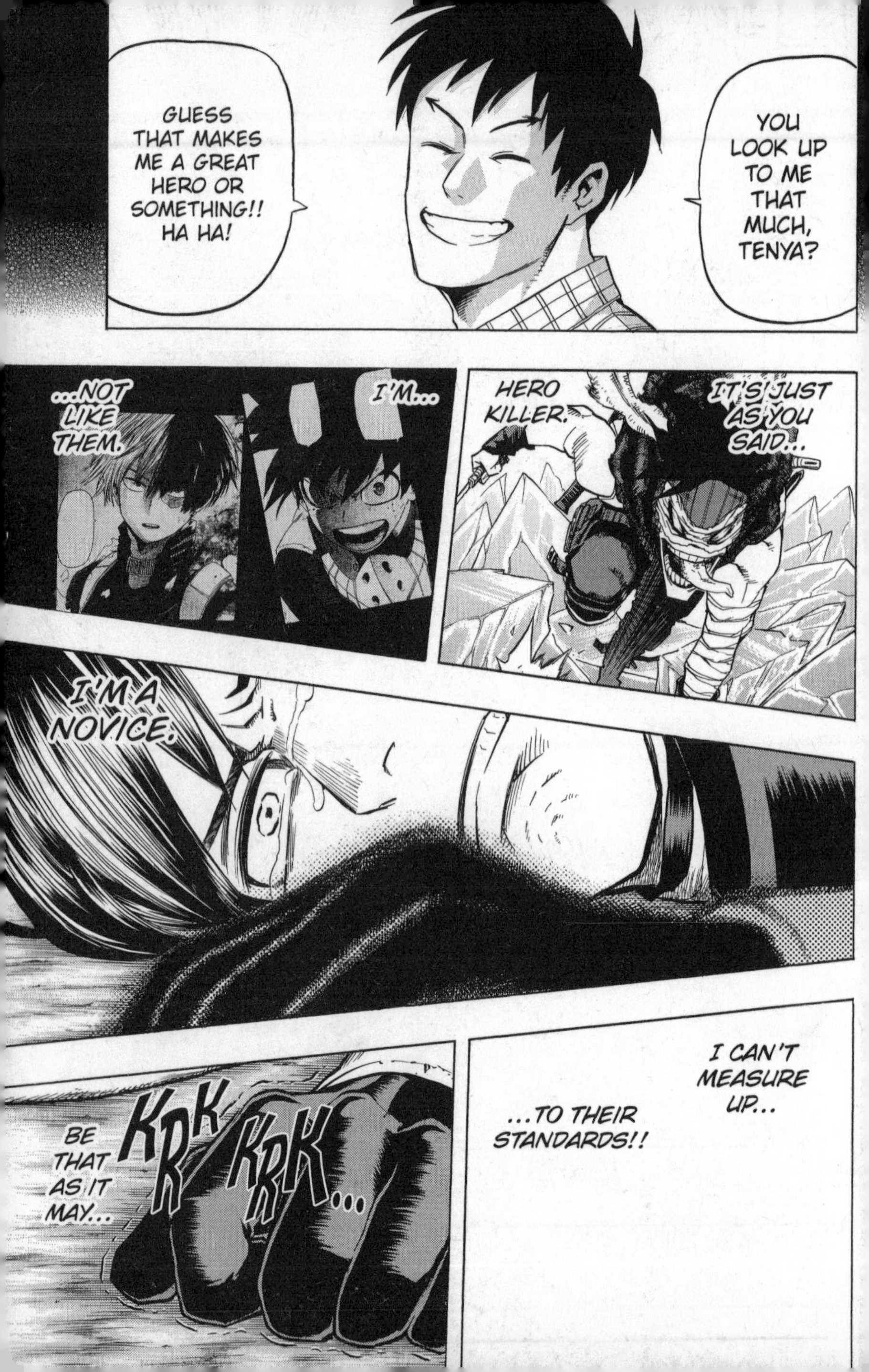
YOU LOOK UP TO ME THAT MUCH, TENYA?
GUESS THAT MAKES ME A GREAT HERO OR SOMETHING!! HA HA!
IT'S JUST AS YOU SAID...
HERO KILLER.
I'M...
...NOT LIKE THEM.
I'M A NOVICE.
I CAN'T MEASURE UP...
...TO THEIR STANDARDS!!
BE THAT AS IT MAY...
KRK KRK...

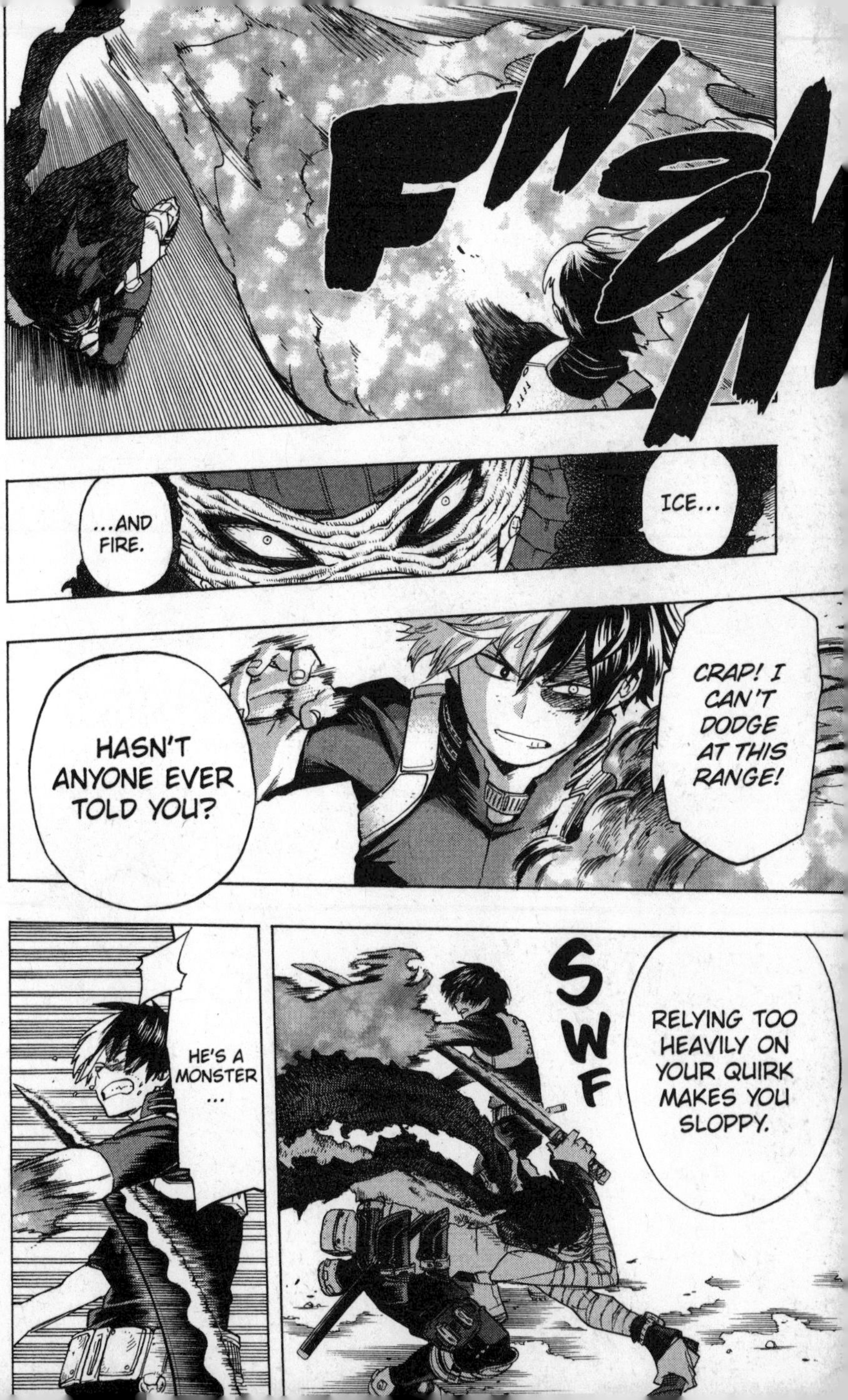
FWOOM
ICE...
...AND FIRE.
CRAP! I CAN'T DODGE AT THIS RANGE!
HASN'T ANYONE EVER TOLD YOU?
RELYING TOO HEAVILY ON YOUR QUIRK MAKES YOU SLOPPY.
SWF
HE'S A MONSTER ...

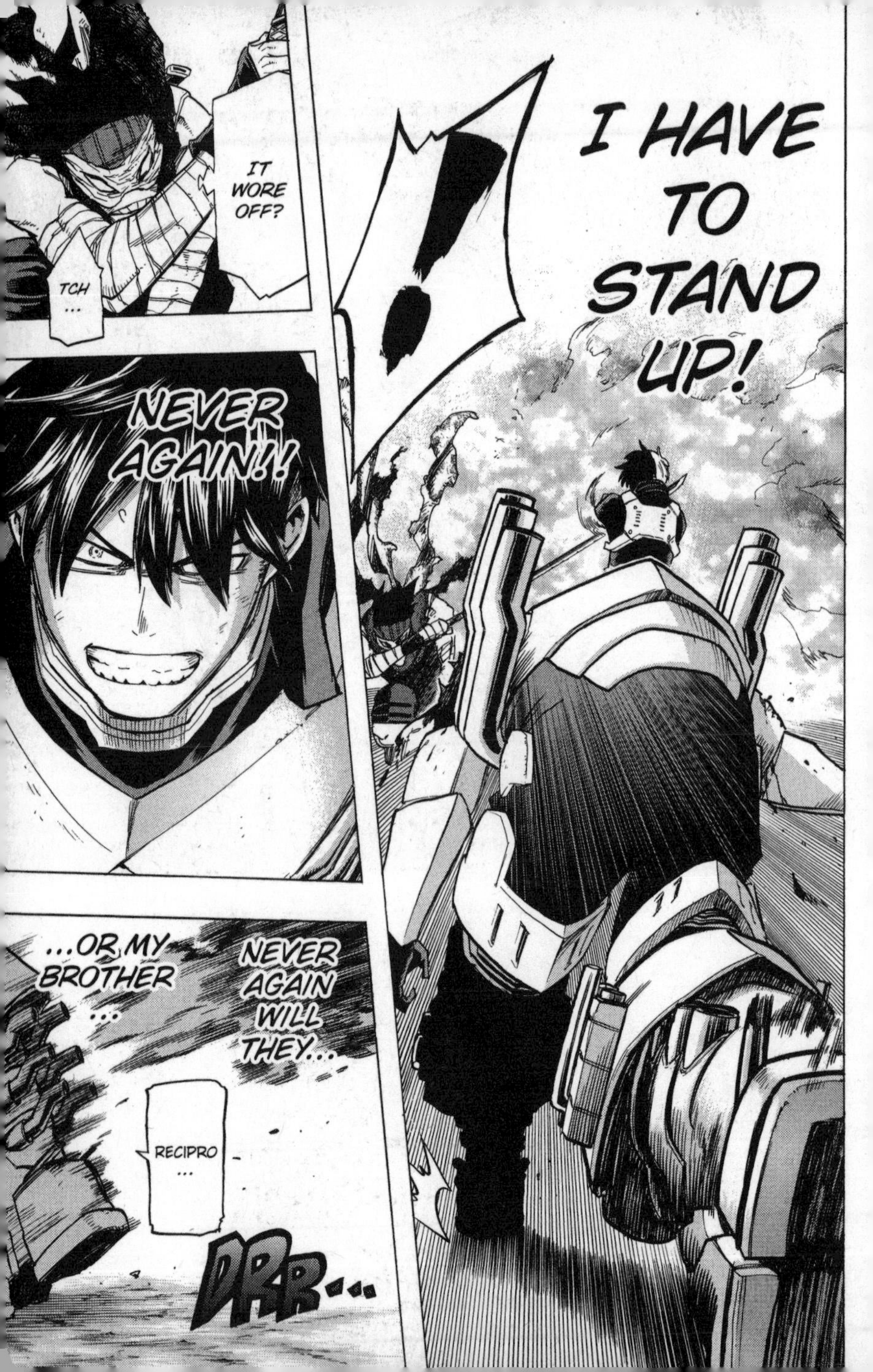
I HAVE TO STAND UP!
!
IT WORE OFF?
TCH ...
NEVER AGAIN!!
NEVER AGAIN WILL THEY...
...OR MY BROTHER ...
RECIPRO ...
DRR...

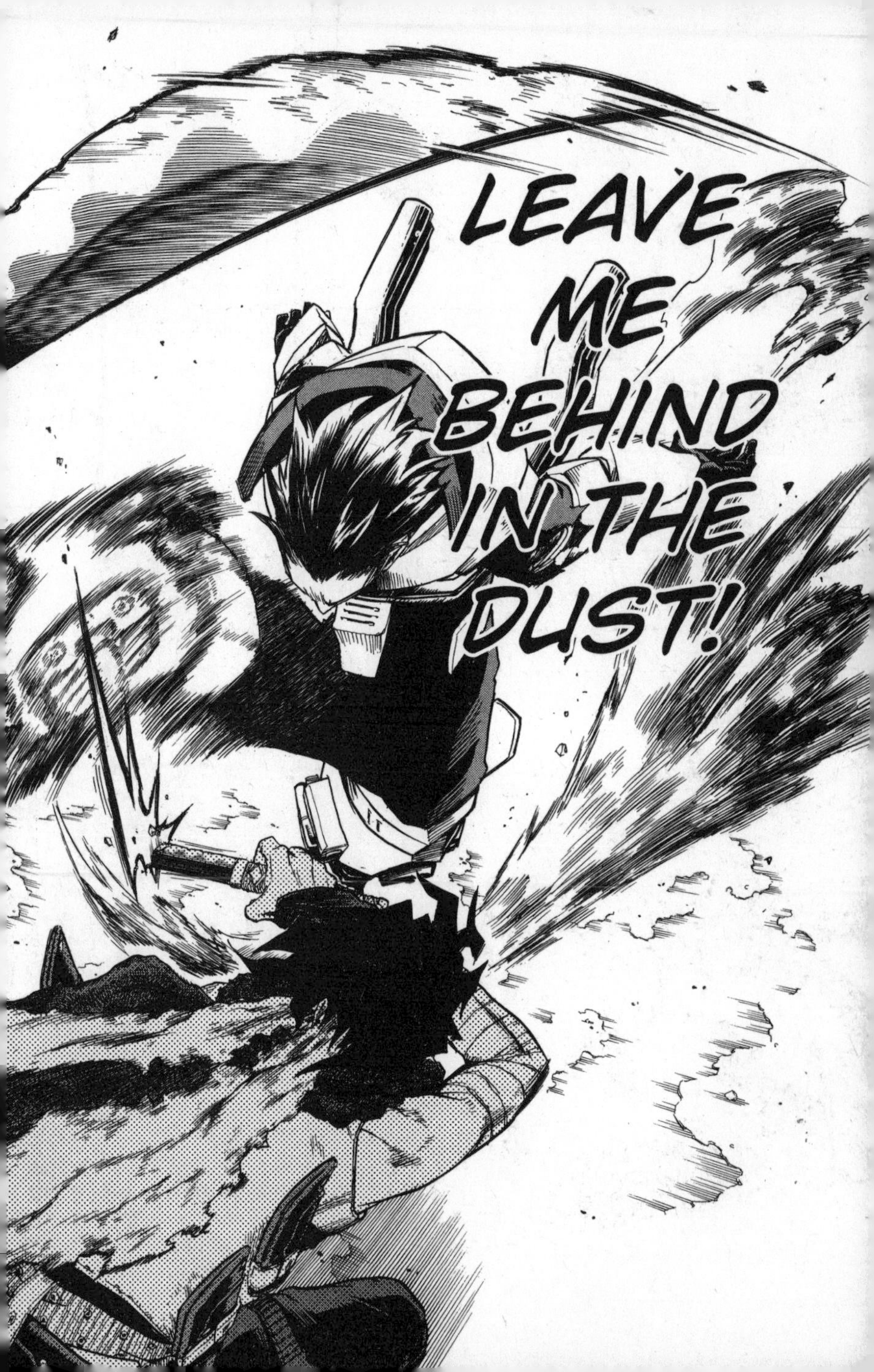
LEAVE ME BEHIND IN THE DUST!

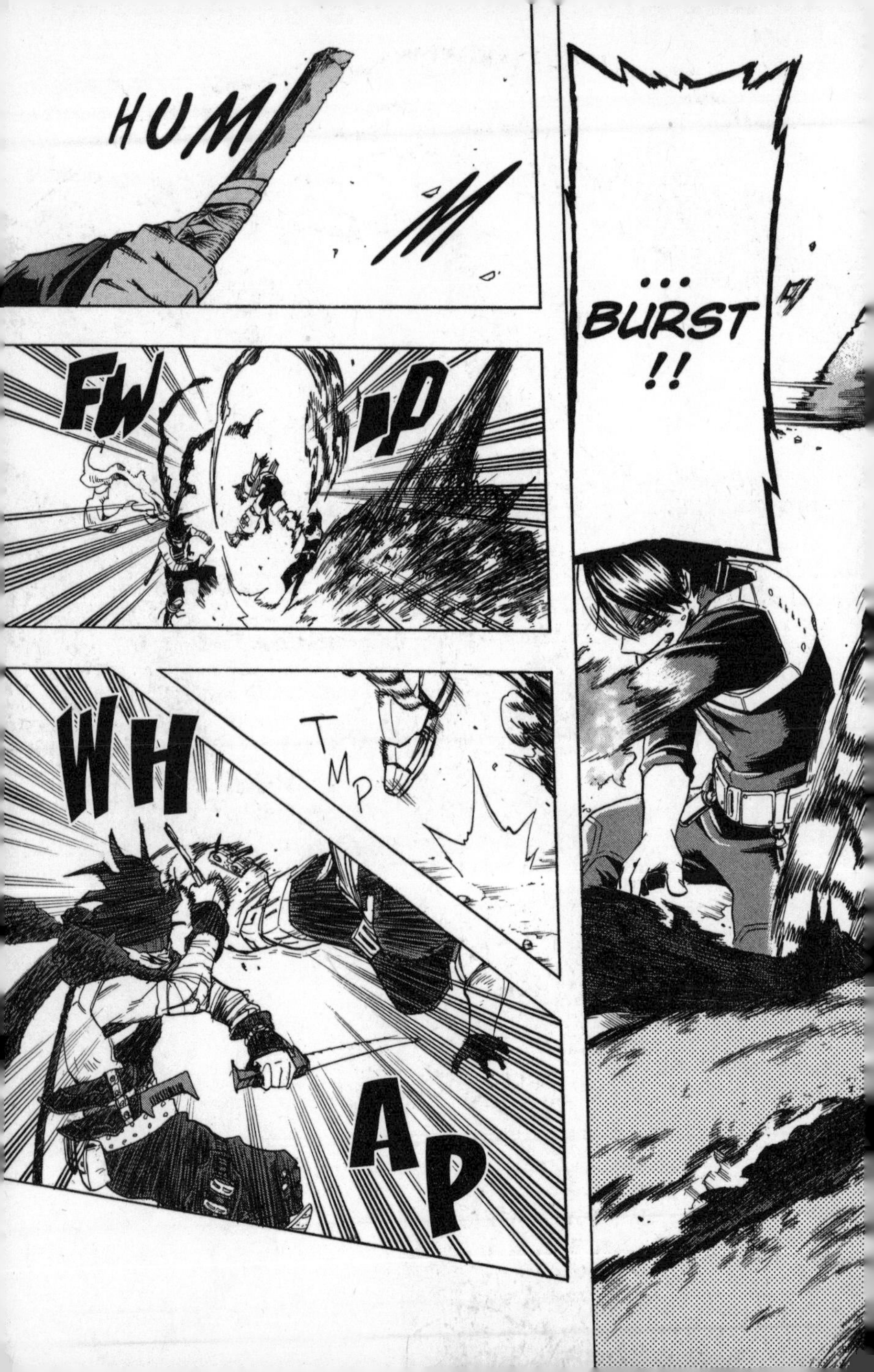
...BÜRST!!
HUM
M
FW
P
WH
TMP
AP

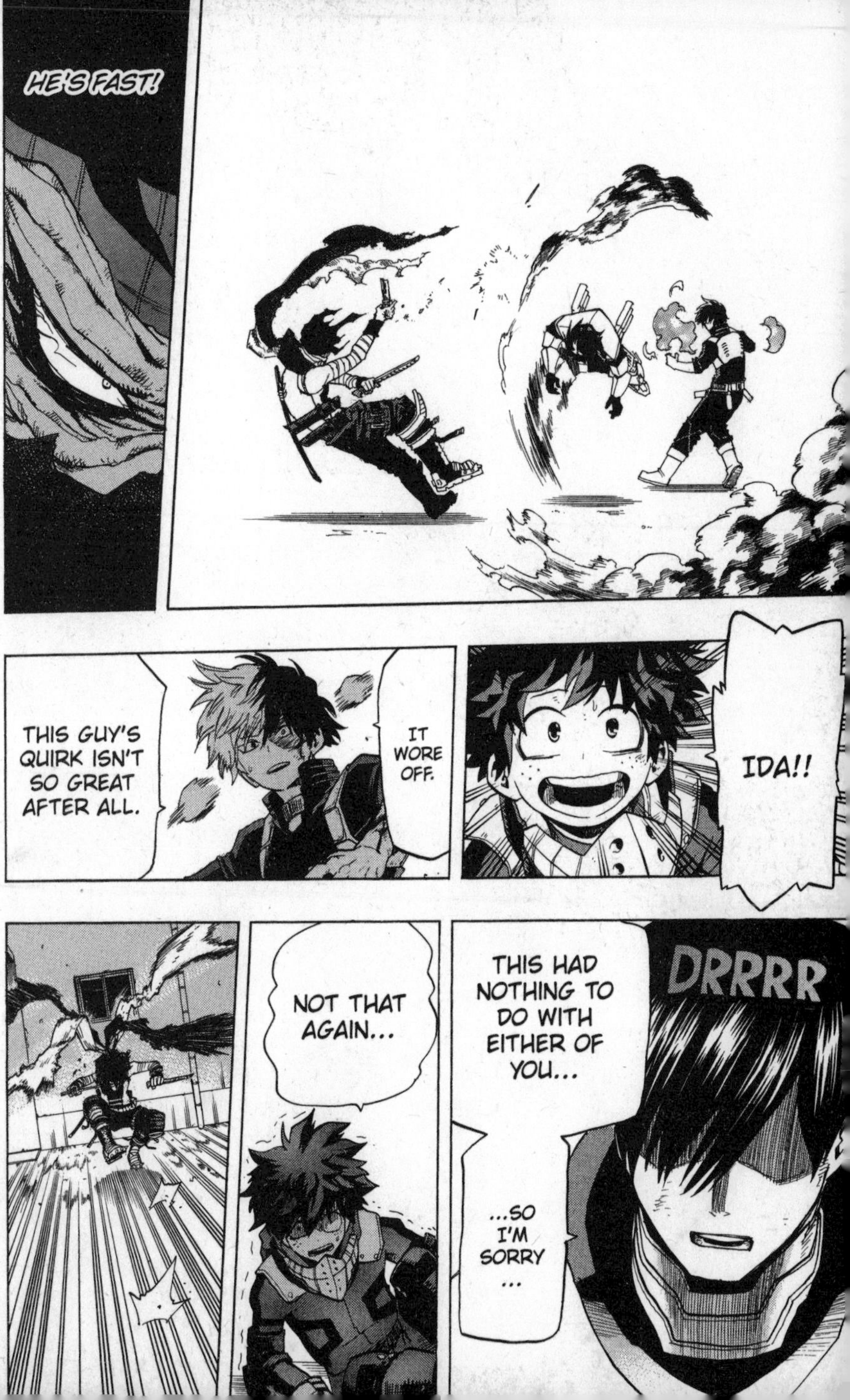
HE'S FAST!
IDA!!
IT WORE OFF.
THIS GUY'S QUIRK ISN'T SO GREAT AFTER ALL.
DRRRR
THIS HAD NOTHING TO DO WITH EITHER OF YOU...
...SO I'M SORRY ...
NOT THAT AGAIN...

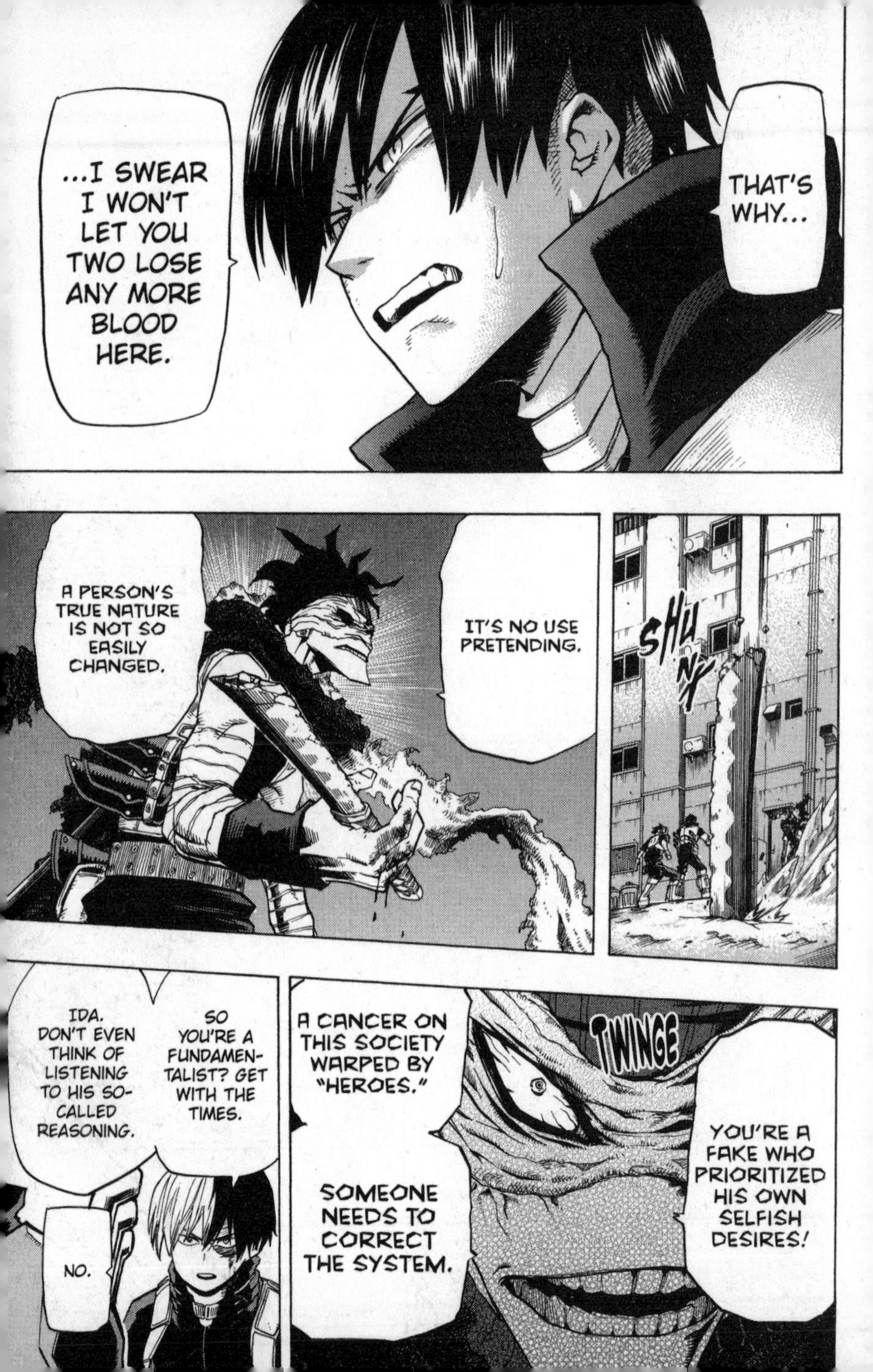
THAT'S WHY...
...I SWEAR I WON'T LET YOU TWO LOSE ANY MORE BLOOD HERE.
SHUNK
IT'S NO USE PRETENDING.
A PERSON'S TRUE NATURE IS NOT SO EASILY CHANGED.
TWINGE
YOU'RE A FAKE WHO PRIORITIZED HIS OWN SELFISH DESIRES!
A CANCER ON THIS SOCIETY WARPED BY "HEROES."
SOMEONE NEEDS TO CORRECT THE SYSTEM.
SO YOU'RE A FUNDAMENTALIST? GET WITH THE TIMES.
IDA. DON'T EVEN THINK OF LISTENING TO HIS SO-CALLED REASONING.
NO.

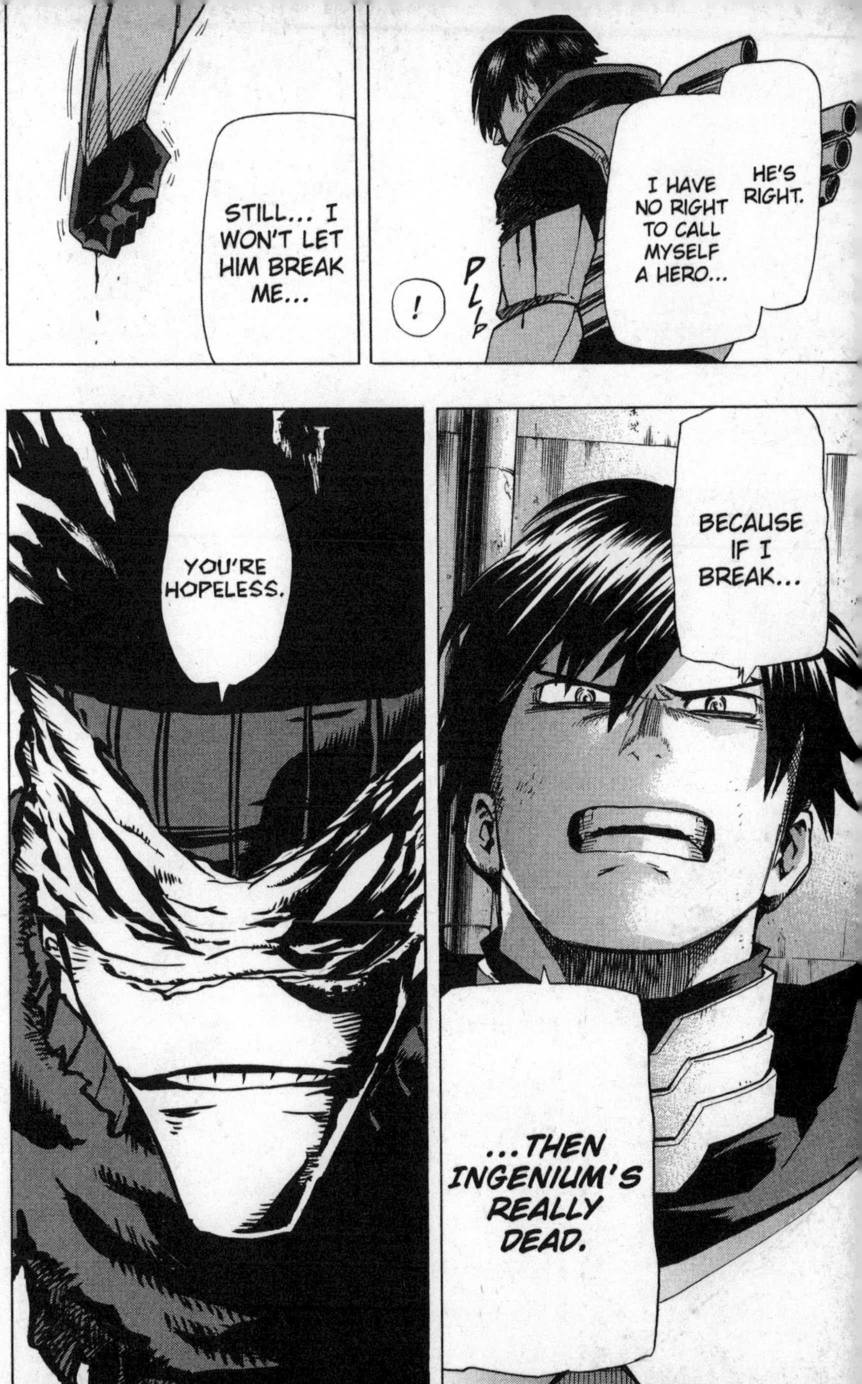
HE'S RIGHT.
I HAVE NO RIGHT TO CALL MYSELF A HERO...
!
PLIP
STILL... I WON'T LET HIM BREAK ME...
BECAUSE IF I BREAK...
...THEN INGENIUM'S REALLY DEAD.
YOU'RE HOPELESS.

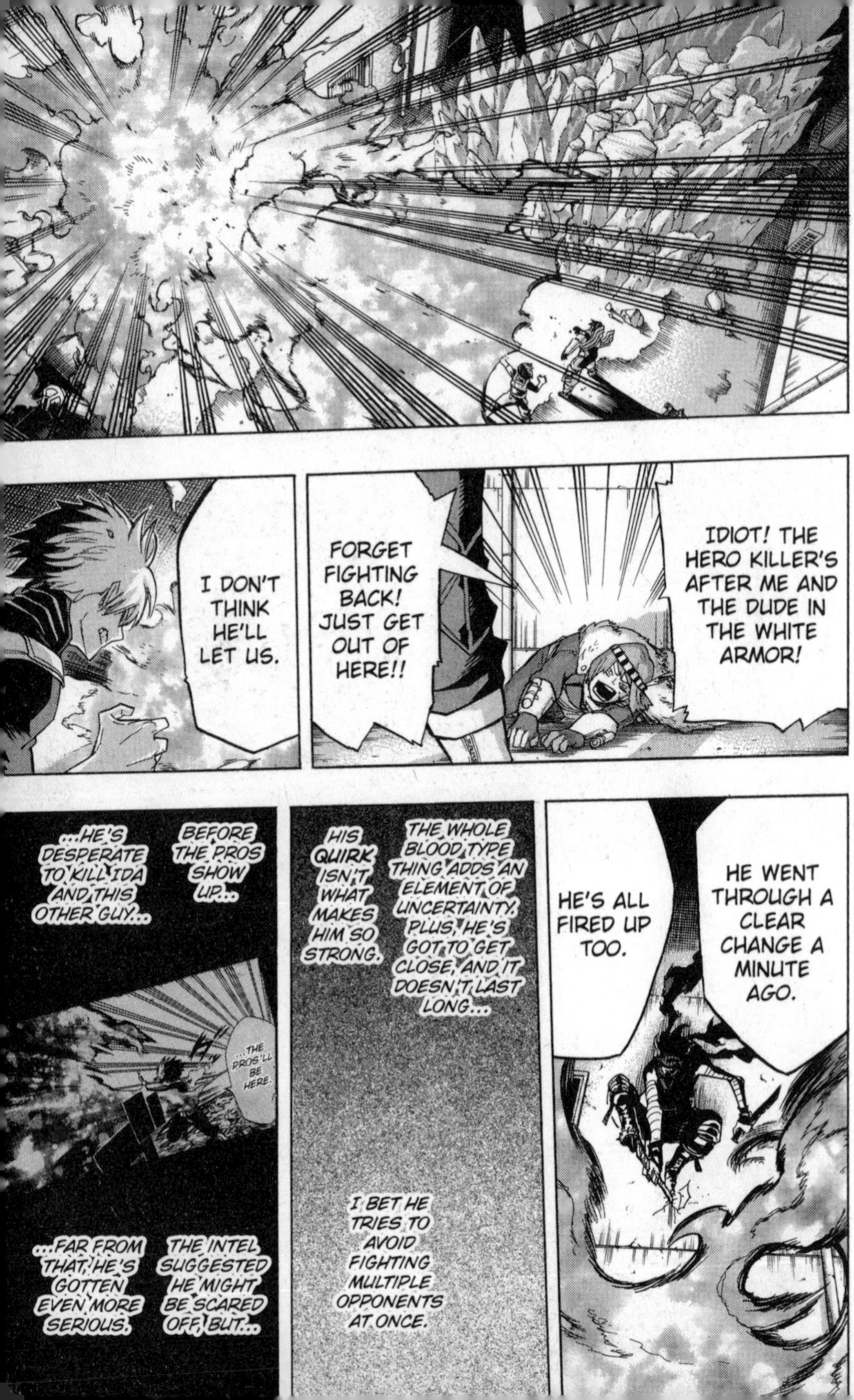
IDIOT! THE HERO KILLER'S AFTER ME AND THE DUDE IN THE WHITE ARMOR!
FORGET FIGHTING BACK! JUST GET OUT OF HERE!!
I DON'T THINK HE'LL LET US.
HE WENT THROUGH A CLEAR CHANGE A MINUTE AGO.
HE'S ALL FIRED UP TOO.
THE WHOLE BLOOD TYPE THING ADDS AN ELEMENT OF UNCERTAINTY. PLUS, HE'S GOT TO GET CLOSE, AND IT DOESN'T LAST LONG...
HIS QUIRK ISN'T WHAT MAKES HIM SO STRONG.
I BET HE TRIES TO AVOID FIGHTING MULTIPLE OPPONENTS AT ONCE.
BEFORE THE PROS SHOW UP...
...HE'S DESPERATE TO KILL IDA AND THIS OTHER GUY...
...THE PROS'LL BE HERE.
THE INTEL SUGGESTED HE MIGHT BE SCARED OFF, BUT...
...FAR FROM THAT, HE'S GOTTEN EVEN MORE SERIOUS.

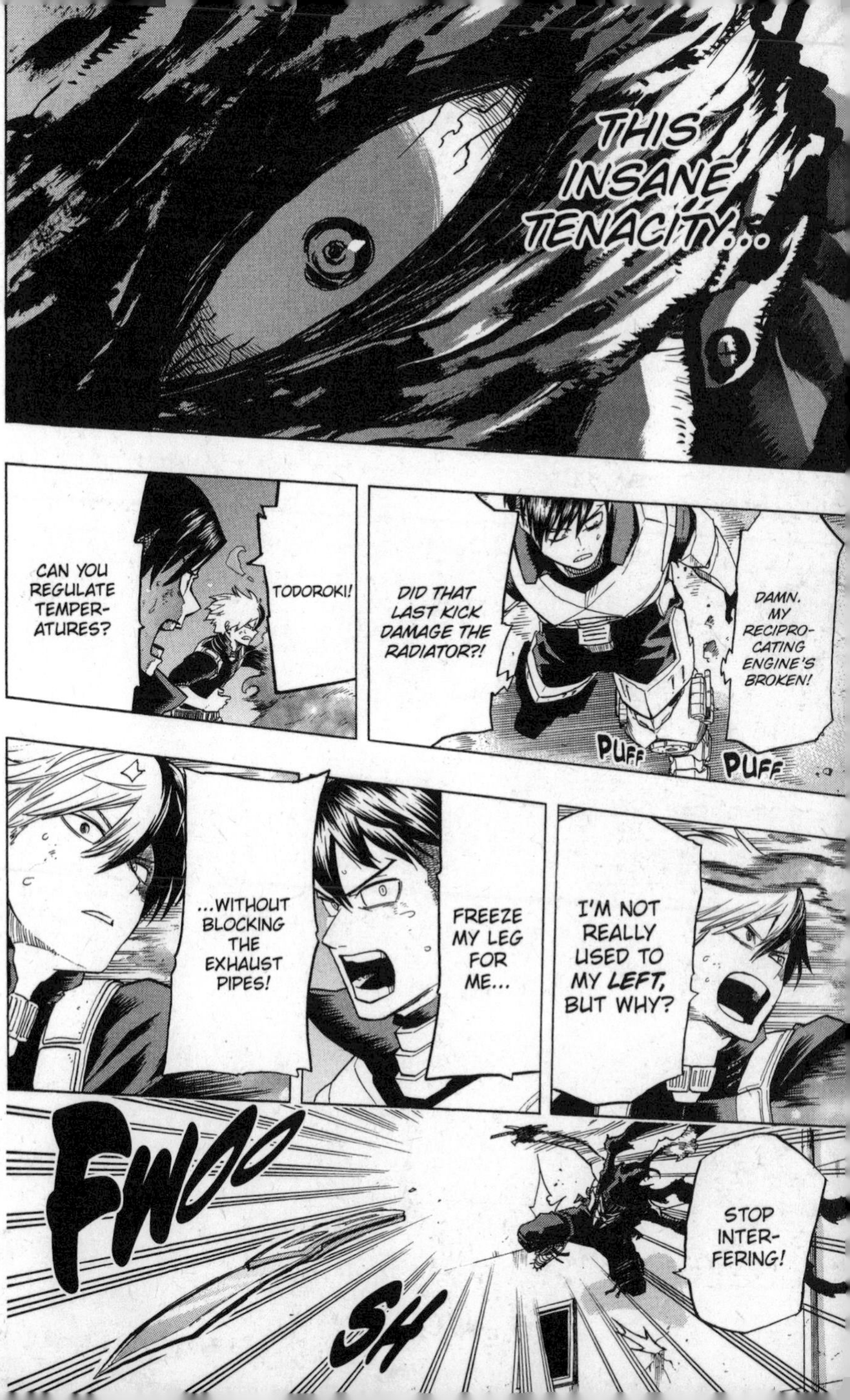
THIS INSANE TENACITY...
DAMN. MY RECIPRO-CATING ENGINE'S BROKEN!
DID THAT LAST KICK DAMAGE THE RADIATOR?!
PUFF
PUFF
TODOROKI!
CAN YOU REGULATE TEMPER-ATURES?
I'M NOT REALLY USED TO MY *LEFT*, BUT WHY?
FREEZE MY LEG FOR ME...
...WITHOUT BLOCKING THE EXHAUST PIPES!
STOP INTER-FERING!
FWOO
SH

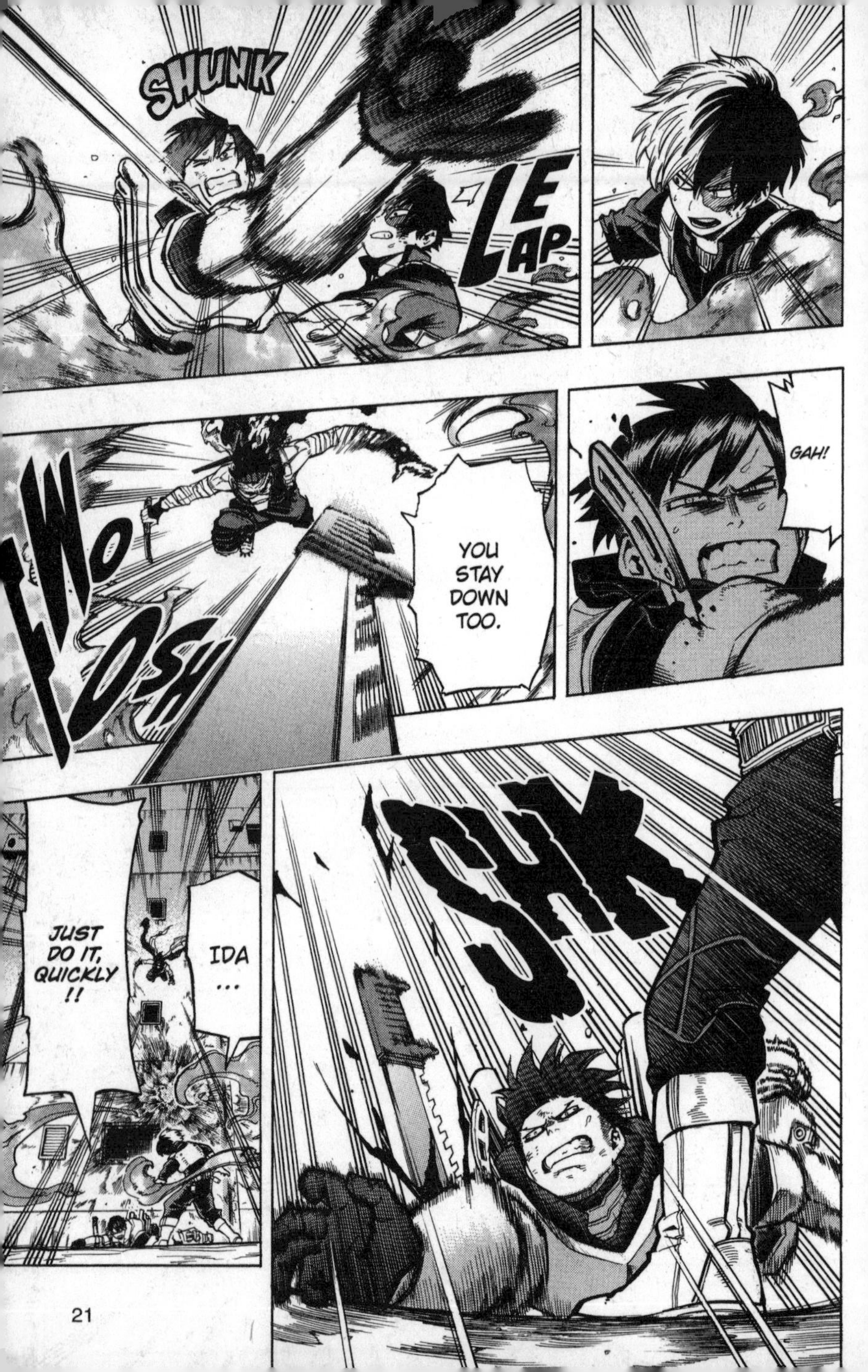
SHUNK
LEAP
GAH!
WOOSH
YOU STAY DOWN TOO.
SHK
IDA...
JUST DO IT, QUICKLY!!

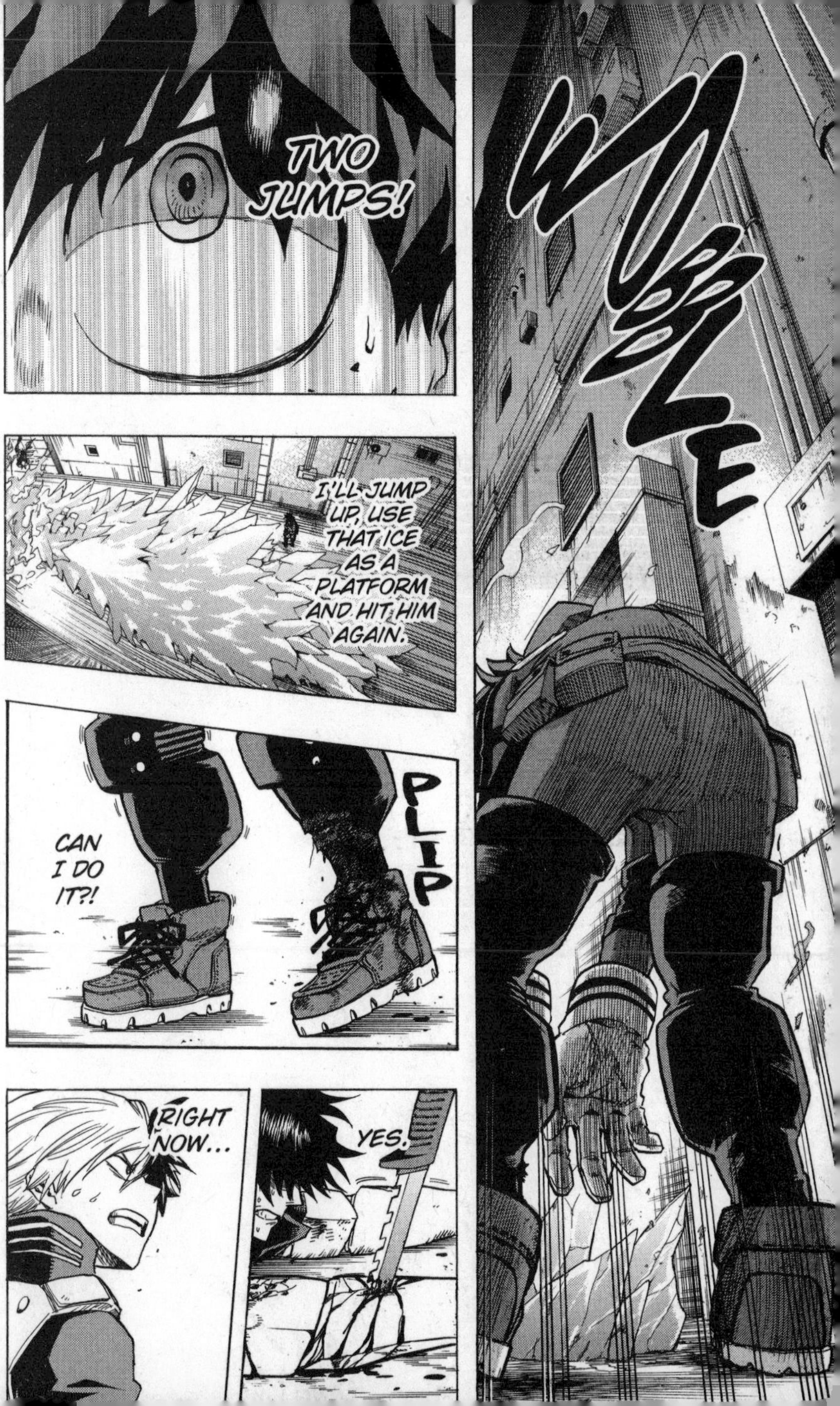
WOBBLE
TWO JUMPS!
I'LL JUMP UP, USE THAT ICE AS A PLATFORM AND HIT HIM AGAIN.
PLIP
CAN I DO IT?!
YES.
RIGHT NOW...

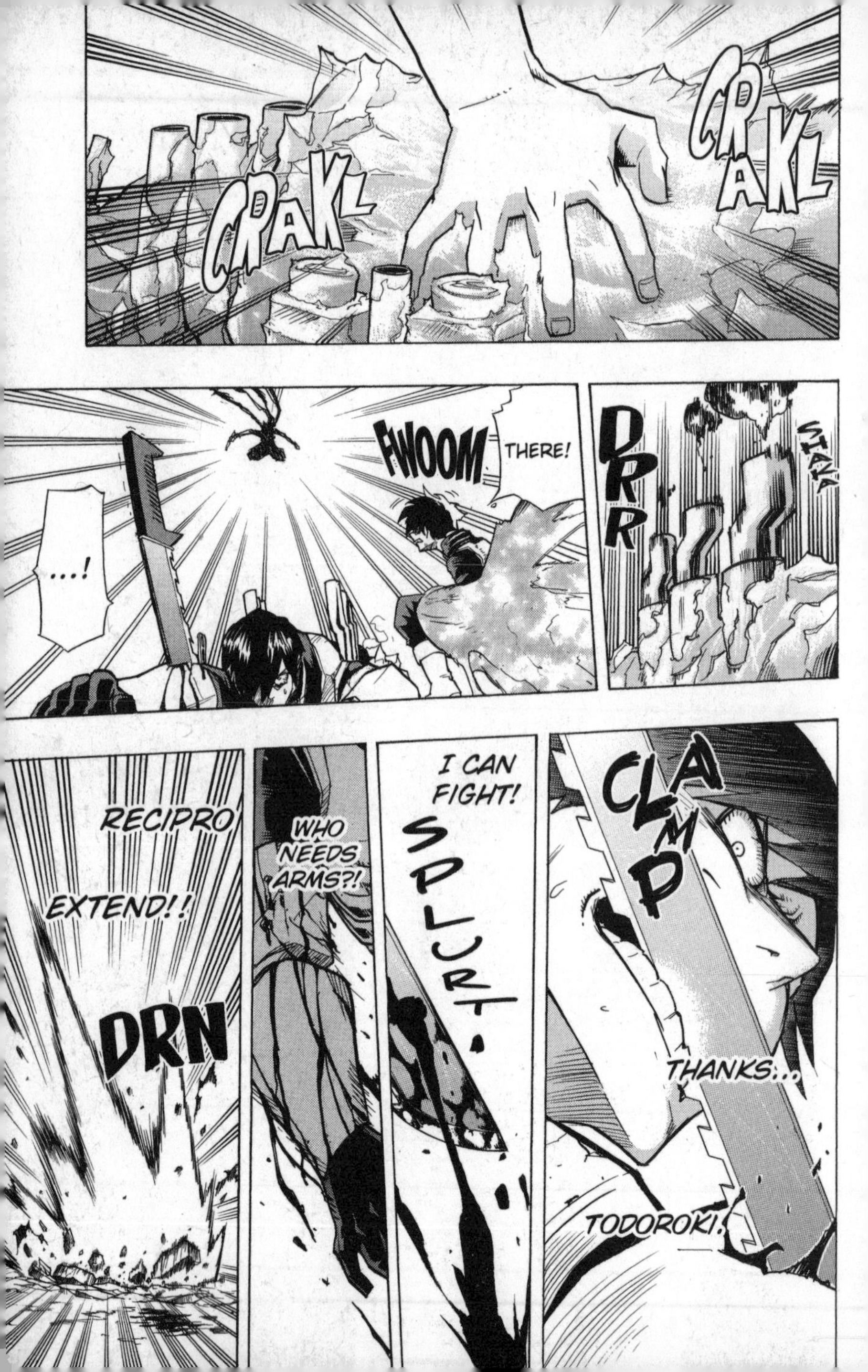
CRAKL
CRAKL
DRR
SHAAA
THERE!
FWOOM
...!
CLAMP
THANKS...
TODOROKI.
I CAN FIGHT!
SPLURT
WHO NEEDS ARMS?!
RECIPRO
EXTEND!!
DRN

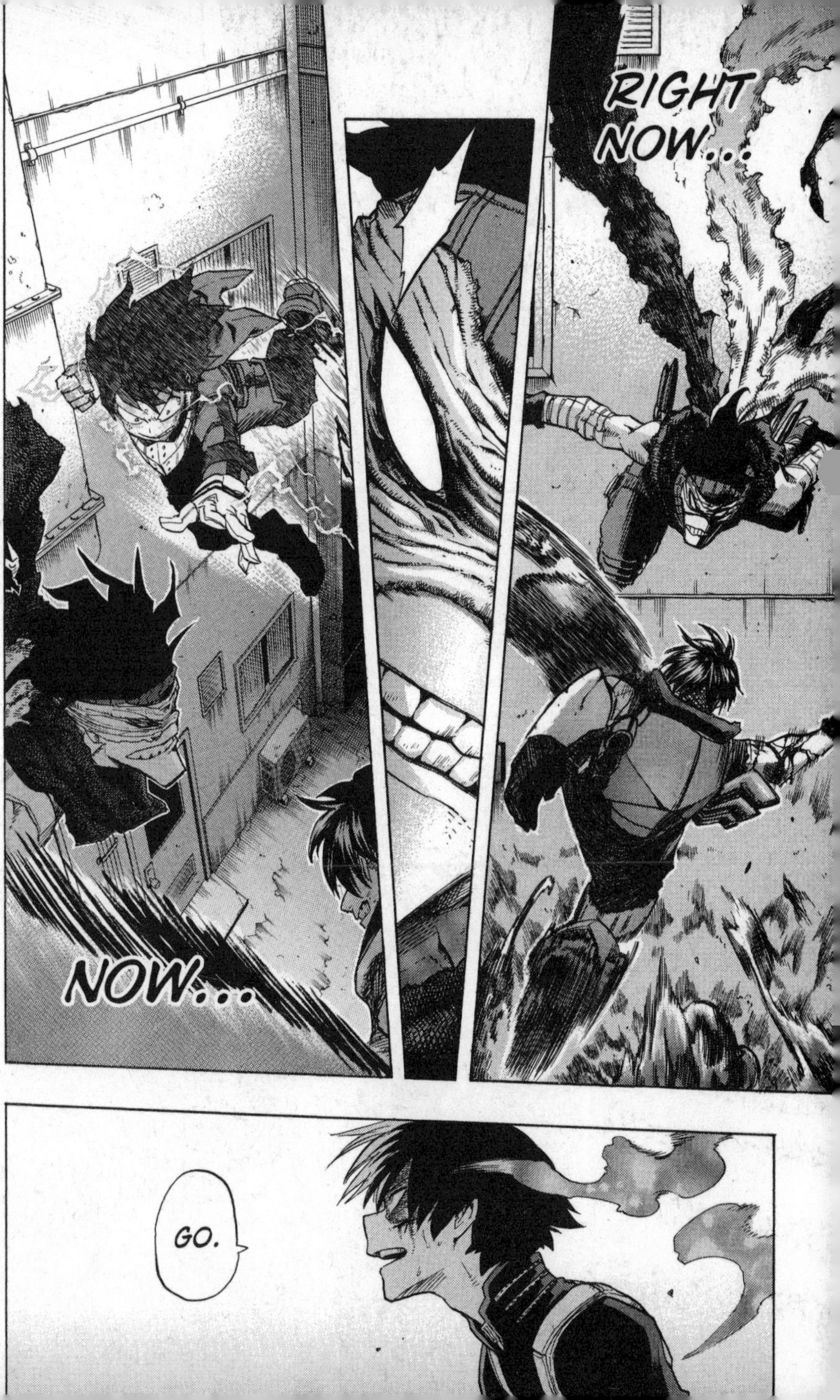
RIGHT NOW...
NOW...
GO.

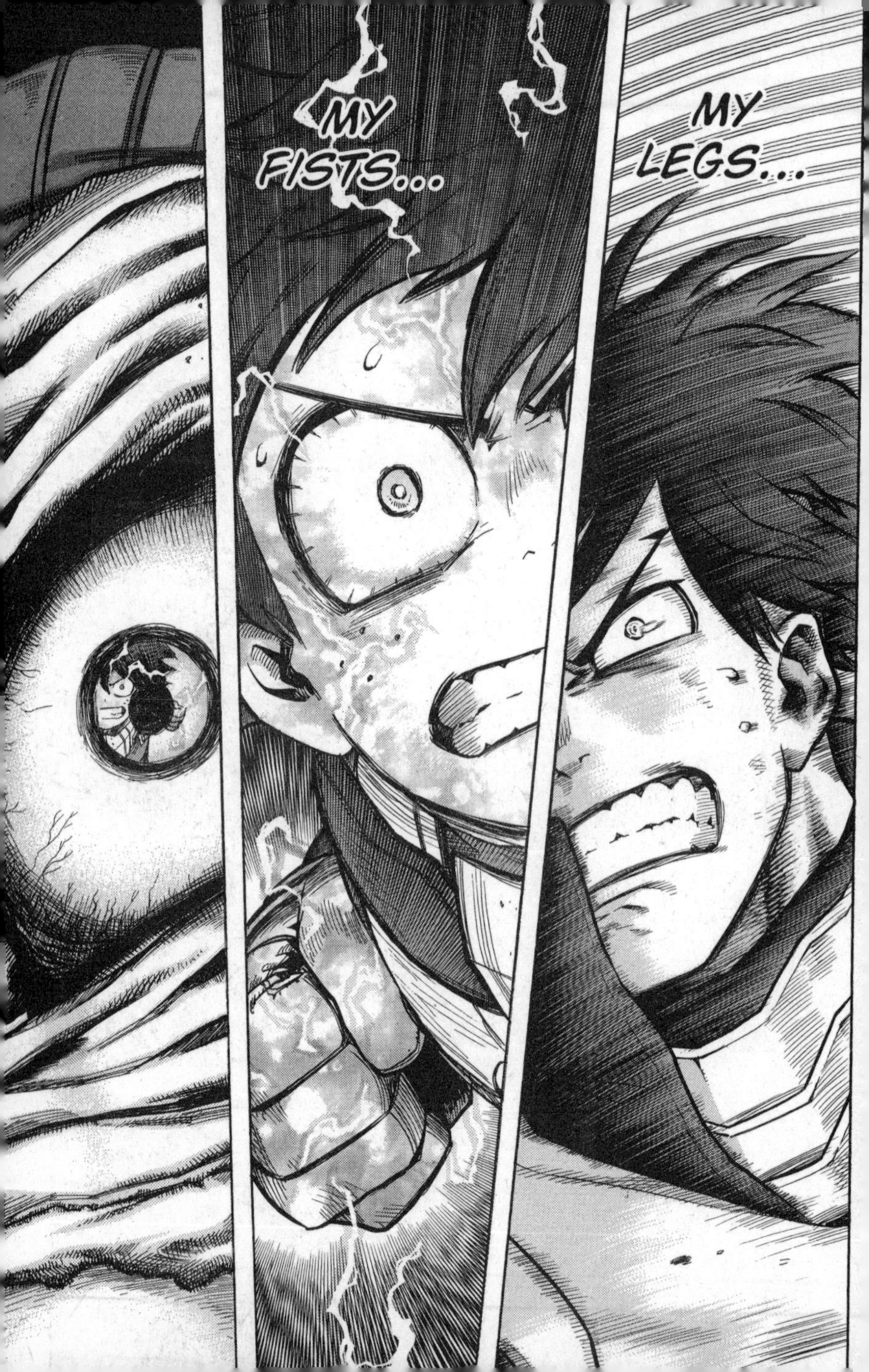
MY LEGS...
MY FISTS...

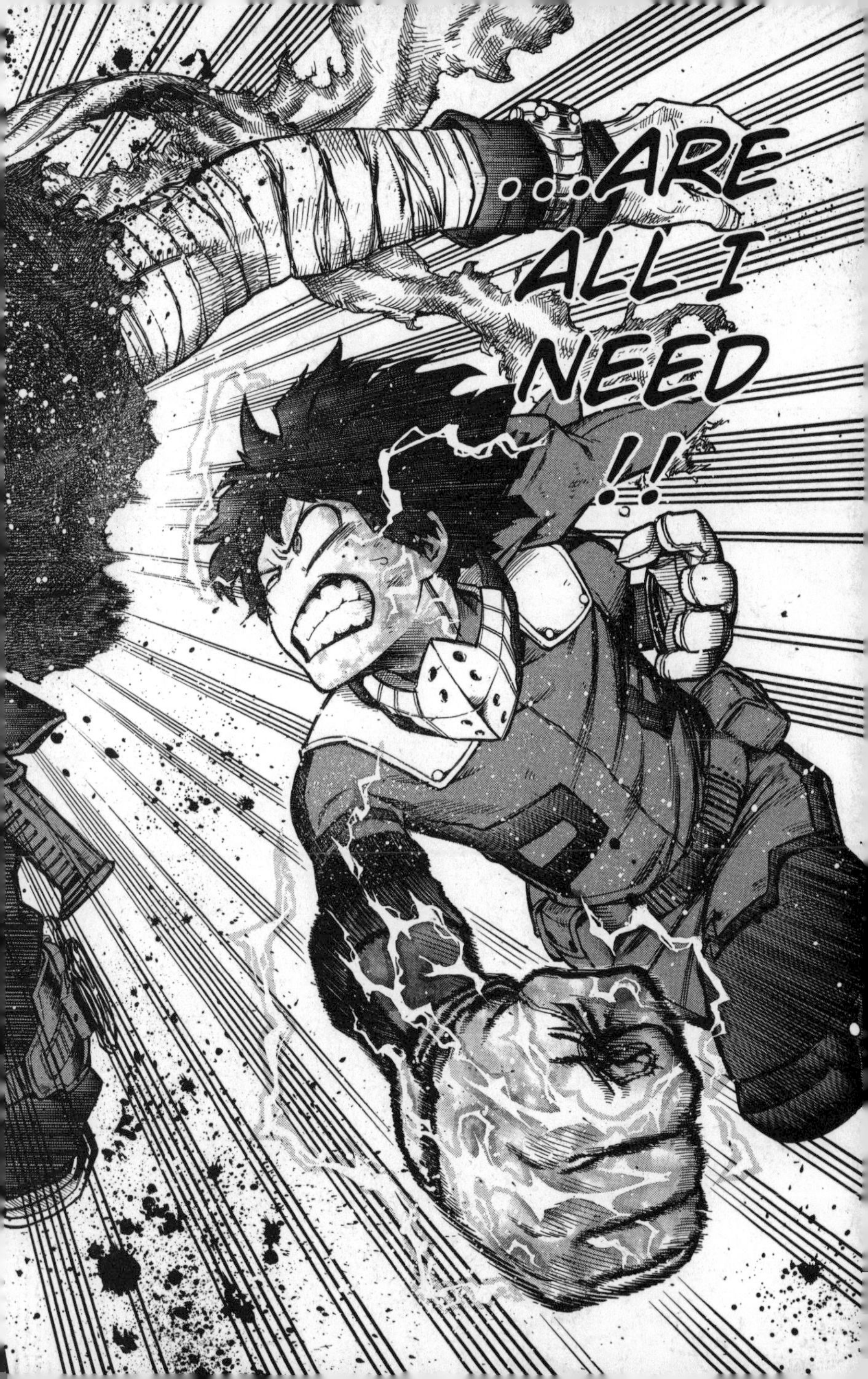
...ARE ALL I NEED!!

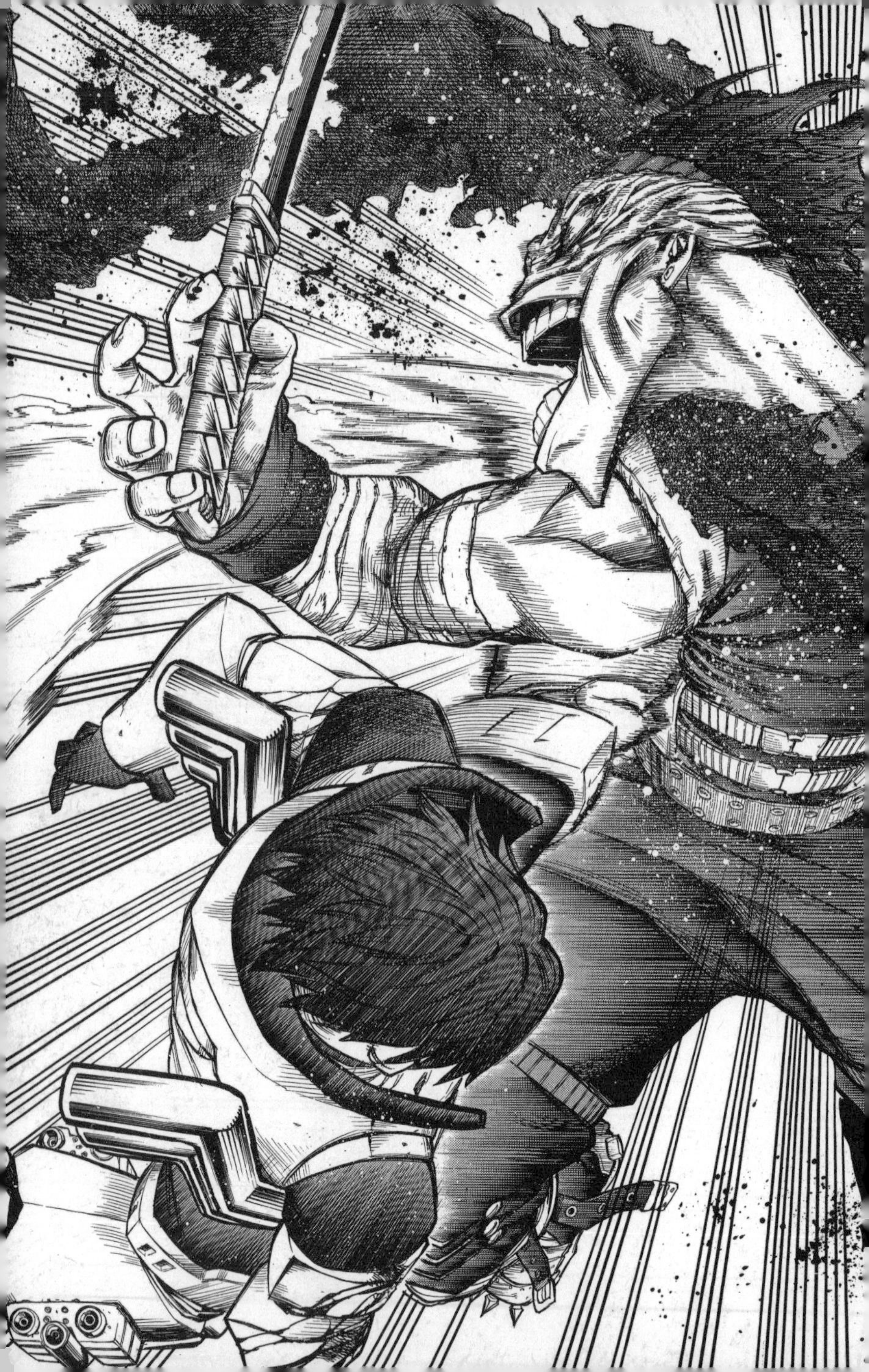

THE "FILL IN THE BLANK PAGES" CORNER (COSTUME EXPLANATION CORNER)

SHOTO TODOROKI'S COSTUME

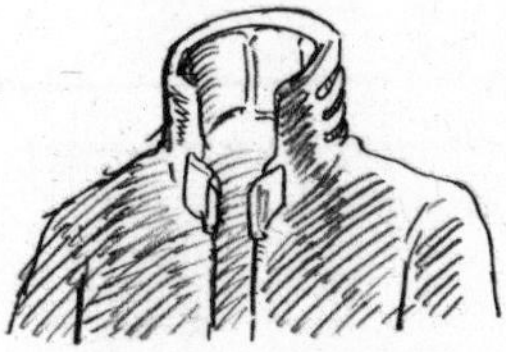

Todoroki Jacket
Made of special heat-resistant fibers. There are cooling/heating devices in the collar. They monitor Todoroki's body temperature and automatically help regulate it, all to keep him operating in tip-top shape.

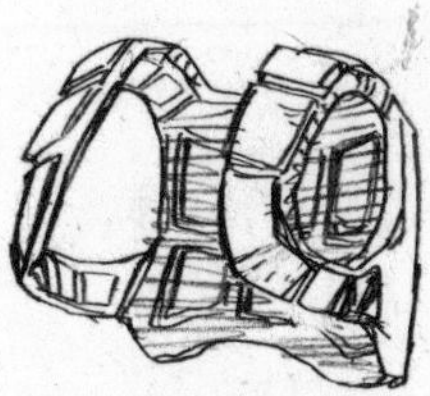

Todoroki Tactical Vest
Monitors Todoroki's body temperature and automatically cools him off or heats him up. It's a heater and radiator in one, whereas the previous model only functioned as a heater.

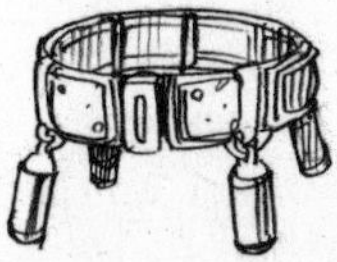

Todoroki Belt
The hanging canisters contain things like water, painkillers, disinfectants, etc. Useful in rescue missions.

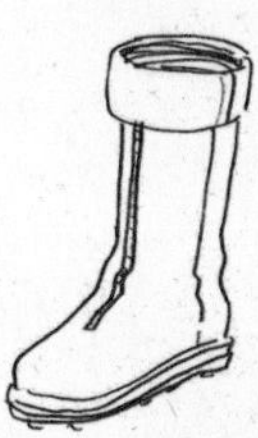

Short Boots
Equipped with spikes to keep him from slipping on icy surfaces.

ALL IN ALL: "ONE COOL COSTUME"

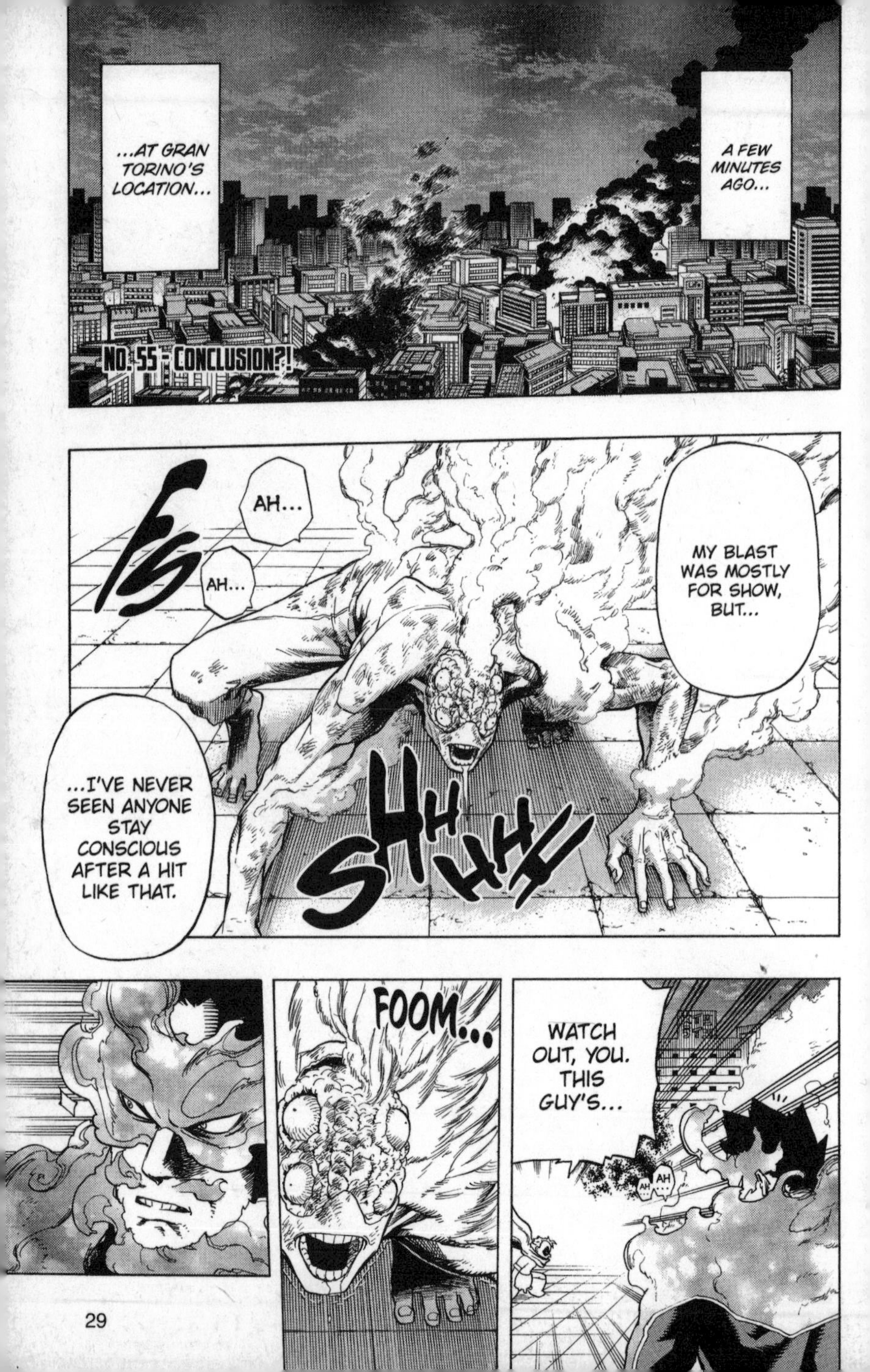
A FEW MINUTES AGO...
...AT GRAN TORINO'S LOCATION...
No. 55 - CONCLUSION?!
MY BLAST WAS MOSTLY FOR SHOW, BUT...
AH...
AH...
...I'VE NEVER SEEN ANYONE STAY CONSCIOUS AFTER A HIT LIKE THAT.
WATCH OUT, YOU. THIS GUY'S...
AH...
AH
FOOM...

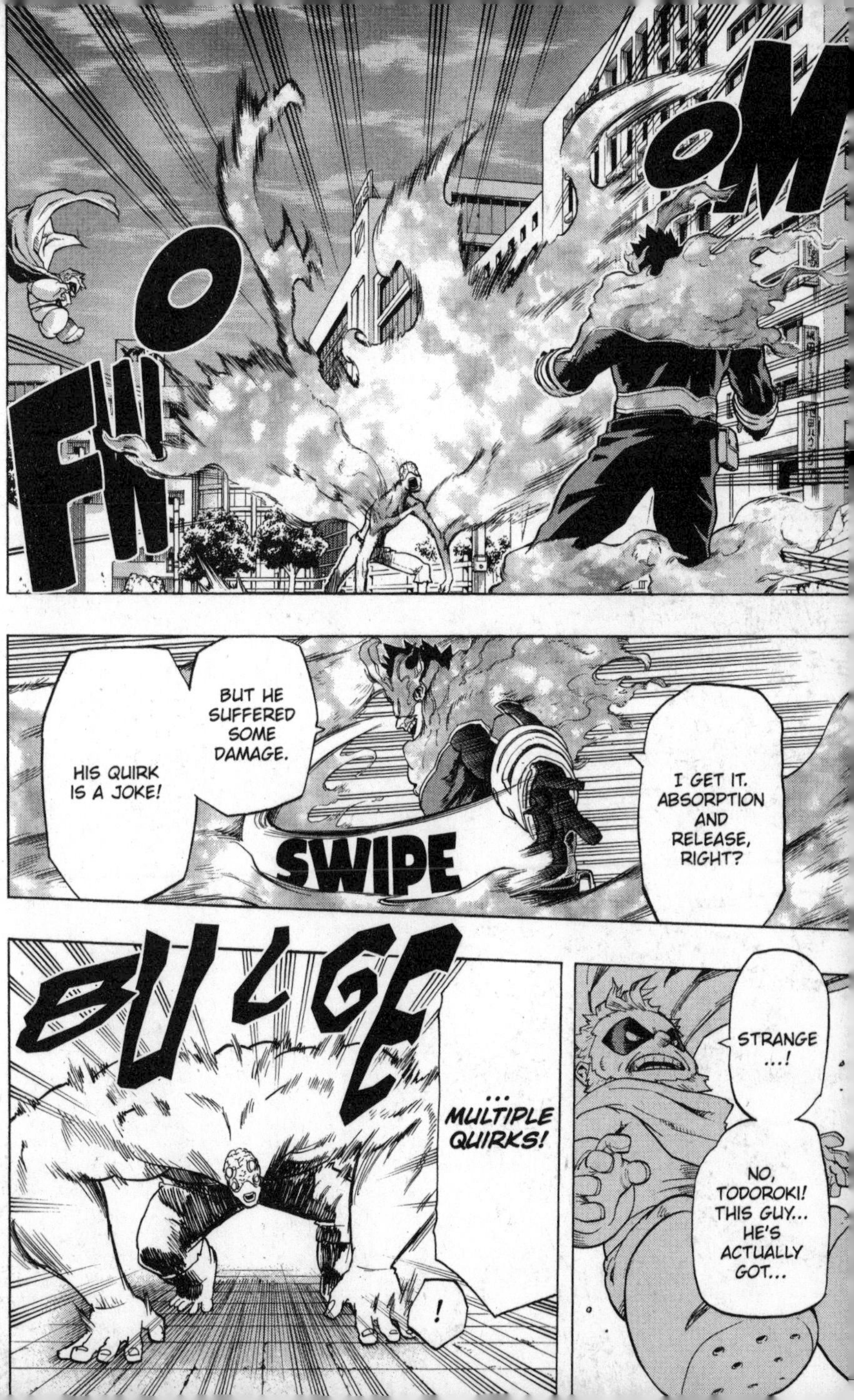
FWOOM
I GET IT. ABSORPTION AND RELEASE, RIGHT?
SWIPE
BUT HE SUFFERED SOME DAMAGE.
HIS QUIRK IS A JOKE!
STRANGE ...!
NO, TODOROKI! THIS GUY... HE'S ACTUALLY GOT...
... MULTIPLE QUIRKS!
BULGE
!

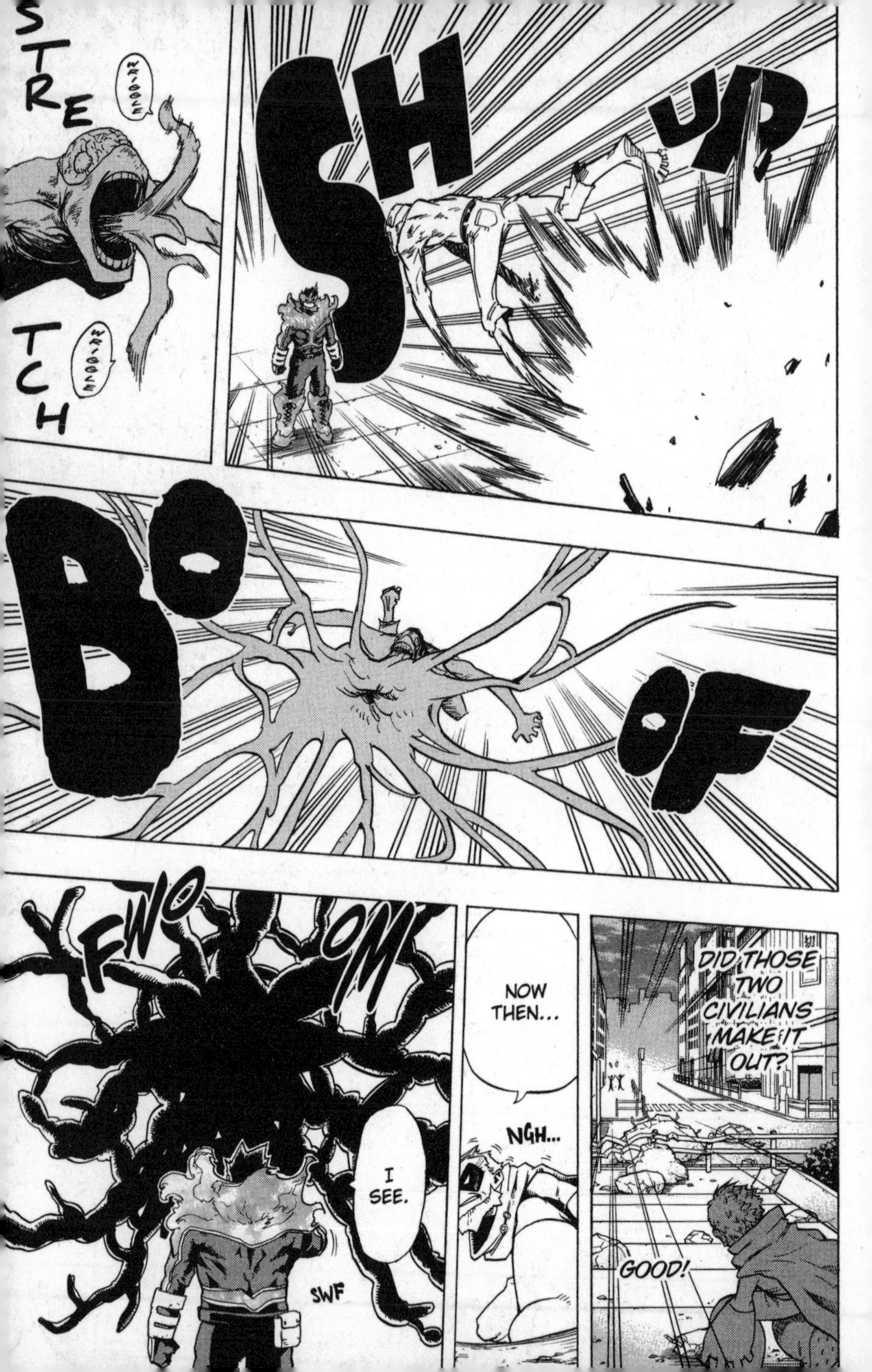
SHUP
STRETCH
WRIGGLE
WRIGGLE
BOOF
DID THOSE TWO CIVILIANS MAKE IT OUT?
GOOD!
NOW THEN...
NGH...
FWOOM
I SEE.
SWF

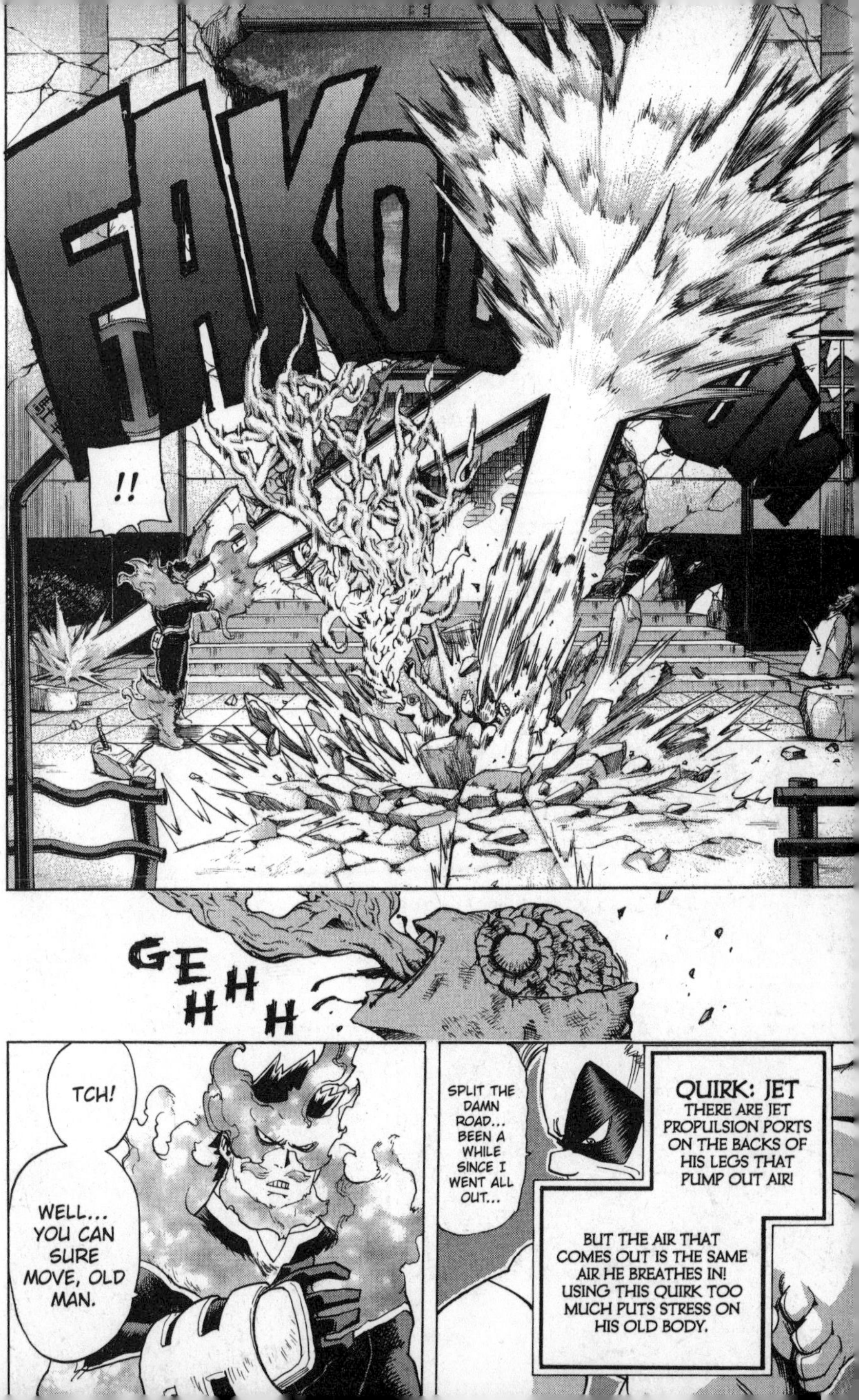
!!
GEHHH
QUIRK: JET
THERE ARE JET PROPULSION PORTS ON THE BACKS OF HIS LEGS THAT PUMP OUT AIR!
SPLIT THE DAMN ROAD... BEEN A WHILE SINCE I WENT ALL OUT...
BUT THE AIR THAT COMES OUT IS THE SAME AIR HE BREATHES IN! USING THIS QUIRK TOO MUCH PUTS STRESS ON HIS OLD BODY.
TCH!
WELL... YOU CAN SURE MOVE, OLD MAN.

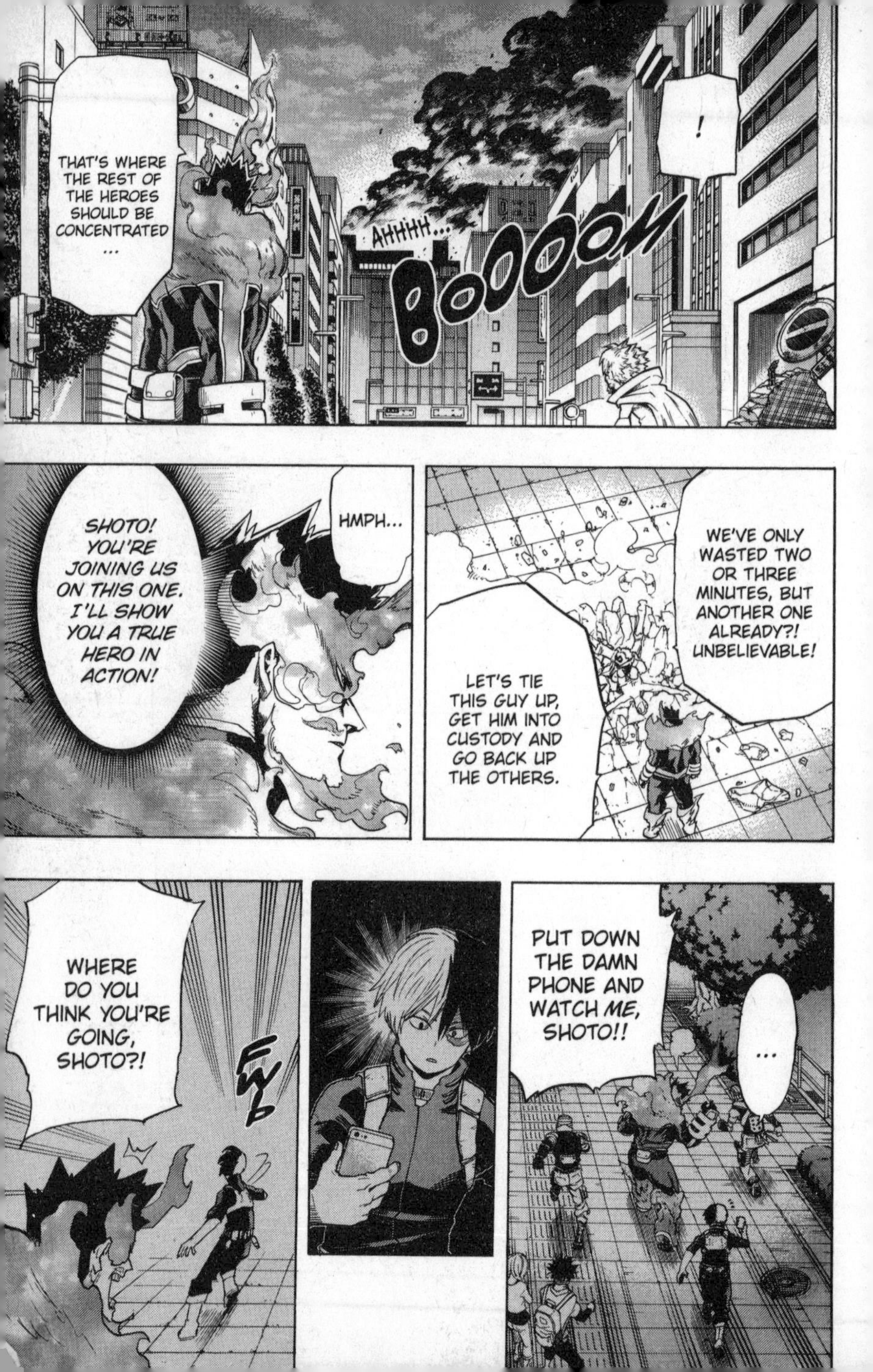
!
THAT'S WHERE THE REST OF THE HEROES SHOULD BE CONCENTRATED ...
AHHHH...
BOOOOOM
WE'VE ONLY WASTED TWO OR THREE MINUTES, BUT ANOTHER ONE ALREADY?! UNBELIEVABLE!
LET'S TIE THIS GUY UP, GET HIM INTO CUSTODY AND GO BACK UP THE OTHERS.
HMPH...
SHOTO! YOU'RE JOINING US ON THIS ONE. I'LL SHOW YOU A TRUE HERO IN ACTION!
PUT DOWN THE DAMN PHONE AND WATCH ME, SHOTO!!
...
WHERE DO YOU THINK YOU'RE GOING, SHOTO?!
FWB

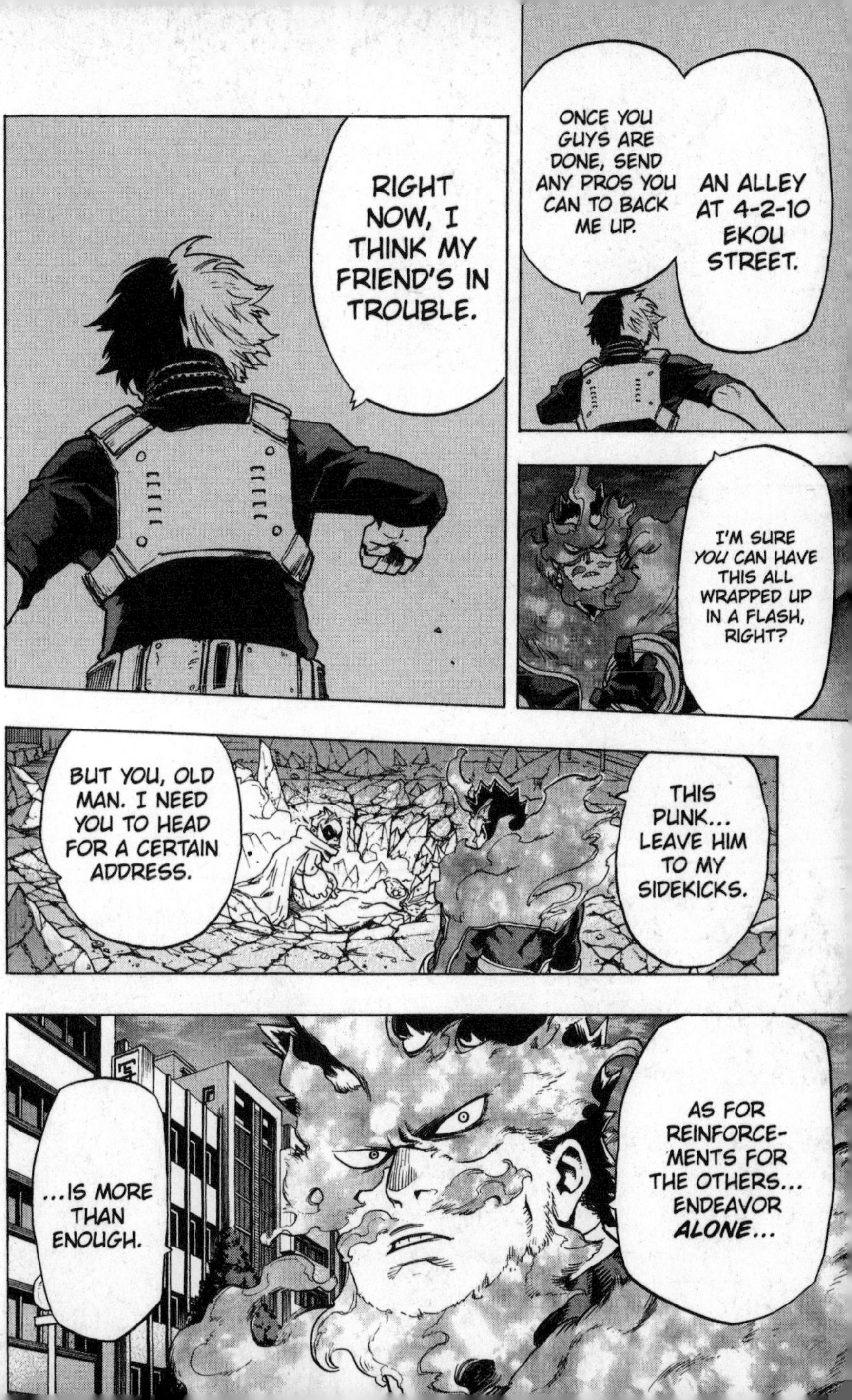
AN ALLEY AT 4-2-10 EKOU STREET.
ONCE YOU GUYS ARE DONE, SEND ANY PROS YOU CAN TO BACK ME UP.
I'M SURE *YOU* CAN HAVE THIS ALL WRAPPED UP IN A FLASH, RIGHT?
RIGHT NOW, I THINK MY FRIEND'S IN TROUBLE.
THIS PUNK... LEAVE HIM TO MY SIDEKICKS.
BUT YOU, OLD MAN. I NEED YOU TO HEAD FOR A CERTAIN ADDRESS.
AS FOR REINFORCE-MENTS FOR THE OTHERS... ENDEAVOR ***ALONE***...
...IS MORE THAN ENOUGH.

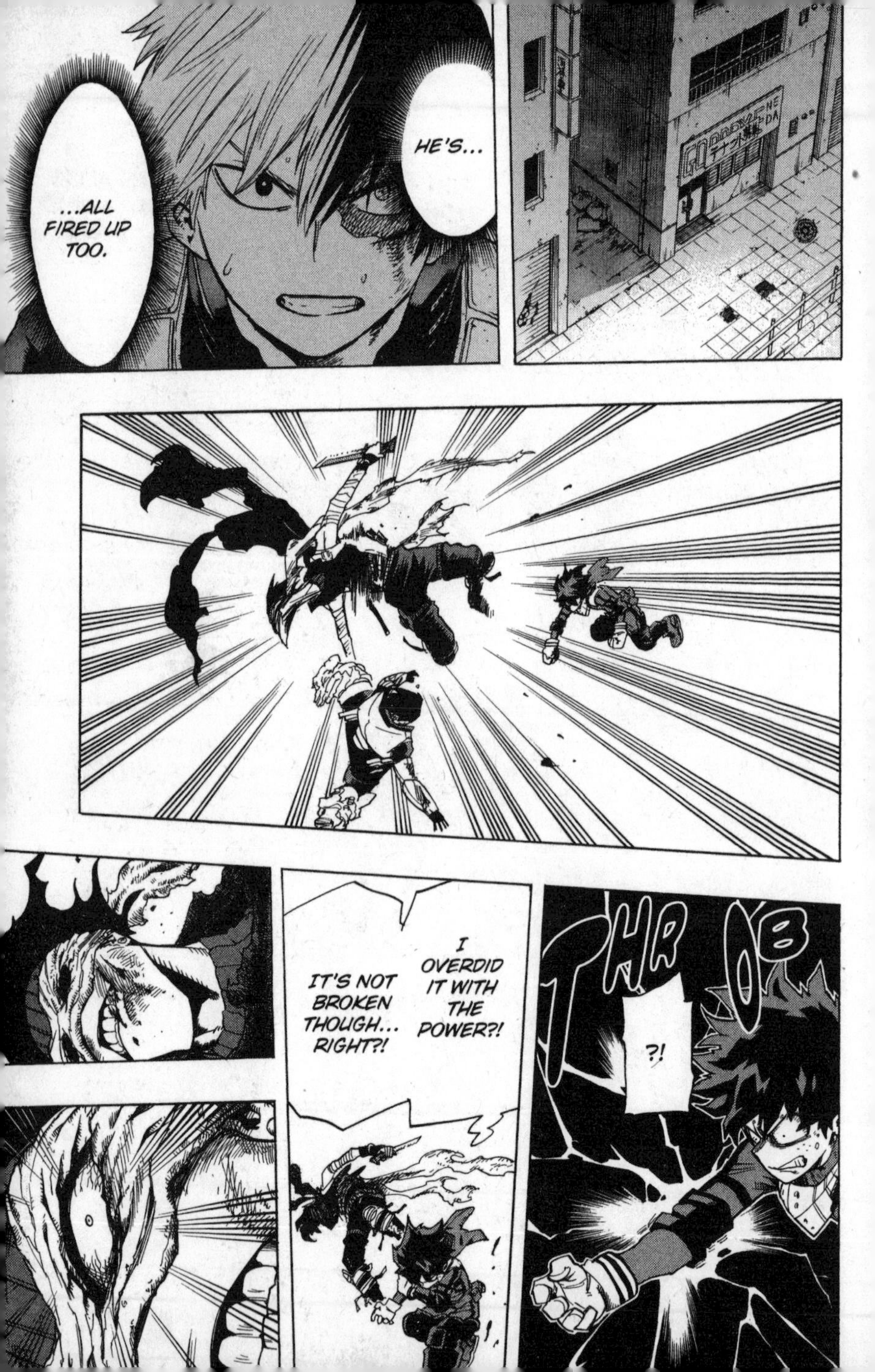
HE'S...
...ALL FIRED UP TOO.
THR OB
?!
I OVERDID IT WITH THE POWER?!
IT'S NOT BROKEN THOUGH... RIGHT?!

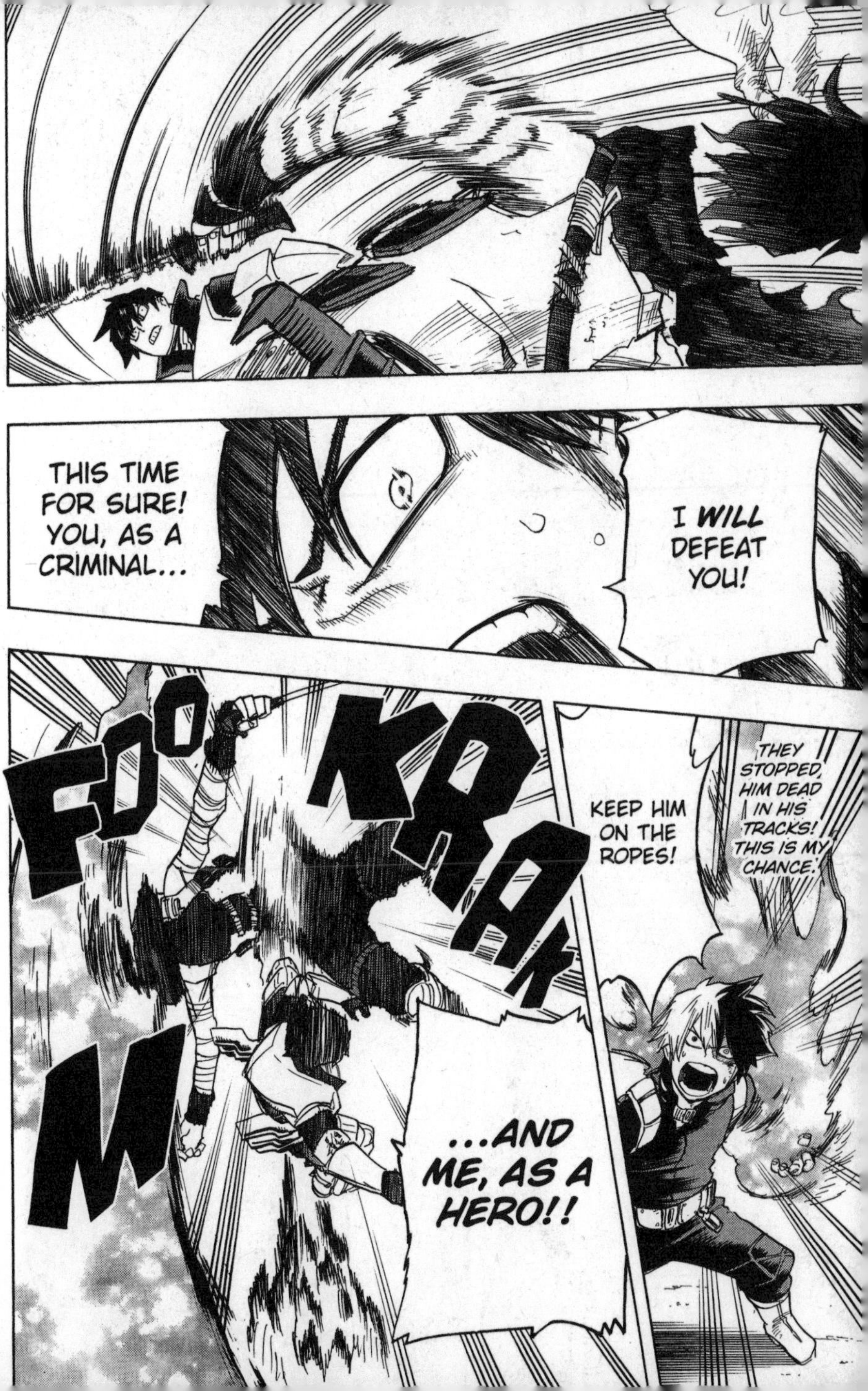
I WILL DEFEAT YOU!
THIS TIME FOR SURE! YOU, AS A CRIMINAL...
THEY STOPPED HIM DEAD IN HIS TRACKS! THIS IS MY CHANCE.
KEEP HIM ON THE ROPES!
FOOM
KRAK
...AND ME, AS A HERO!!

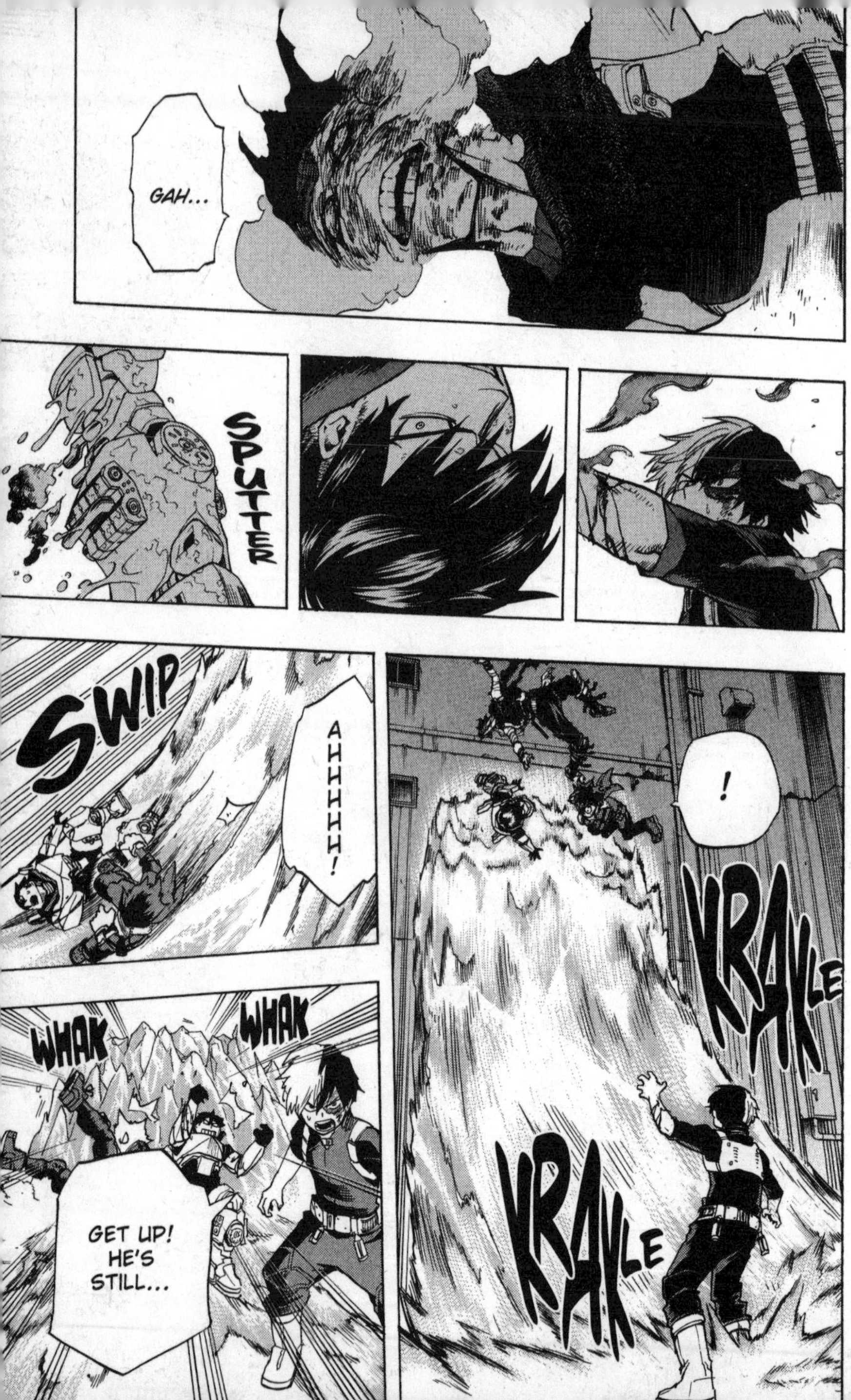
GAH...
SPUTTER
!
KRAKLE
KRAKLE
SWIP
AHHHHHH!
WHAK
WHAK
GET UP! HE'S STILL...

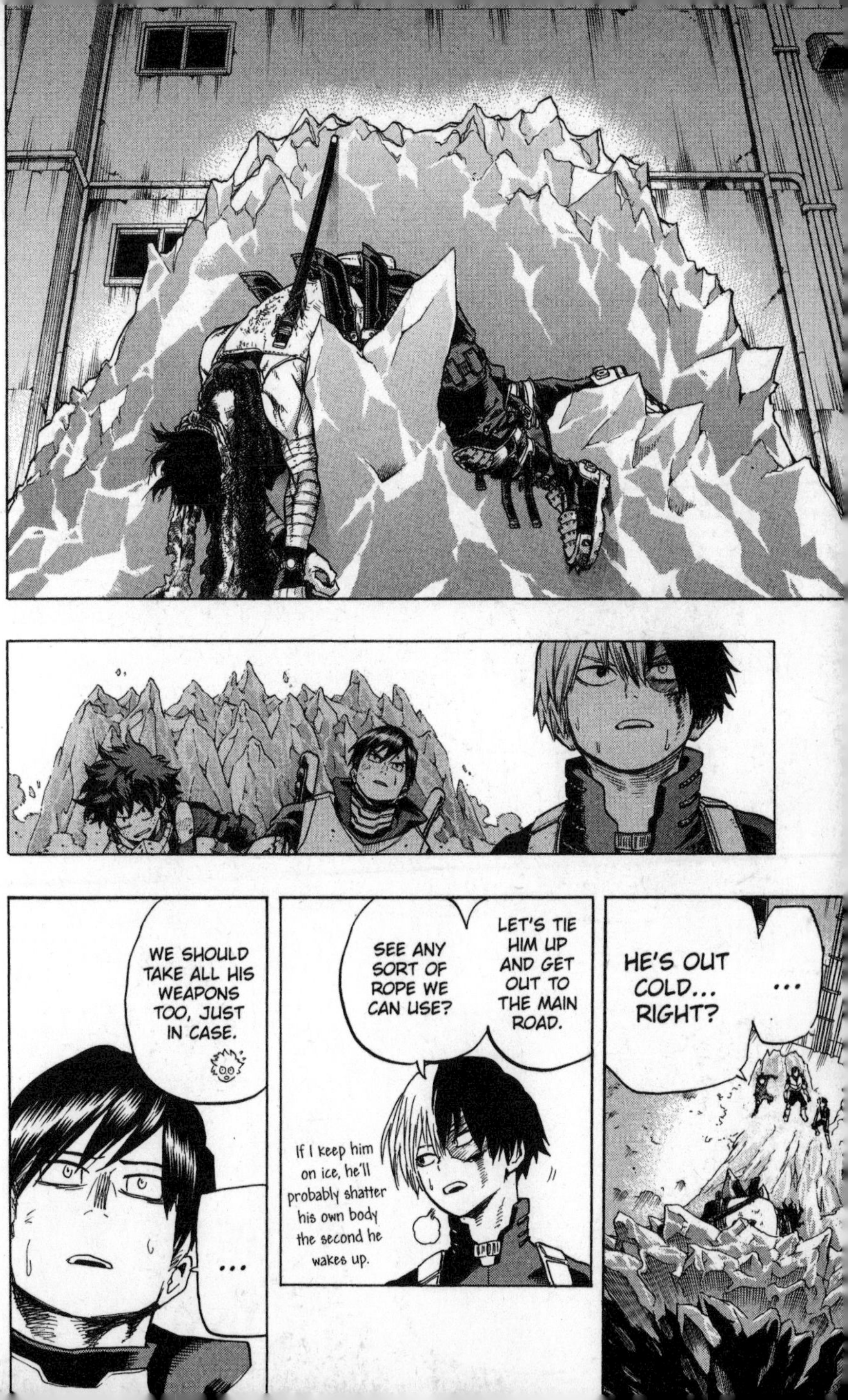
HE'S OUT COLD... RIGHT?
...
LET'S TIE HIM UP AND GET OUT TO THE MAIN ROAD.
SEE ANY SORT OF ROPE WE CAN USE?
If I keep him on ice, he'll probably shatter his own body the second he wakes up.
WE SHOULD TAKE ALL HIS WEAPONS TOO, JUST IN CASE.
...

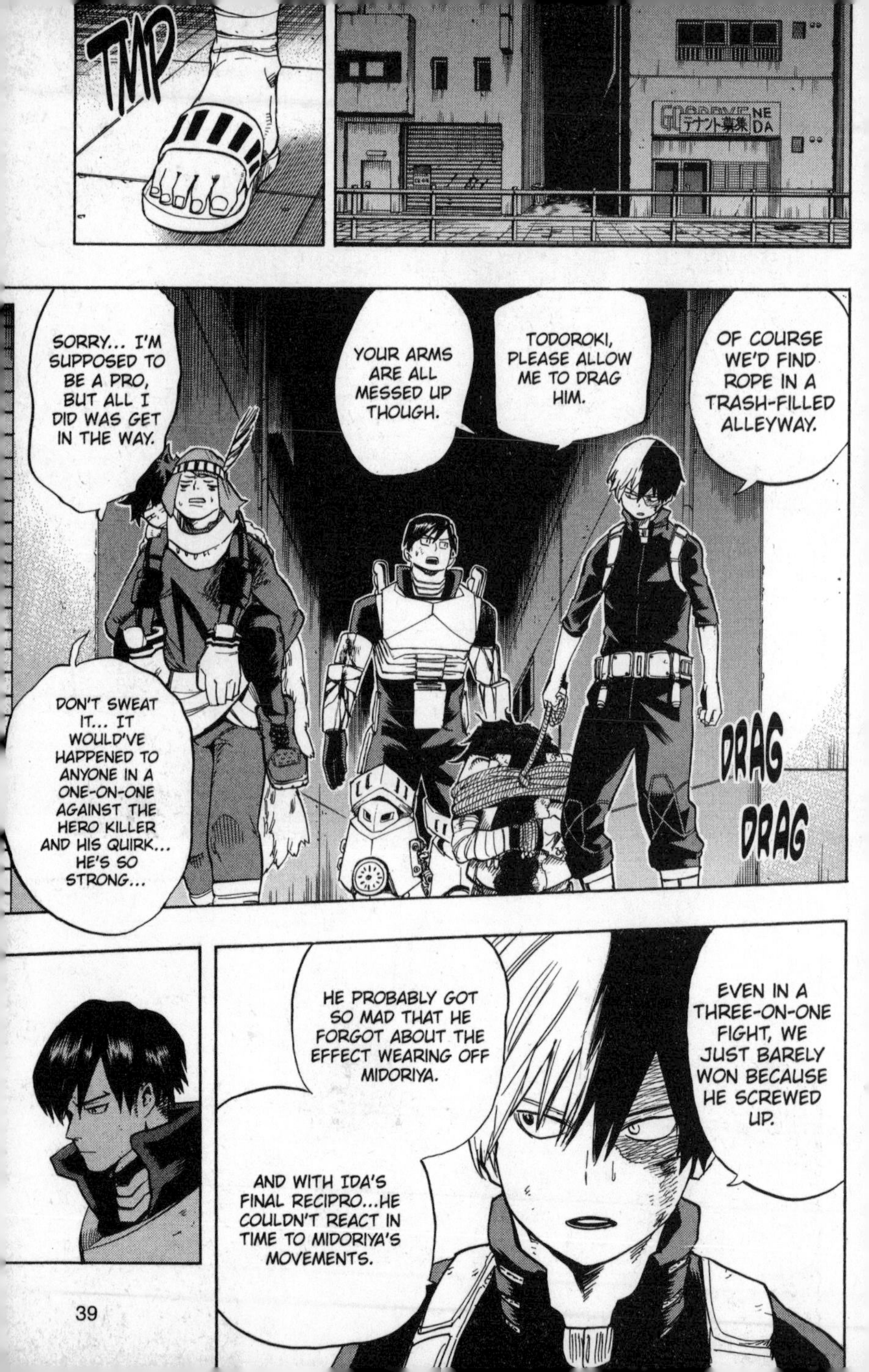

テナント募集
TMP
OF COURSE WE'D FIND ROPE IN A TRASH-FILLED ALLEYWAY.
TODOROKI, PLEASE ALLOW ME TO DRAG HIM.
YOUR ARMS ARE ALL MESSED UP THOUGH.
SORRY... I'M SUPPOSED TO BE A PRO, BUT ALL I DID WAS GET IN THE WAY.
DRAG DRAG
DON'T SWEAT IT... IT WOULD'VE HAPPENED TO ANYONE IN A ONE-ON-ONE AGAINST THE HERO KILLER AND HIS QUIRK... HE'S SO STRONG...
EVEN IN A THREE-ON-ONE FIGHT, WE JUST BARELY WON BECAUSE HE SCREWED UP.
HE PROBABLY GOT SO MAD THAT HE FORGOT ABOUT THE EFFECT WEARING OFF MIDORIYA.
AND WITH IDA'S FINAL RECIPRO...HE COULDN'T REACT IN TIME TO MIDORIYA'S MOVEMENTS.

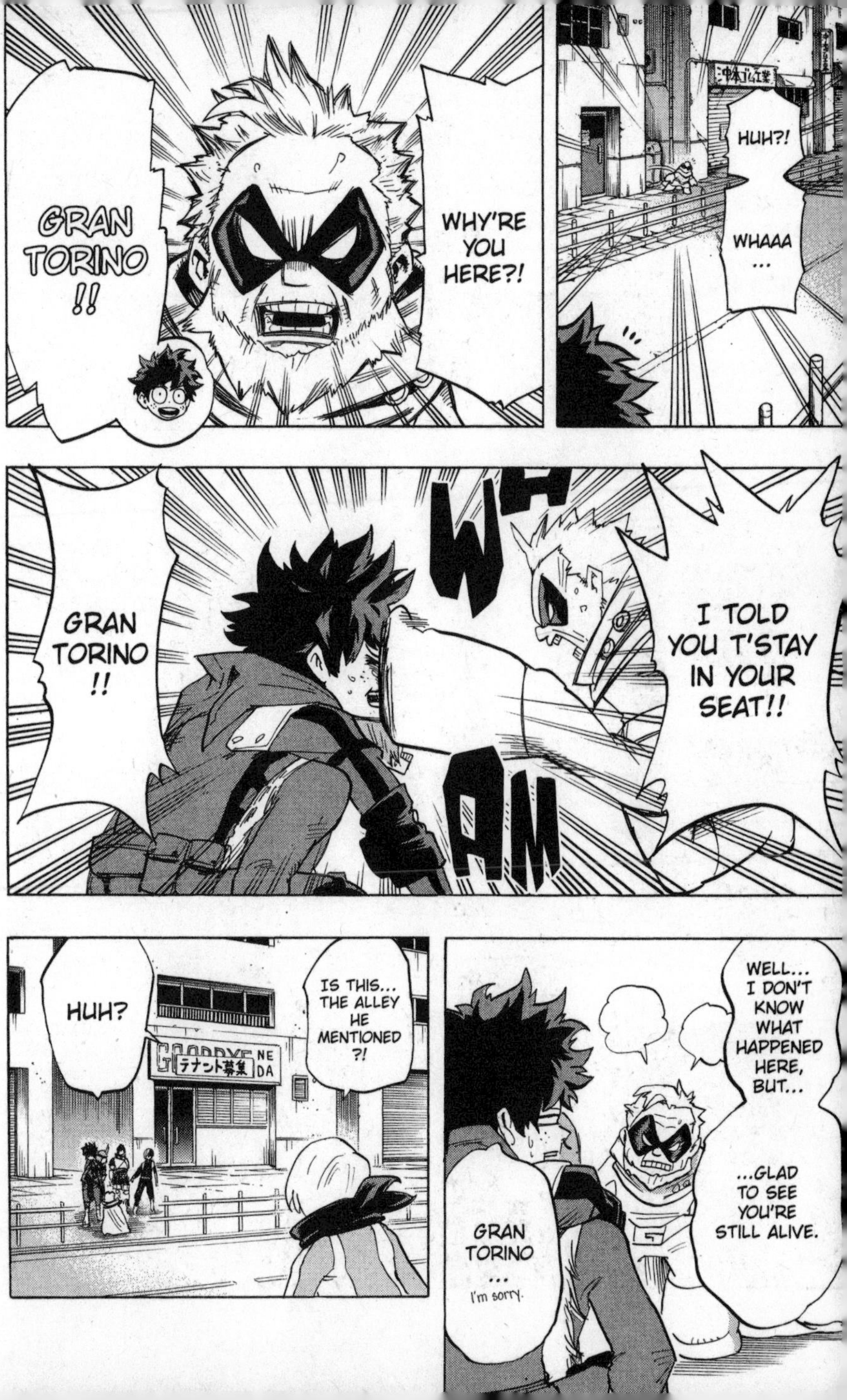
HUH?!
WHAAA...
WHY'RE YOU HERE?!
GRAN TORINO!!
I TOLD YOU T'STAY IN YOUR SEAT!!
WHAM
GRAN TORINO!!
WELL... I DON'T KNOW WHAT HAPPENED HERE, BUT...
...GLAD TO SEE YOU'RE STILL ALIVE.
GRAN TORINO... I'm sorry.
IS THIS... THE ALLEY HE MENTIONED?!
HUH?
テナント募集
NE DA

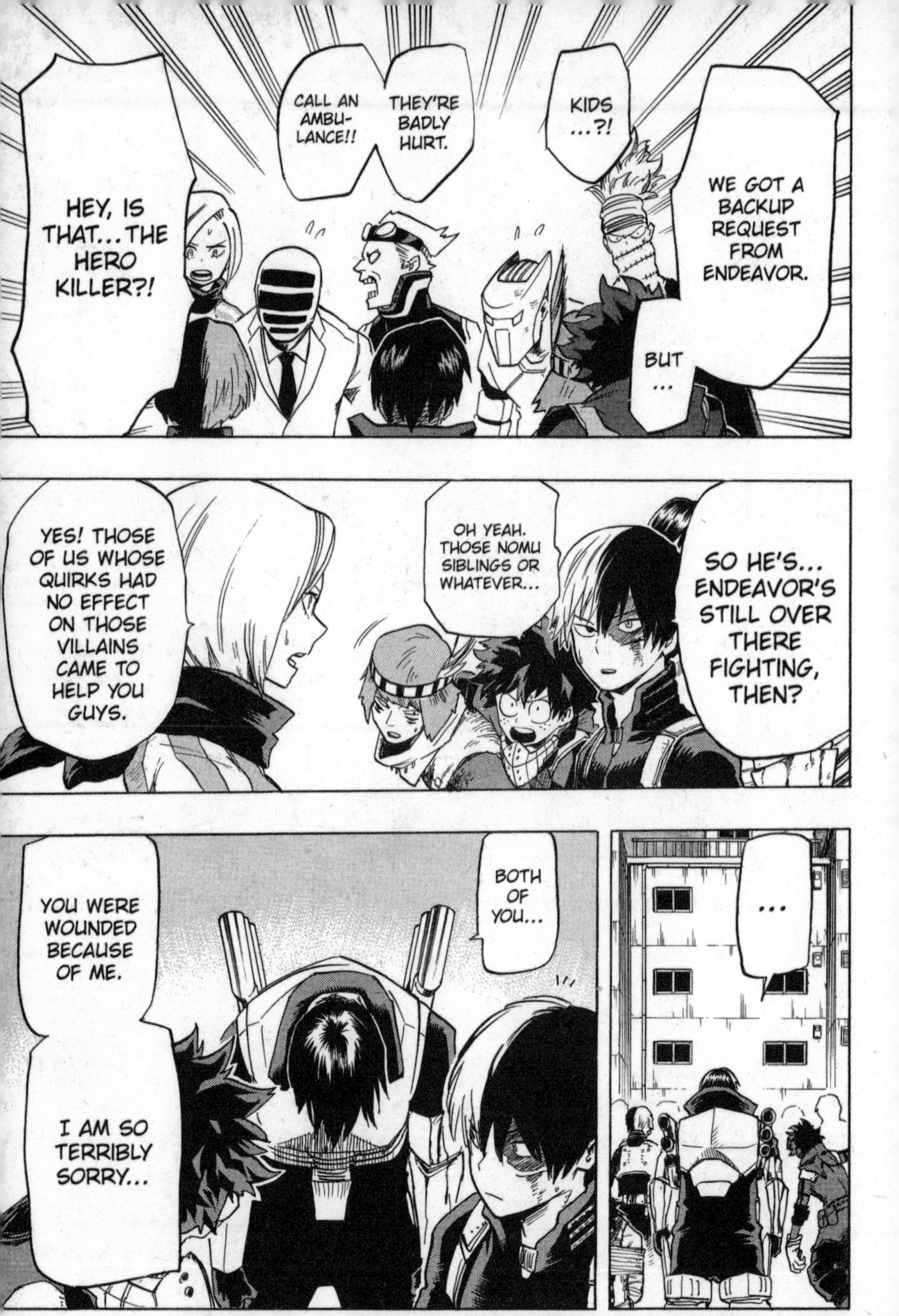
WE GOT A BACKUP REQUEST FROM ENDEAVOR.
BUT...
KIDS...?!
THEY'RE BADLY HURT.
CALL AN AMBU-LANCE!!
HEY, IS THAT...THE HERO KILLER?!
SO HE'S... ENDEAVOR'S STILL OVER THERE FIGHTING, THEN?
OH YEAH. THOSE NOMU SIBLINGS OR WHATEVER...
YES! THOSE OF US WHOSE QUIRKS HAD NO EFFECT ON THOSE VILLAINS CAME TO HELP YOU GUYS.
...
BOTH OF YOU...
YOU WERE WOUNDED BECAUSE OF ME.
I AM SO TERRIBLY SORRY...

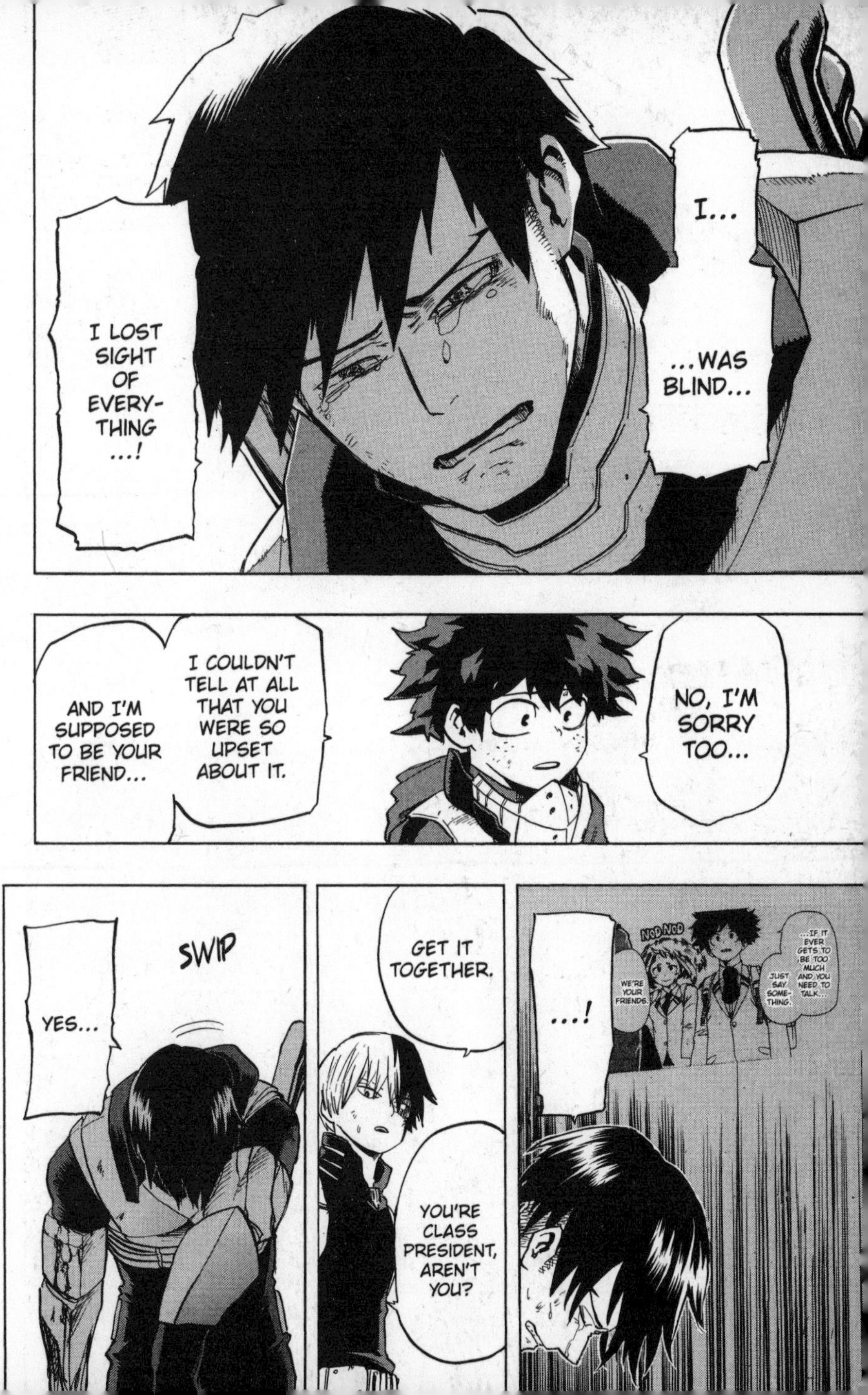

I...
...WAS BLIND...
I LOST SIGHT OF EVERYTHING...!
NO, I'M SORRY TOO...
I COULDN'T TELL AT ALL THAT YOU WERE SO UPSET ABOUT IT.
AND I'M SUPPOSED TO BE YOUR FRIEND...
NOD NOD
...IF IT EVER GETS TO BE TOO MUCH AND YOU NEED TO TALK...
JUST SAY SOMETHING.
WE'RE YOUR FRIENDS.
...!
GET IT TOGETHER.
YOU'RE CLASS PRESIDENT, AREN'T YOU?
SWIP
YES...

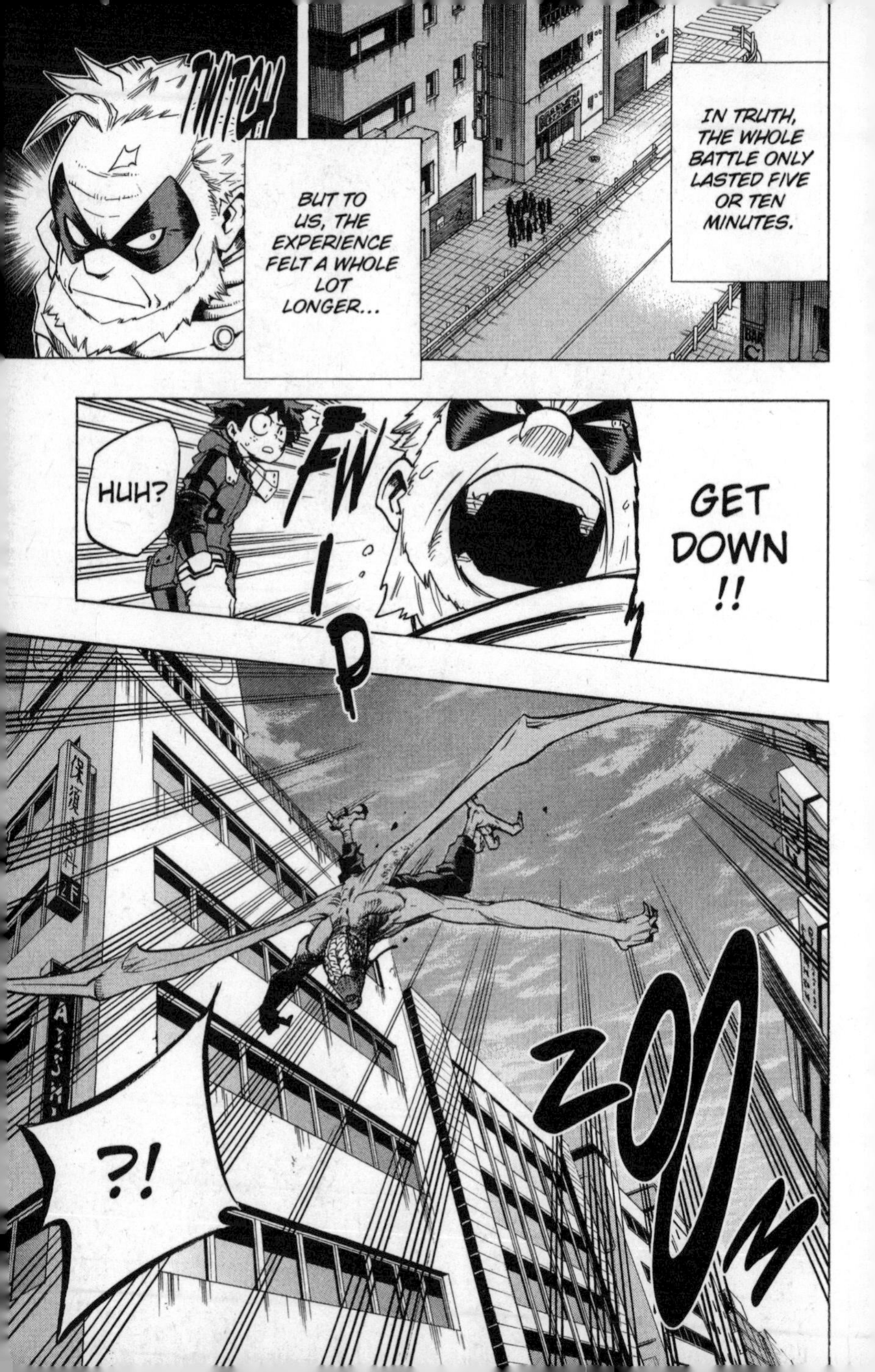
IN TRUTH, THE WHOLE BATTLE ONLY LASTED FIVE OR TEN MINUTES.
BUT TO US, THE EXPERIENCE FELT A WHOLE LOT LONGER...
TWITCH
GET DOWN !!
FWIP
HUH?
ZOOM
?!

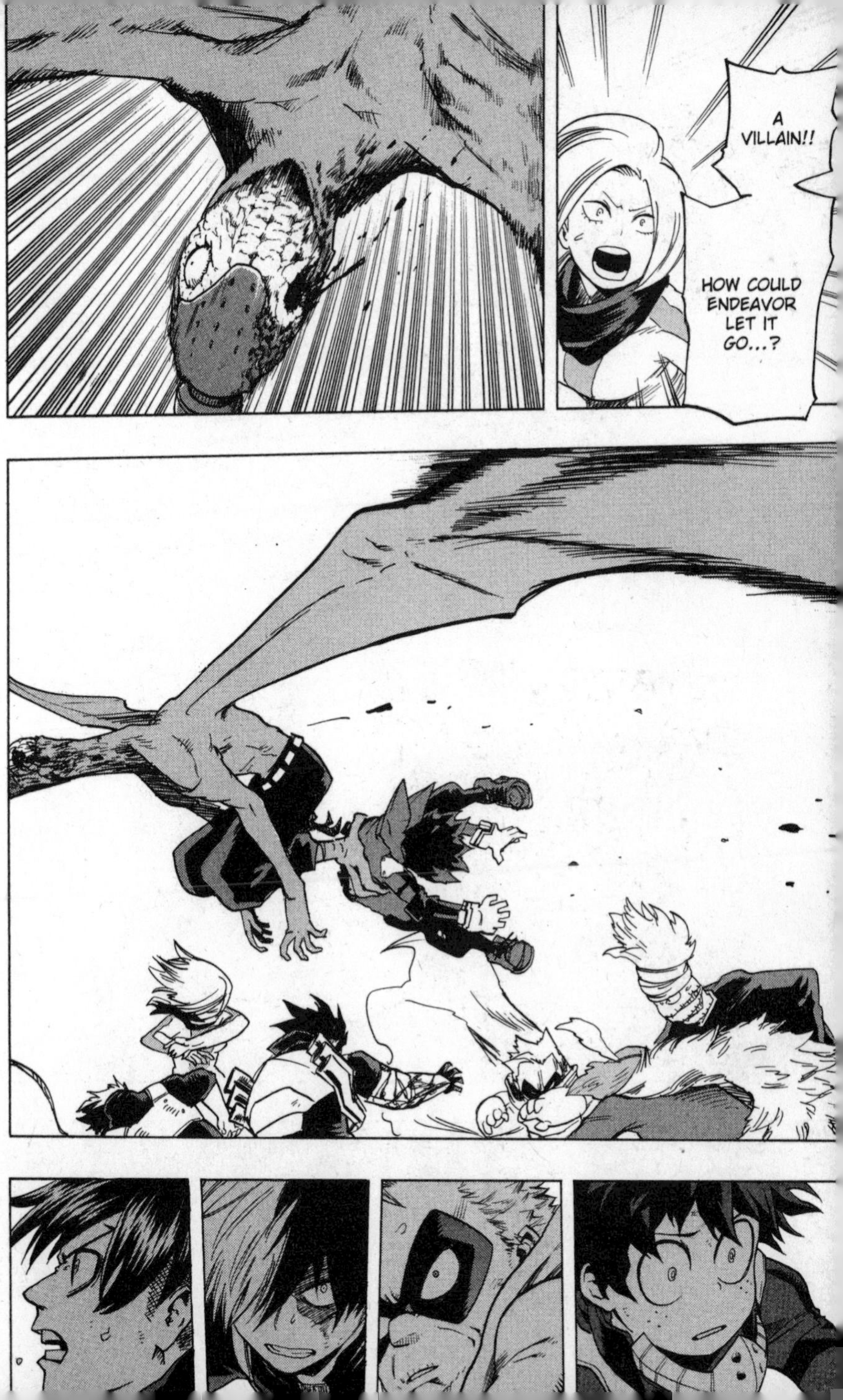
A VILLAIN!!
HOW COULD ENDEAVOR LET IT GO...?

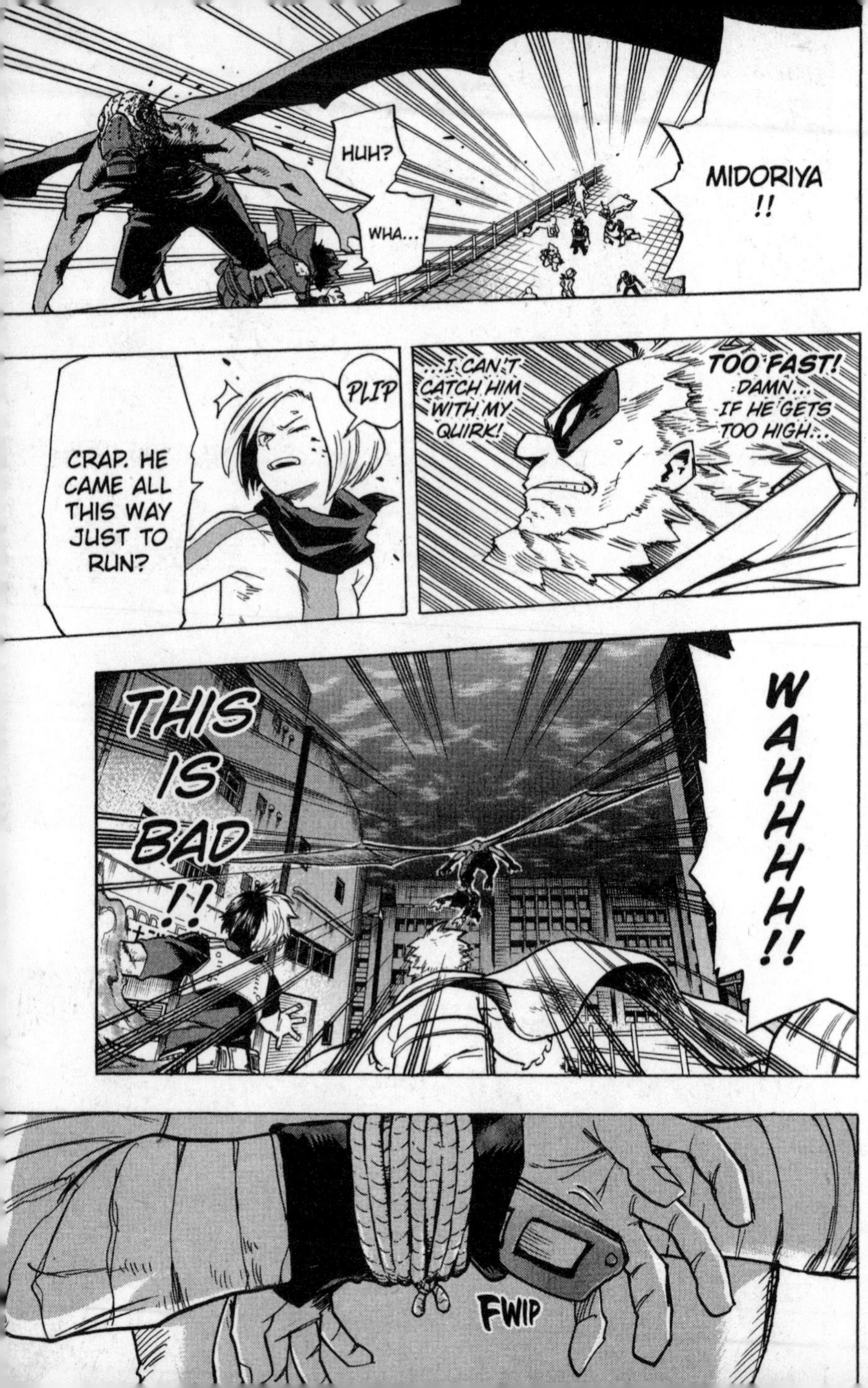
MIDORIYA!!
HUH?
WHA...
TOO FAST! DAMN... IF HE GETS TOO HIGH...
...I CAN'T CATCH HIM WITH MY QUIRK!
PLIP
CRAP. HE CAME ALL THIS WAY JUST TO RUN?
WAHHHHH!!
THIS IS BAD!!
FWIP

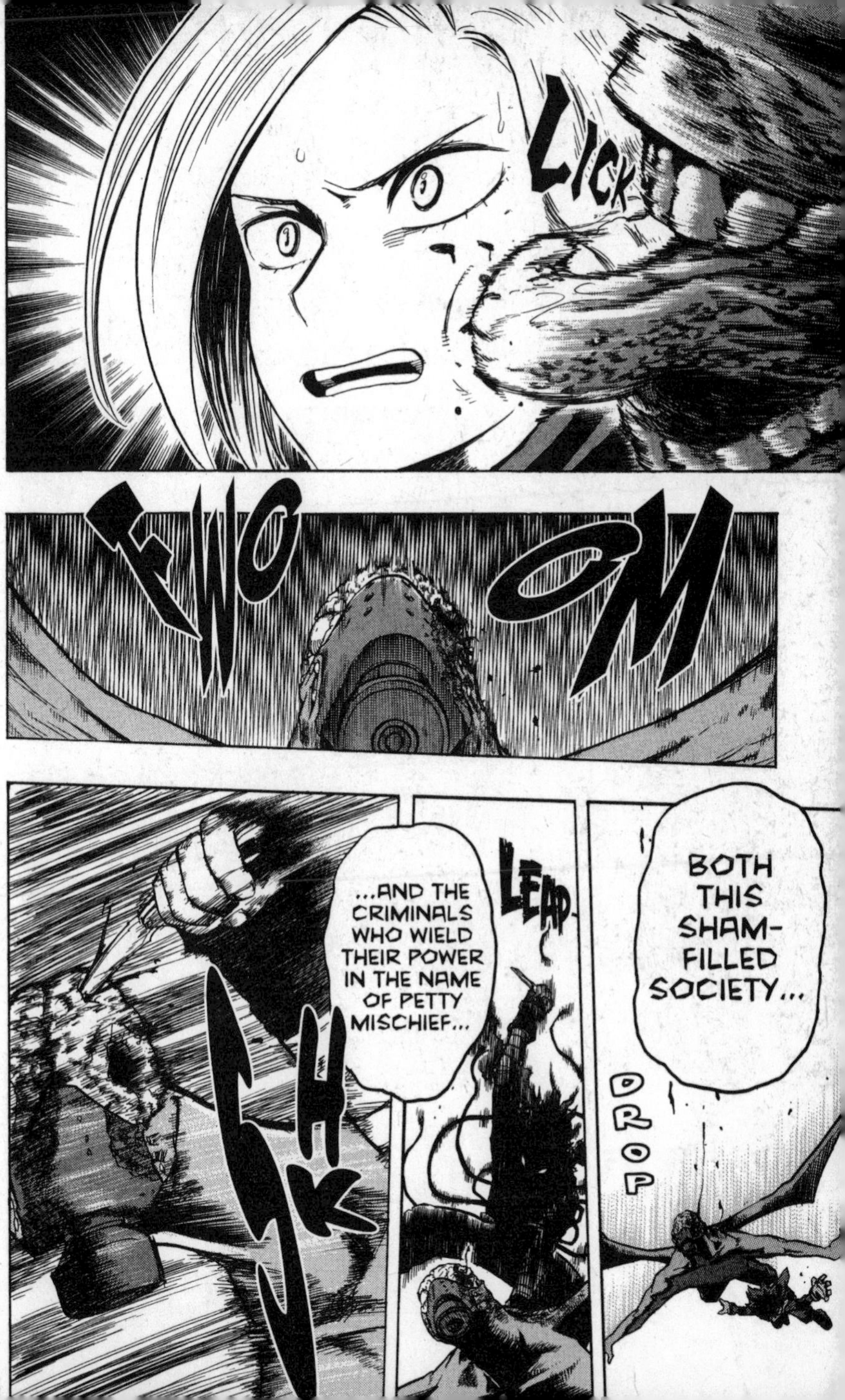
LICK
FWOOM
BOTH THIS SHAM-FILLED SOCIETY...
DROP
LEAP
...AND THE CRIMINALS WHO WIELD THEIR POWER IN THE NAME OF PETTY MISCHIEF...
SHK

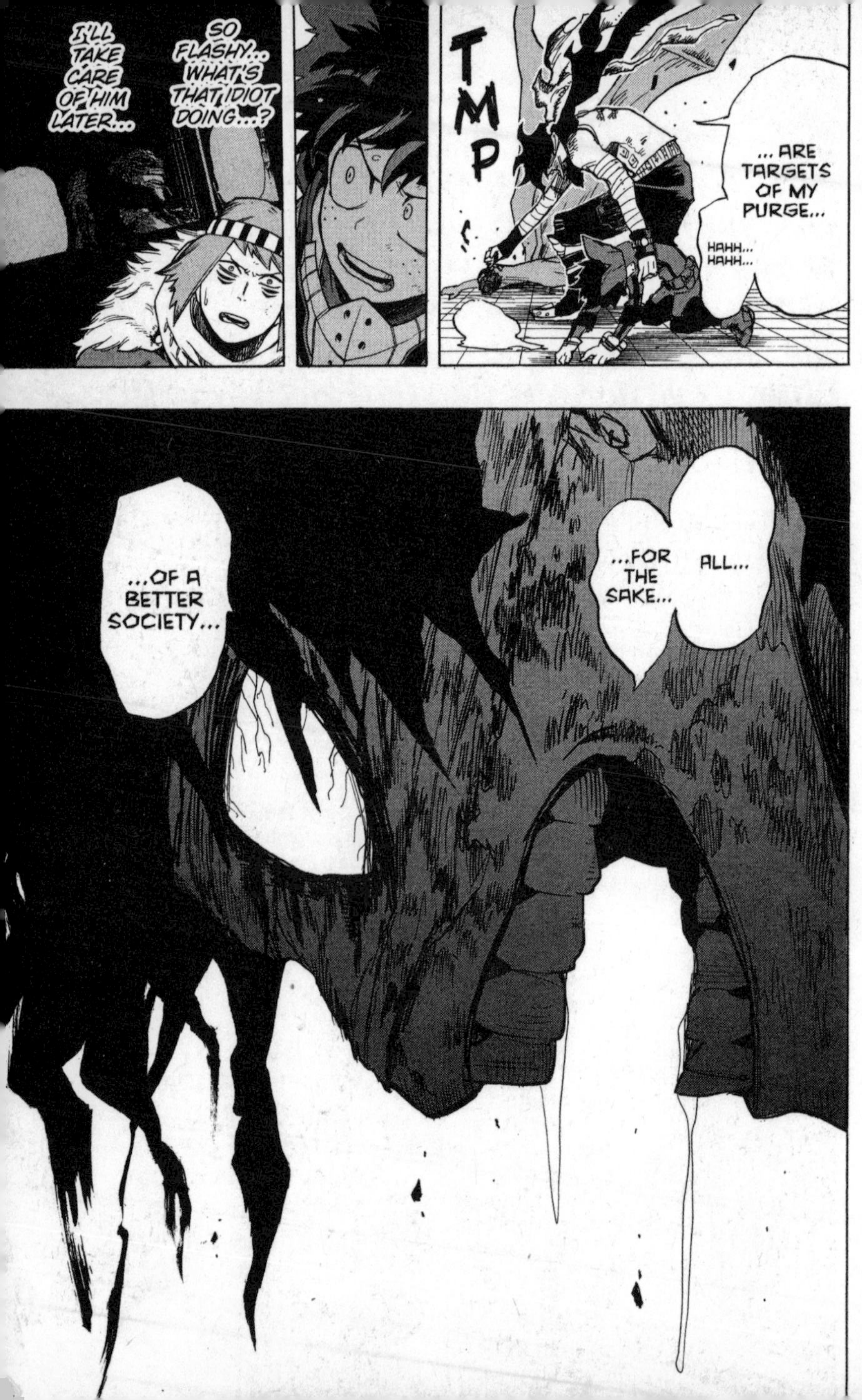
TMP
... ARE TARGETS OF MY PURGE...
HAHH... HAHH...
SO FLASHY... WHAT'S THAT IDIOT DOING...?
I'LL TAKE CARE OF HIM LATER...
ALL...
...FOR THE SAKE...
...OF A BETTER SOCIETY...

THE "IT'S NOT LIKE THERE'S A HARD-AND-FAST RULE THAT SAYS I GOTTA FILL THIS SPACE, BUT WHEN I WAS A KID, I'D ALWAYS GET JUST A LITTLE DISAPPOINTED WHEN I SAW BLANK PAGES IN A MANGA VOLUME I BOUGHT, SO I'M GOING ALL OUT TO COME UP WITH SOMETHING TO PUT HERE, SO AS NOT TO DISAPPOINT READERS WHO FEEL THE SAME WAY" CORNER

TENYA IDA'S COSTUME

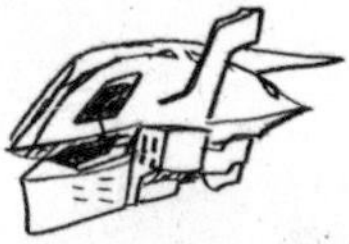

Ingenimet
To reduce drag.

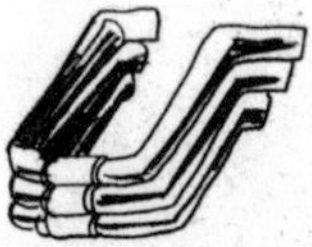

Ingenimuffler
Decorative.

Other Pieces
Most of the armor is just there as decoration, under the pretense of reducing drag. Much lighter than it looks.

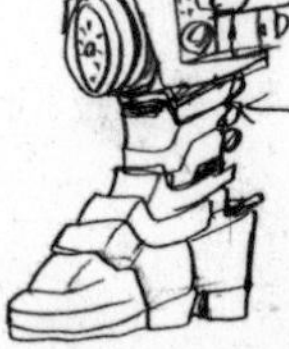

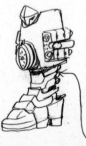

Ingenifoot
Equipped with a cooling function. Also supplements his leg engines and gives him better mileage. Exhaust comes out here.

ALL IN ALL: THE IMAGE IDA'S GOING FOR IN THE FUTURE IS PRETTY MUCH SET IN STONE, SO THERE'S A HEAVY EMPHASIS ON THE VISUALS.

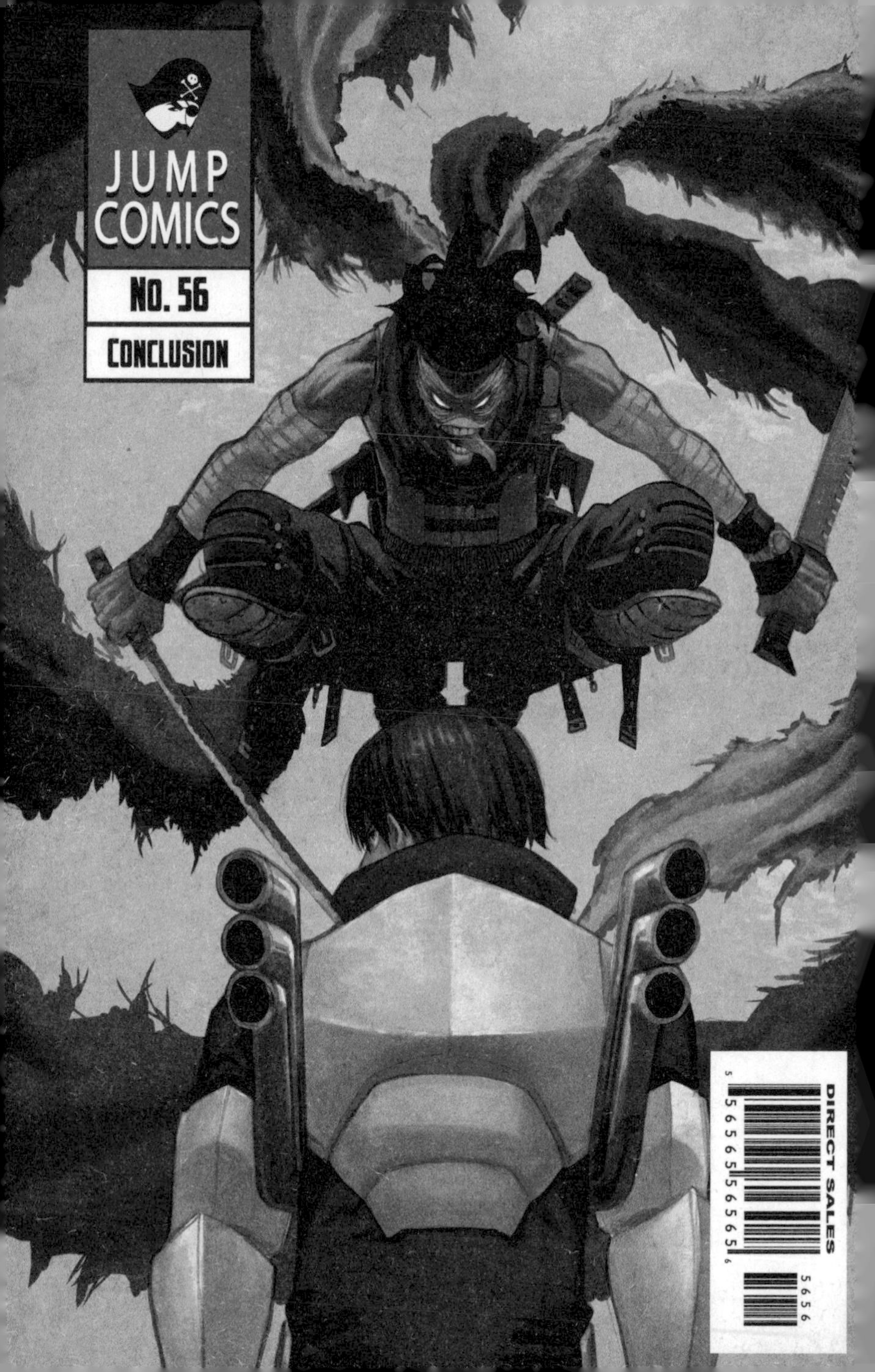
JUMP COMICS
NO. 56
CONCLUSION
DIRECT SALES

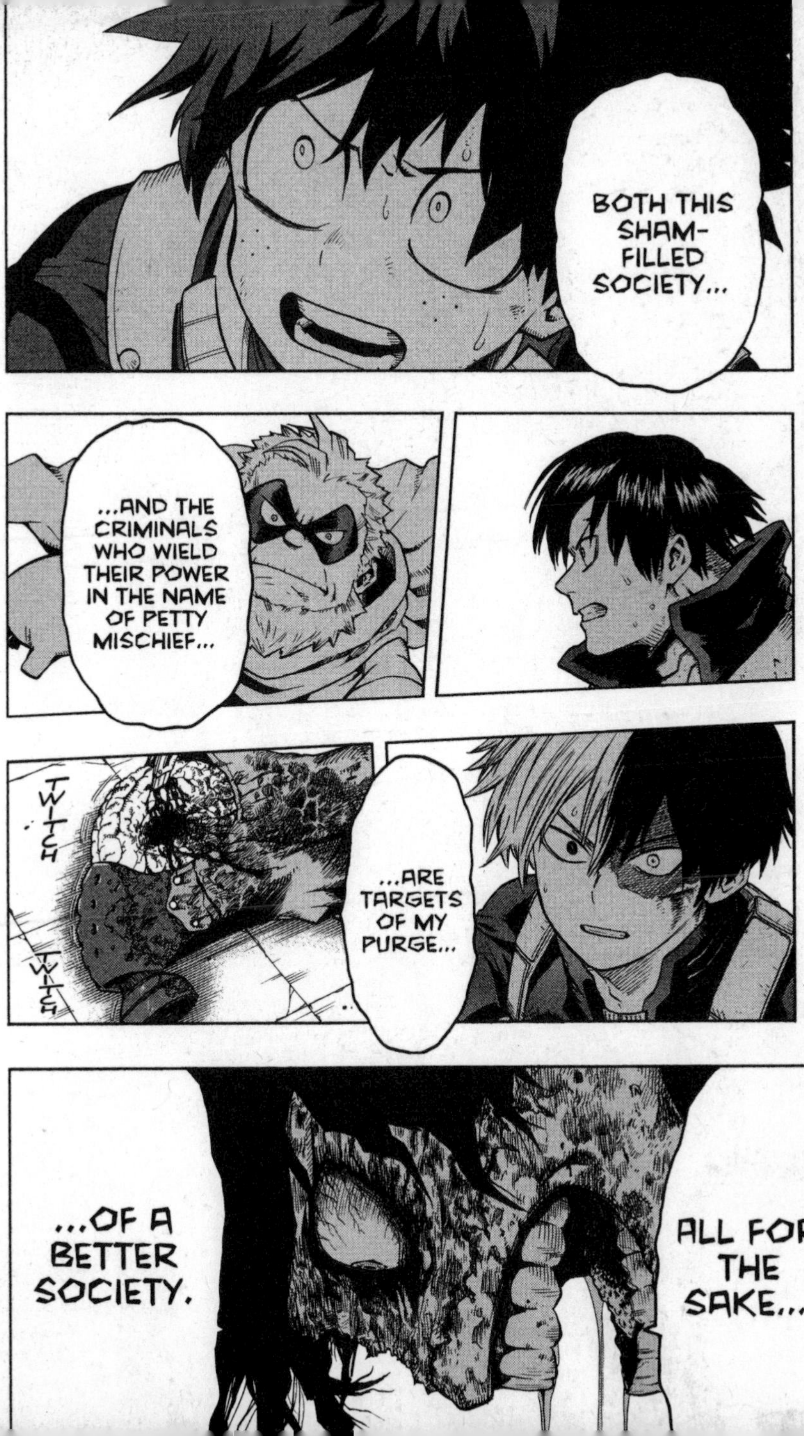
BOTH THIS SHAM-FILLED SOCIETY...
...AND THE CRIMINALS WHO WIELD THEIR POWER IN THE NAME OF PETTY MISCHIEF...
...ARE TARGETS OF MY PURGE...
TWITCH
TWITCH
ALL FOR THE SAKE...
...OF A BETTER SOCIETY.

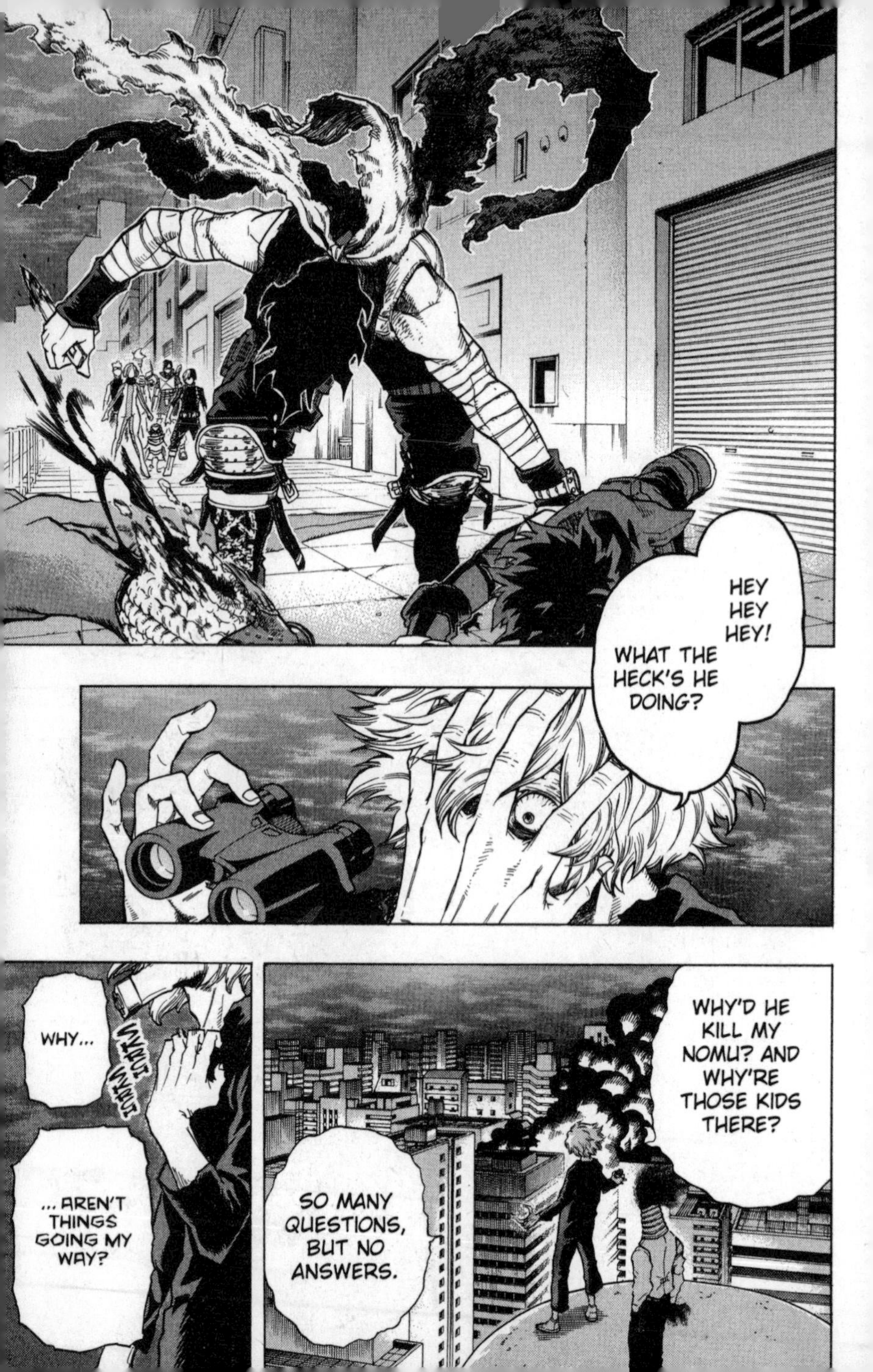
HEY HEY HEY! WHAT THE HECK'S HE DOING?
WHY'D HE KILL MY NOMU? AND WHY'RE THOSE KIDS THERE?
SO MANY QUESTIONS, BUT NO ANSWERS.
WHY...
...AREN'T THINGS GOING MY WAY?

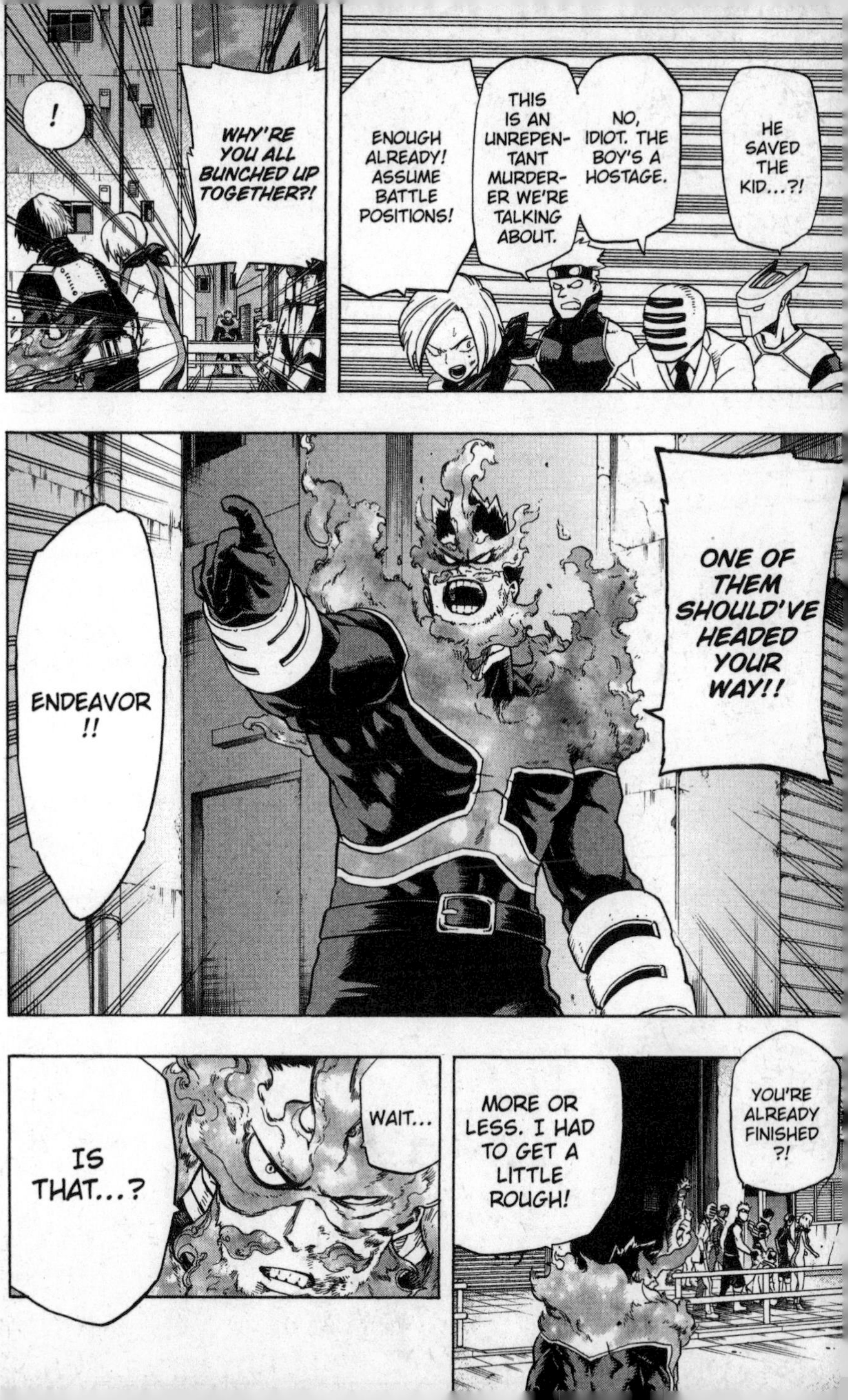
HE SAVED THE KID...?!
NO, IDIOT. THE BOY'S A HOSTAGE.
THIS IS AN UNREPEN-TANT MURDER-ER WE'RE TALKING ABOUT.
ENOUGH ALREADY! ASSUME BATTLE POSITIONS!
WHY'RE YOU ALL BUNCHED UP TOGETHER?!
!
ONE OF THEM SHOULD'VE HEADED YOUR WAY!!
ENDEAVOR !!
YOU'RE ALREADY FINISHED ?!
MORE OR LESS. I HAD TO GET A LITTLE ROUGH!
WAIT...
IS THAT...?

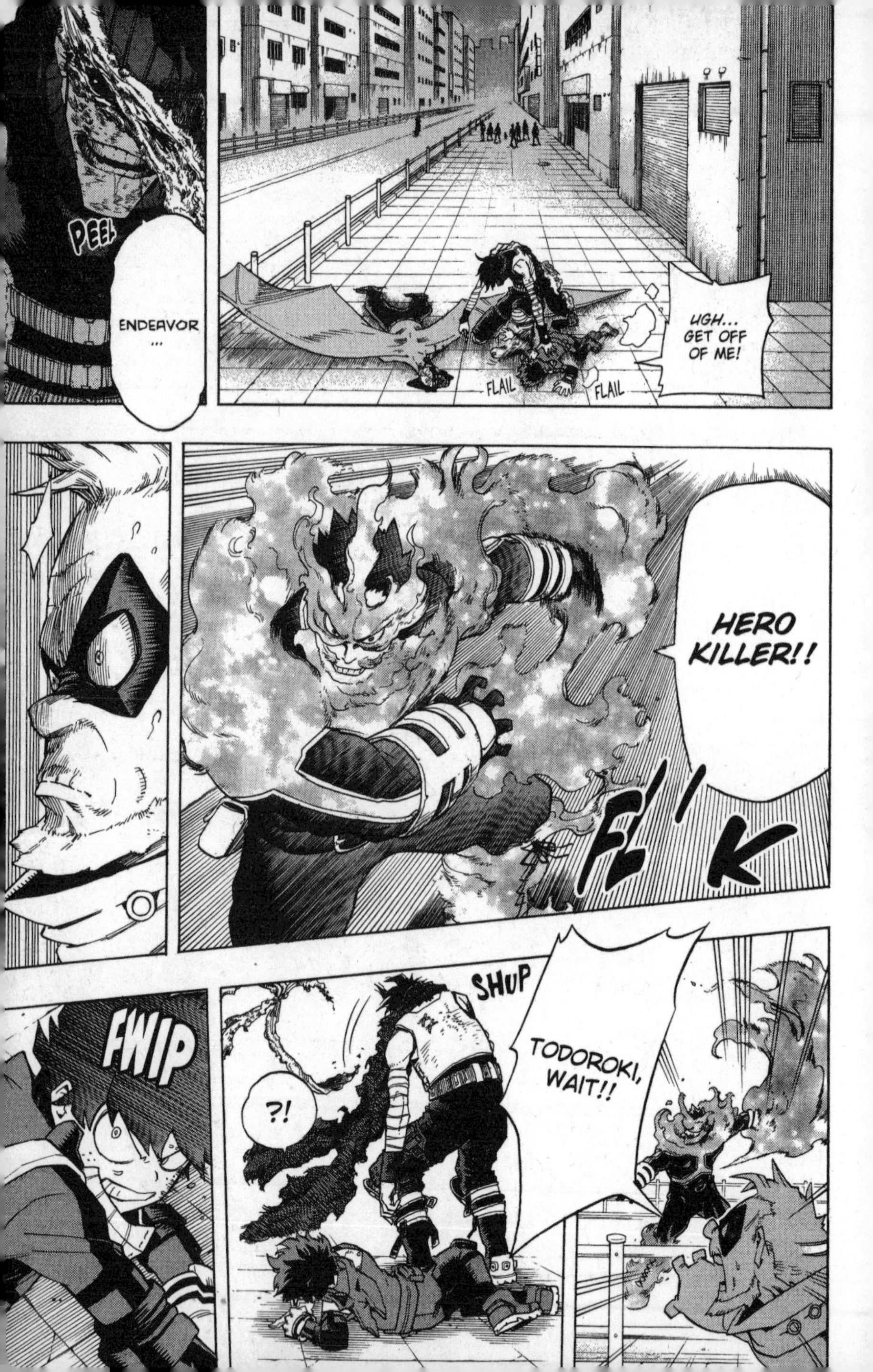
UGH... GET OFF OF ME!
FLAIL
FLAIL
PEEL
ENDEAVOR ...
HERO KILLER!!
FL'K
TODOROKI, WAIT!!
SHUP
?!
FWIP

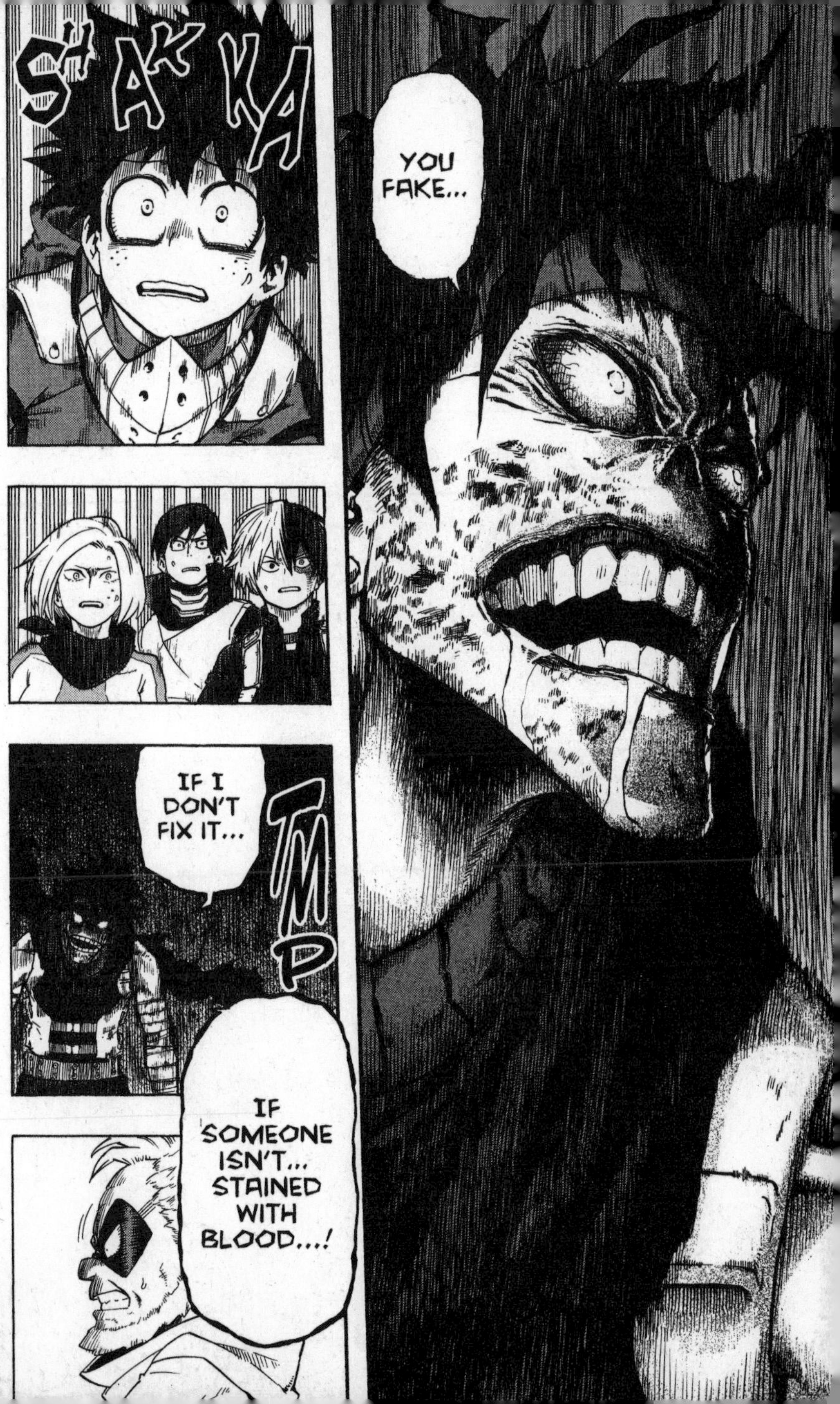
YOU FAKE...
SHAKKA
IF I DON'T FIX IT...
TMP
IF SOMEONE ISN'T... STAINED WITH BLOOD...!

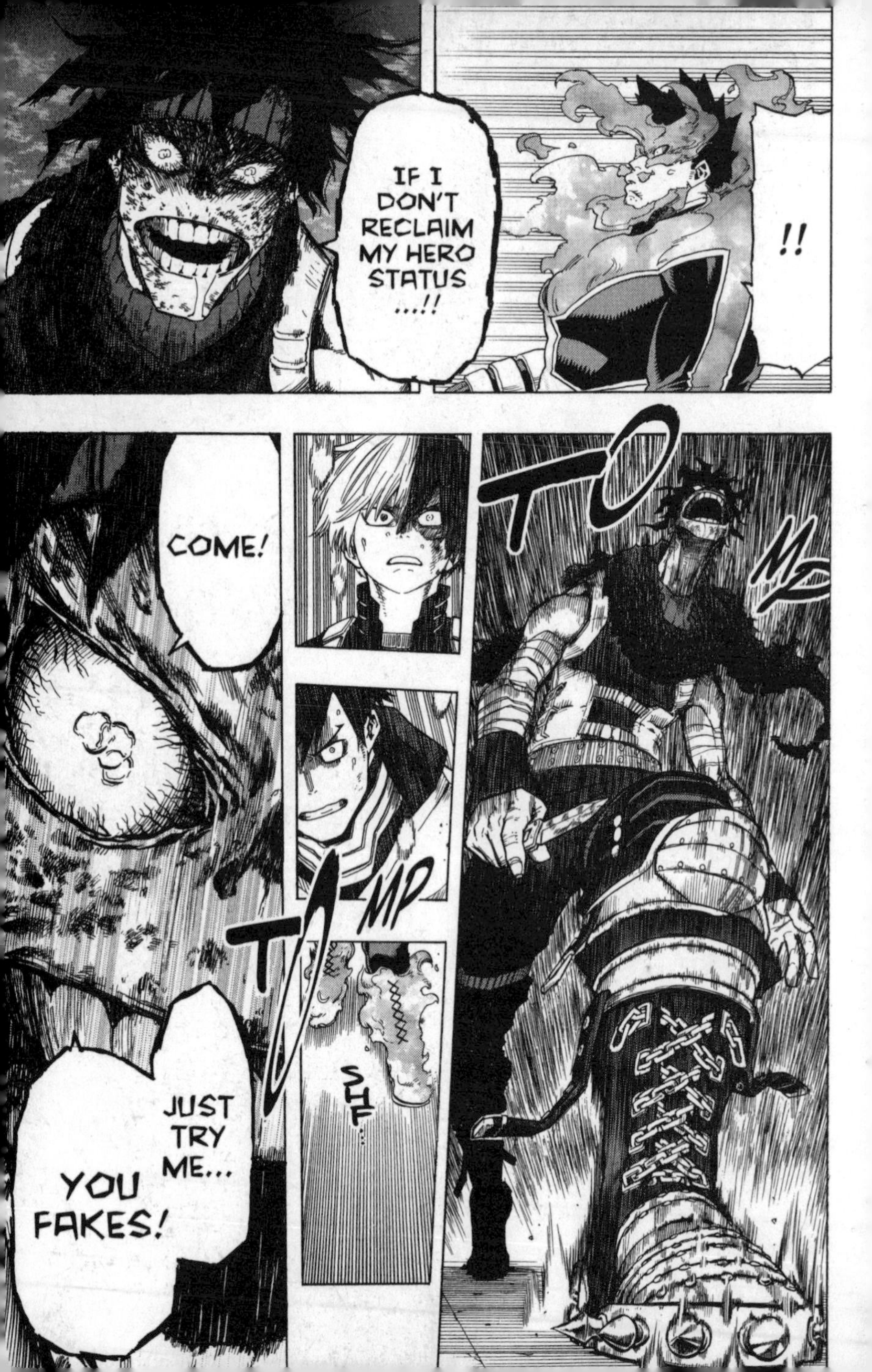
!!
IF I DON'T RECLAIM MY HERO STATUS ...!!
TOMP
TOMP
SHF...
COME!
JUST TRY ME...
YOU FAKES!

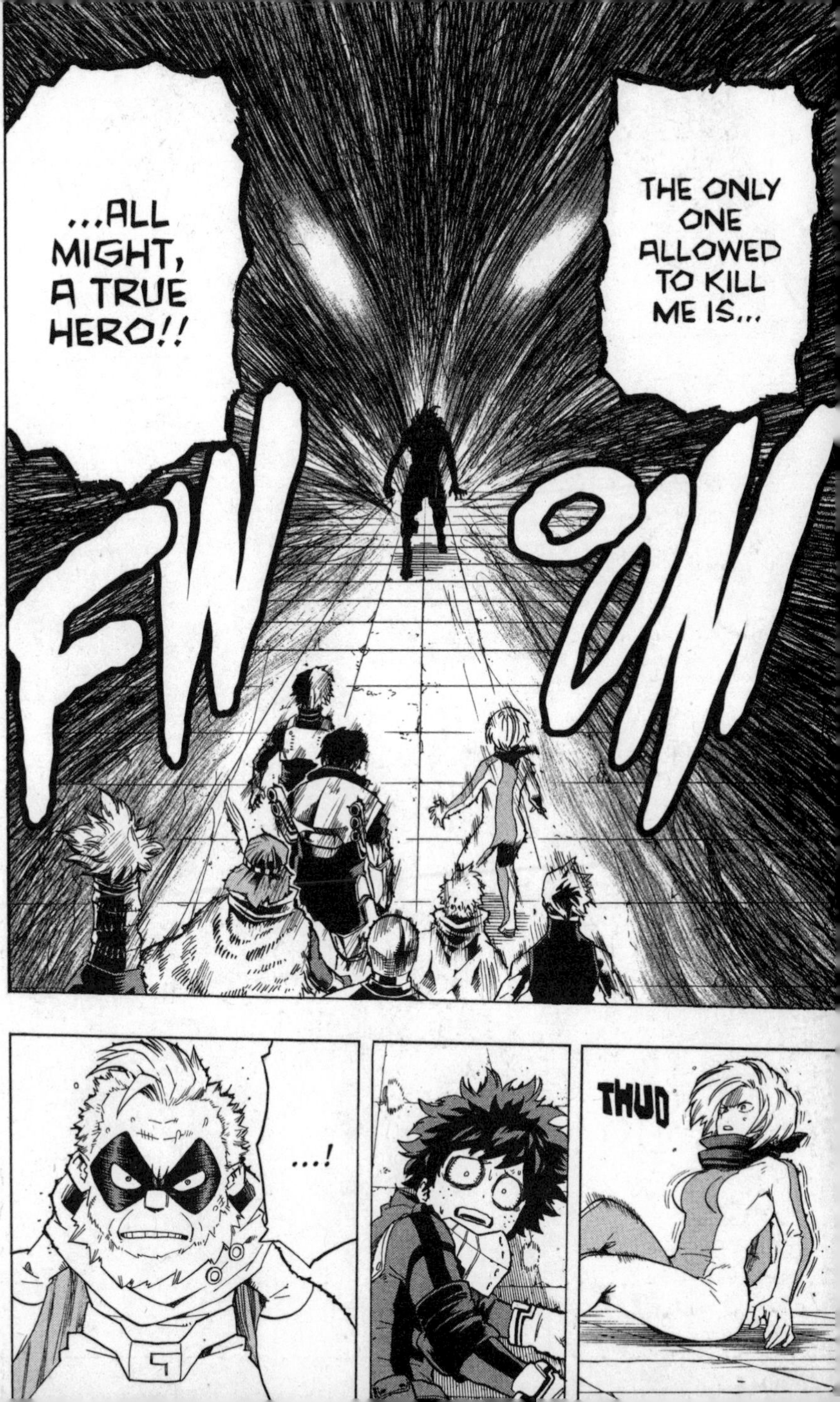
THE ONLY ONE ALLOWED TO KILL ME IS...
...ALL MIGHT, A TRUE HERO!!
FWOOM
THUD
...!

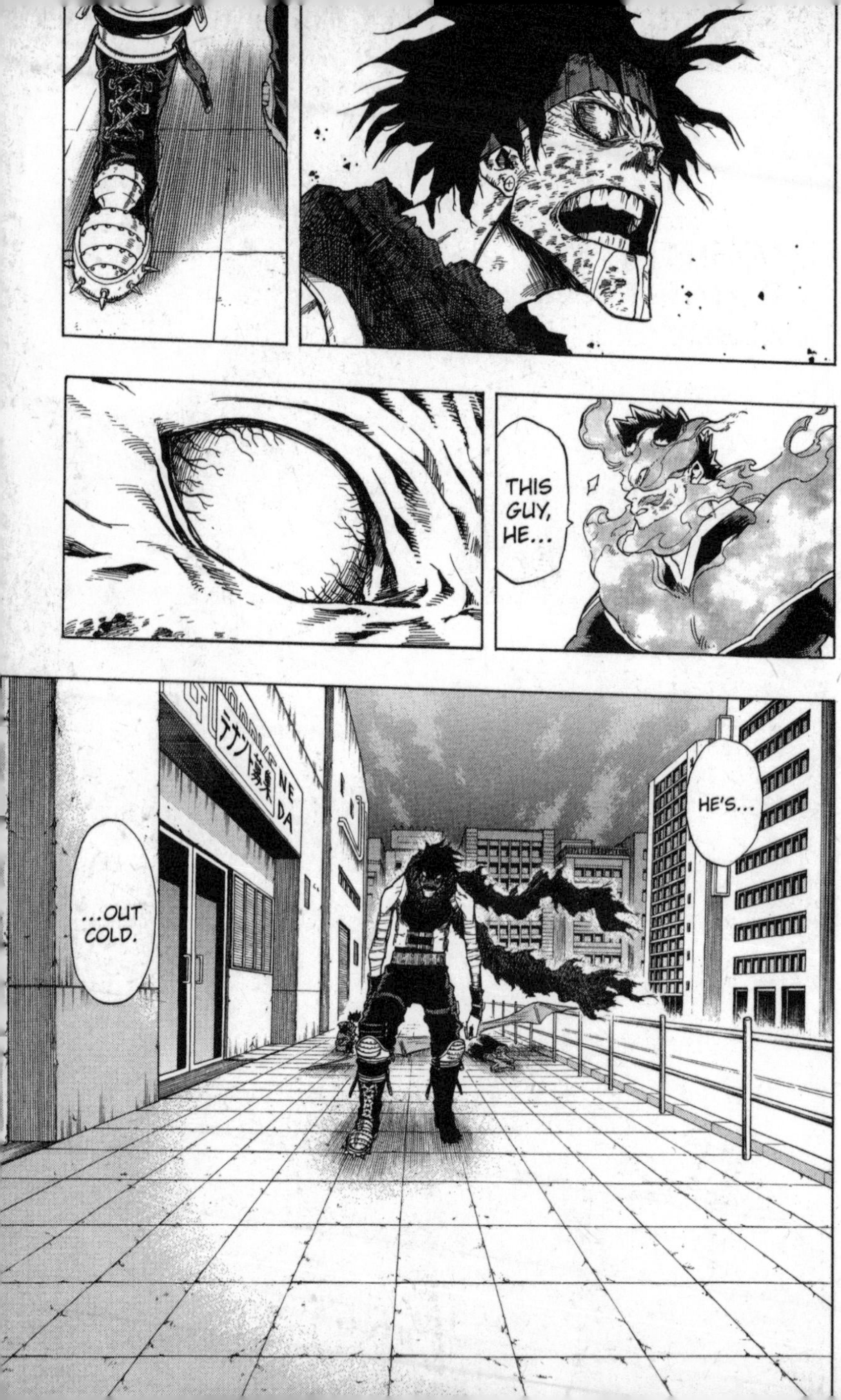
THIS GUY, HE...
HE'S...
テナント募集
NE
DA
...OUT COLD.

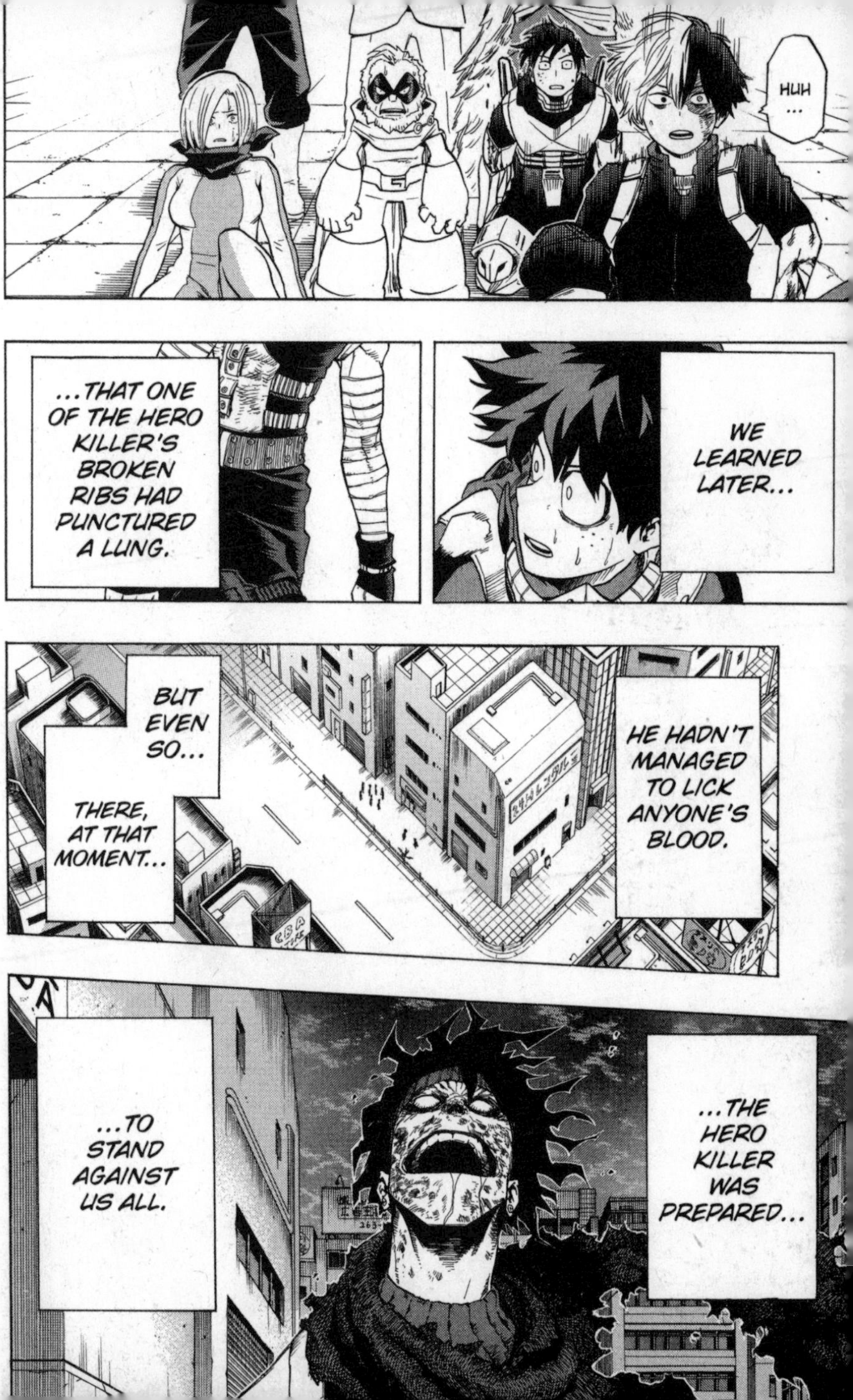
HUH ...
WE LEARNED LATER...
...THAT ONE OF THE HERO KILLER'S BROKEN RIBS HAD PUNCTURED A LUNG.
HE HADN'T MANAGED TO LICK ANYONE'S BLOOD.
BUT EVEN SO...
THERE, AT THAT MOMENT...
...THE HERO KILLER WAS PREPARED...
...TO STAND AGAINST US ALL.

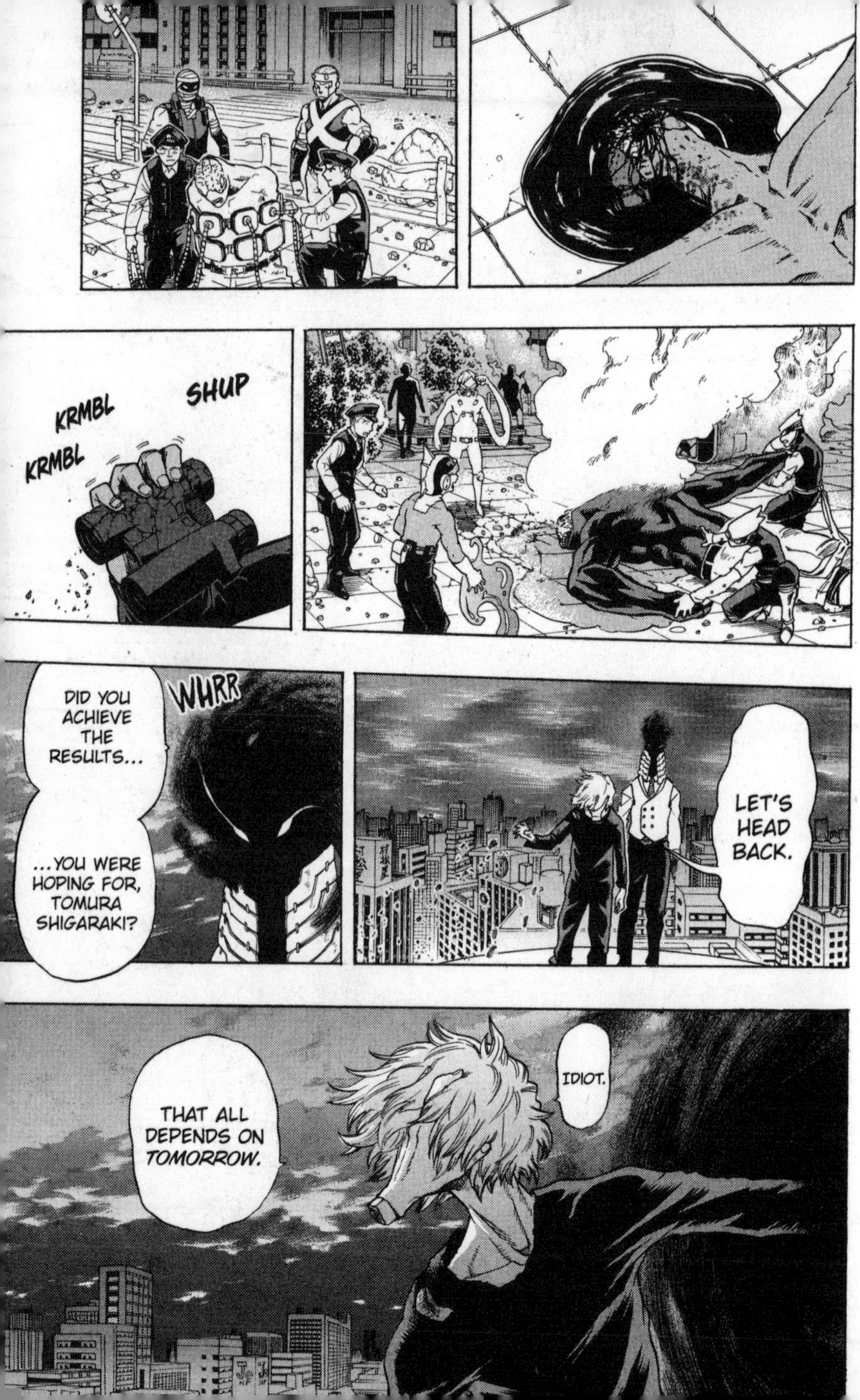
SHUP
KRMBL
KRMBL
LET'S HEAD BACK.
WHRR
DID YOU ACHIEVE THE RESULTS...
...YOU WERE HOPING FOR, TOMURA SHIGARAKI?
IDIOT.
THAT ALL DEPENDS ON *TOMORROW.*

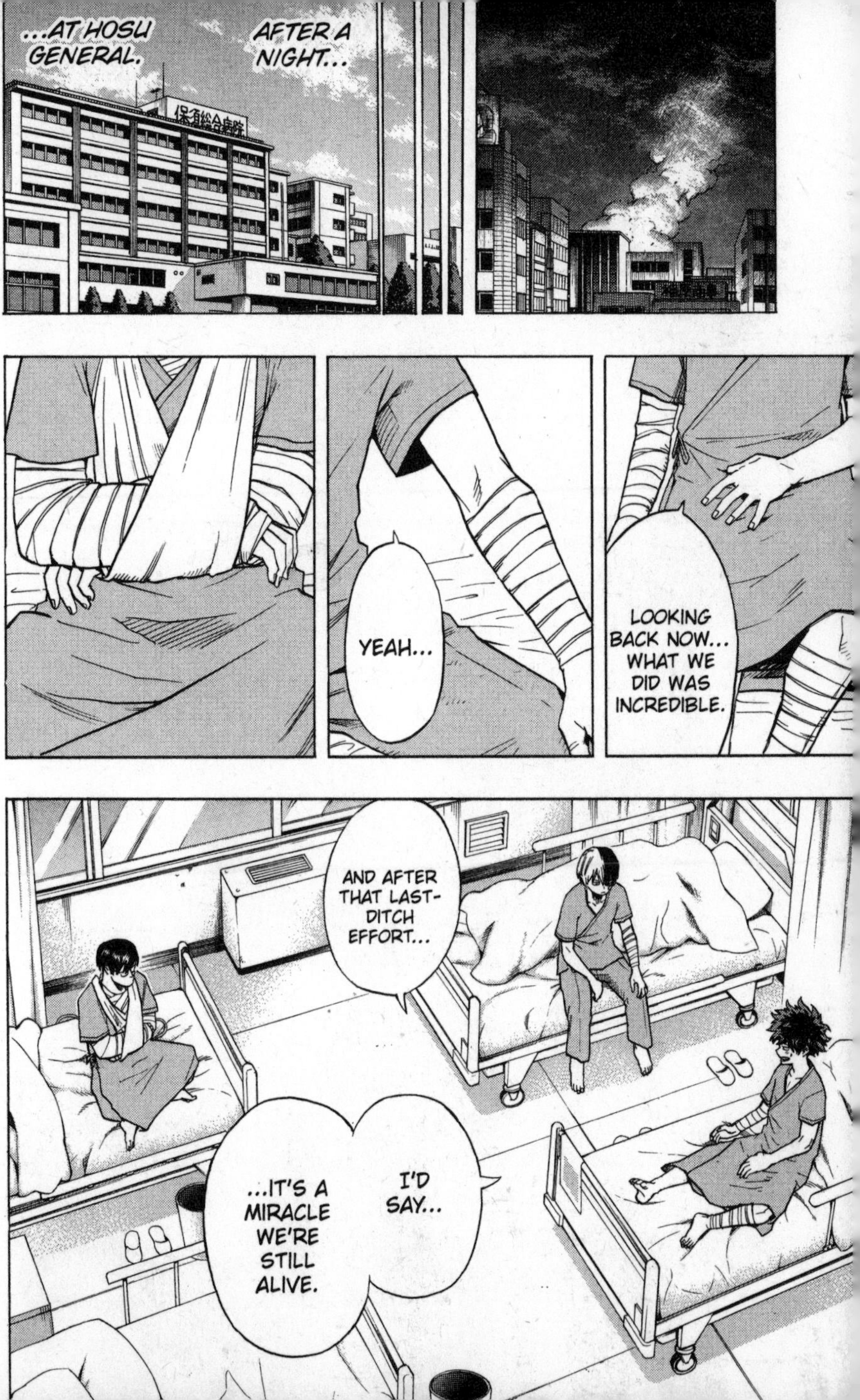
AFTER A NIGHT...
...AT HOSU GENERAL.
LOOKING BACK NOW... WHAT WE DID WAS INCREDIBLE.
YEAH...
AND AFTER THAT LAST-DITCH EFFORT...
I'D SAY...
...IT'S A MIRACLE WE'RE STILL ALIVE.

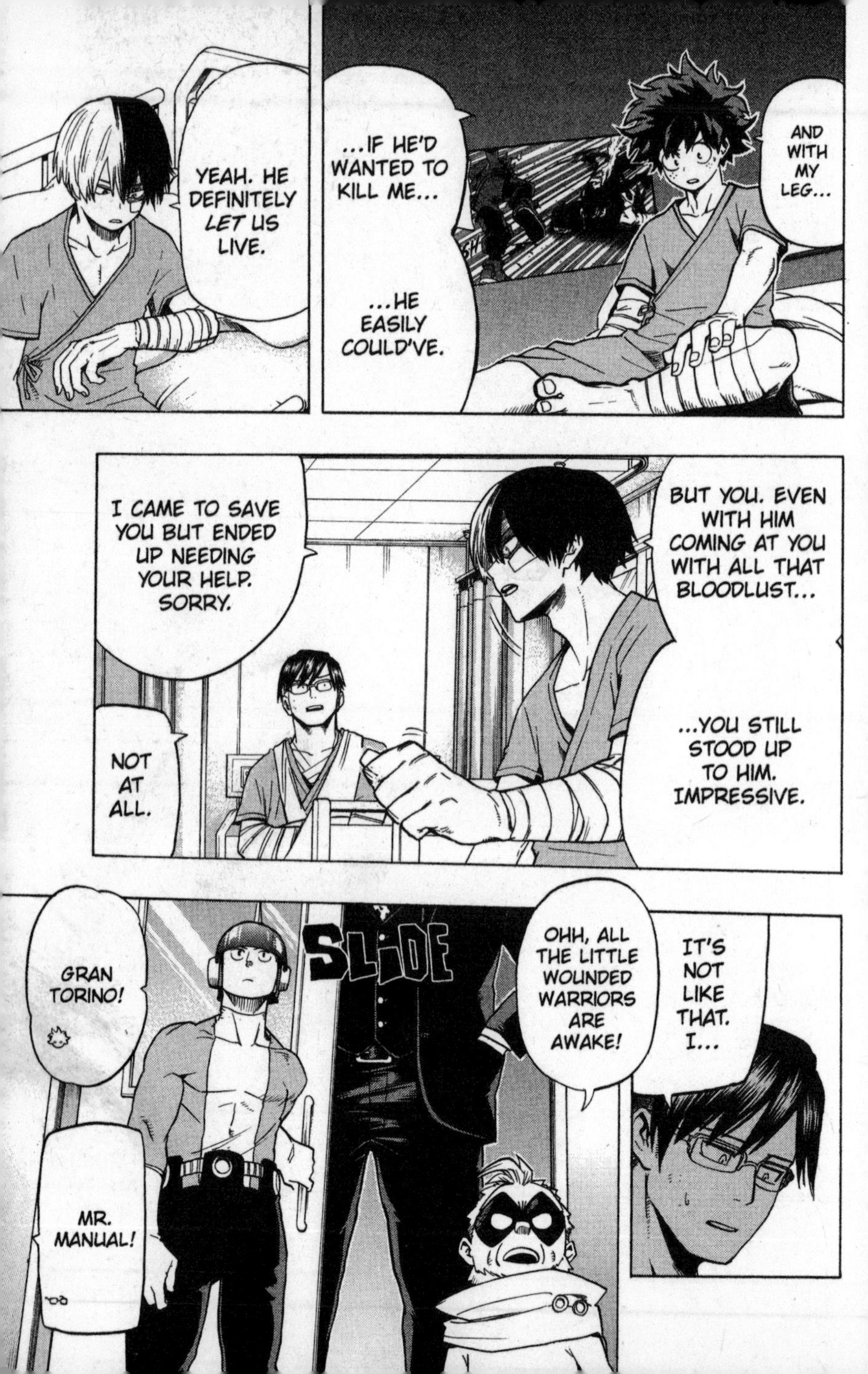
AND WITH MY LEG...
...IF HE'D WANTED TO KILL ME...
...HE EASILY COULD'VE.
YEAH. HE DEFINITELY *LET* US LIVE.
BUT YOU. EVEN WITH HIM COMING AT YOU WITH ALL THAT BLOODLUST...
...YOU STILL STOOD UP TO HIM. IMPRESSIVE.
I CAME TO SAVE YOU BUT ENDED UP NEEDING YOUR HELP. SORRY.
NOT AT ALL.
IT'S NOT LIKE THAT. I...
SLIDE
OHH, ALL THE LITTLE WOUNDED WARRIORS ARE AWAKE!
GRAN TORINO!
MR. MANUAL!

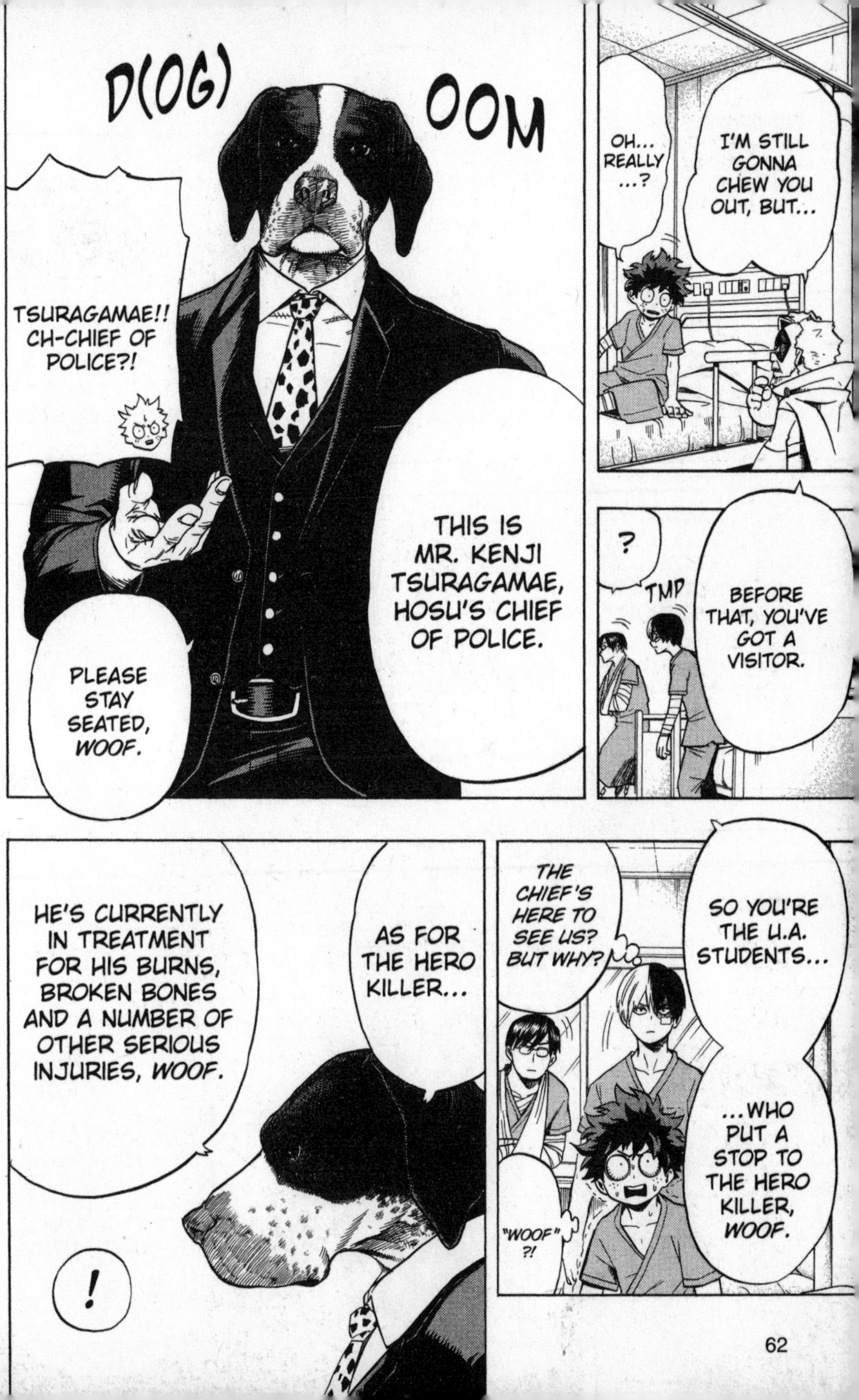
I'M STILL GONNA CHEW YOU OUT, BUT...
OH... REALLY ...?
BEFORE THAT, YOU'VE GOT A VISITOR.
TMP
?
D(OG) OOM
THIS IS MR. KENJI TSURAGAMAE, HOSU'S CHIEF OF POLICE.
TSURAGAMAE!! CH-CHIEF OF POLICE?!
PLEASE STAY SEATED, *WOOF.*
SO YOU'RE THE U.A. STUDENTS...
...WHO PUT A STOP TO THE HERO KILLER, *WOOF.*
THE CHIEF'S HERE TO SEE US? BUT WHY?
"WOOF" ?!
AS FOR THE HERO KILLER...
HE'S CURRENTLY IN TREATMENT FOR HIS BURNS, BROKEN BONES AND A NUMBER OF OTHER SERIOUS INJURIES, *WOOF.*
!

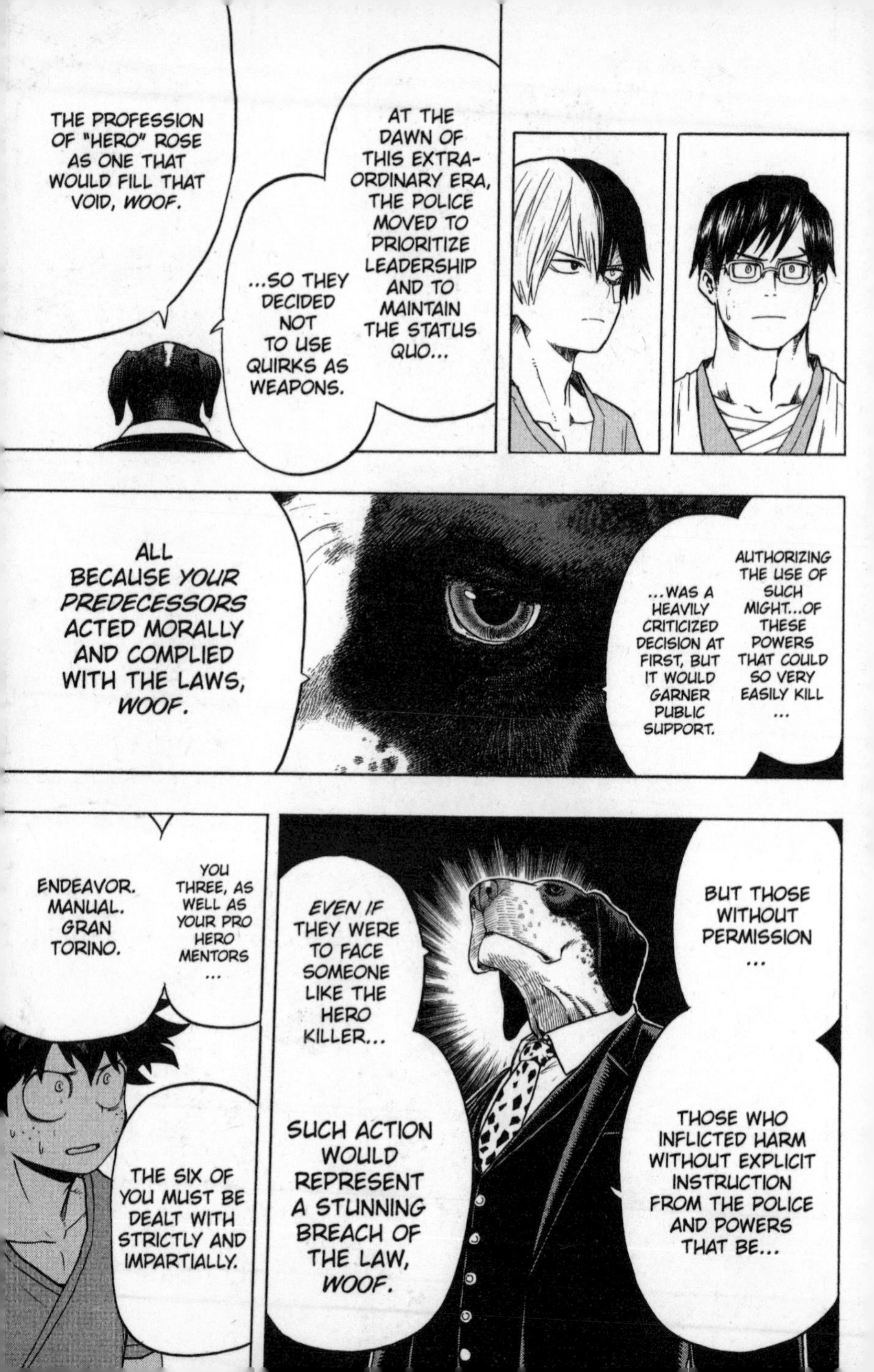
AT THE DAWN OF THIS EXTRA-ORDINARY ERA, THE POLICE MOVED TO PRIORITIZE LEADERSHIP AND TO MAINTAIN THE STATUS QUO...
...SO THEY DECIDED NOT TO USE QUIRKS AS WEAPONS.
THE PROFESSION OF "HERO" ROSE AS ONE THAT WOULD FILL THAT VOID, *WOOF*.
AUTHORIZING THE USE OF SUCH MIGHT...OF THESE POWERS THAT COULD SO VERY EASILY KILL ...
...WAS A HEAVILY CRITICIZED DECISION AT FIRST, BUT IT WOULD GARNER PUBLIC SUPPORT.
ALL BECAUSE *YOUR PREDECESSORS* ACTED MORALLY AND COMPLIED WITH THE LAWS, *WOOF*.
BUT THOSE WITHOUT PERMISSION ...
THOSE WHO INFLICTED HARM WITHOUT EXPLICIT INSTRUCTION FROM THE POLICE AND POWERS THAT BE...
EVEN IF THEY WERE TO FACE SOMEONE LIKE THE HERO KILLER...
SUCH ACTION WOULD REPRESENT A STUNNING BREACH OF THE LAW, *WOOF*.
YOU THREE, AS WELL AS YOUR PRO HERO MENTORS ...
ENDEAVOR. MANUAL. GRAN TORINO.
THE SIX OF YOU MUST BE DEALT WITH STRICTLY AND IMPARTIALLY.

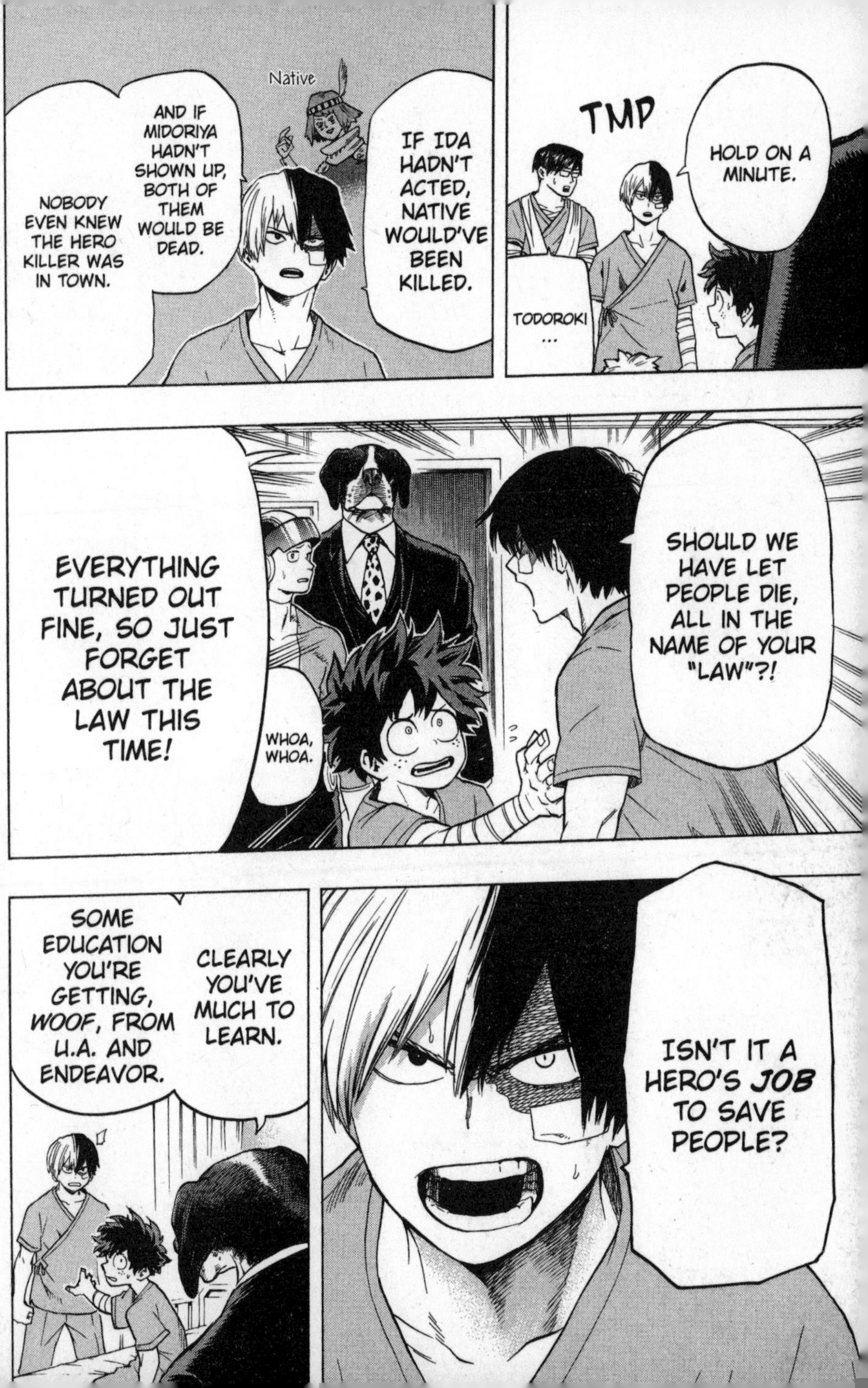
TMP
HOLD ON A MINUTE.
TODOROKI ...
IF IDA HADN'T ACTED, NATIVE WOULD'VE BEEN KILLED.
Native
AND IF MIDORIYA HADN'T SHOWN UP, BOTH OF THEM WOULD BE DEAD.
NOBODY EVEN KNEW THE HERO KILLER WAS IN TOWN.
SHOULD WE HAVE LET PEOPLE DIE, ALL IN THE NAME OF YOUR "LAW"?!
WHOA, WHOA.
EVERYTHING TURNED OUT FINE, SO JUST FORGET ABOUT THE LAW THIS TIME!
ISN'T IT A HERO'S *JOB* TO SAVE PEOPLE?
CLEARLY YOU'VE MUCH TO LEARN.
SOME EDUCATION YOU'RE GETTING, *WOOF*, FROM U.A. AND ENDEAVOR.

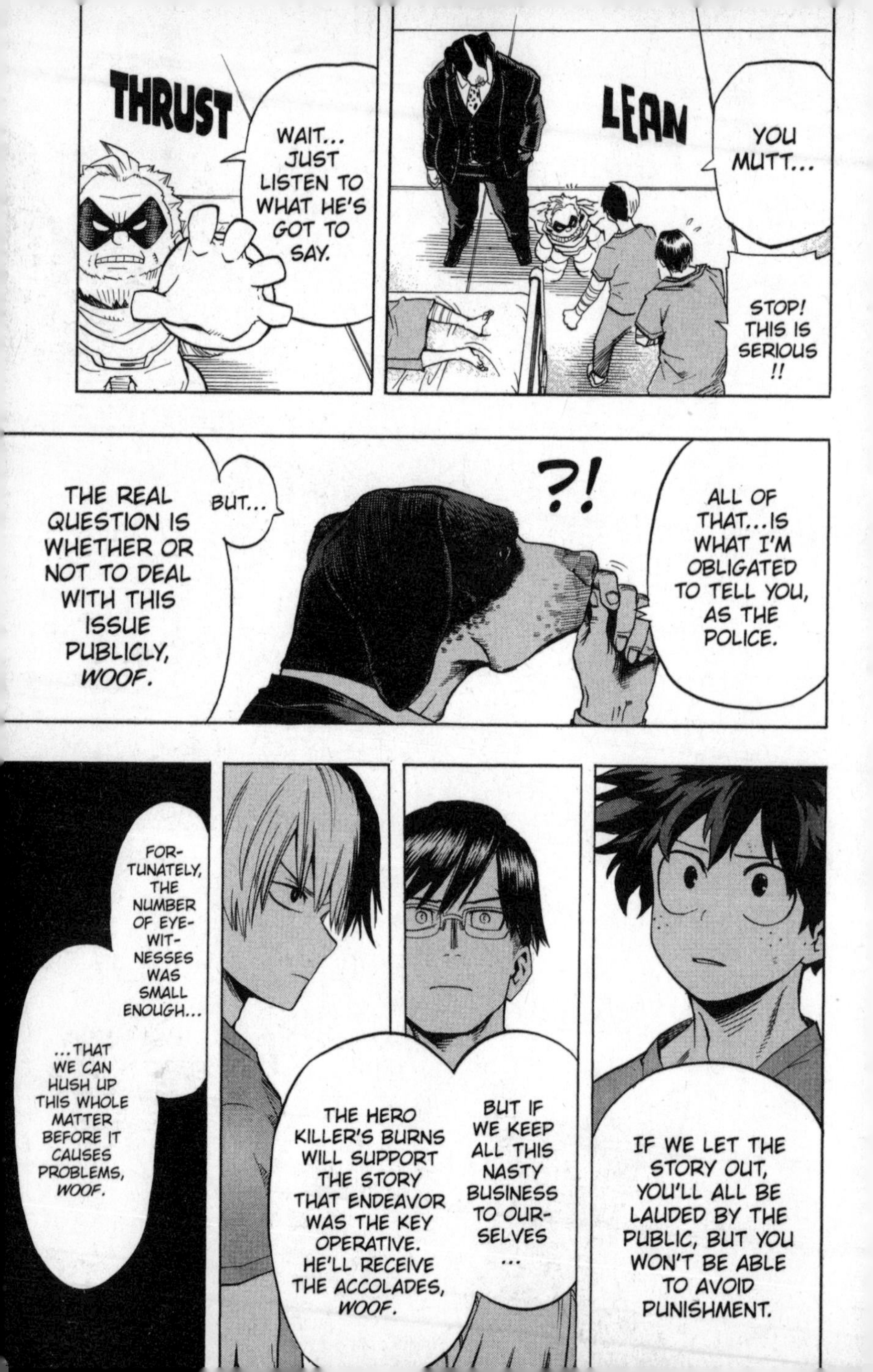
LEAN
YOU MUTT...
STOP! THIS IS SERIOUS !!
THRUST
WAIT... JUST LISTEN TO WHAT HE'S GOT TO SAY.
ALL OF THAT...IS WHAT I'M OBLIGATED TO TELL YOU, AS THE POLICE.
?!
BUT...
THE REAL QUESTION IS WHETHER OR NOT TO DEAL WITH THIS ISSUE PUBLICLY, *WOOF.*
IF WE LET THE STORY OUT, YOU'LL ALL BE LAUDED BY THE PUBLIC, BUT YOU WON'T BE ABLE TO AVOID PUNISHMENT.
BUT IF WE KEEP ALL THIS NASTY BUSINESS TO OURSELVES ...
THE HERO KILLER'S BURNS WILL SUPPORT THE STORY THAT ENDEAVOR WAS THE KEY OPERATIVE. HE'LL RECEIVE THE ACCOLADES, *WOOF.*
FORTUNATELY, THE NUMBER OF EYEWITNESSES WAS SMALL ENOUGH...
...THAT WE CAN HUSH UP THIS WHOLE MATTER BEFORE IT CAUSES PROBLEMS, *WOOF.*

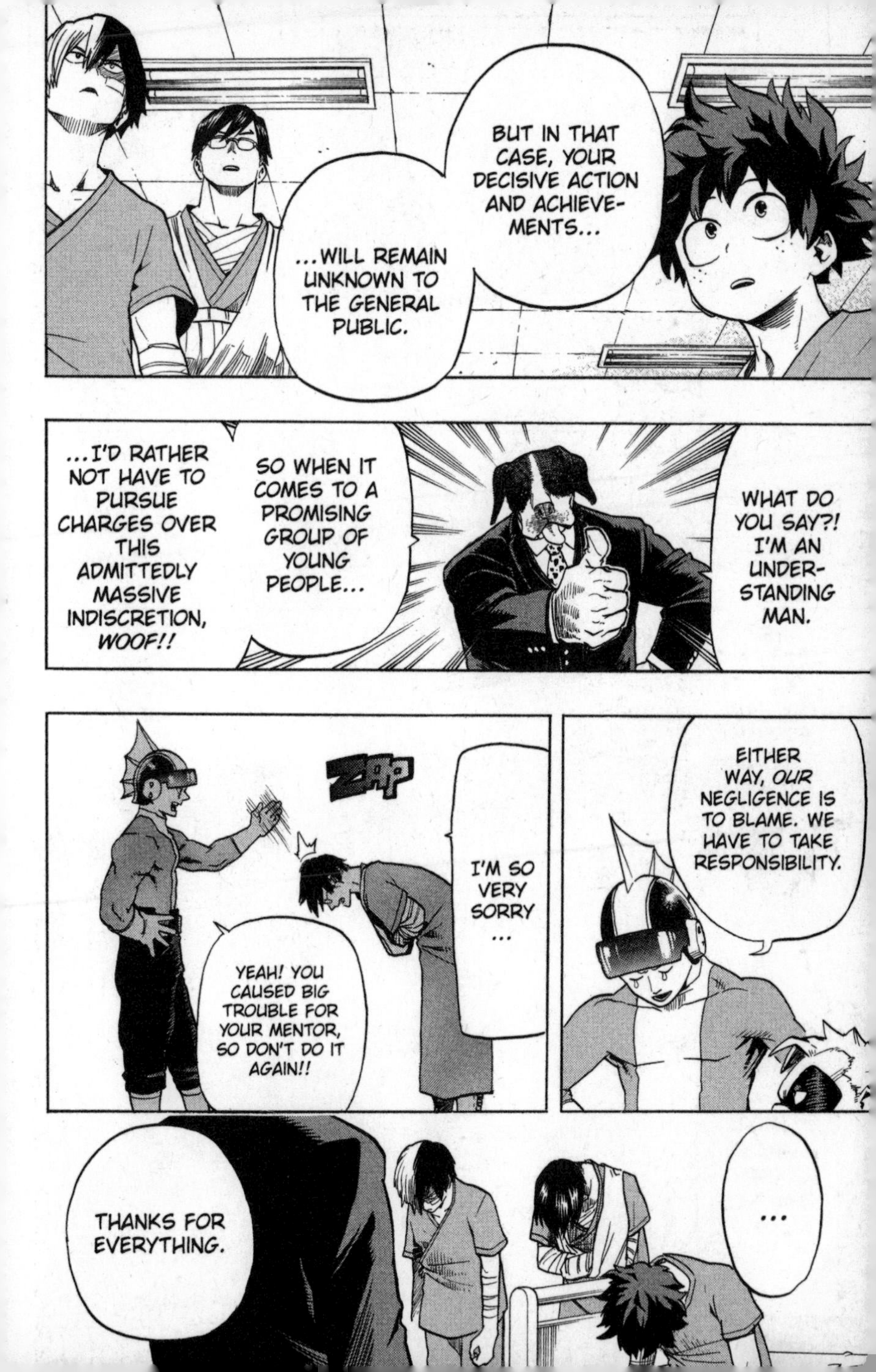
BUT IN THAT CASE, YOUR DECISIVE ACTION AND ACHIEVEMENTS...
...WILL REMAIN UNKNOWN TO THE GENERAL PUBLIC.
WHAT DO YOU SAY?! I'M AN UNDERSTANDING MAN.
SO WHEN IT COMES TO A PROMISING GROUP OF YOUNG PEOPLE...
...I'D RATHER NOT HAVE TO PURSUE CHARGES OVER THIS ADMITTEDLY MASSIVE INDISCRETION, *WOOF!!*
EITHER WAY, *OUR* NEGLIGENCE IS TO BLAME. WE HAVE TO TAKE RESPONSIBILITY.
I'M SO VERY SORRY ...
ZAP
YEAH! YOU CAUSED BIG TROUBLE FOR YOUR MENTOR, SO DON'T DO IT AGAIN!!
...
THANKS FOR EVERYTHING.

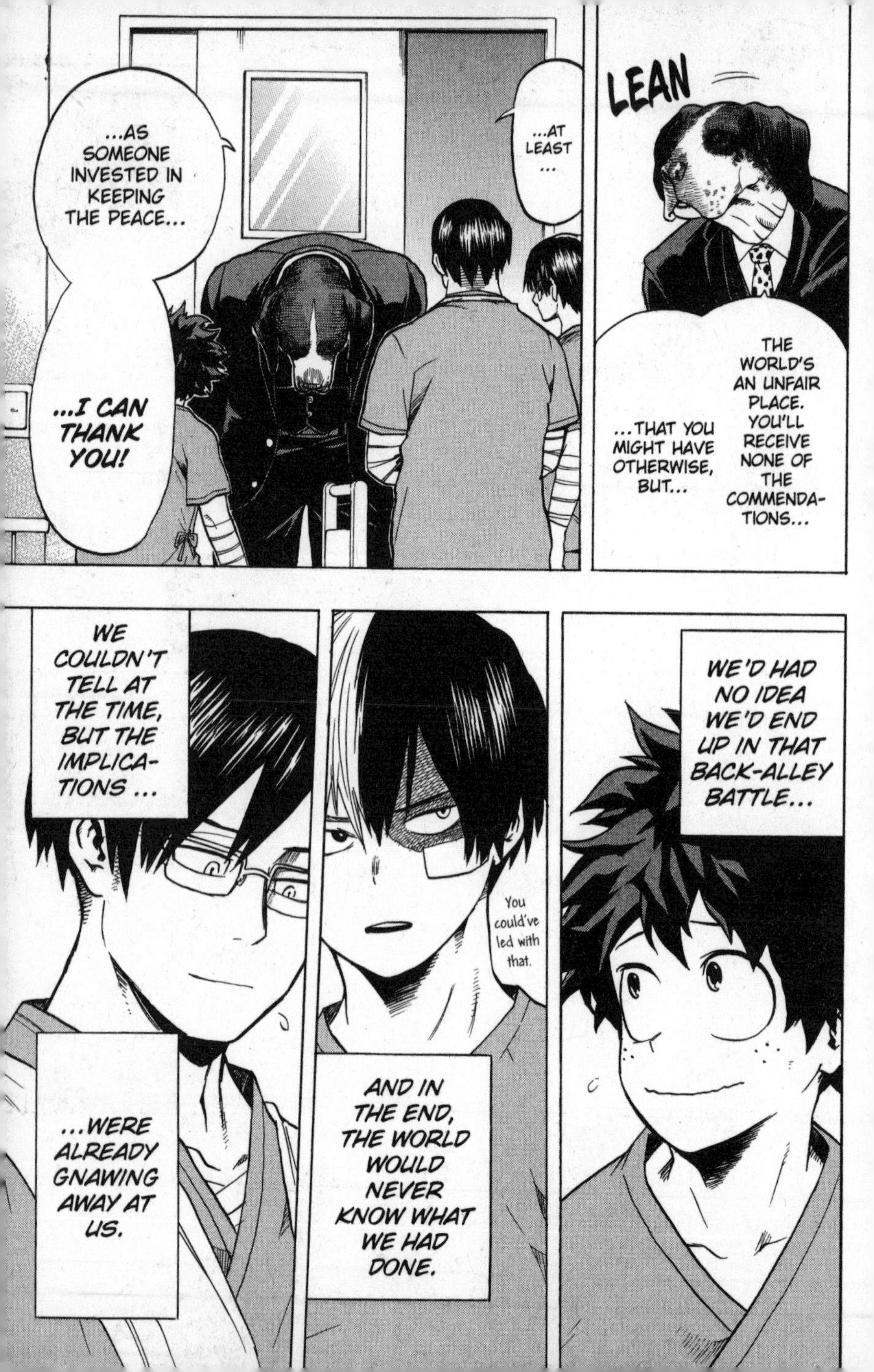
LEAN
THE WORLD'S AN UNFAIR PLACE. YOU'LL RECEIVE NONE OF THE COMMENDATIONS...
...THAT YOU MIGHT HAVE OTHERWISE, BUT...
...AT LEAST...
...AS SOMEONE INVESTED IN KEEPING THE PEACE...
...I CAN THANK YOU!
WE'D HAD NO IDEA WE'D END UP IN THAT BACK-ALLEY BATTLE...
You could've led with that.
AND IN THE END, THE WORLD WOULD NEVER KNOW WHAT WE HAD DONE.
WE COULDN'T TELL AT THE TIME, BUT THE IMPLICATIONS ...
...WERE ALREADY GNAWING AWAY AT US.

THE "WHY'D THE WINGED NOMU PICK MIDORIYA OUT OF THAT CROWD, SPECIFICALLY?! HERE'S SOMETHING LIKE A HINT" CORNER

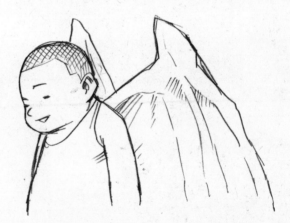

I'm hoping to dive into a more detailed discussion of the Nomu at some point. Working hard to that end.

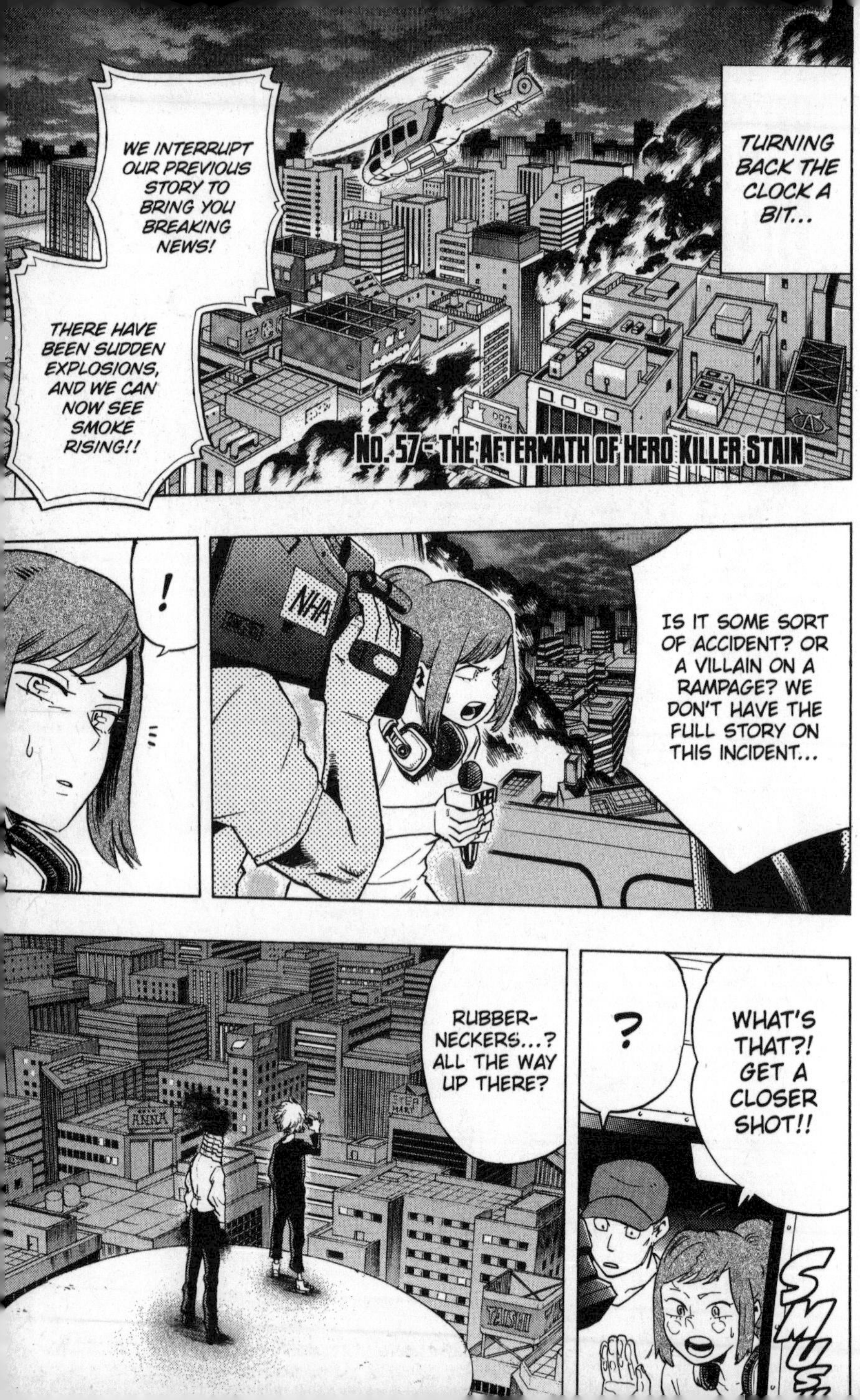
TURNING BACK THE CLOCK A BIT...
WE INTERRUPT OUR PREVIOUS STORY TO BRING YOU BREAKING NEWS!
THERE HAVE BEEN SUDDEN EXPLOSIONS, AND WE CAN NOW SEE SMOKE RISING!!
No. 57 - The Aftermath of Hero Killer Stain
IS IT SOME SORT OF ACCIDENT? OR A VILLAIN ON A RAMPAGE? WE DON'T HAVE THE FULL STORY ON THIS INCIDENT...
!
WHAT'S THAT?! GET A CLOSER SHOT!!
?
RUBBER-NECKERS...? ALL THE WAY UP THERE?

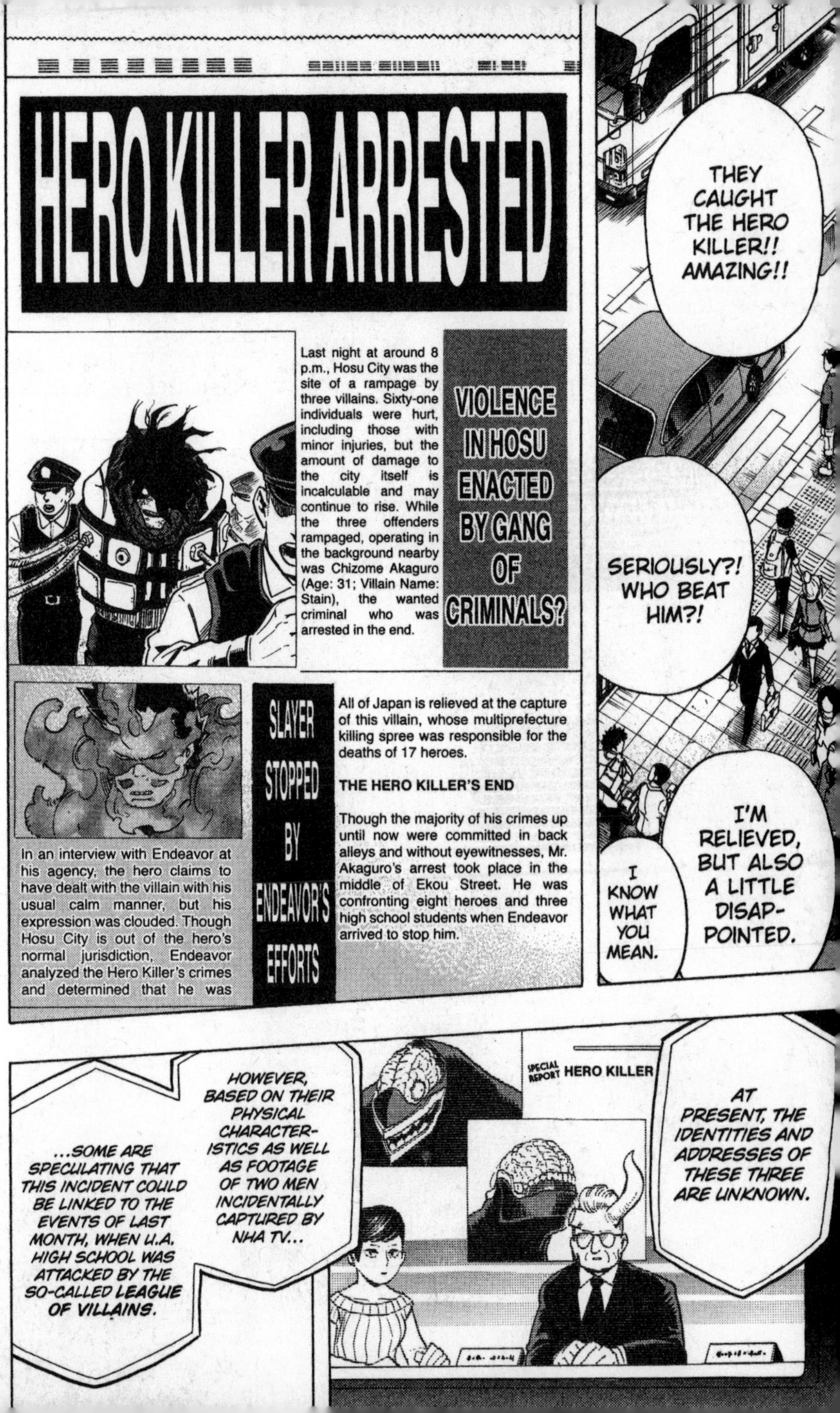
THEY CAUGHT THE HERO KILLER!! AMAZING!!
SERIOUSLY?! WHO BEAT HIM?!
I'M RELIEVED, BUT ALSO A LITTLE DISAP-POINTED.
I KNOW WHAT YOU MEAN.
HERO KILLER ARRESTED
VIOLENCE IN HOSU ENACTED BY GANG OF CRIMINALS?
Last night at around 8 p.m., Hosu City was the site of a rampage by three villains. Sixty-one individuals were hurt, including those with minor injuries, but the amount of damage to the city itself is incalculable and may continue to rise. While the three offenders rampaged, operating in the background nearby was Chizome Akaguro (Age: 31; Villain Name: Stain), the wanted criminal who was arrested in the end.
SLAYER STOPPED BY ENDEAVOR'S EFFORTS
All of Japan is relieved at the capture of this villain, whose multiprefecture killing spree was responsible for the deaths of 17 heroes.
THE HERO KILLER'S END
Though the majority of his crimes up until now were committed in back alleys and without eyewitnesses, Mr. Akaguro's arrest took place in the middle of Ekou Street. He was confronting eight heroes and three high school students when Endeavor arrived to stop him.
In an interview with Endeavor at his agency, the hero claims to have dealt with the villain with his usual calm manner, but his expression was clouded. Though Hosu City is out of the hero's normal jurisdiction, Endeavor analyzed the Hero Killer's crimes and determined that he was
SPECIAL REPORT HERO KILLER
AT PRESENT, THE IDENTITIES AND ADDRESSES OF THESE THREE ARE UNKNOWN.
HOWEVER, BASED ON THEIR PHYSICAL CHARACTER-ISTICS AS WELL AS FOOTAGE OF TWO MEN INCIDENTALLY CAPTURED BY NHA TV...
...SOME ARE SPECULATING THAT THIS INCIDENT COULD BE LINKED TO THE EVENTS OF LAST MONTH, WHEN U.A. HIGH SCHOOL WAS ATTACKED BY THE SO-CALLED LEAGUE OF VILLAINS.

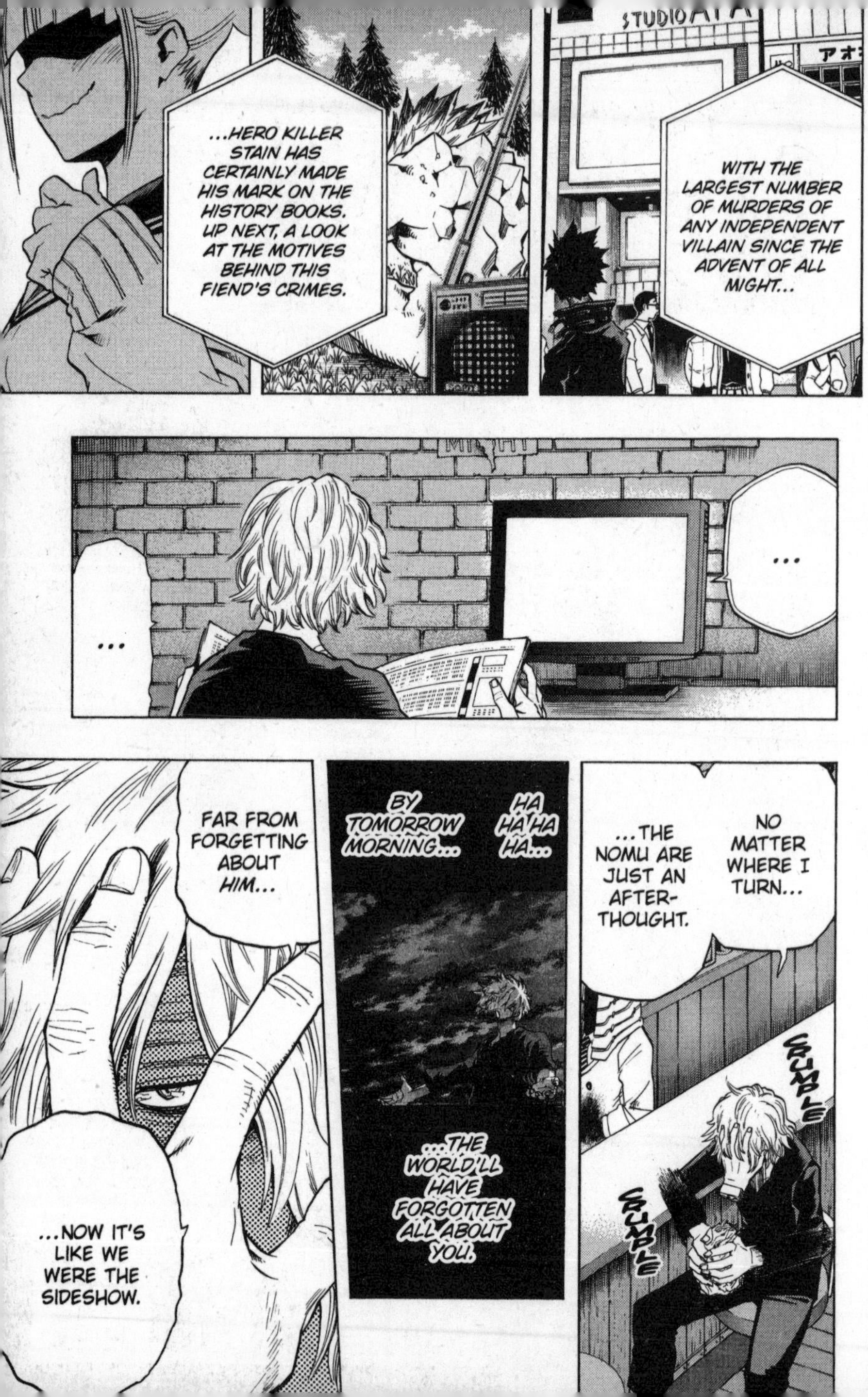
WITH THE LARGEST NUMBER OF MURDERS OF ANY INDEPENDENT VILLAIN SINCE THE ADVENT OF ALL MIGHT...
...HERO KILLER STAIN HAS CERTAINLY MADE HIS MARK ON THE HISTORY BOOKS. UP NEXT, A LOOK AT THE MOTIVES BEHIND THIS FIEND'S CRIMES.
...
...
NO MATTER WHERE I TURN...
...THE NOMU ARE JUST AN AFTER-THOUGHT.
CRUMPLE
CRUMPLE
HA HA HA HA...
BY TOMORROW MORNING...
...THE WORLD'LL HAVE FORGOTTEN ALL ABOUT YOU.
FAR FROM FORGETTING ABOUT HIM...
...NOW IT'S LIKE WE WERE THE SIDESHOW.

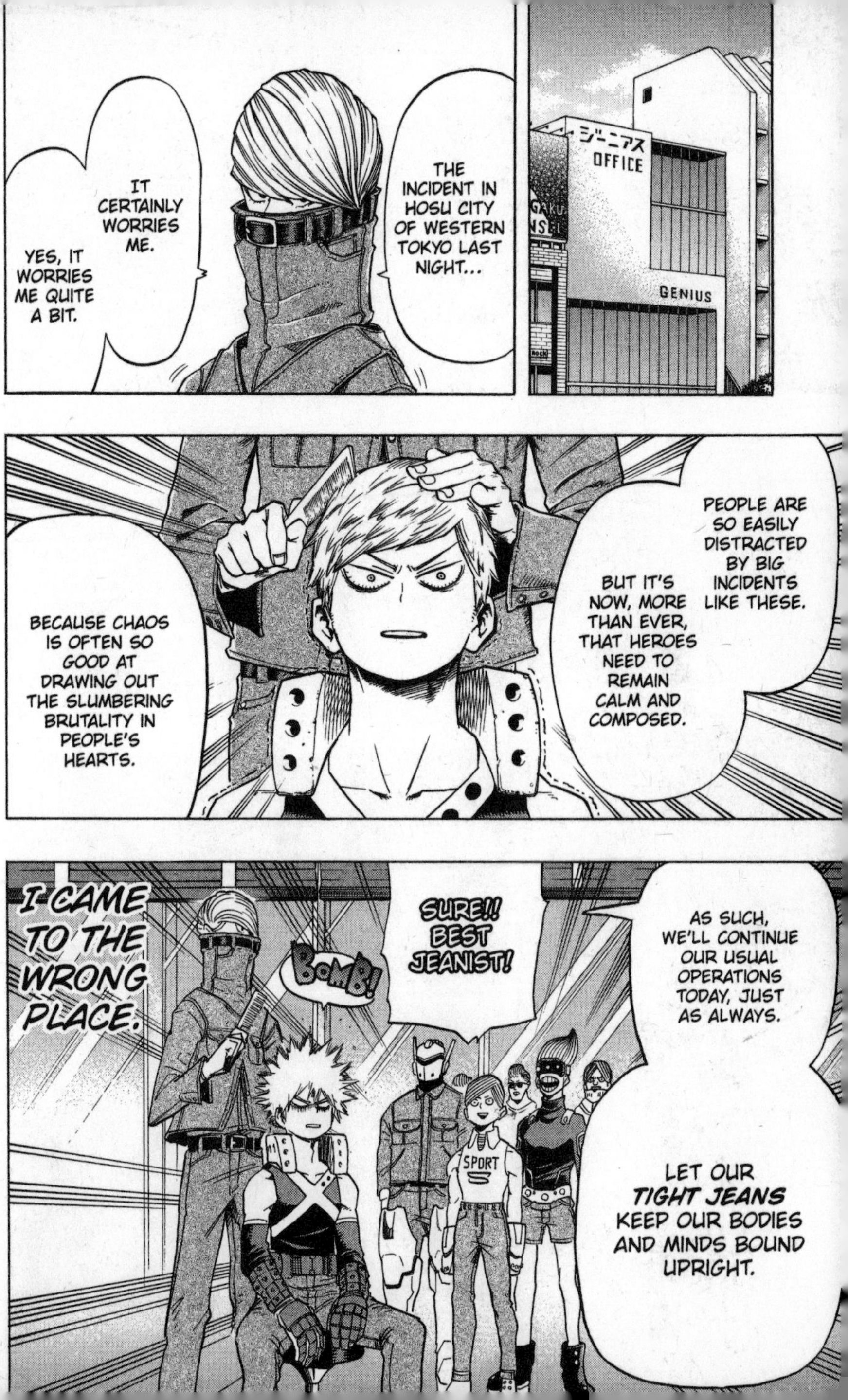

ジーニアス
OFFICE
GENIUS
THE INCIDENT IN HOSU CITY OF WESTERN TOKYO LAST NIGHT...
IT CERTAINLY WORRIES ME.
YES, IT WORRIES ME QUITE A BIT.
PEOPLE ARE SO EASILY DISTRACTED BY BIG INCIDENTS LIKE THESE.
BUT IT'S NOW, MORE THAN EVER, THAT HEROES NEED TO REMAIN CALM AND COMPOSED.
BECAUSE CHAOS IS OFTEN SO GOOD AT DRAWING OUT THE SLUMBERING BRUTALITY IN PEOPLE'S HEARTS.
AS SUCH, WE'LL CONTINUE OUR USUAL OPERATIONS TODAY, JUST AS ALWAYS.
LET OUR *TIGHT JEANS* KEEP OUR BODIES AND MINDS BOUND UPRIGHT.
SURE!! BEST JEANIST!
BOMB!
SPORT
I CAME TO THE WRONG PLACE.

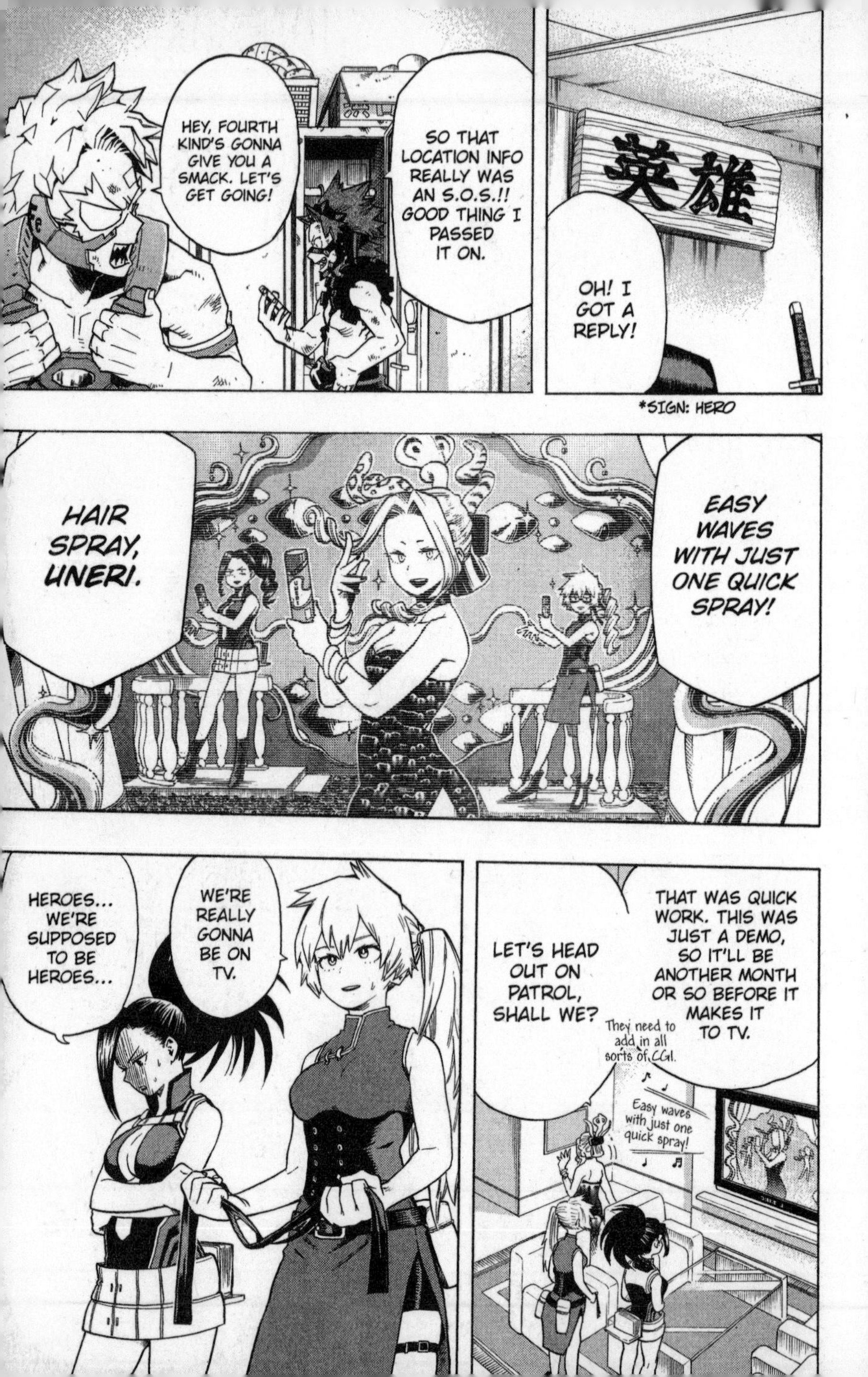
英雄
OH! I GOT A REPLY!
SO THAT LOCATION INFO REALLY WAS AN S.O.S.!! GOOD THING I PASSED IT ON.
HEY, FOURTH KIND'S GONNA GIVE YOU A SMACK. LET'S GET GOING!
*SIGN: HERO
EASY WAVES WITH JUST ONE QUICK SPRAY!
HAIR SPRAY, UNERI.
THAT WAS QUICK WORK. THIS WAS JUST A DEMO, SO IT'LL BE ANOTHER MONTH OR SO BEFORE IT MAKES IT TO TV.
LET'S HEAD OUT ON PATROL, SHALL WE?
They need to add in all sorts of CGI.
Easy waves with just one quick spray!
WE'RE REALLY GONNA BE ON TV.
HEROES... WE'RE SUPPOSED TO BE HEROES...

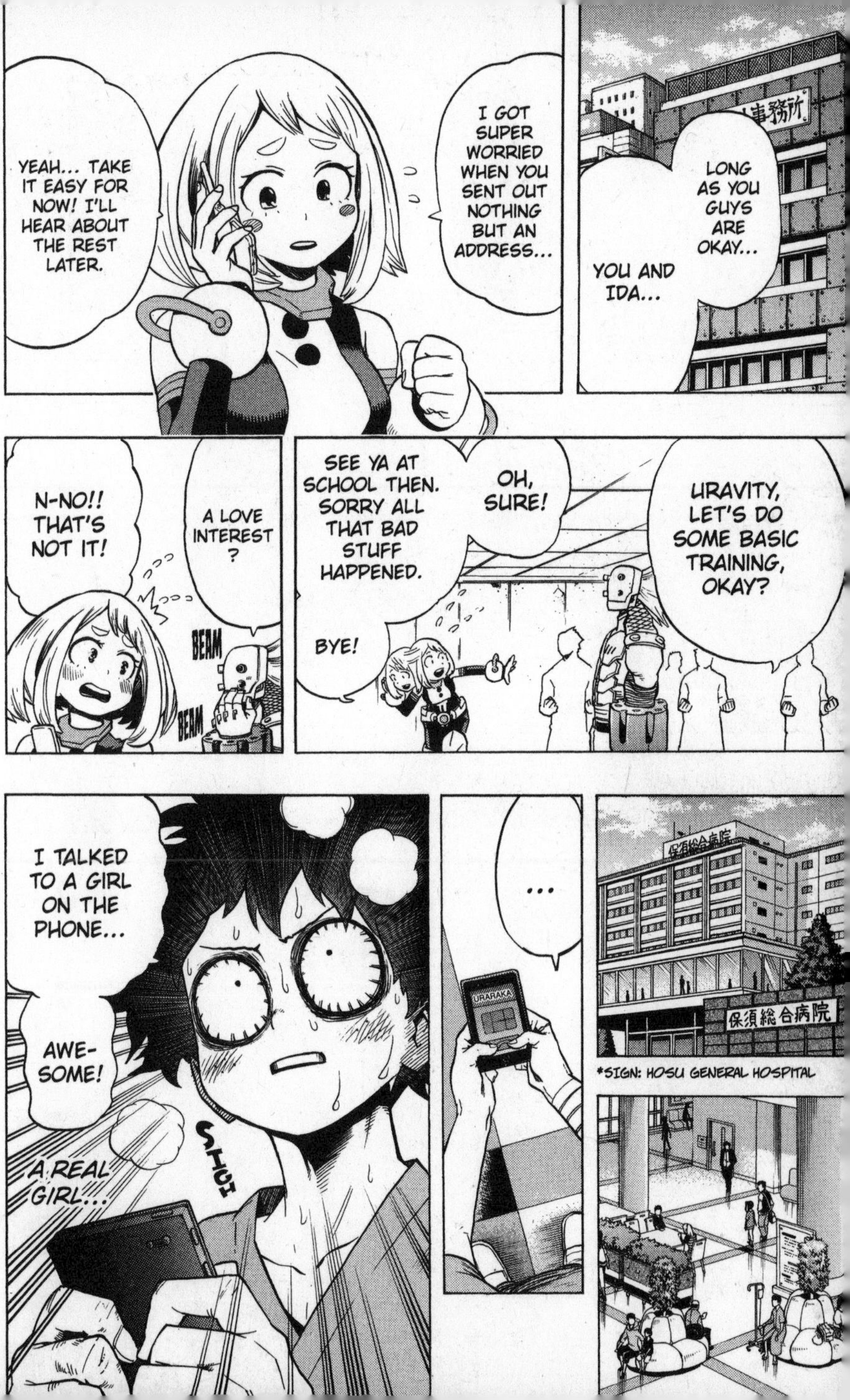
事務所
LONG AS YOU GUYS ARE OKAY...
YOU AND IDA...
I GOT SUPER WORRIED WHEN YOU SENT OUT NOTHING BUT AN ADDRESS...
YEAH... TAKE IT EASY FOR NOW! I'LL HEAR ABOUT THE REST LATER.
URAVITY, LET'S DO SOME BASIC TRAINING, OKAY?
OH, SURE!
SEE YA AT SCHOOL THEN. SORRY ALL THAT BAD STUFF HAPPENED.
BYE!
A LOVE INTEREST?
N-NO!! THAT'S NOT IT!
BEAM
BEAM
保須総合病院
保須総合病院
*SIGN: HOSU GENERAL HOSPITAL
...
URARAKA
I TALKED TO A GIRL ON THE PHONE...
AWE-SOME!
SIGH
A REAL GIRL...

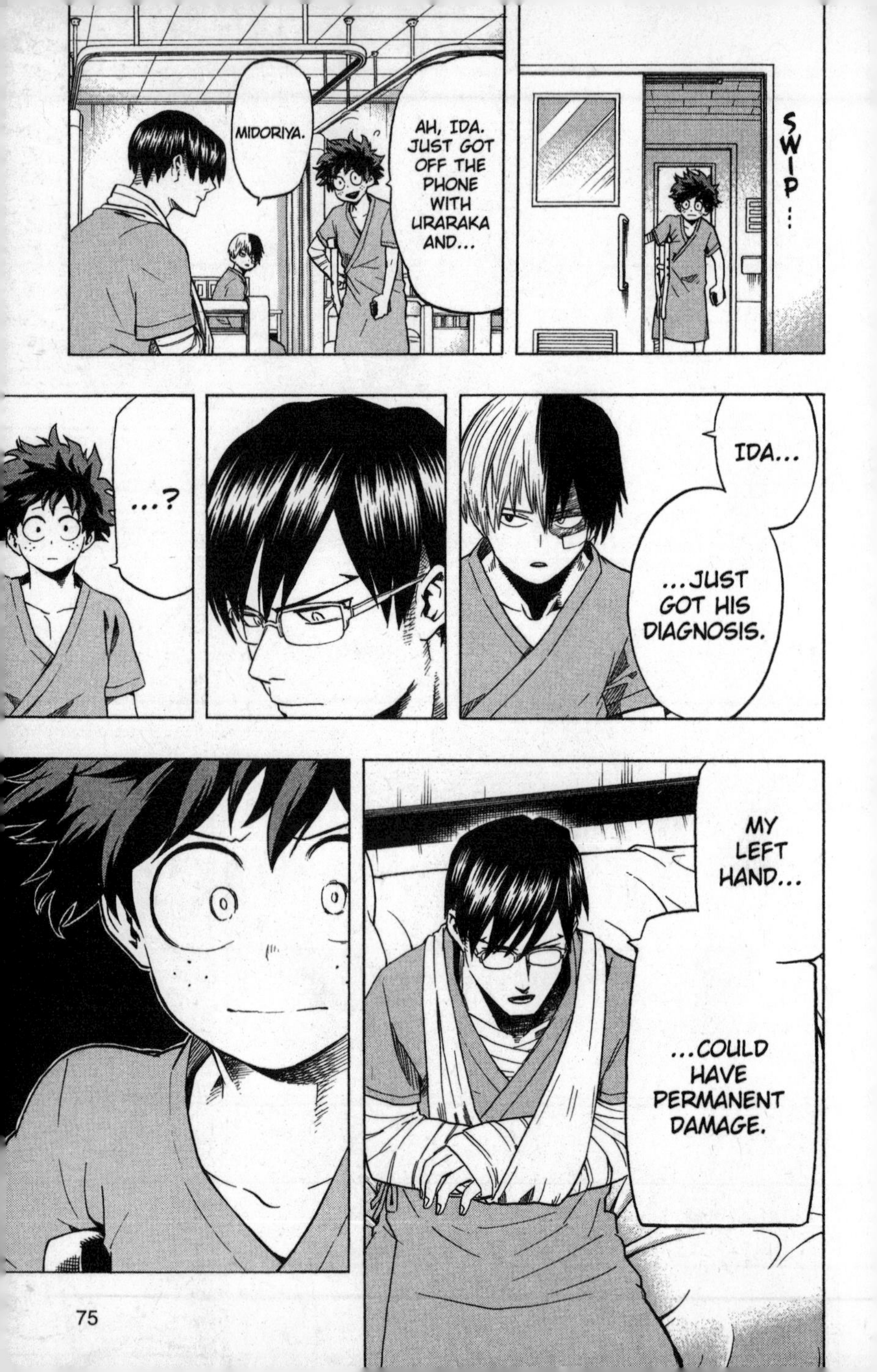
SWIP...
AH, IDA. JUST GOT OFF THE PHONE WITH URARAKA AND...
MIDORIYA.
IDA...
...JUST GOT HIS DIAGNOSIS.
...?
MY LEFT HAND...
...COULD HAVE PERMANENT DAMAGE.

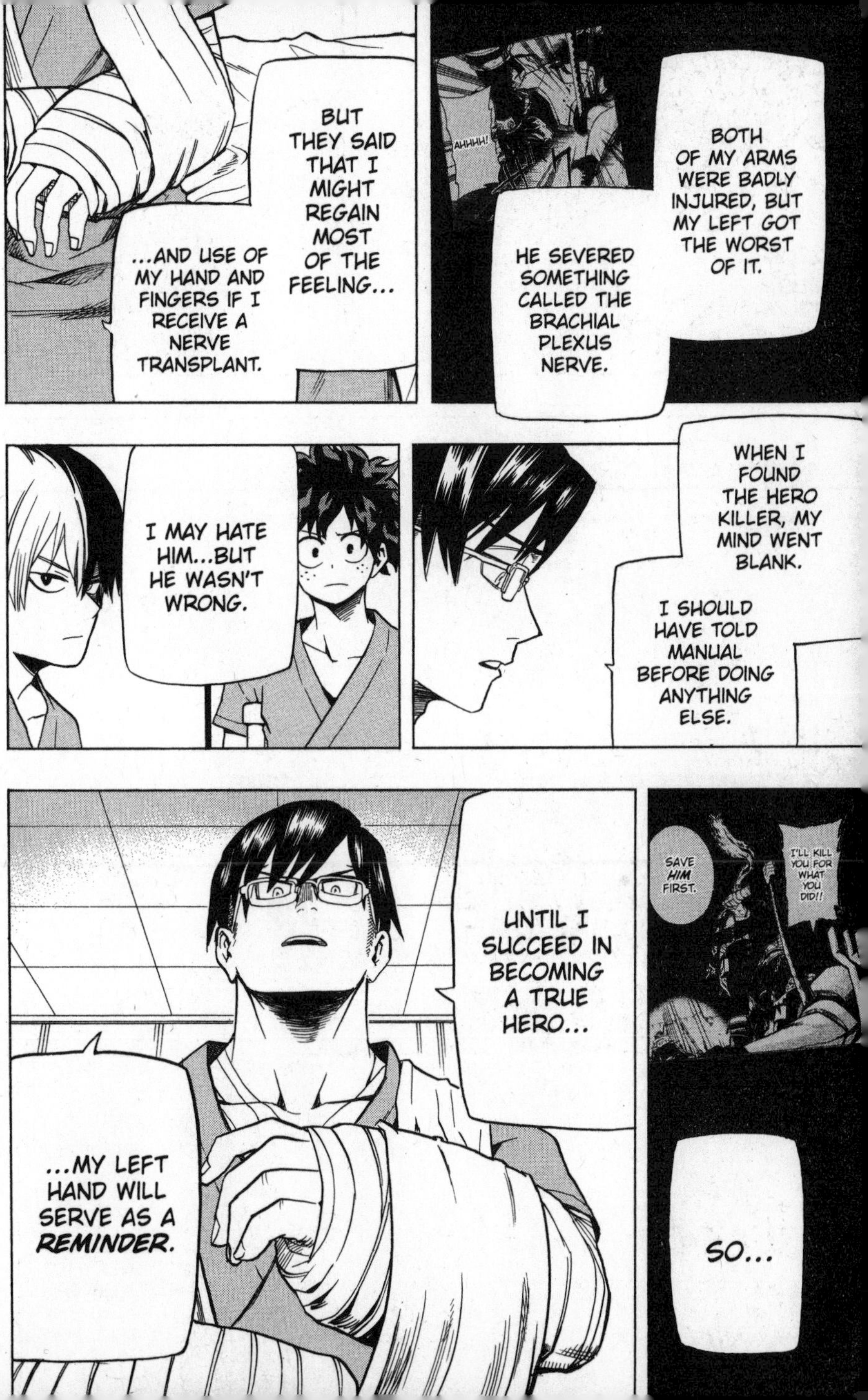
BOTH OF MY ARMS WERE BADLY INJURED, BUT MY LEFT GOT THE WORST OF IT.
AHHHH!
HE SEVERED SOMETHING CALLED THE BRACHIAL PLEXUS NERVE.
BUT THEY SAID THAT I MIGHT REGAIN MOST OF THE FEELING...
...AND USE OF MY HAND AND FINGERS IF I RECEIVE A NERVE TRANSPLANT.
WHEN I FOUND THE HERO KILLER, MY MIND WENT BLANK.
I SHOULD HAVE TOLD MANUAL BEFORE DOING ANYTHING ELSE.
I MAY HATE HIM...BUT HE WASN'T WRONG.
I'LL KILL YOU FOR WHAT YOU DID!!
SAVE *HIM* FIRST.
SO...
UNTIL I SUCCEED IN BECOMING A TRUE HERO...
...MY LEFT HAND WILL SERVE AS A *REMINDER*.

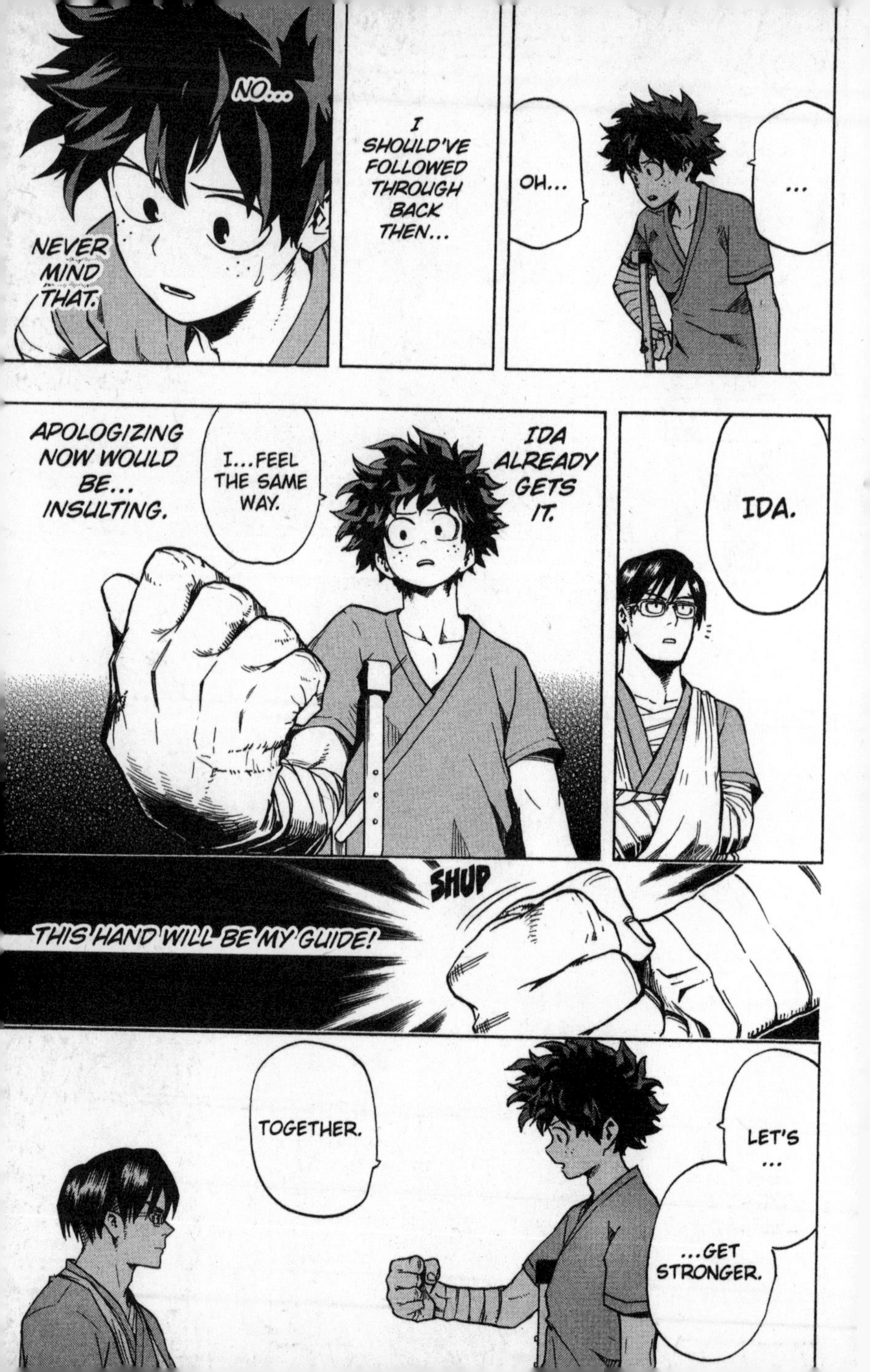
...
OH...
I SHOULD'VE FOLLOWED THROUGH BACK THEN...
NO...
NEVER MIND THAT.
IDA.
IDA ALREADY GETS IT.
I...FEEL THE SAME WAY.
APOLOGIZING NOW WOULD BE... INSULTING.
SHUP
THIS HAND WILL BE MY GUIDE!
LET'S...
...GET STRONGER.
TOGETHER.

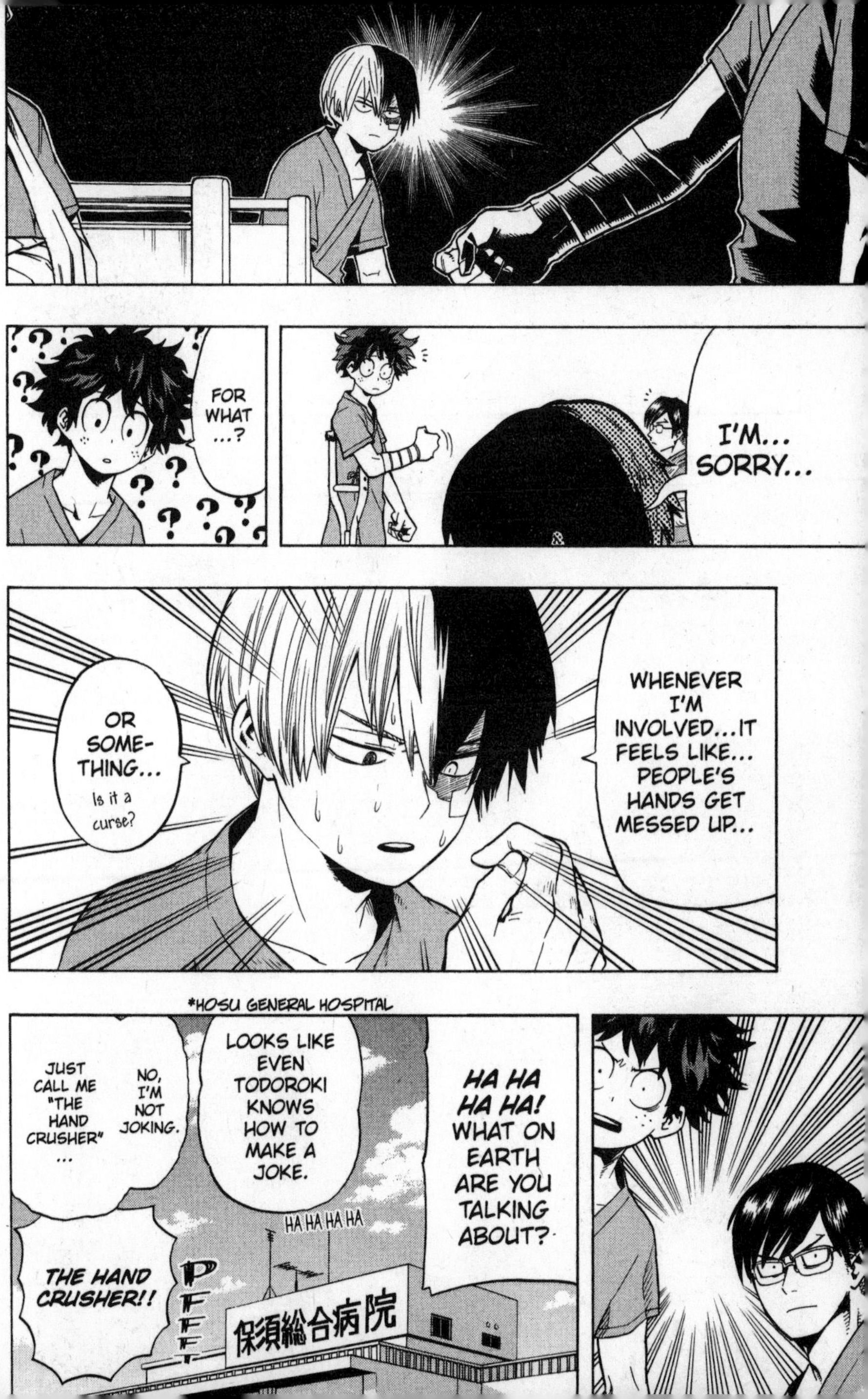
I'M... SORRY...
FOR WHAT ...?
WHENEVER I'M INVOLVED...IT FEELS LIKE... PEOPLE'S HANDS GET MESSED UP...
OR SOME-THING...
Is it a curse?
*HOSU GENERAL HOSPITAL
HA HA HA HA! WHAT ON EARTH ARE YOU TALKING ABOUT?
LOOKS LIKE EVEN TODOROKI KNOWS HOW TO MAKE A JOKE.
HA HA HA HA
NO, I'M NOT JOKING.
JUST CALL ME "THE HAND CRUSHER" ...
保須総合病院
PFFFT
THE HAND CRUSHER!!

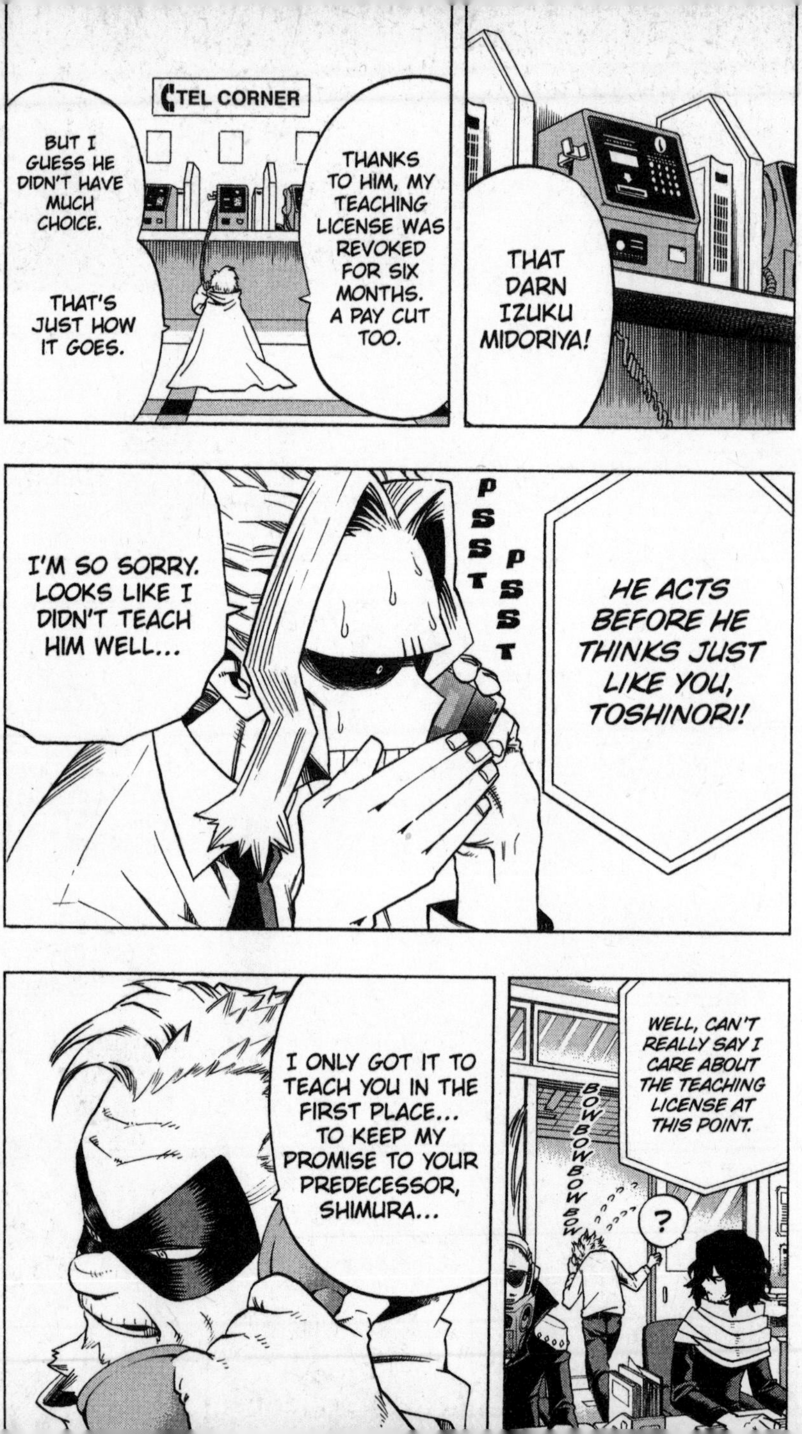
THAT DARN IZUKU MIDORIYA!
TEL CORNER
THANKS TO HIM, MY TEACHING LICENSE WAS REVOKED FOR SIX MONTHS. A PAY CUT TOO.
BUT I GUESS HE DIDN'T HAVE MUCH CHOICE.
THAT'S JUST HOW IT GOES.
HE ACTS BEFORE HE THINKS JUST LIKE YOU, TOSHINORI!
PSST PSST
I'M SO SORRY. LOOKS LIKE I DIDN'T TEACH HIM WELL...
WELL, CAN'T REALLY SAY I CARE ABOUT THE TEACHING LICENSE AT THIS POINT.
BOW BOW BOW BOW
?
I ONLY GOT IT TO TEACH YOU IN THE FIRST PLACE... TO KEEP MY PROMISE TO YOUR PREDECESSOR, SHIMURA...

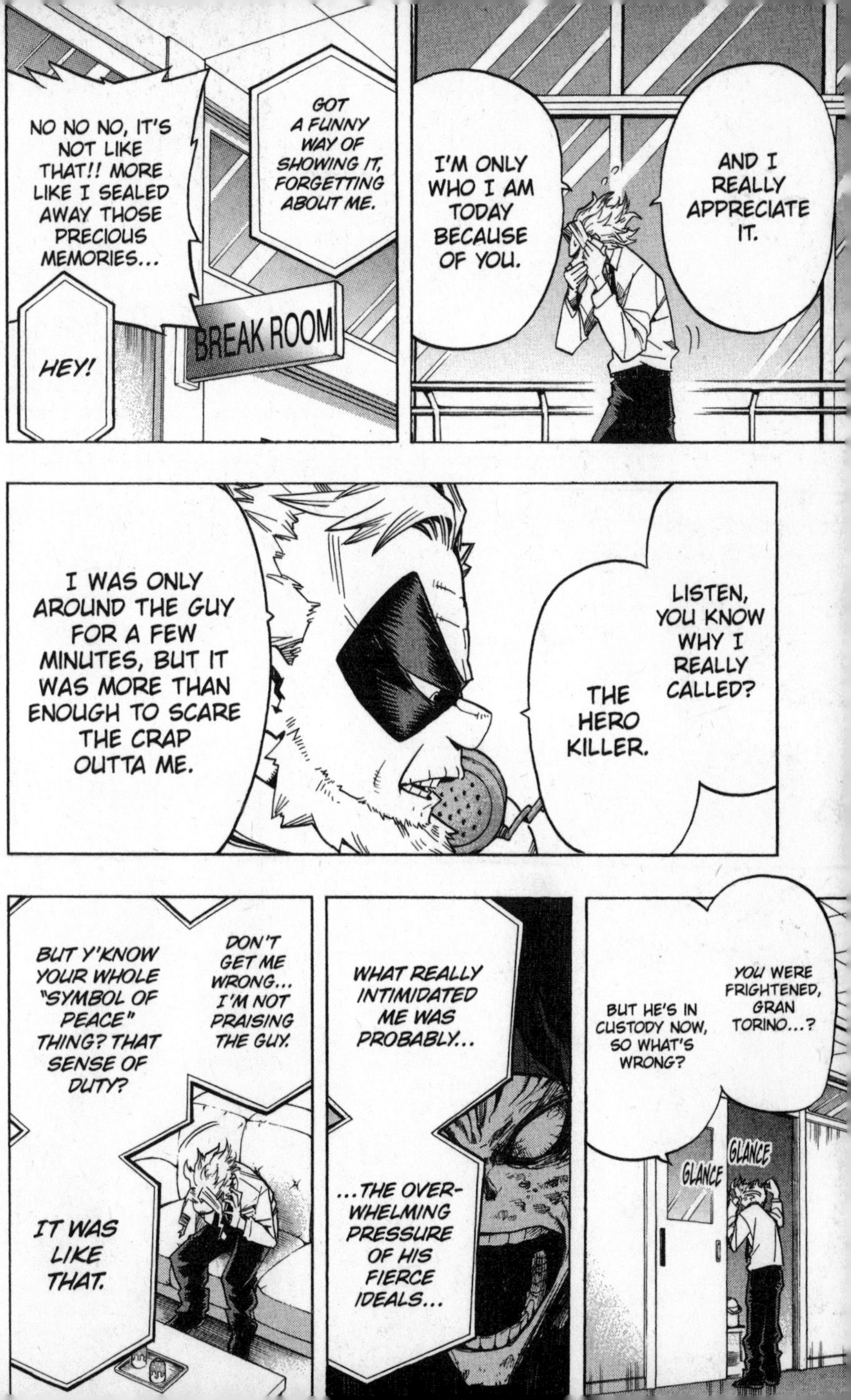
I'M ONLY WHO I AM TODAY BECAUSE OF YOU.
AND I REALLY APPRECIATE IT.
GOT A FUNNY WAY OF SHOWING IT, FORGETTING ABOUT ME.
NO NO NO, IT'S NOT LIKE THAT!! MORE LIKE I SEALED AWAY THOSE PRECIOUS MEMORIES...
BREAK ROOM
HEY!
LISTEN, YOU KNOW WHY I REALLY CALLED?
THE HERO KILLER.
I WAS ONLY AROUND THE GUY FOR A FEW MINUTES, BUT IT WAS MORE THAN ENOUGH TO SCARE THE CRAP OUTTA ME.
YOU WERE FRIGHTENED, GRAN TORINO...?
BUT HE'S IN CUSTODY NOW, SO WHAT'S WRONG?
GLANCE
GLANCE
WHAT REALLY INTIMIDATED ME WAS PROBABLY...
...THE OVER-WHELMING PRESSURE OF HIS FIERCE IDEALS...
DON'T GET ME WRONG... I'M NOT PRAISING THE GUY.
BUT Y'KNOW YOUR WHOLE "SYMBOL OF PEACE" THING? THAT SENSE OF DUTY?
IT WAS LIKE THAT.

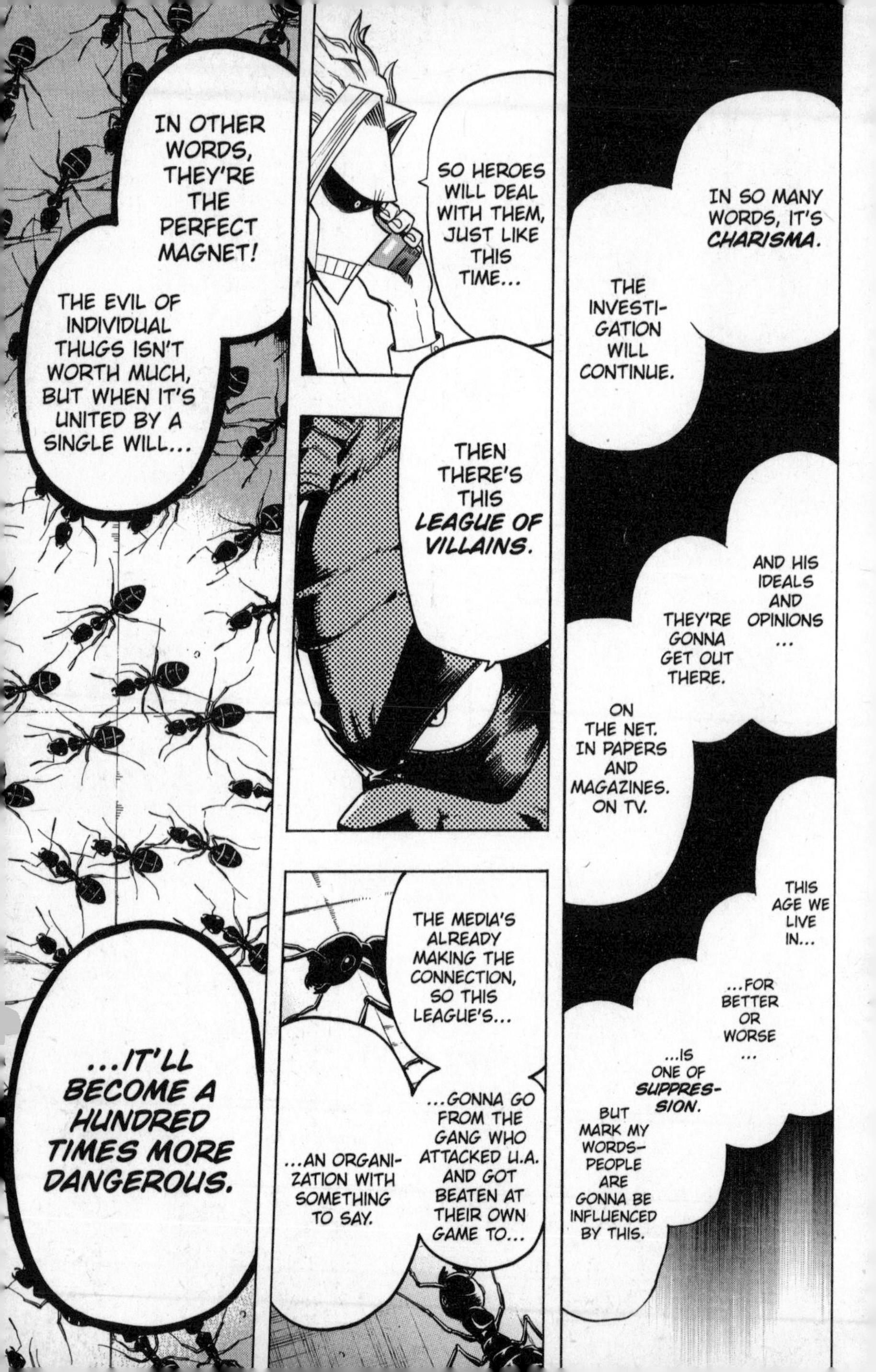

IN SO MANY WORDS, IT'S CHARISMA.
THE INVESTI-GATION WILL CONTINUE.
AND HIS IDEALS AND OPINIONS...
THEY'RE GONNA GET OUT THERE.
ON THE NET. IN PAPERS AND MAGAZINES. ON TV.
THIS AGE WE LIVE IN...
...FOR BETTER OR WORSE...
...IS ONE OF SUPPRES-SION.
BUT MARK MY WORDS— PEOPLE ARE GONNA BE INFLUENCED BY THIS.
SO HEROES WILL DEAL WITH THEM, JUST LIKE THIS TIME...
THEN THERE'S THIS LEAGUE OF VILLAINS.
THE MEDIA'S ALREADY MAKING THE CONNECTION, SO THIS LEAGUE'S...
...GONNA GO FROM THE GANG WHO ATTACKED U.A. AND GOT BEATEN AT THEIR OWN GAME TO...
...AN ORGANI-ZATION WITH SOMETHING TO SAY.
IN OTHER WORDS, THEY'RE THE PERFECT MAGNET!
THE EVIL OF INDIVIDUAL THUGS ISN'T WORTH MUCH, BUT WHEN IT'S UNITED BY A SINGLE WILL...
...IT'LL BECOME A HUNDRED TIMES MORE DANGEROUS.

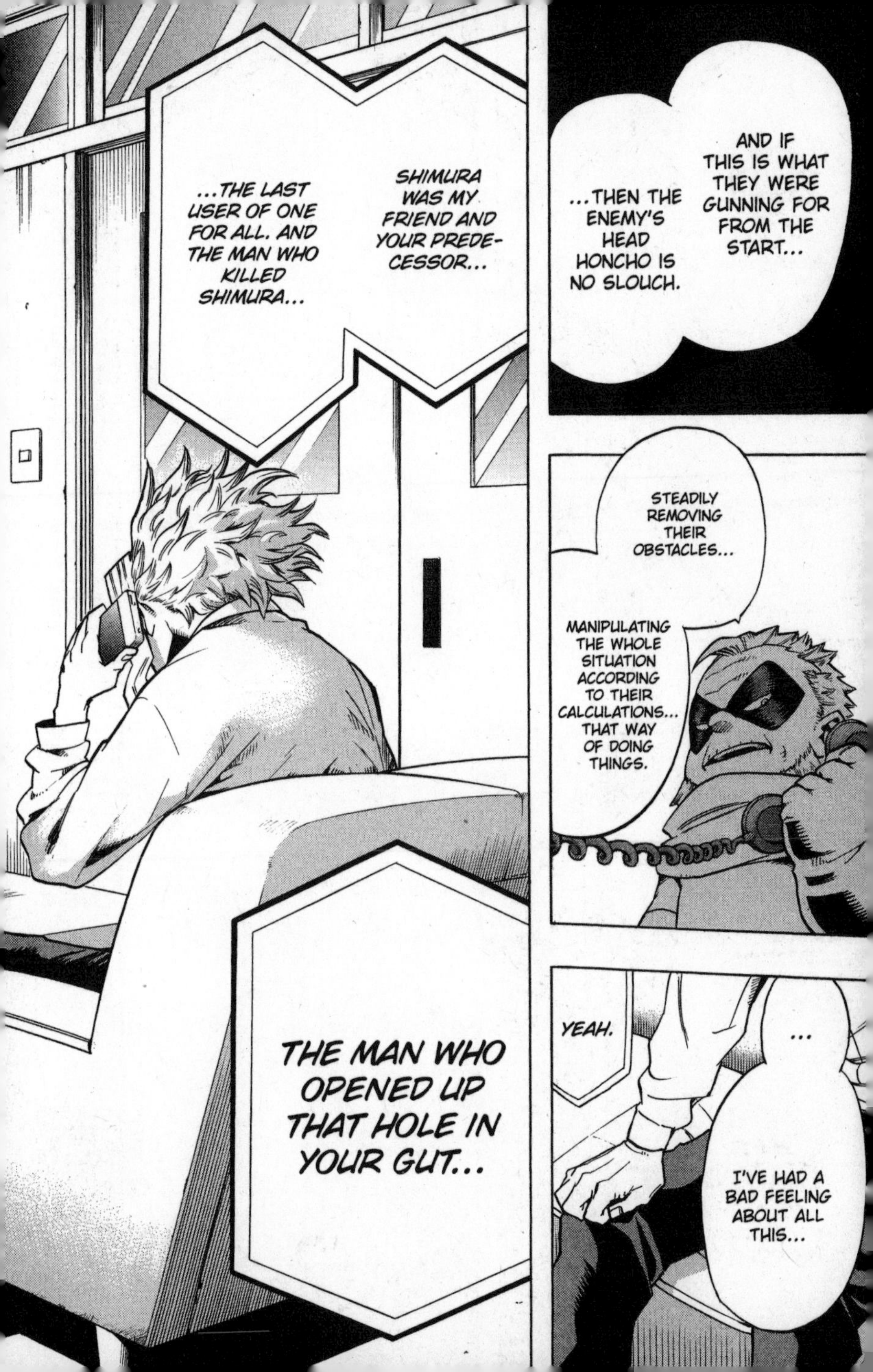
AND IF THIS IS WHAT THEY WERE GUNNING FOR FROM THE START...
...THEN THE ENEMY'S HEAD HONCHO IS NO SLOUCH.
STEADILY REMOVING THEIR OBSTACLES...
MANIPULATING THE WHOLE SITUATION ACCORDING TO THEIR CALCULATIONS... THAT WAY OF DOING THINGS.
...
YEAH.
I'VE HAD A BAD FEELING ABOUT ALL THIS...
SHIMURA WAS MY FRIEND AND YOUR PREDECESSOR...
...THE LAST USER OF ONE FOR ALL. AND THE MAN WHO KILLED SHIMURA...
THE MAN WHO OPENED UP THAT HOLE IN YOUR GUT...

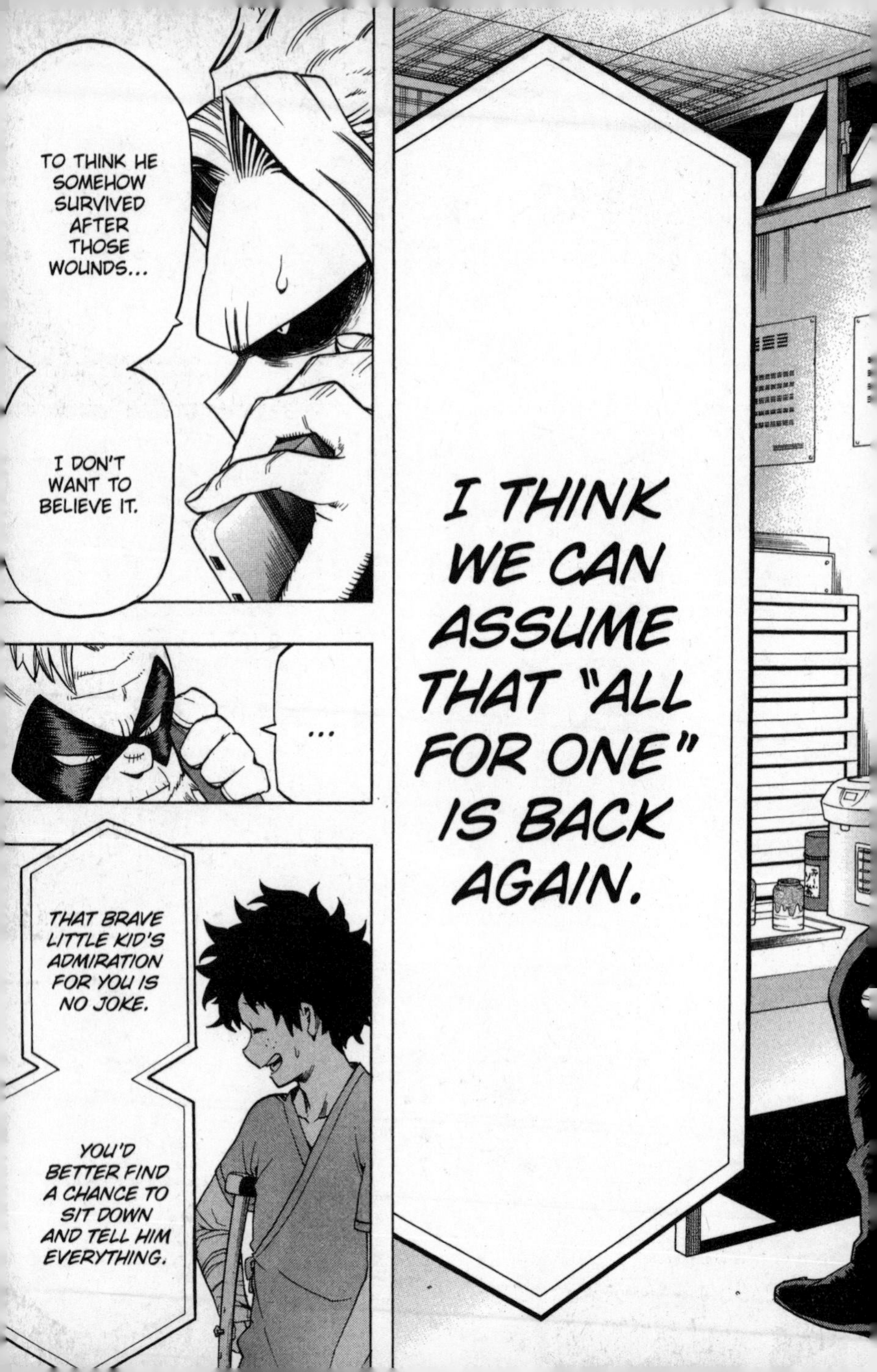
I THINK WE CAN ASSUME THAT "ALL FOR ONE" IS BACK AGAIN.
TO THINK HE SOMEHOW SURVIVED AFTER THOSE WOUNDS...
I DON'T WANT TO BELIEVE IT.
...
THAT BRAVE LITTLE KID'S ADMIRATION FOR YOU IS NO JOKE.
YOU'D BETTER FIND A CHANCE TO SIT DOWN AND TELL HIM EVERYTHING.

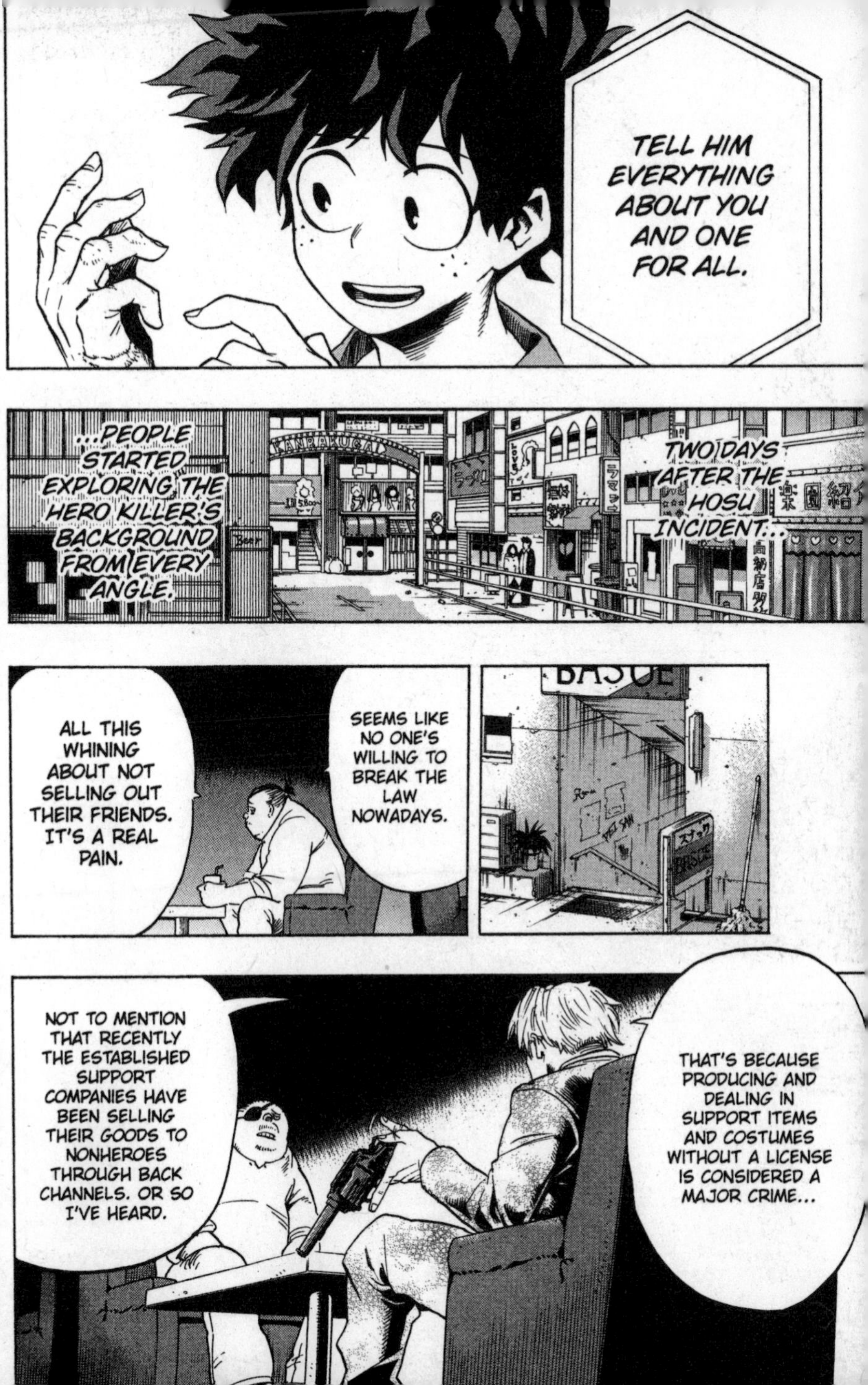
TELL HIM EVERYTHING ABOUT YOU AND ONE FOR ALL.
TWO DAYS AFTER THE HOSU INCIDENT...
...PEOPLE STARTED EXPLORING THE HERO KILLER'S BACKGROUND FROM EVERY ANGLE.
SEEMS LIKE NO ONE'S WILLING TO BREAK THE LAW NOWADAYS.
ALL THIS WHINING ABOUT NOT SELLING OUT THEIR FRIENDS. IT'S A REAL PAIN.
THAT'S BECAUSE PRODUCING AND DEALING IN SUPPORT ITEMS AND COSTUMES WITHOUT A LICENSE IS CONSIDERED A MAJOR CRIME...
NOT TO MENTION THAT RECENTLY THE ESTABLISHED SUPPORT COMPANIES HAVE BEEN SELLING THEIR GOODS TO NONHEROES THROUGH BACK CHANNELS. OR SO I'VE HEARD.

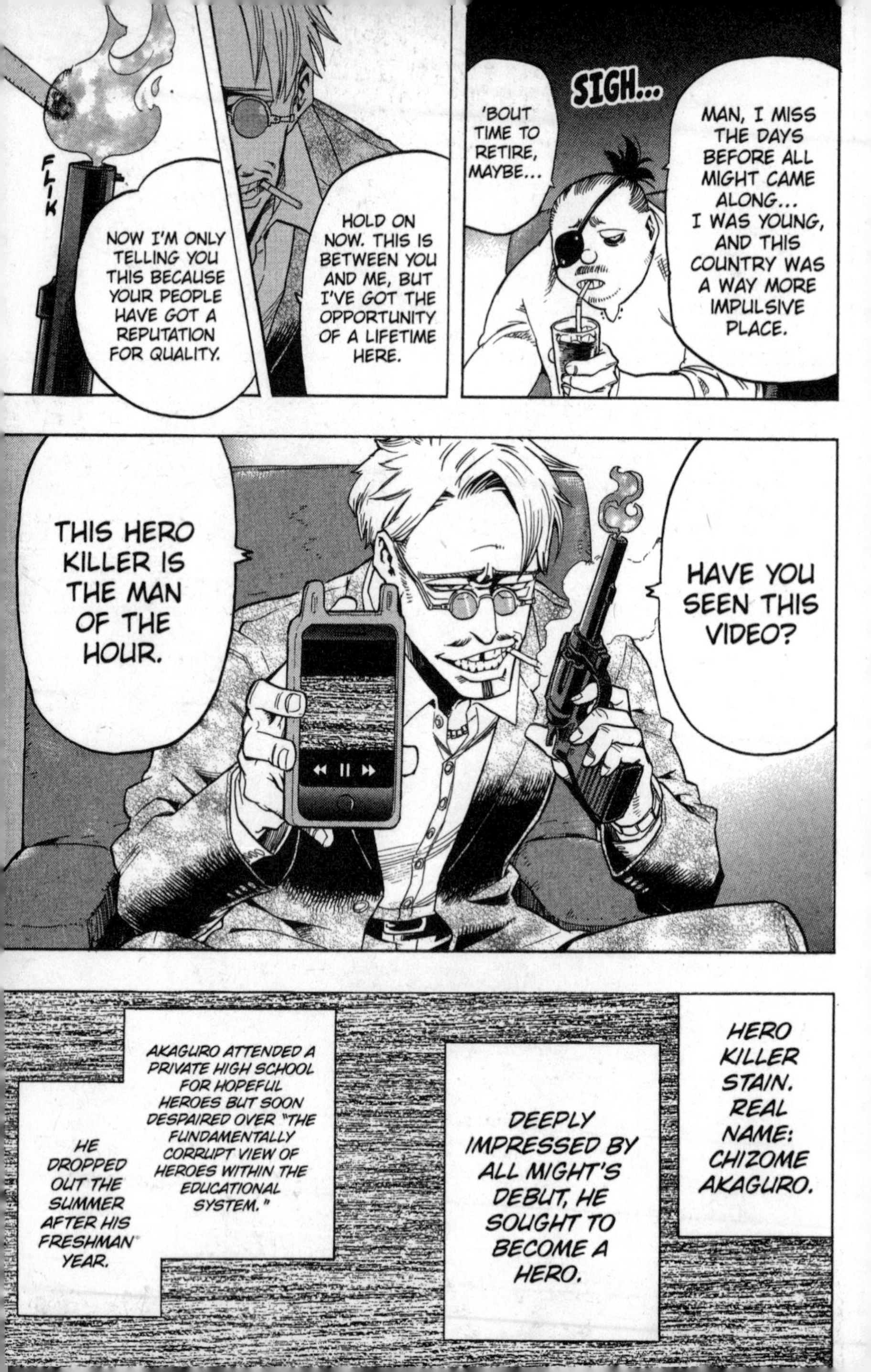
MAN, I MISS THE DAYS BEFORE ALL MIGHT CAME ALONG... I WAS YOUNG, AND THIS COUNTRY WAS A WAY MORE IMPULSIVE PLACE.
SIGH...
'BOUT TIME TO RETIRE, MAYBE...
HOLD ON NOW. THIS IS BETWEEN YOU AND ME, BUT I'VE GOT THE OPPORTUNITY OF A LIFETIME HERE.
NOW I'M ONLY TELLING YOU THIS BECAUSE YOUR PEOPLE HAVE GOT A REPUTATION FOR QUALITY.
FLIK
HAVE YOU SEEN THIS VIDEO?
THIS HERO KILLER IS THE MAN OF THE HOUR.
HERO KILLER STAIN. REAL NAME: CHIZOME AKAGURO.
DEEPLY IMPRESSED BY ALL MIGHT'S DEBUT, HE SOUGHT TO BECOME A HERO.
AKAGURO ATTENDED A PRIVATE HIGH SCHOOL FOR HOPEFUL HEROES BUT SOON DESPAIRED OVER "THE FUNDAMENTALLY CORRUPT VIEW OF HEROES WITHIN THE EDUCATIONAL SYSTEM."
HE DROPPED OUT THE SUMMER AFTER HIS FRESHMAN YEAR.

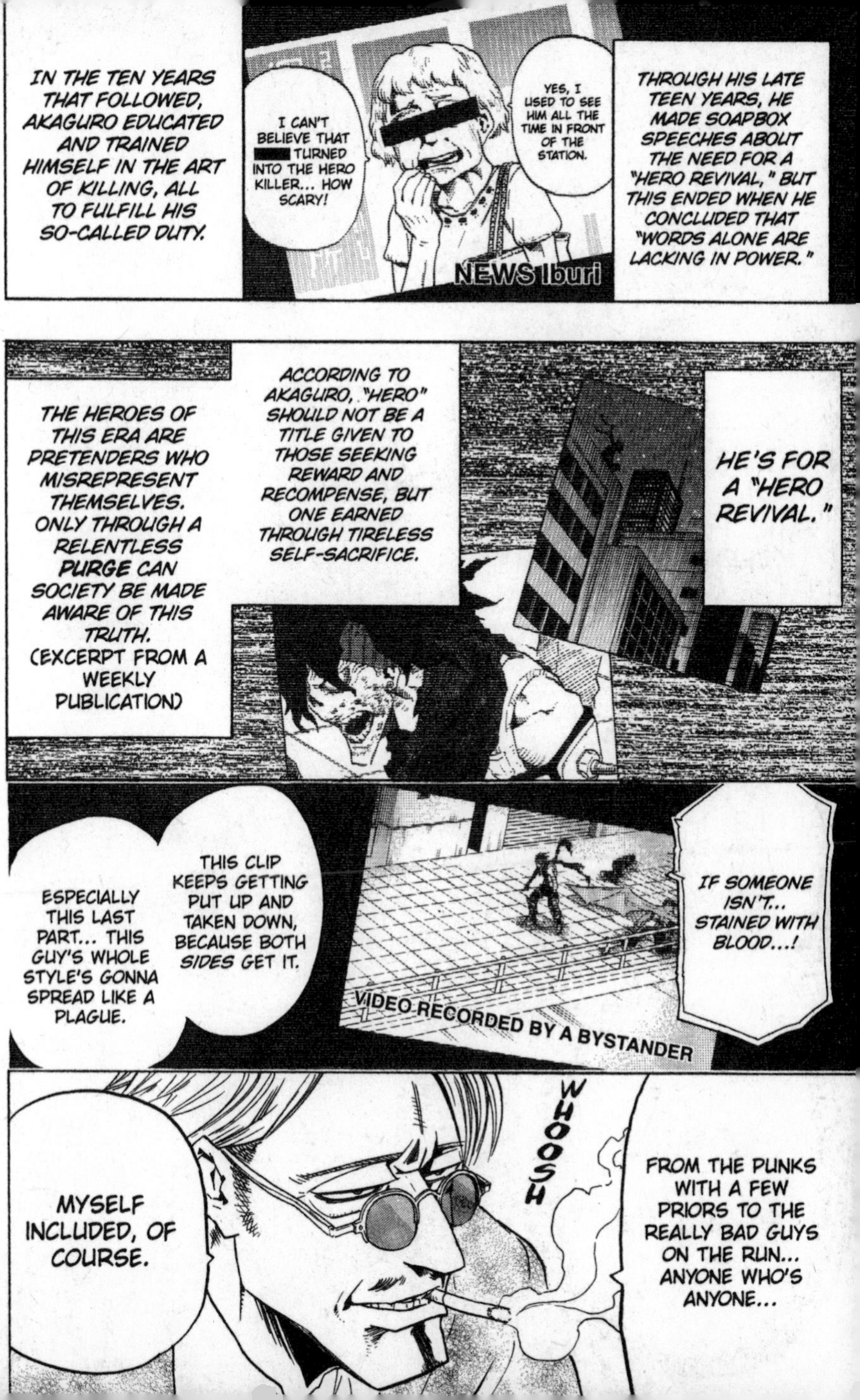
THROUGH HIS LATE TEEN YEARS, HE MADE SOAPBOX SPEECHES ABOUT THE NEED FOR A "HERO REVIVAL," BUT THIS ENDED WHEN HE CONCLUDED THAT "WORDS ALONE ARE LACKING IN POWER."
YES, I USED TO SEE HIM ALL THE TIME IN FRONT OF THE STATION.
I CAN'T BELIEVE THAT [redacted] TURNED INTO THE HERO KILLER... HOW SCARY!
NEWS Iburi
IN THE TEN YEARS THAT FOLLOWED, AKAGURO EDUCATED AND TRAINED HIMSELF IN THE ART OF KILLING, ALL TO FULFILL HIS SO-CALLED DUTY.
HE'S FOR A "HERO REVIVAL."
ACCORDING TO AKAGURO, "HERO" SHOULD NOT BE A TITLE GIVEN TO THOSE SEEKING REWARD AND RECOMPENSE, BUT ONE EARNED THROUGH TIRELESS SELF-SACRIFICE.
THE HEROES OF THIS ERA ARE PRETENDERS WHO MISREPRESENT THEMSELVES. ONLY THROUGH A RELENTLESS PURGE CAN SOCIETY BE MADE AWARE OF THIS TRUTH. (EXCERPT FROM A WEEKLY PUBLICATION)
IF SOMEONE ISN'T... STAINED WITH BLOOD...!
VIDEO RECORDED BY A BYSTANDER
THIS CLIP KEEPS GETTING PUT UP AND TAKEN DOWN, BECAUSE BOTH SIDES GET IT.
ESPECIALLY THIS LAST PART... THIS GUY'S WHOLE STYLE'S GONNA SPREAD LIKE A PLAGUE.
FROM THE PUNKS WITH A FEW PRIORS TO THE REALLY BAD GUYS ON THE RUN... ANYONE WHO'S ANYONE...
WHOOOSH
MYSELF INCLUDED, OF COURSE.

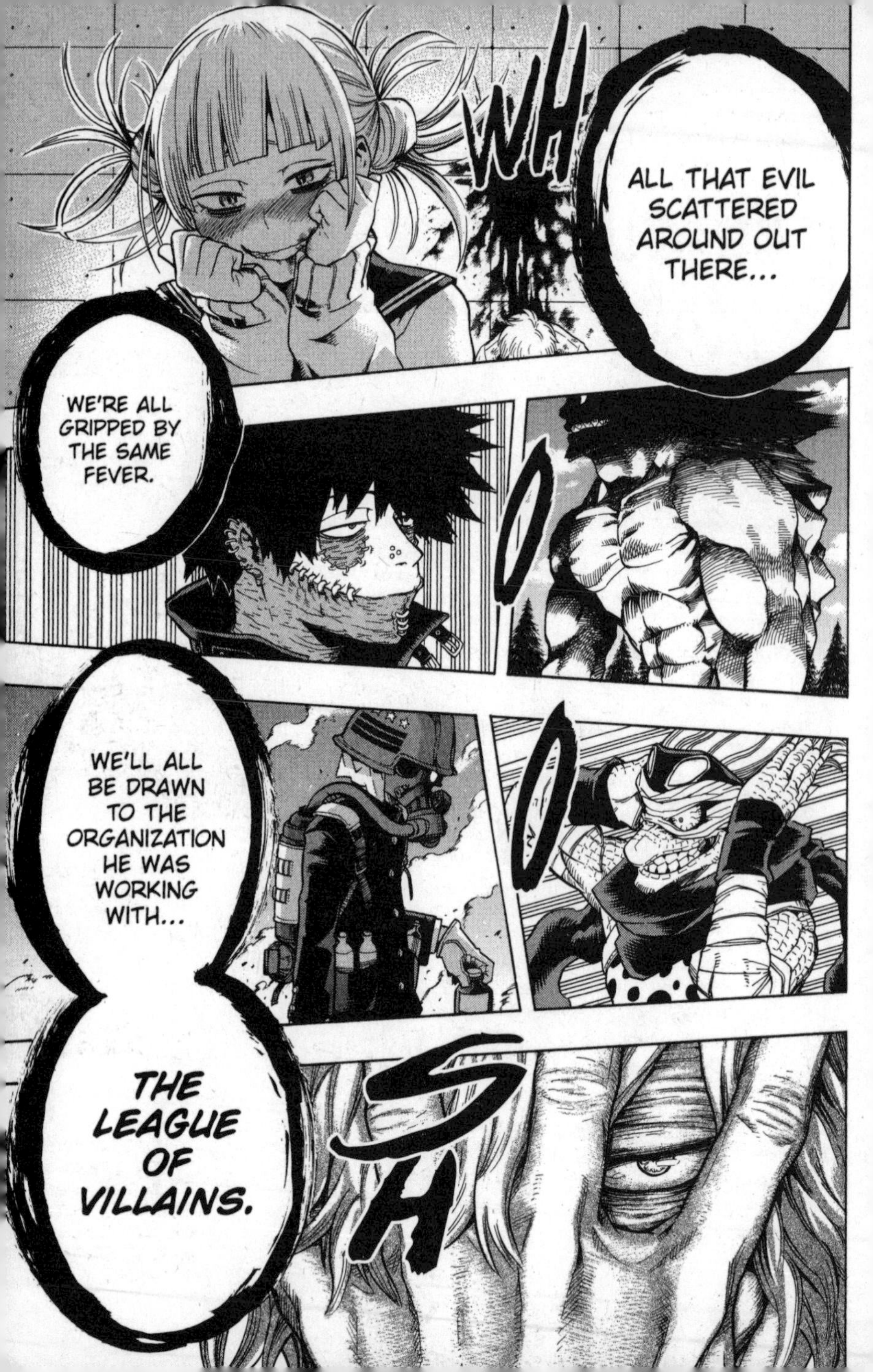
WH
ALL THAT EVIL SCATTERED AROUND OUT THERE...
O
WE'RE ALL GRIPPED BY THE SAME FEVER.
O
WE'LL ALL BE DRAWN TO THE ORGANIZATION HE WAS WORKING WITH...
SH
THE LEAGUE OF VILLAINS.

THE SUPPORTING CAST SIDEBAR CORNER

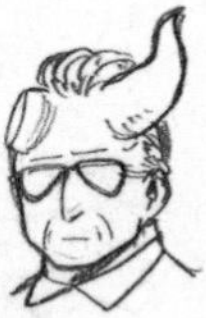

This is the anchorman who appeared in chapter 57.
His name is Daikaku Miyagi.

He reports the news from a fair and impartial viewpoint, using precise and easily understood language. As such, he has the trust of many a household throughout the country. However, the enormous horns granted him by his Quirk, "Big Horn," used to often get in the way of Miyagi's newscasts and visual presentations.

In order to better do his job, he voluntarily had one of his impressive horns removed.

Never one to rest on his laurels, Miyagi always pays due mind to his viewing audience—a style that has garnered him much praise from society on the whole. However, a certain human rights group has condemned him, claiming that, "Daikaku Miyagi's act was a rejection of his Quirk. A sign that he doesn't respect Quirks. Decisions such as his foster discrimination and are linked to an overall rejection of our Quirk-based society!"

Despite this, Miyagi continues to report the news.

In a superpowered society full of Quirks of all kinds, professional heroes are not the only ones fighting the good fight. There is simply nothing in this world that *everyone* will find acceptable, so all we can do is believe in ourselves and walk our chosen paths.
Fight on, Daikaku Miyagi!

[Main characters are one thing, but I also like to think about the lives and stories behind some of the minor characters. Even ones who only make one or two appearances.]

NO. 58 - INTERNSHIP'S END

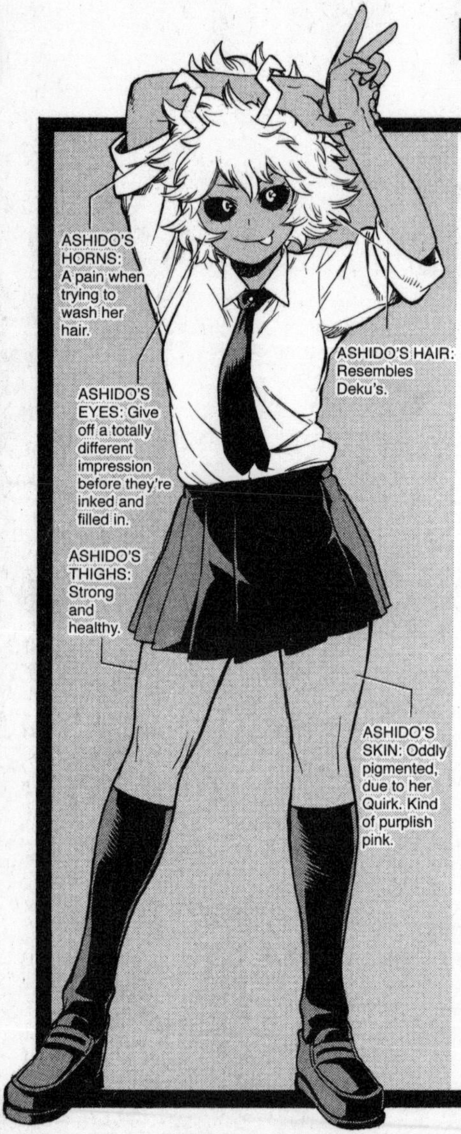
ASHIDO'S HORNS: A pain when trying to wash her hair.
ASHIDO'S HAIR: Resembles Deku's.
ASHIDO'S EYES: Give off a totally different impression before they're inked and filled in.
ASHIDO'S THIGHS: Strong and healthy.
ASHIDO'S SKIN: Oddly pigmented, due to her Quirk. Kind of purplish pink.

U.A. FILE.07

CLASS No.02

MINA ASHIDO

QUIRK

ACID

She can secrete a corrosive liquid from her body! She can even control how corrosive or sticky it is! Besides allowing her to attack in some nasty ways, she can make the ground slick and slide across it quickly or even melt right through walls and floors, making her great at stealthy spy missions. One wrong move, though, and her fickle Quirk could melt the clothes right off her body!

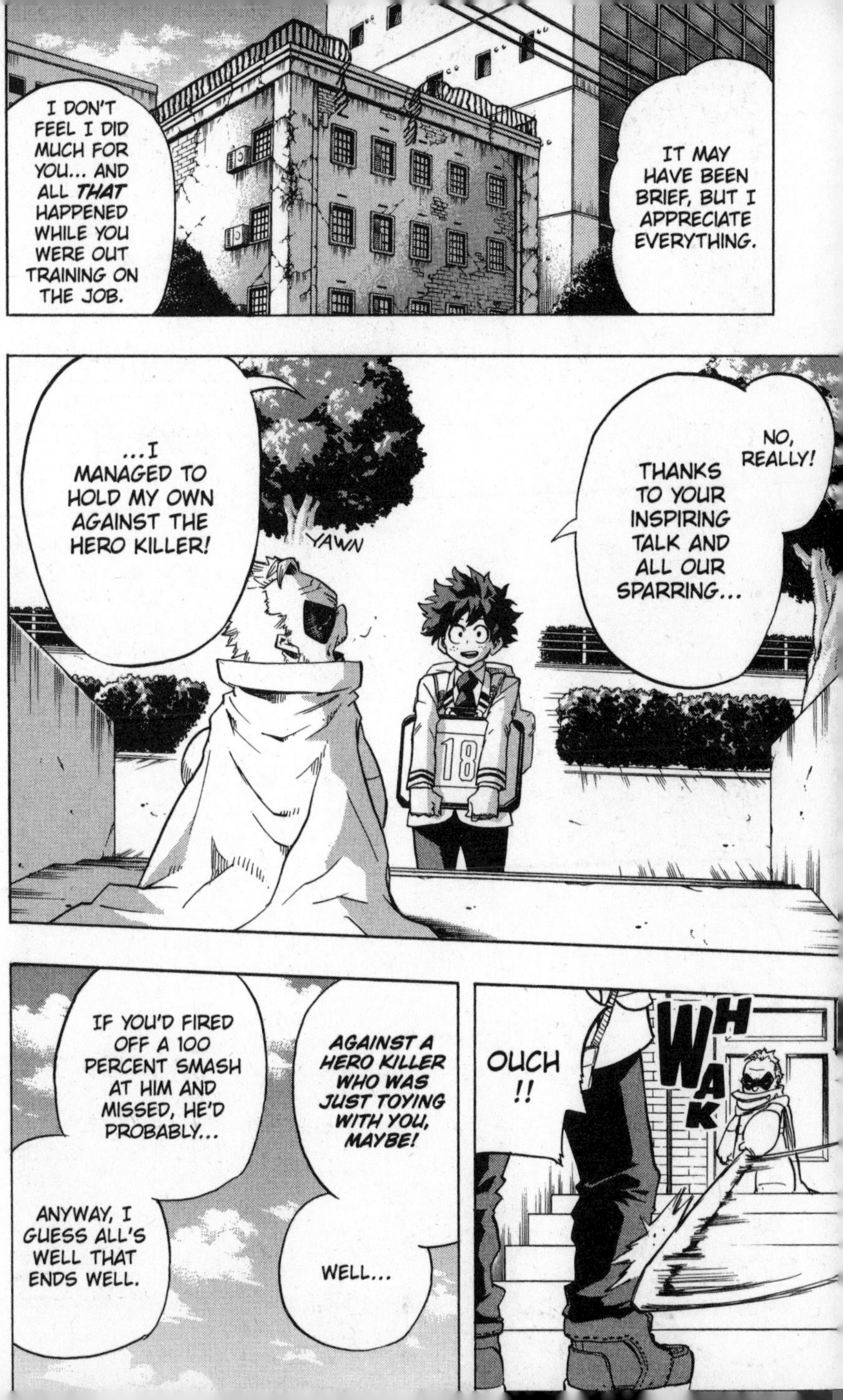
IT MAY HAVE BEEN BRIEF, BUT I APPRECIATE EVERYTHING.
I DON'T FEEL I DID MUCH FOR YOU... AND ALL *THAT* HAPPENED WHILE YOU WERE OUT TRAINING ON THE JOB.
NO, REALLY!
THANKS TO YOUR INSPIRING TALK AND ALL OUR SPARRING...
...I MANAGED TO HOLD MY OWN AGAINST THE HERO KILLER!
YAWN
WHAK
OUCH !!
AGAINST A HERO KILLER WHO WAS JUST TOYING WITH YOU, MAYBE!
IF YOU'D FIRED OFF A 100 PERCENT SMASH AT HIM AND MISSED, HE'D PROBABLY...
WELL...
ANYWAY, I GUESS ALL'S WELL THAT ENDS WELL.

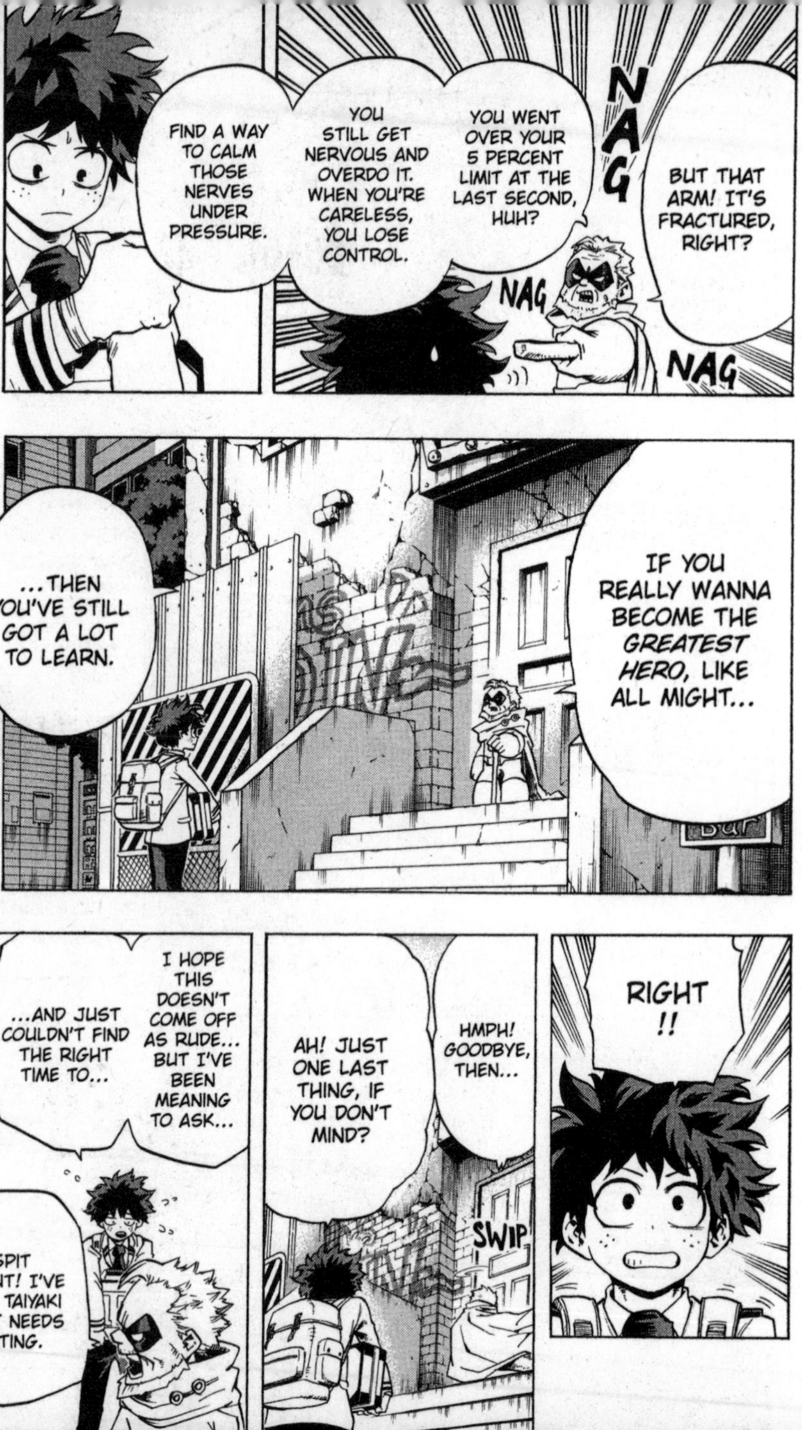
BUT THAT ARM! IT'S FRACTURED, RIGHT?
NAG NAG
YOU WENT OVER YOUR 5 PERCENT LIMIT AT THE LAST SECOND, HUH?
NAG
YOU STILL GET NERVOUS AND OVERDO IT. WHEN YOU'RE CARELESS, YOU LOSE CONTROL.
NAG
FIND A WAY TO CALM THOSE NERVES UNDER PRESSURE.
IF YOU REALLY WANNA BECOME THE *GREATEST HERO*, LIKE ALL MIGHT...
...THEN YOU'VE STILL GOT A LOT TO LEARN.
RIGHT !!
HMPH! GOODBYE, THEN...
SWIP
AH! JUST ONE LAST THING, IF YOU DON'T MIND?
I HOPE THIS DOESN'T COME OFF AS RUDE... BUT I'VE BEEN MEANING TO ASK...
...AND JUST COULDN'T FIND THE RIGHT TIME TO...
SPIT IT OUT! I'VE GOT TAIYAKI THAT NEEDS EATING.

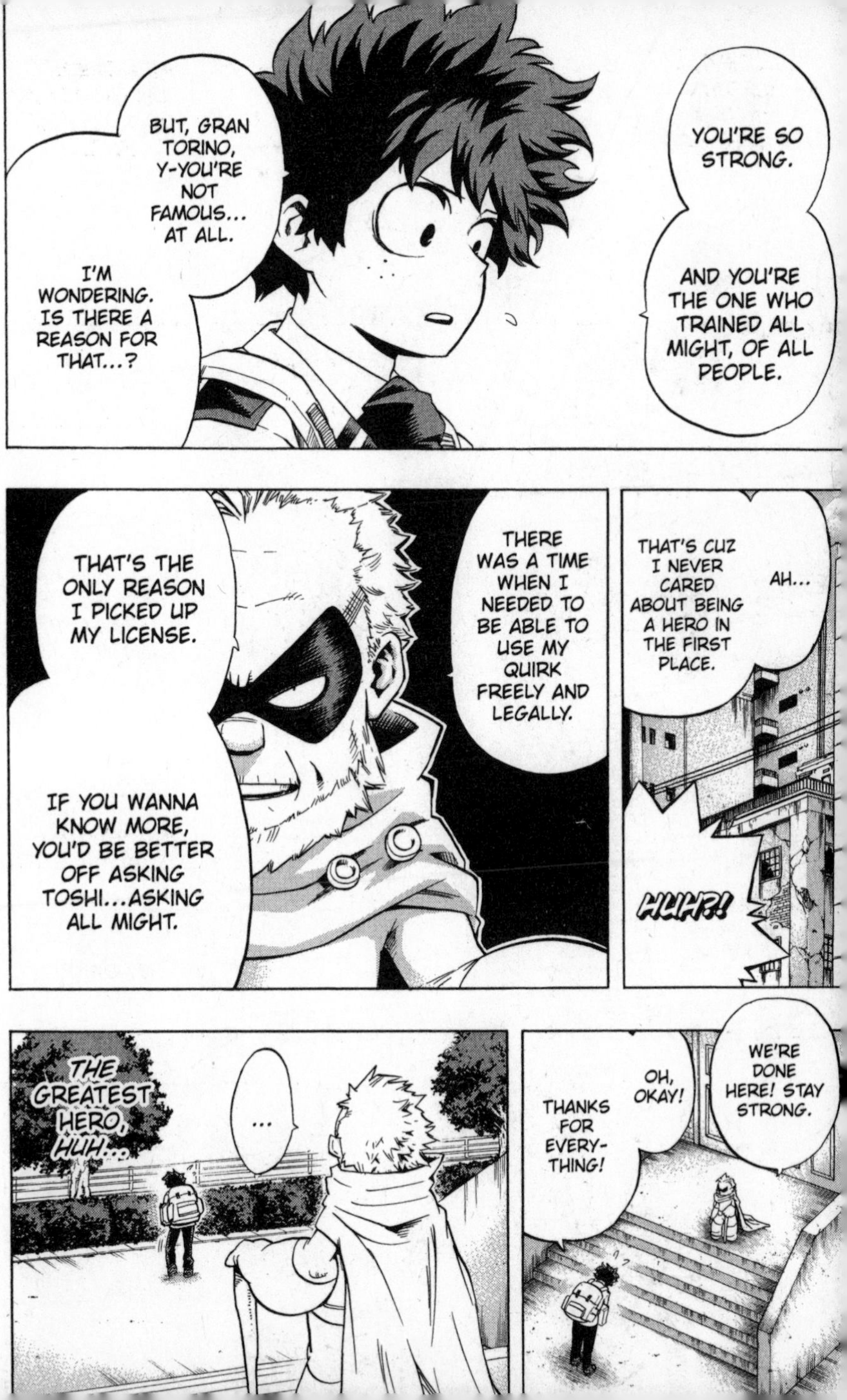
YOU'RE SO STRONG.
AND YOU'RE THE ONE WHO TRAINED ALL MIGHT, OF ALL PEOPLE.
BUT, GRAN TORINO, Y-YOU'RE NOT FAMOUS... AT ALL.
I'M WONDERING. IS THERE A REASON FOR THAT...?
AH...
THAT'S CUZ I NEVER CARED ABOUT BEING A HERO IN THE FIRST PLACE.
HUH?!
THERE WAS A TIME WHEN I NEEDED TO BE ABLE TO USE MY QUIRK FREELY AND LEGALLY.
THAT'S THE ONLY REASON I PICKED UP MY LICENSE.
IF YOU WANNA KNOW MORE, YOU'D BE BETTER OFF ASKING TOSHI...ASKING ALL MIGHT.
WE'RE DONE HERE! STAY STRONG.
OH, OKAY!
THANKS FOR EVERY-THING!
...
THE GREATEST HERO, HUH...

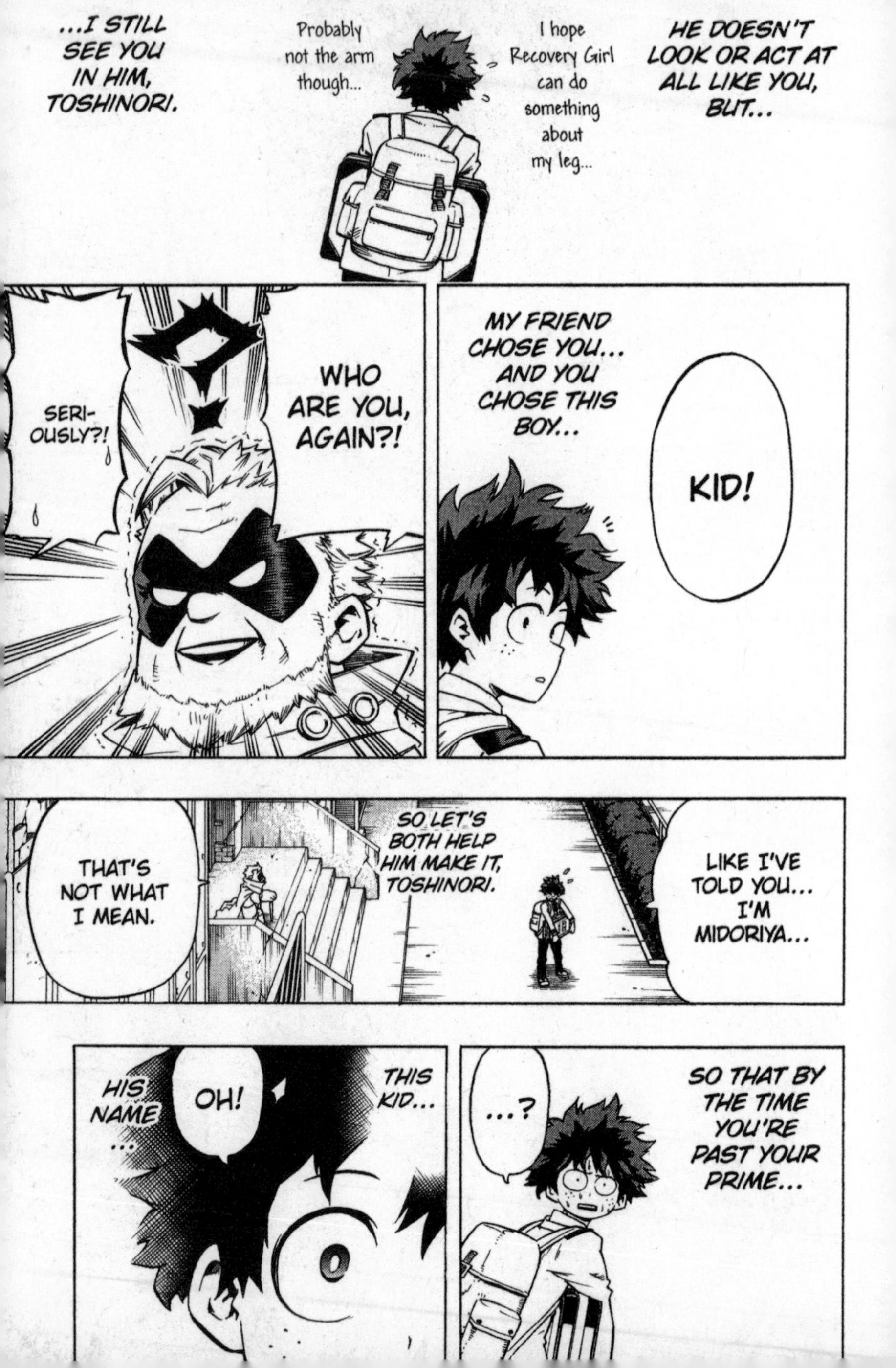
HE DOESN'T LOOK OR ACT AT ALL LIKE YOU, BUT...
I hope Recovery Girl can do something about my leg...
Probably not the arm though...
...I STILL SEE YOU IN HIM, TOSHINORI.
MY FRIEND CHOSE YOU... AND YOU CHOSE THIS BOY...
KID!
WHO ARE YOU, AGAIN?!
SERI-OUSLY?!
LIKE I'VE TOLD YOU... I'M MIDORIYA...
SO LET'S BOTH HELP HIM MAKE IT, TOSHINORI.
THAT'S NOT WHAT I MEAN.
SO THAT BY THE TIME YOU'RE PAST YOUR PRIME...
...?
THIS KID...
OH!
HIS NAME...

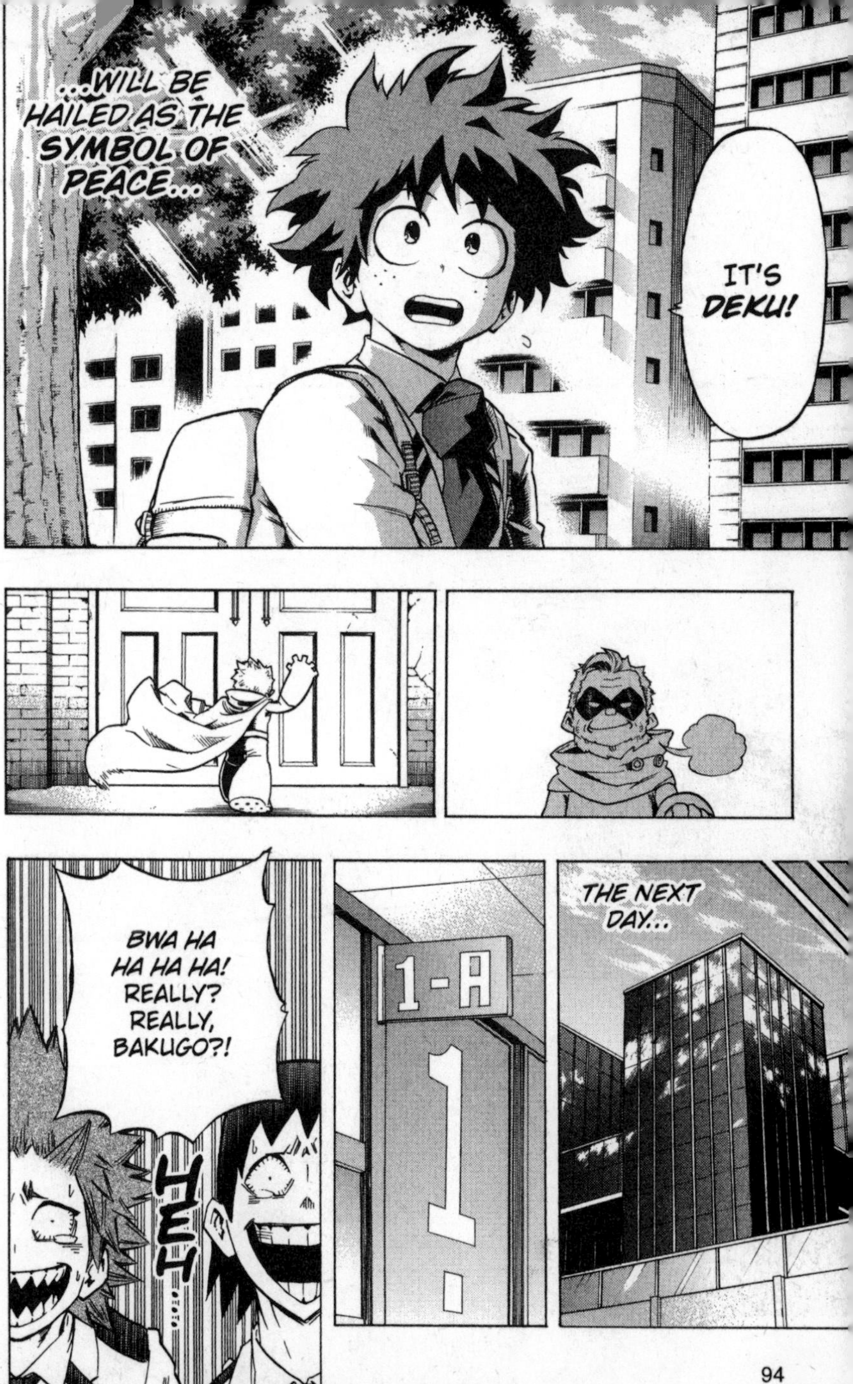
...WILL BE HAILED AS THE SYMBOL OF PEACE...
IT'S DEKU!
THE NEXT DAY...
1-A
1
BWA HA HA HA HA! REALLY? REALLY, BAKUGO?!
HEH...

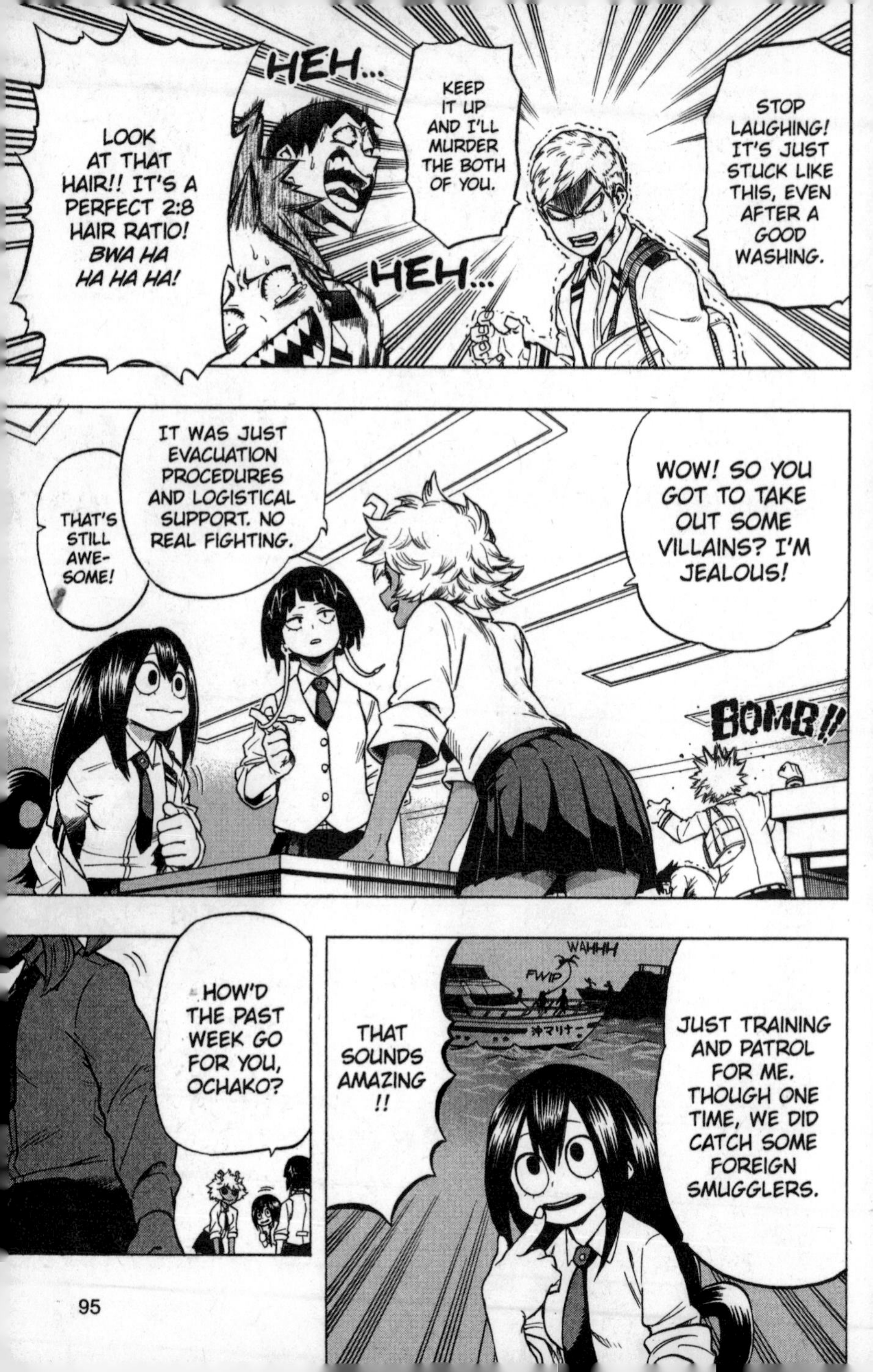
STOP LAUGHING! IT'S JUST STUCK LIKE THIS, EVEN AFTER A GOOD WASHING.
KEEP IT UP AND I'LL MURDER THE BOTH OF YOU.
HEH...
LOOK AT THAT HAIR!! IT'S A PERFECT 2:8 HAIR RATIO! *BWA HA HA HA HA!*
HEH...
WOW! SO YOU GOT TO TAKE OUT SOME VILLAINS? I'M JEALOUS!
BOMB!!
IT WAS JUST EVACUATION PROCEDURES AND LOGISTICAL SUPPORT. NO REAL FIGHTING.
THAT'S STILL AWE-SOME!
JUST TRAINING AND PATROL FOR ME. THOUGH ONE TIME, WE DID CATCH SOME FOREIGN SMUGGLERS.
WAHHH
FWIP
沖マリナ
THAT SOUNDS AMAZING !!
HOW'D THE PAST WEEK GO FOR YOU, OCHAKO?

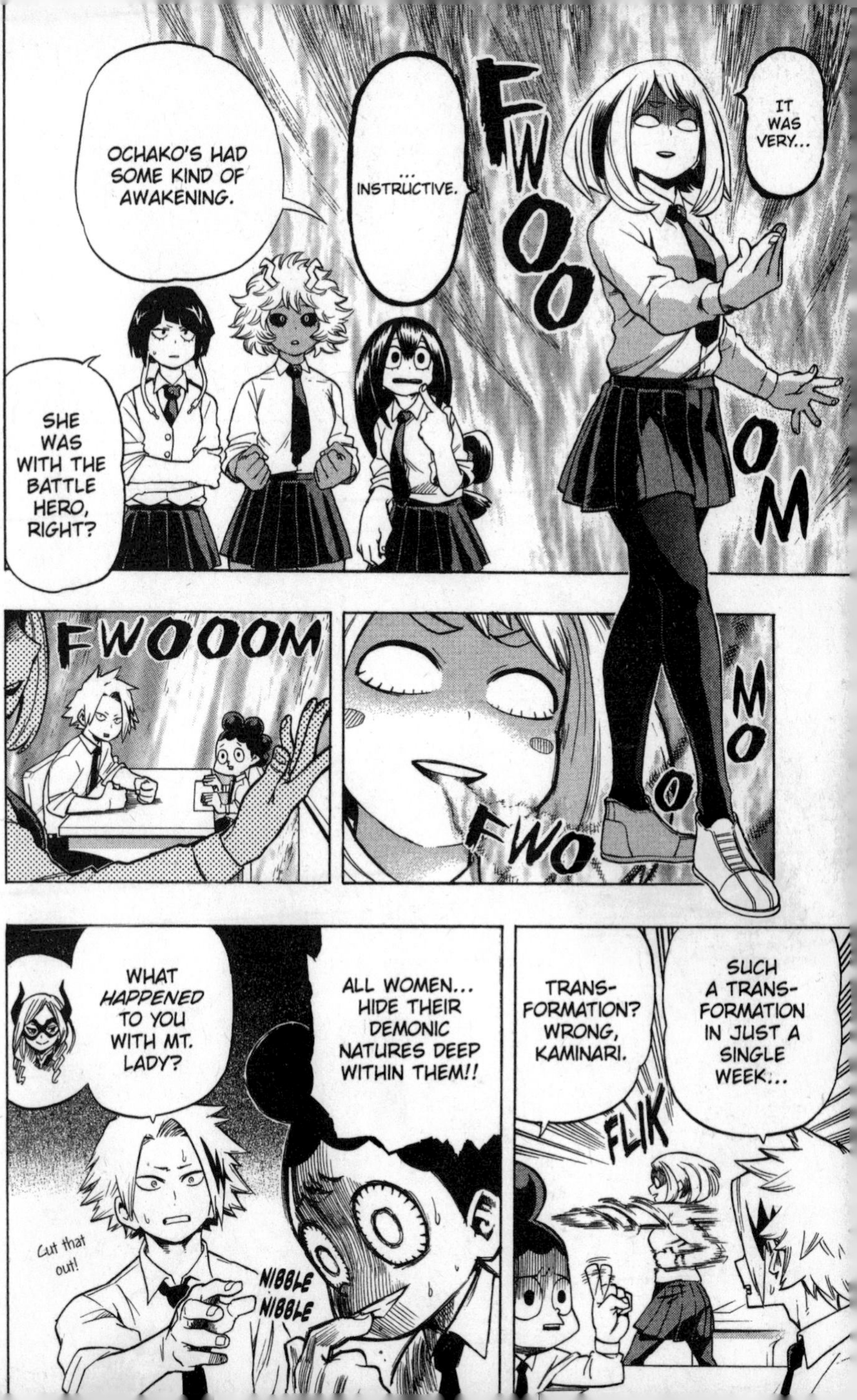
IT WAS VERY...
FWOO
OM
... INSTRUCTIVE.
OCHAKO'S HAD SOME KIND OF AWAKENING.
SHE WAS WITH THE BATTLE HERO, RIGHT?
MO
O
FWO
FWOOOM
SUCH A TRANS-FORMATION IN JUST A SINGLE WEEK...
TRANS-FORMATION? WRONG, KAMINARI.
FLIK
ALL WOMEN... HIDE THEIR DEMONIC NATURES DEEP WITHIN THEM!!
WHAT HAPPENED TO YOU WITH MT. LADY?
NIBBLE NIBBLE
Cut that out!

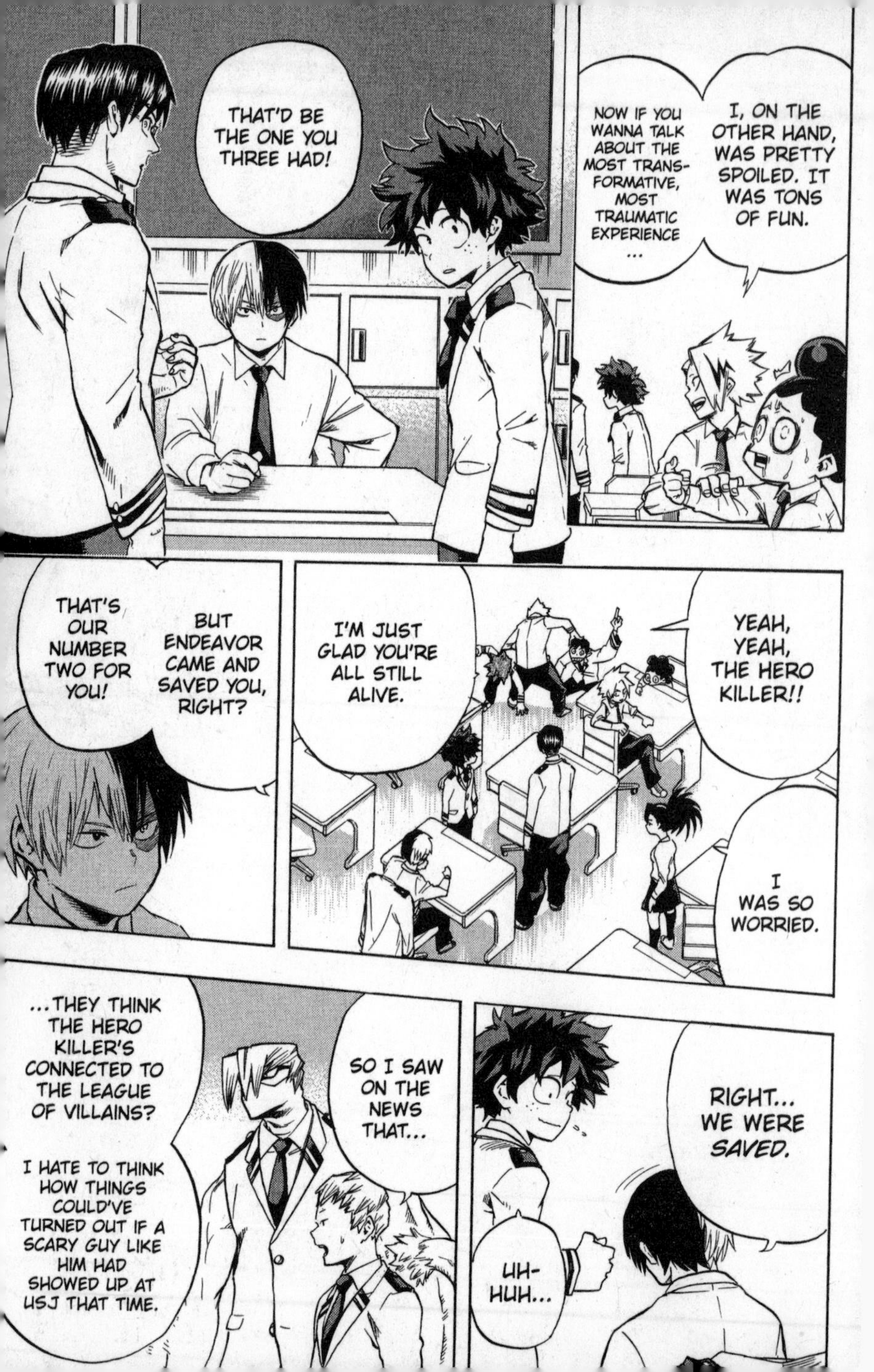
I, ON THE OTHER HAND, WAS PRETTY SPOILED. IT WAS TONS OF FUN.
NOW IF YOU WANNA TALK ABOUT THE MOST TRANS-FORMATIVE, MOST TRAUMATIC EXPERIENCE...
THAT'D BE THE ONE YOU THREE HAD!
YEAH, YEAH, THE HERO KILLER!!
I WAS SO WORRIED.
I'M JUST GLAD YOU'RE ALL STILL ALIVE.
BUT ENDEAVOR CAME AND SAVED YOU, RIGHT?
THAT'S OUR NUMBER TWO FOR YOU!
RIGHT... WE WERE SAVED.
UH-HUH...
SO I SAW ON THE NEWS THAT...
...THEY THINK THE HERO KILLER'S CONNECTED TO THE LEAGUE OF VILLAINS?
I HATE TO THINK HOW THINGS COULD'VE TURNED OUT IF A SCARY GUY LIKE HIM HAD SHOWED UP AT USJ THAT TIME.

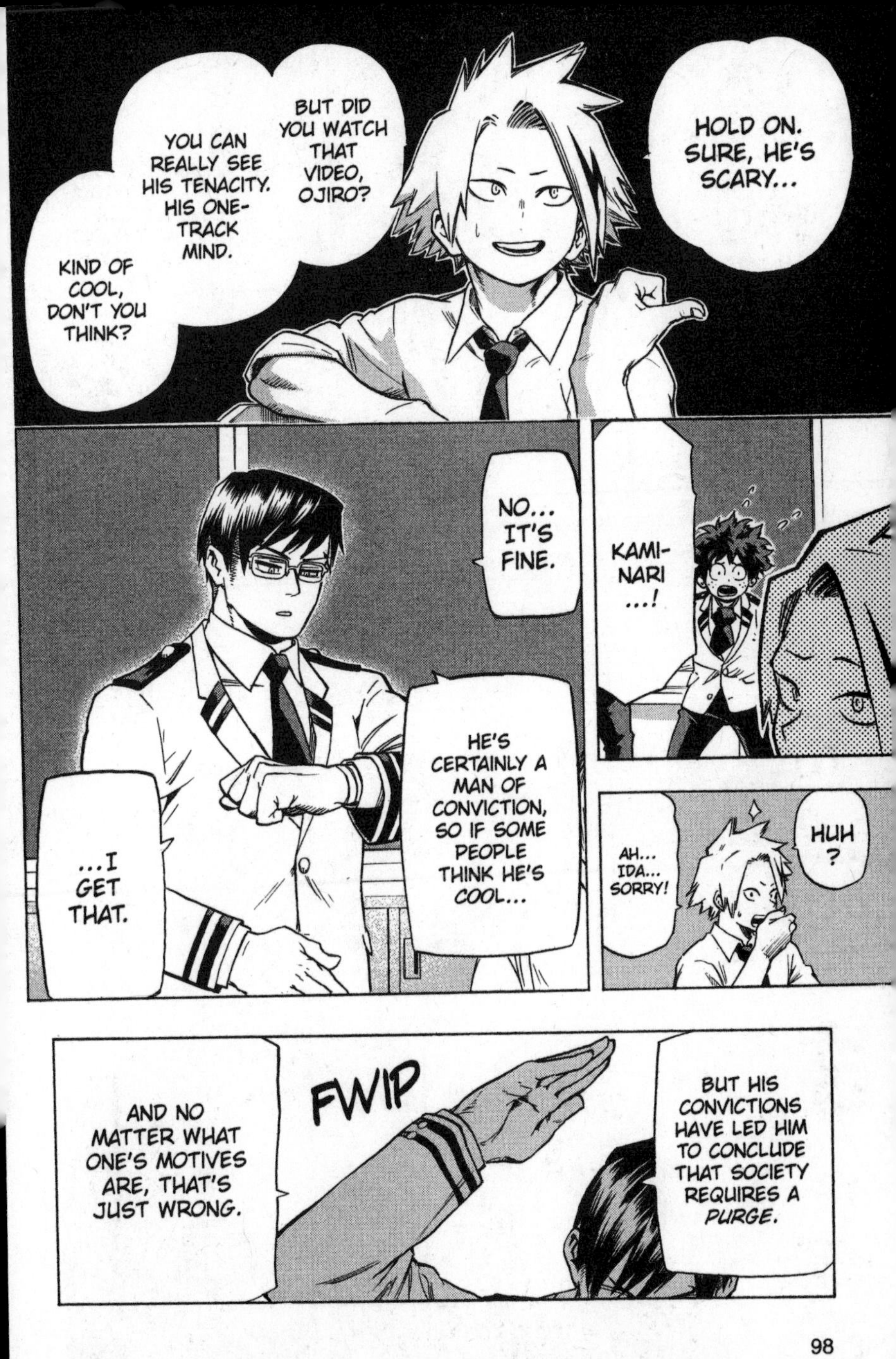
HOLD ON. SURE, HE'S SCARY...
BUT DID YOU WATCH THAT VIDEO, OJIRO?
YOU CAN REALLY SEE HIS TENACITY. HIS ONE-TRACK MIND.
KIND OF COOL, DON'T YOU THINK?
KAMI-NARI ...!
HUH?
AH... IDA... SORRY!
NO... IT'S FINE.
HE'S CERTAINLY A MAN OF CONVICTION, SO IF SOME PEOPLE THINK HE'S COOL...
...I GET THAT.
BUT HIS CONVICTIONS HAVE LED HIM TO CONCLUDE THAT SOCIETY REQUIRES A *PURGE*.
FWIP
AND NO MATTER WHAT ONE'S MOTIVES ARE, THAT'S JUST WRONG.

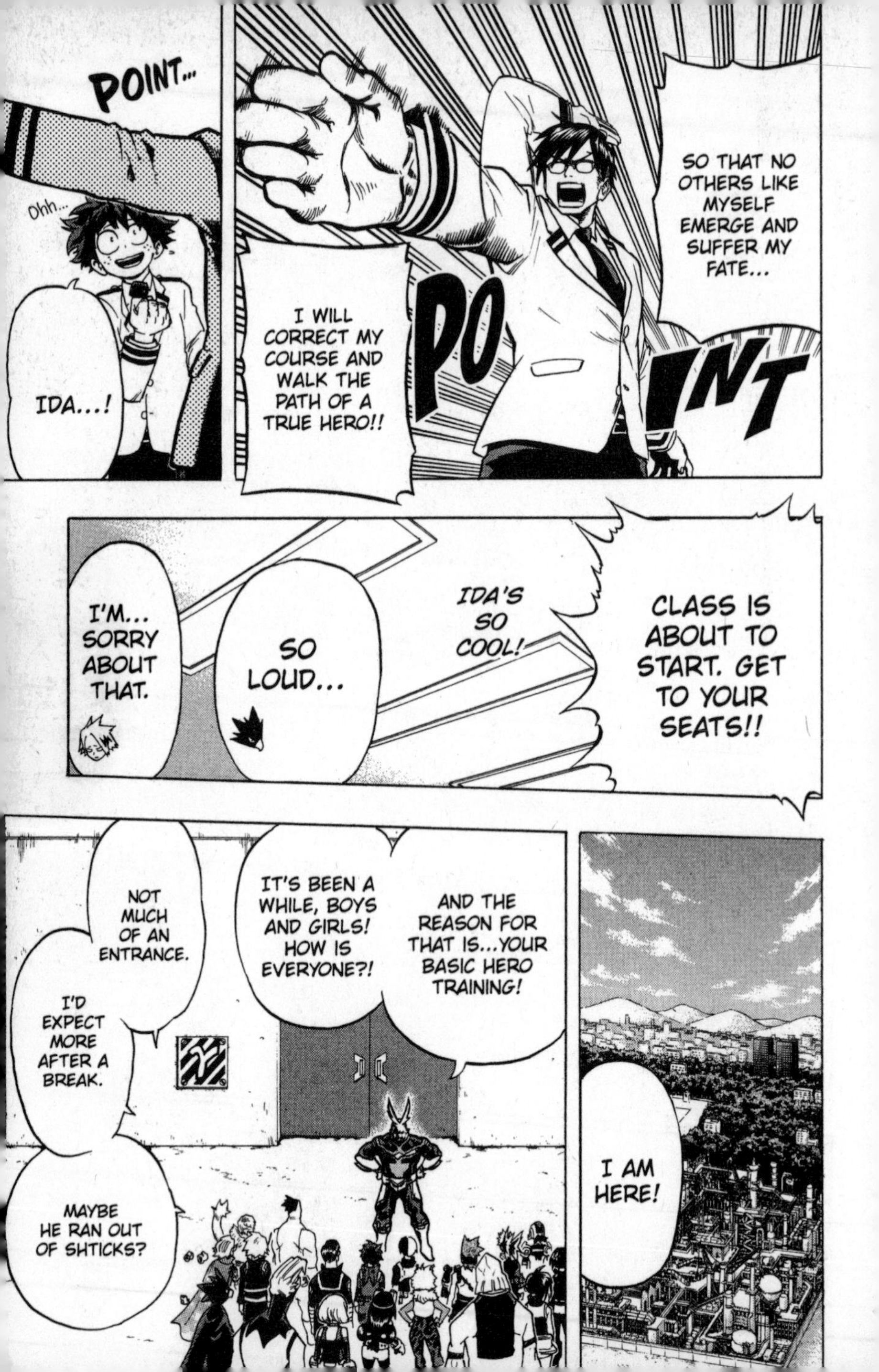
SO THAT NO OTHERS LIKE MYSELF EMERGE AND SUFFER MY FATE...
I WILL CORRECT MY COURSE AND WALK THE PATH OF A TRUE HERO!!
POINT
POINT...
Ohh...
IDA...!
CLASS IS ABOUT TO START. GET TO YOUR SEATS!!
IDA'S SO COOL!
SO LOUD...
I'M... SORRY ABOUT THAT.
I AM HERE!
IT'S BEEN A WHILE, BOYS AND GIRLS! HOW IS EVERYONE?!
AND THE REASON FOR THAT IS...YOUR BASIC HERO TRAINING!
NOT MUCH OF AN ENTRANCE.
I'D EXPECT MORE AFTER A BREAK.
MAYBE HE RAN OUT OF SHTICKS?

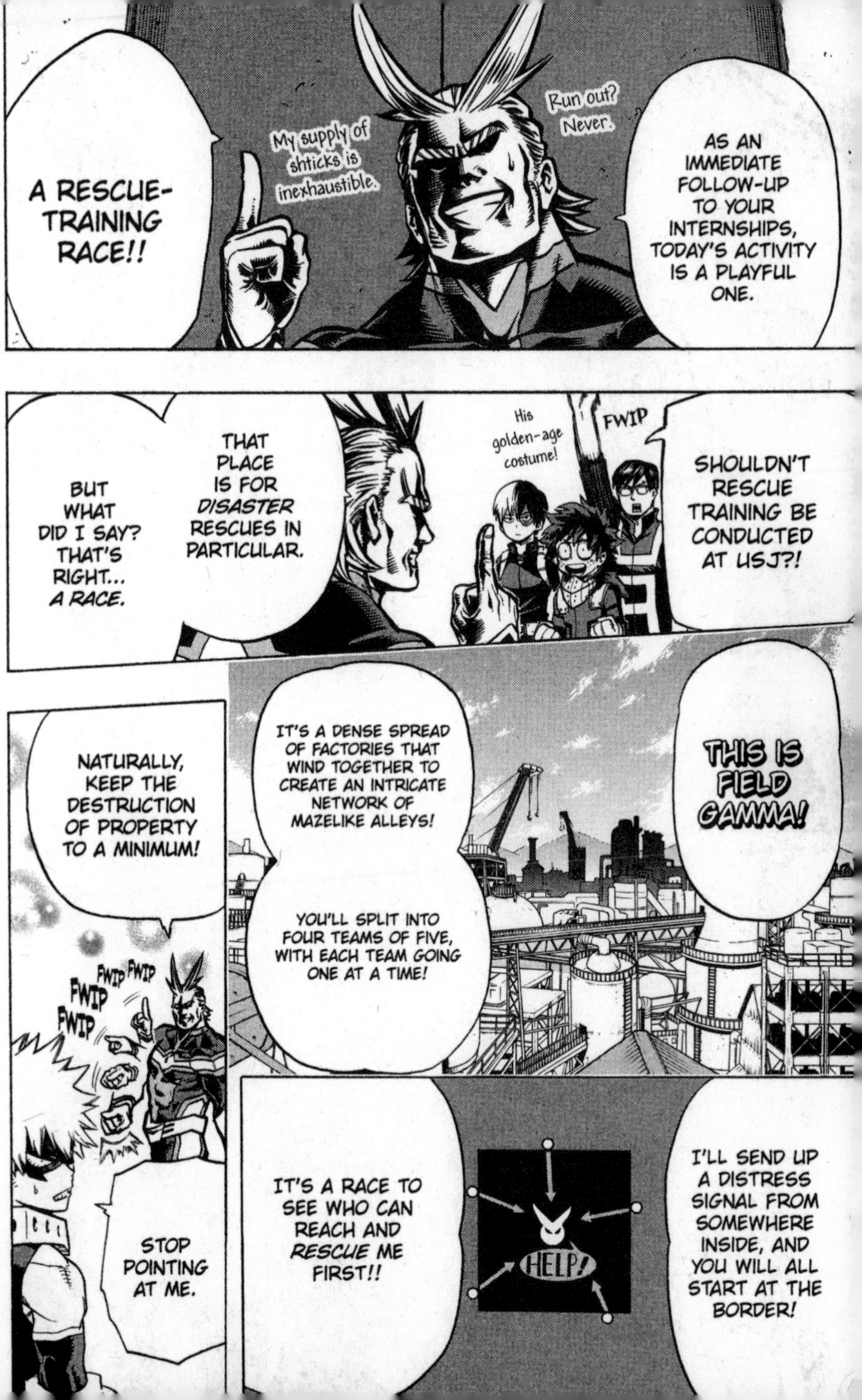
AS AN IMMEDIATE FOLLOW-UP TO YOUR INTERNSHIPS, TODAY'S ACTIVITY IS A PLAYFUL ONE.
Run out? Never.
My supply of shticks is inexhaustible.
A RESCUE-TRAINING RACE!!
SHOULDN'T RESCUE TRAINING BE CONDUCTED AT USJ?!
FWIP
His golden-age costume!
THAT PLACE IS FOR DISASTER RESCUES IN PARTICULAR.
BUT WHAT DID I SAY? THAT'S RIGHT... A RACE.
THIS IS FIELD GAMMA!
IT'S A DENSE SPREAD OF FACTORIES THAT WIND TOGETHER TO CREATE AN INTRICATE NETWORK OF MAZELIKE ALLEYS!
YOU'LL SPLIT INTO FOUR TEAMS OF FIVE, WITH EACH TEAM GOING ONE AT A TIME!
I'LL SEND UP A DISTRESS SIGNAL FROM SOMEWHERE INSIDE, AND YOU WILL ALL START AT THE BORDER!
HELP!
IT'S A RACE TO SEE WHO CAN REACH AND RESCUE ME FIRST!!
NATURALLY, KEEP THE DESTRUCTION OF PROPERTY TO A MINIMUM!
FWIP FWIP
FWIP
FWIP
STOP POINTING AT ME.

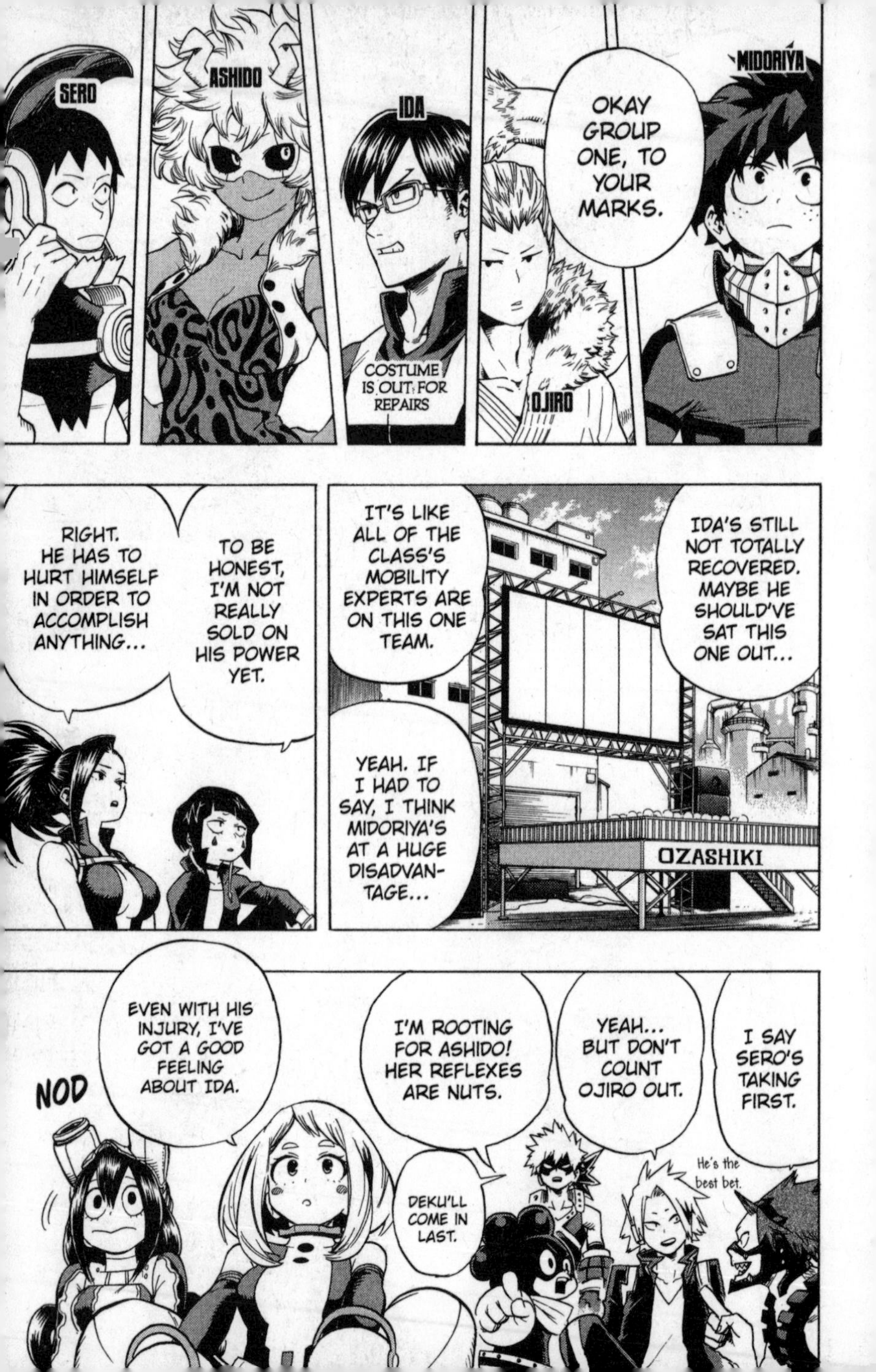
MIDORIYA
OKAY GROUP ONE, TO YOUR MARKS.
OJIRO
IDA
COSTUME IS OUT FOR REPAIRS
ASHIDO
SERO
IDA'S STILL NOT TOTALLY RECOVERED. MAYBE HE SHOULD'VE SAT THIS ONE OUT...
IT'S LIKE ALL OF THE CLASS'S MOBILITY EXPERTS ARE ON THIS ONE TEAM.
YEAH. IF I HAD TO SAY, I THINK MIDORIYA'S AT A HUGE DISADVANTAGE...
OZASHIKI
TO BE HONEST, I'M NOT REALLY SOLD ON HIS POWER YET.
RIGHT. HE HAS TO HURT HIMSELF IN ORDER TO ACCOMPLISH ANYTHING...
I SAY SERO'S TAKING FIRST.
He's the best bet.
YEAH... BUT DON'T COUNT OJIRO OUT.
I'M ROOTING FOR ASHIDO! HER REFLEXES ARE NUTS.
DEKU'LL COME IN LAST.
EVEN WITH HIS INJURY, I'VE GOT A GOOD FEELING ABOUT IDA.
NOD

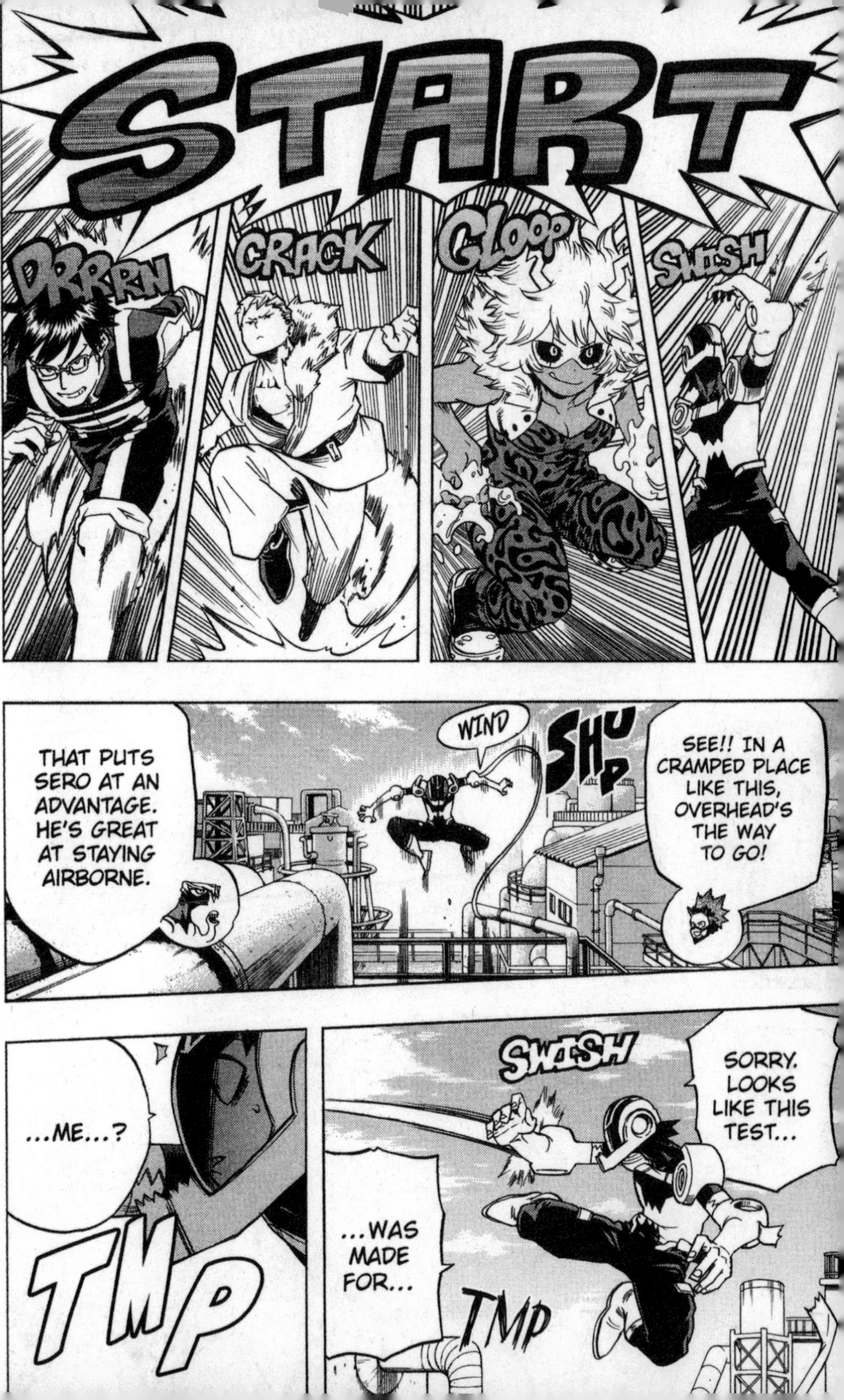
START
SWISH
GLOOP
CRACK
DRRRN
SEE!! IN A CRAMPED PLACE LIKE THIS, OVERHEAD'S THE WAY TO GO!
SHUD
WIND
THAT PUTS SERO AT AN ADVANTAGE. HE'S GREAT AT STAYING AIRBORNE.
SWISH
SORRY. LOOKS LIKE THIS TEST...
...WAS MADE FOR...
TMP
...ME...?
TMP

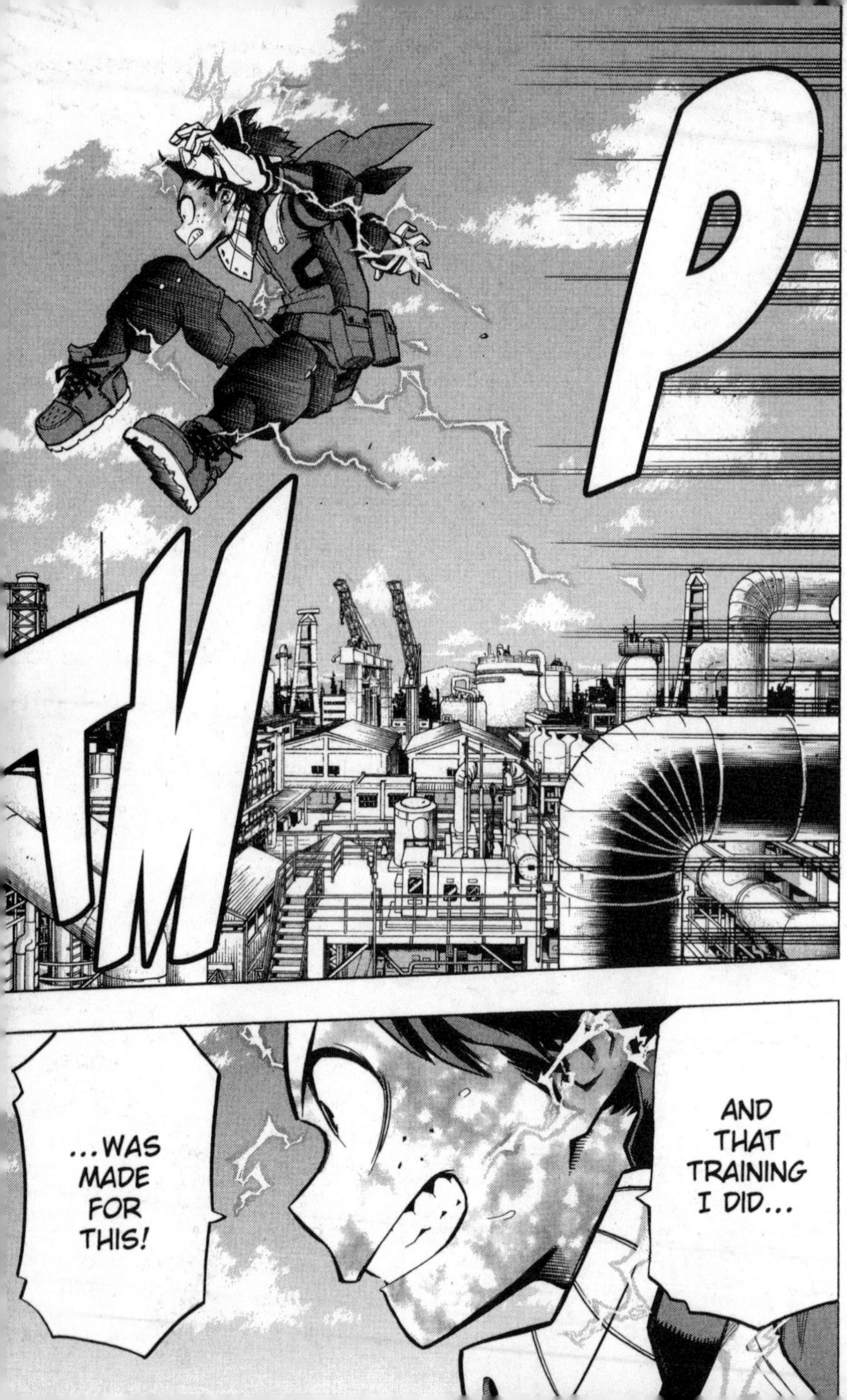
TMP
AND THAT TRAINING I DID...
...WAS MADE FOR THIS!

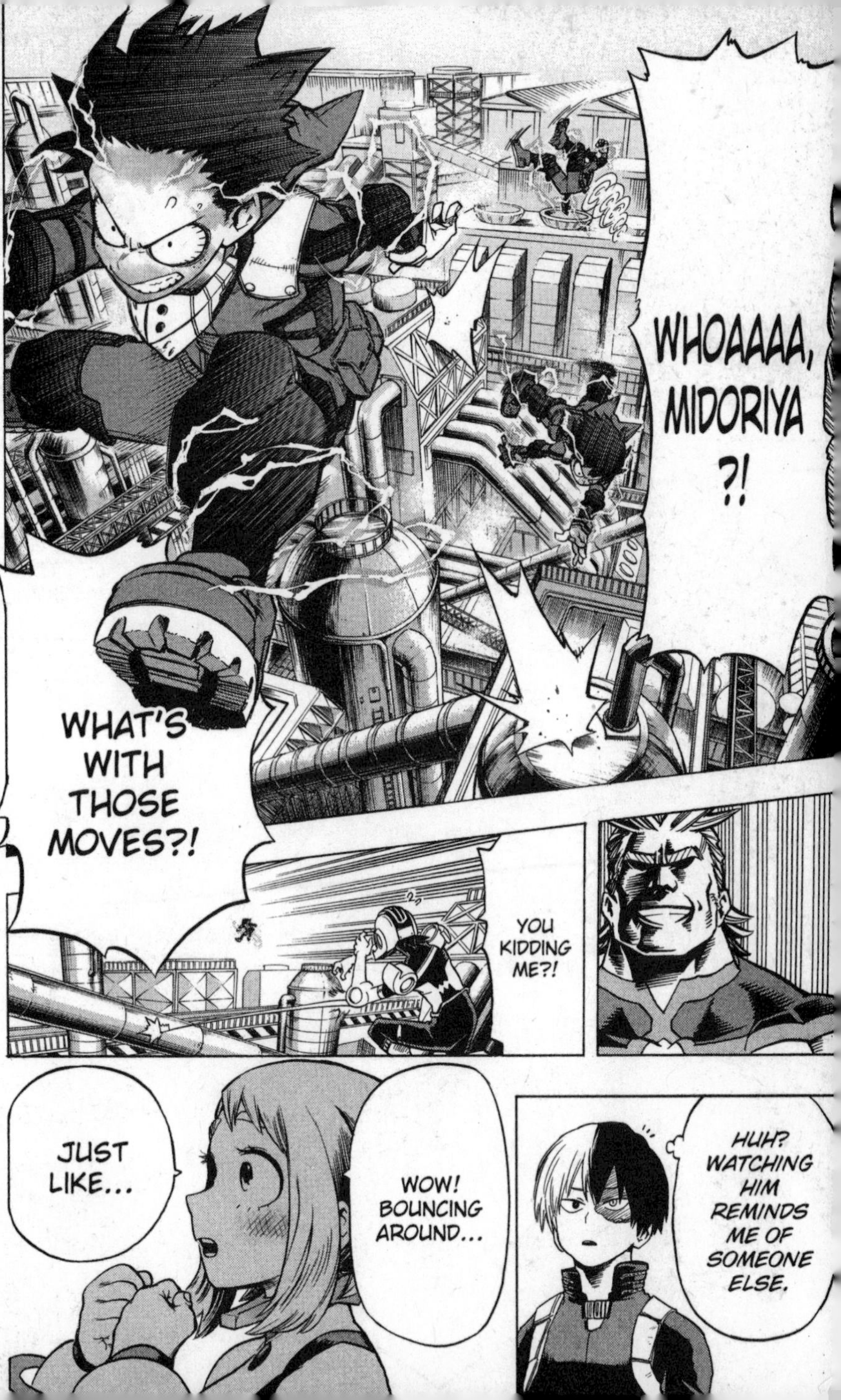
WHOAAAA, MIDORIYA?!
WHAT'S WITH THOSE MOVES?!
YOU KIDDING ME?!
HUH? WATCHING HIM REMINDS ME OF SOMEONE ELSE.
WOW! BOUNCING AROUND...
JUST LIKE...

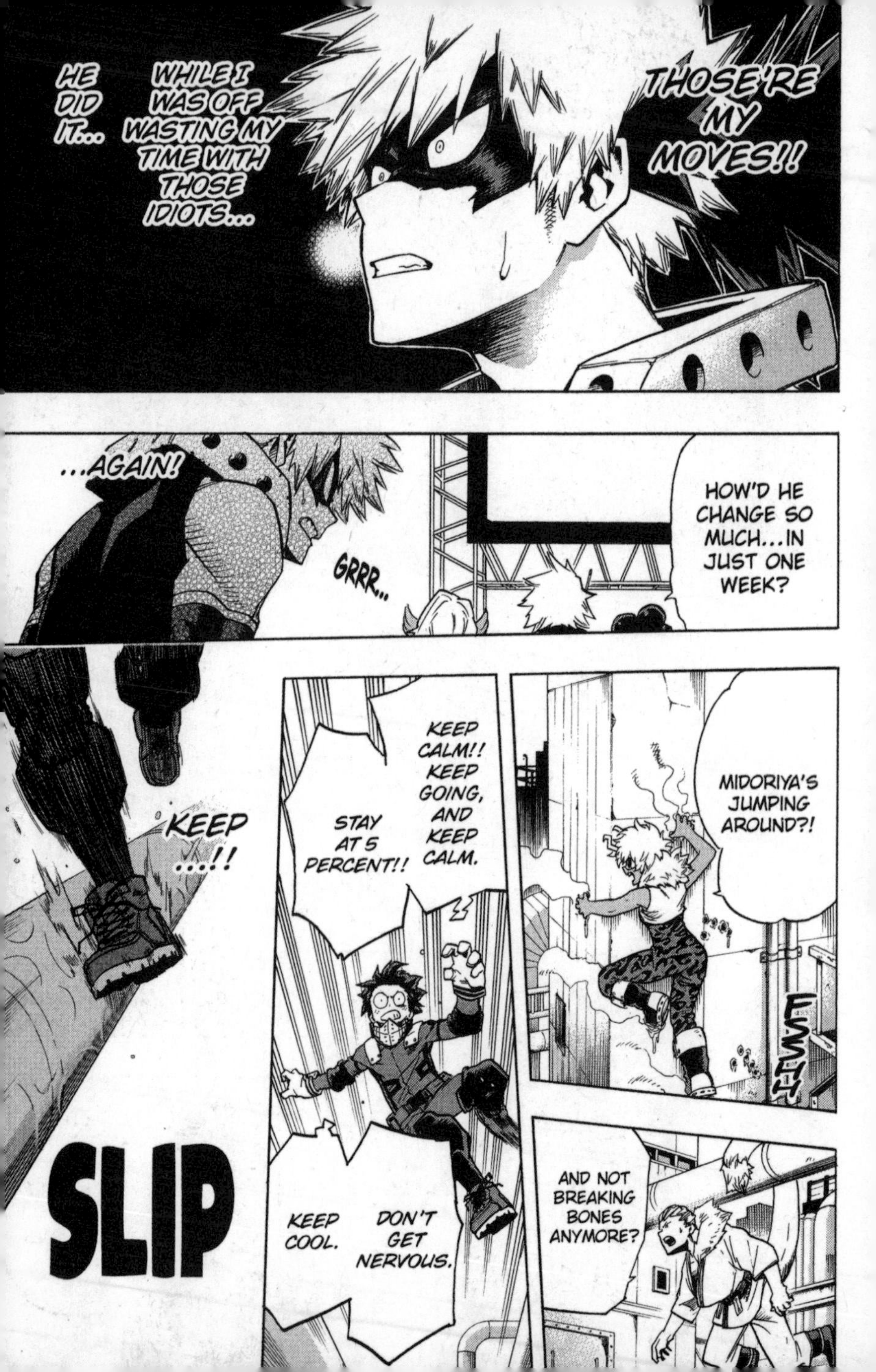
THOSE'RE MY MOVES!!
WHILE I WAS OFF WASTING MY TIME WITH THOSE IDIOTS...
HE DID IT...
HOW'D HE CHANGE SO MUCH...IN JUST ONE WEEK?
GRRR...
...AGAIN!
MIDORIYA'S JUMPING AROUND?!
FSSH
AND NOT BREAKING BONES ANYMORE?
KEEP CALM!! KEEP GOING, AND KEEP CALM.
STAY AT 5 PERCENT!!
DON'T GET NERVOUS.
KEEP COOL.
KEEP ...!!
SLIP

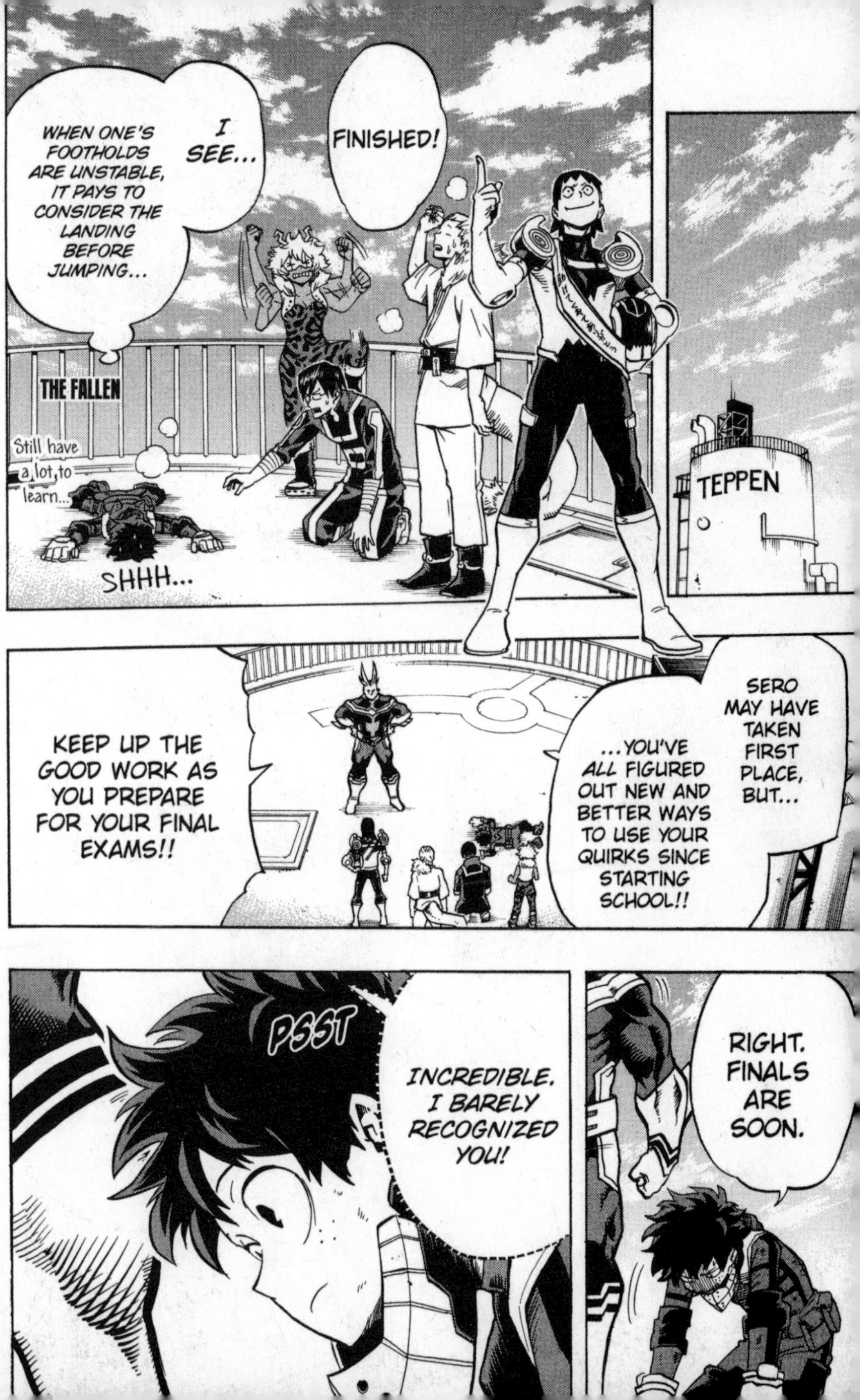
TEPPEN
FINISHED!
I SEE...
WHEN ONE'S FOOTHOLDS ARE UNSTABLE, IT PAYS TO CONSIDER THE LANDING BEFORE JUMPING...
THE FALLEN
Still have a lot to learn...
SHHH...
SERO MAY HAVE TAKEN FIRST PLACE, BUT...
...YOU'VE ALL FIGURED OUT NEW AND BETTER WAYS TO USE YOUR QUIRKS SINCE STARTING SCHOOL!!
KEEP UP THE GOOD WORK AS YOU PREPARE FOR YOUR FINAL EXAMS!!
RIGHT. FINALS ARE SOON.
PSST
INCREDIBLE. I BARELY RECOGNIZED YOU!

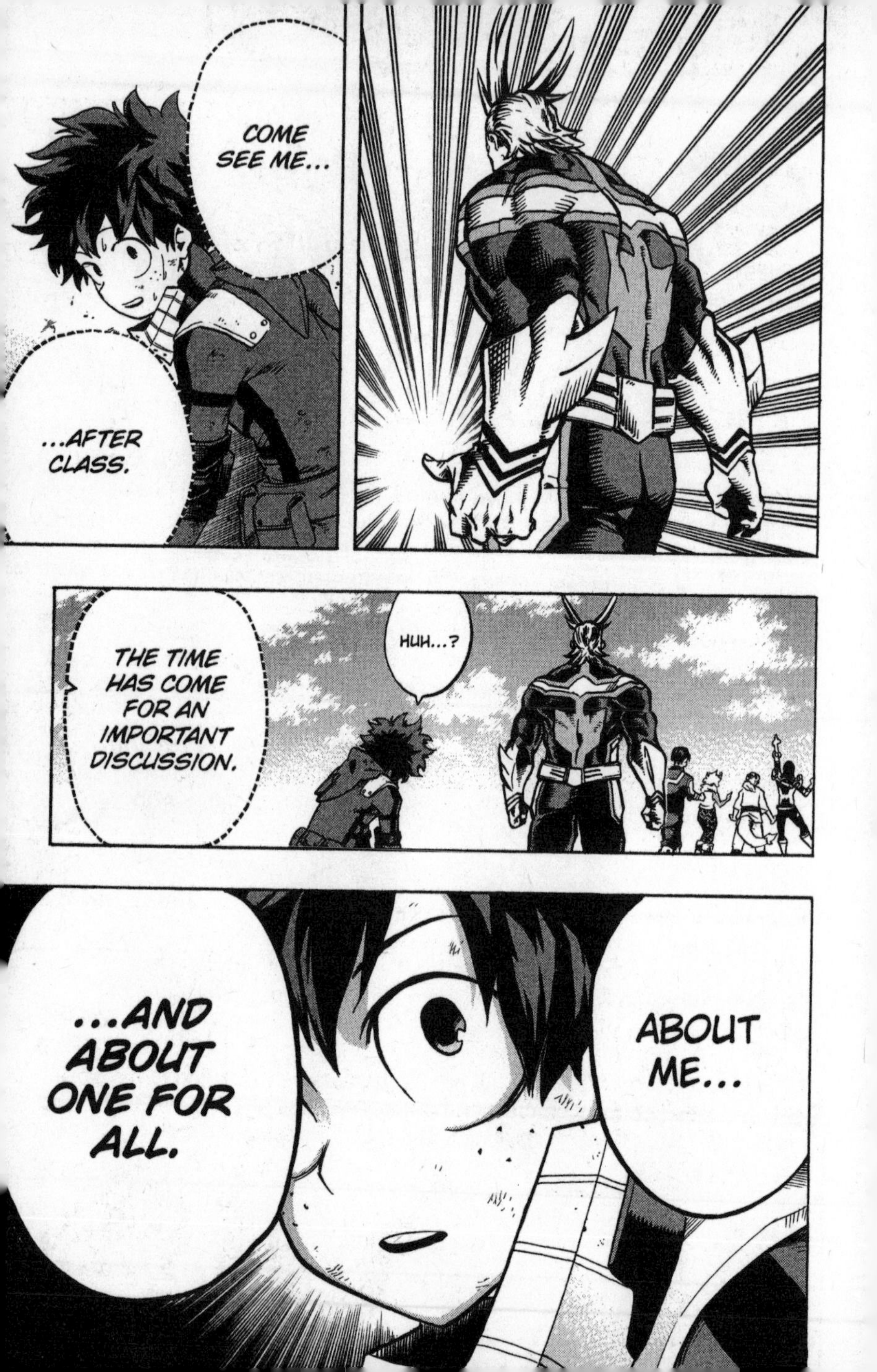
COME SEE ME...
...AFTER CLASS.
HUH...?
THE TIME HAS COME FOR AN IMPORTANT DISCUSSION.
ABOUT ME...
...AND ABOUT ONE FOR ALL.

STAIN

THE COMPLAINT CORNER

Whenever there's a new character in the story, I usually use this blank page to do a proper character introduction, but as the number of new characters has dwindled, I've started to go on some crazy tangents, here. Some of you may be thinking, "What about all the villains?" but for the time being, I have no intention of writing about them. I do the introductions because I personally like those sorts of behind-the-scenes things, and also because I want my readers to feel a connection to the characters. But with villains, I decided I can't have them too likable. They're supposed to be terrifying.

Anyway, Stain got beaten. Drawing him was a pain. I've always been the type to design characters without necessarily thinking about how they'll have to move within the manga, so I end up going way over capacity in terms of detail.

Illustrating and making manga are two very different things.
For instance, I packed a ton of textural detail into Stain's scarf, but then the final version in *JUMP* wound up mostly filled in with black. That showed me that I still have a lot to learn about having a long-running series in *JUMP*.

Stain may have been beaten, but he's a character who's going to have long and lasting effects on the world within the story, so I hope all the readers out there don't go forgetting about him. I appreciate it.

NO. 59 - LISTEN UP!! A TALE FROM THE PAST

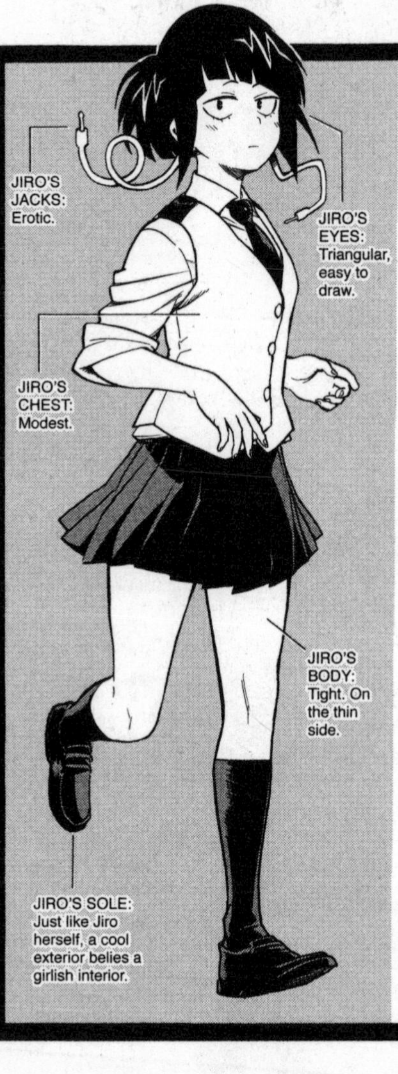

JIRO'S JACKS: Erotic.
JIRO'S EYES: Triangular, easy to draw.
JIRO'S CHEST: Modest.
JIRO'S BODY: Tight. On the thin side.
JIRO'S SOLE: Just like Jiro herself, a cool exterior belies a girlish interior.

U.A. FILE.08

CLASS No. 12
KYOKA JIRO

QUIRK

EARPHONE JACK

She can plug the jacks hanging from her earlobes into all sorts of things and amplify the sound of her heartbeat through them. The vibrations can destroy things from the inside!

She's also great at picking up sounds, even if they're coming through thick walls. The perfect eavesdropper!

Thanks to retractable, winding cords, her jacks can stretch out about six meters! While not very powerful, they can be handy, all-purpose tools within a six-meter radius.

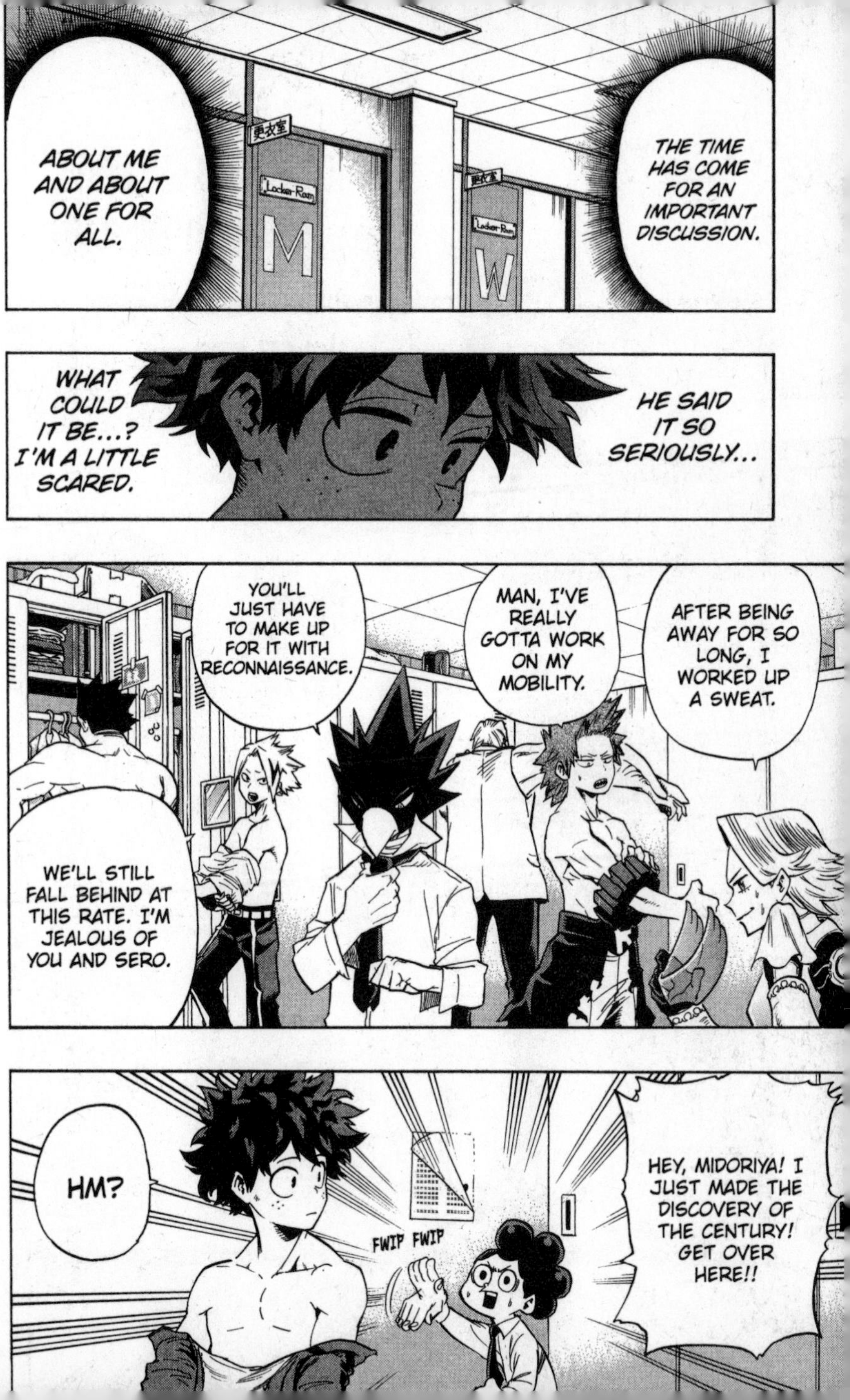
THE TIME HAS COME FOR AN IMPORTANT DISCUSSION.
ABOUT ME AND ABOUT ONE FOR ALL.
HE SAID IT SO SERIOUSLY...
WHAT COULD IT BE...? I'M A LITTLE SCARED.
AFTER BEING AWAY FOR SO LONG, I WORKED UP A SWEAT.
MAN, I'VE REALLY GOTTA WORK ON MY MOBILITY.
YOU'LL JUST HAVE TO MAKE UP FOR IT WITH RECONNAISSANCE.
WE'LL STILL FALL BEHIND AT THIS RATE. I'M JEALOUS OF YOU AND SERO.
HEY, MIDORIYA! I JUST MADE THE DISCOVERY OF THE CENTURY! GET OVER HERE!!
FWIP FWIP
HM?

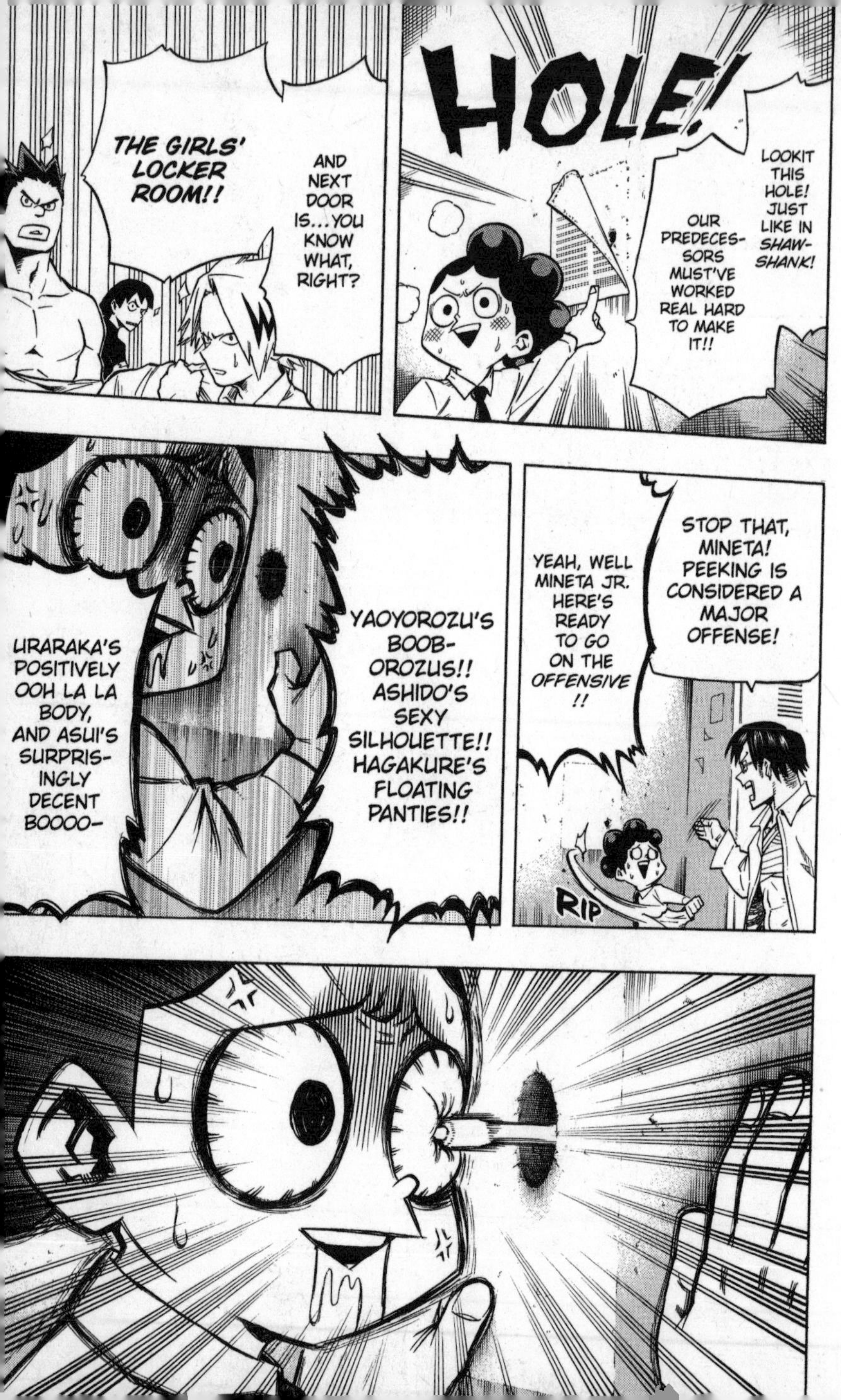
HOLE!
LOOKIT THIS HOLE! JUST LIKE IN SHAWSHANK!
OUR PREDECESSORS MUST'VE WORKED REAL HARD TO MAKE IT!!
AND NEXT DOOR IS...YOU KNOW WHAT, RIGHT?
THE GIRLS' LOCKER ROOM!!
STOP THAT, MINETA! PEEKING IS CONSIDERED A MAJOR OFFENSE!
YEAH, WELL MINETA JR. HERE'S READY TO GO ON THE OFFENSIVE!!
RIP
YAOYOROZU'S BOOB-OROZUS!! ASHIDO'S SEXY SILHOUETTE!! HAGAKURE'S FLOATING PANTIES!!
URARAKA'S POSITIVELY OOH LA LA BODY, AND ASUI'S SURPRISINGLY DECENT BOOOO-

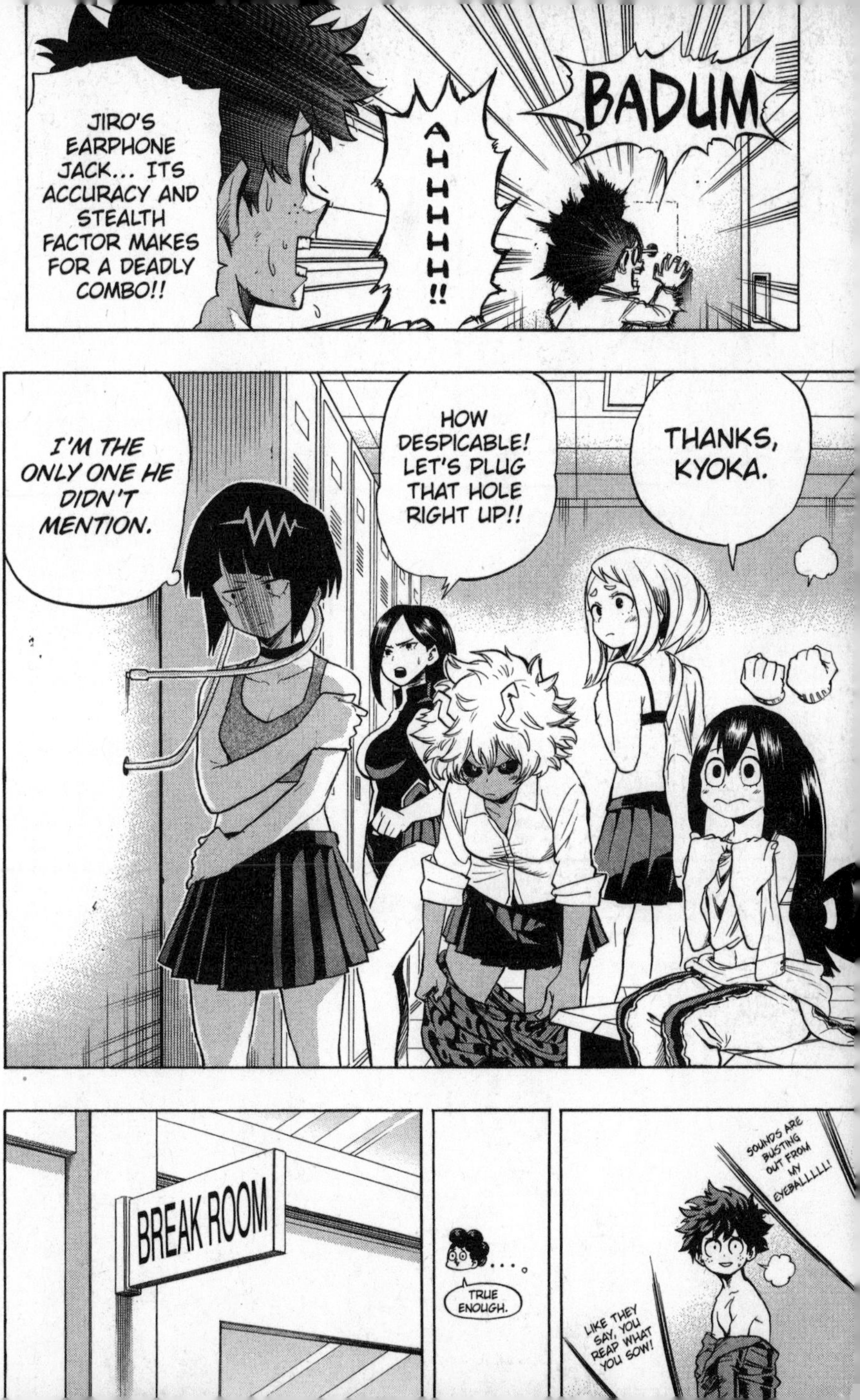
BADUM
AHHHHH!!
JIRO'S EARPHONE JACK... ITS ACCURACY AND STEALTH FACTOR MAKES FOR A DEADLY COMBO!!
THANKS, KYOKA.
HOW DESPICABLE! LET'S PLUG THAT HOLE RIGHT UP!!
I'M THE ONLY ONE HE DIDN'T MENTION.
SOUNDS ARE BUSTING OUT FROM MY EYEBALLLLLL!
LIKE THEY SAY, YOU REAP WHAT YOU SOW!
...
TRUE ENOUGH.
BREAK ROOM

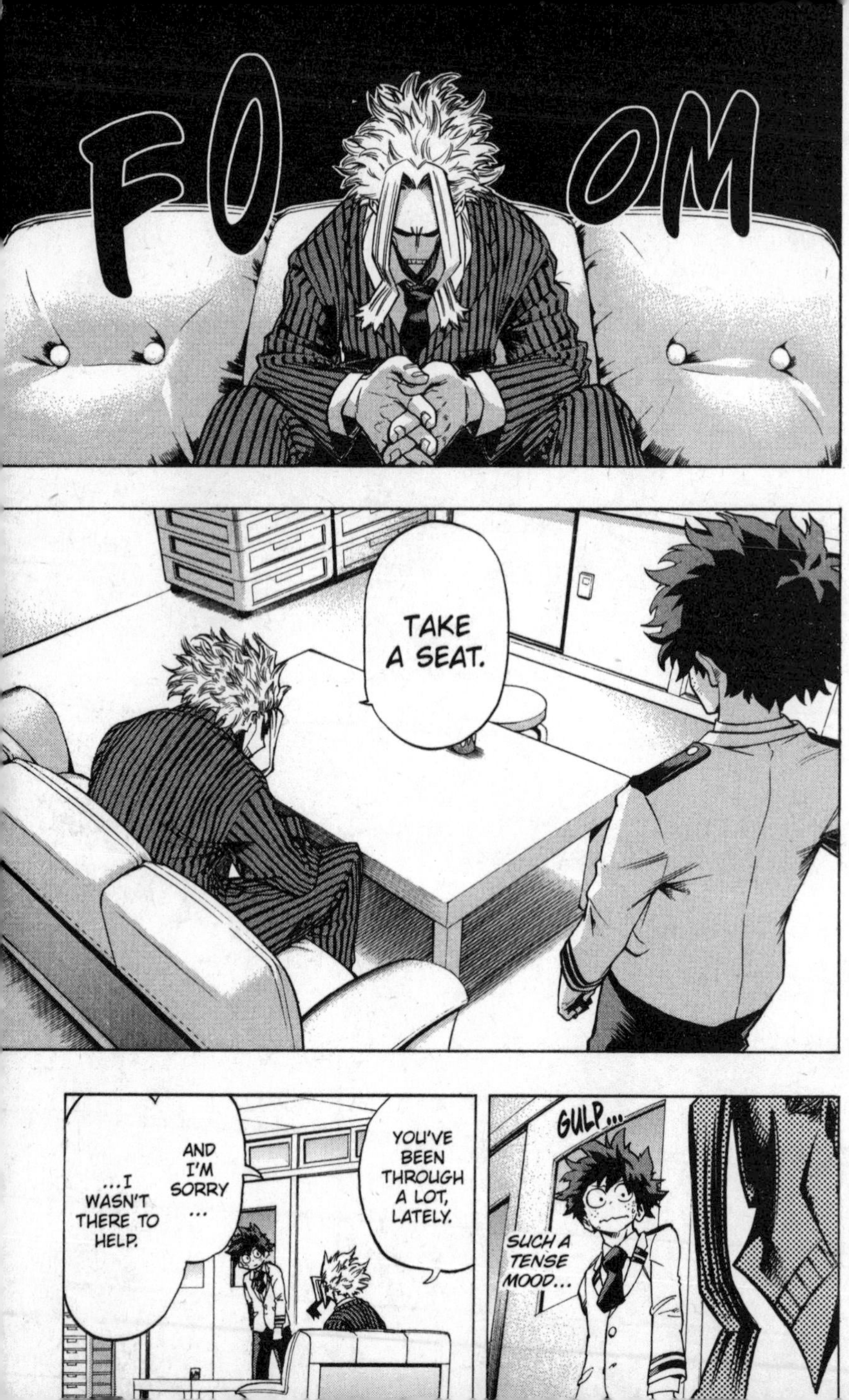
FOOM
TAKE A SEAT.
GULP...
SUCH A TENSE MOOD...
YOU'VE BEEN THROUGH A LOT, LATELY.
AND I'M SORRY ...
...I WASN'T THERE TO HELP.

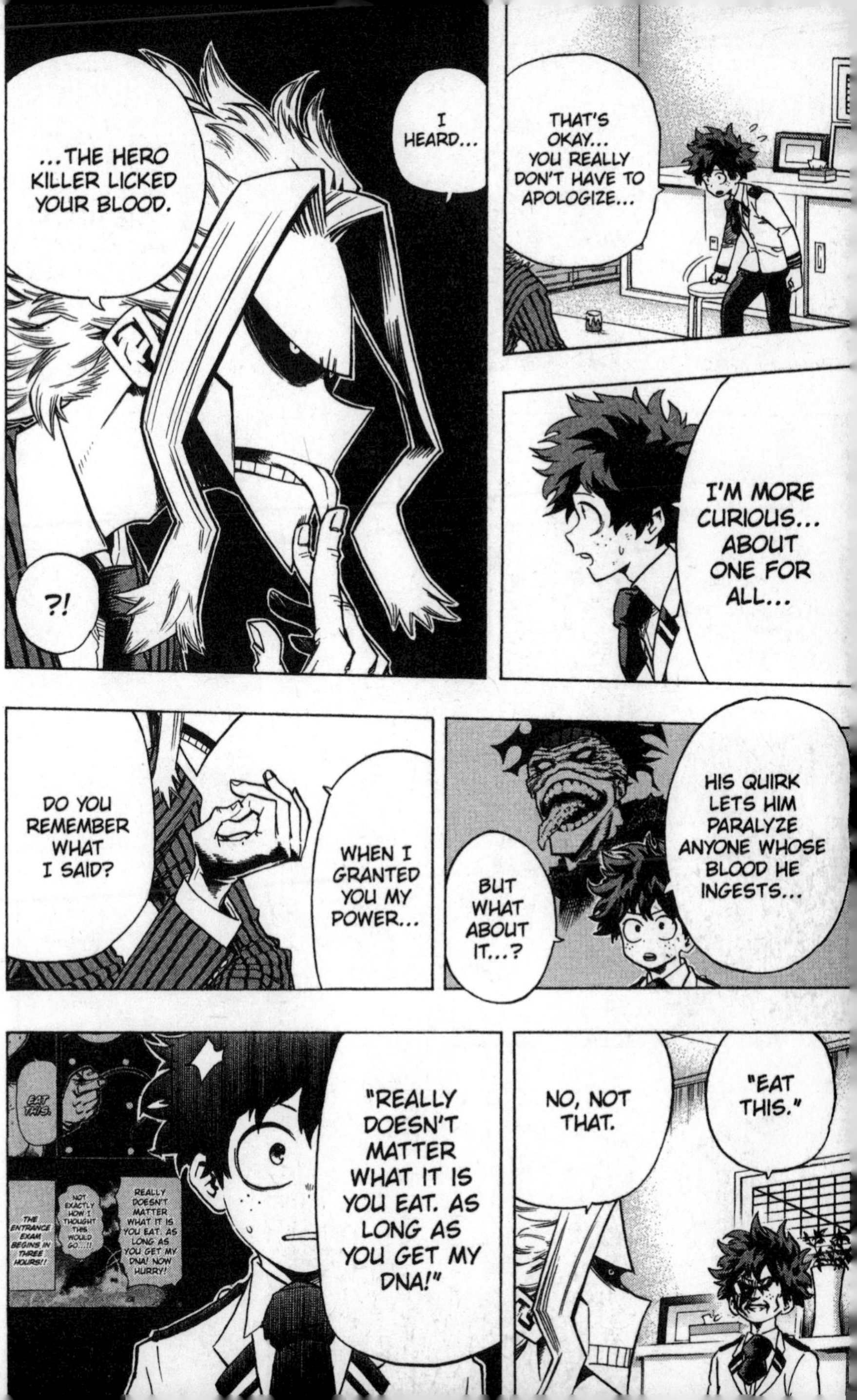
THAT'S OKAY... YOU REALLY DON'T HAVE TO APOLOGIZE...
I'M MORE CURIOUS... ABOUT ONE FOR ALL...
I HEARD...
...THE HERO KILLER LICKED YOUR BLOOD.
?!
HIS QUIRK LETS HIM PARALYZE ANYONE WHOSE BLOOD HE INGESTS...
BUT WHAT ABOUT IT...?
WHEN I GRANTED YOU MY POWER...
DO YOU REMEMBER WHAT I SAID?
"EAT THIS."
NO, NOT THAT.
"REALLY DOESN'T MATTER WHAT IT IS YOU EAT. AS LONG AS YOU GET MY DNA!"
EAT THIS.
REALLY DOESN'T MATTER WHAT IT IS YOU EAT. AS LONG AS YOU GET MY DNA! NOW HURRY!
NOT EXACTLY HOW I THOUGHT THIS WOULD GO...!!
THE ENTRANCE EXAM BEGINS IN THREE HOURS!!

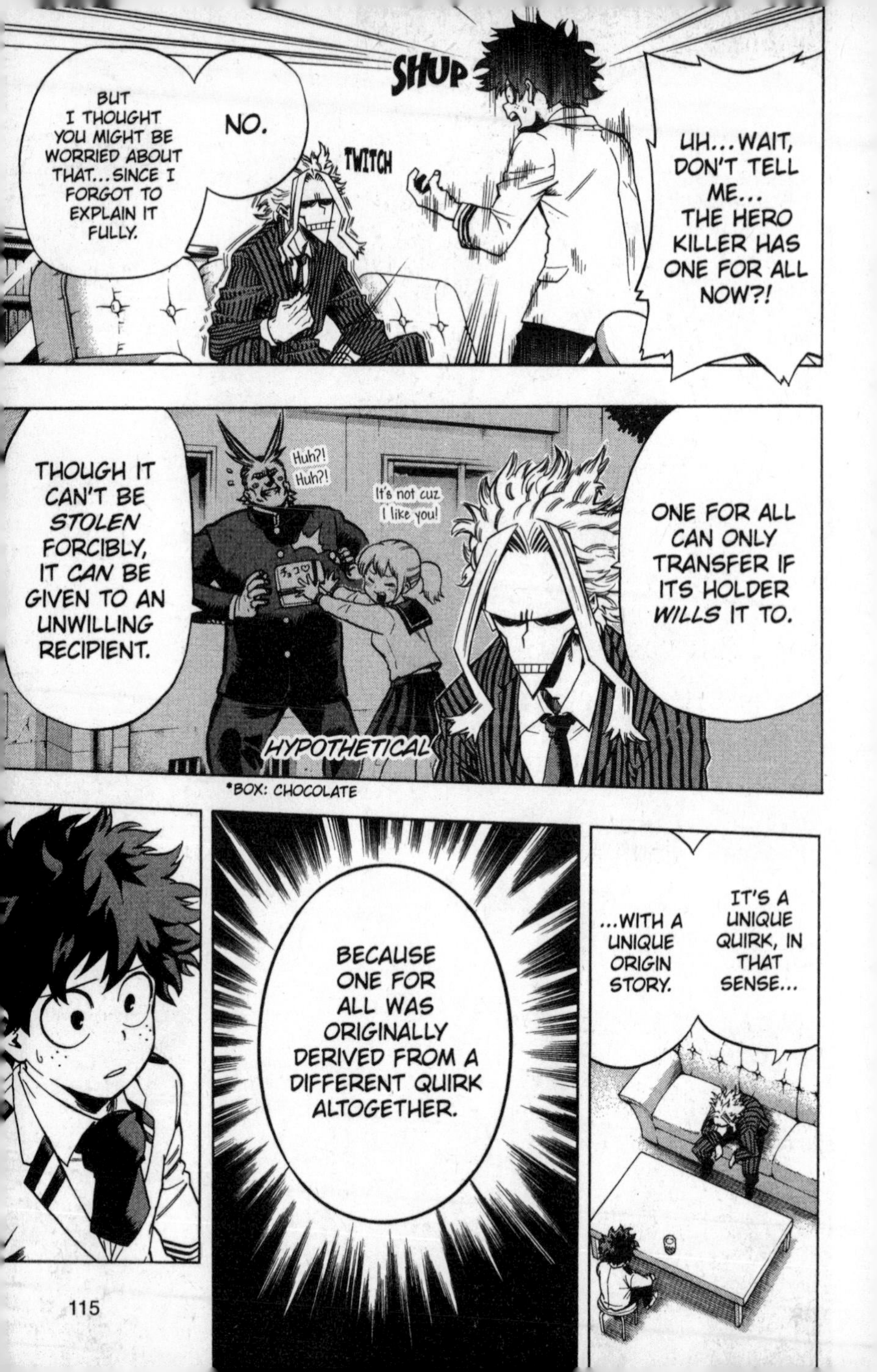
UH...WAIT, DON'T TELL ME... THE HERO KILLER HAS ONE FOR ALL NOW?!
SHUP
NO.
TWITCH
BUT I THOUGHT YOU MIGHT BE WORRIED ABOUT THAT...SINCE I FORGOT TO EXPLAIN IT FULLY.
ONE FOR ALL CAN ONLY TRANSFER IF ITS HOLDER *WILLS* IT TO.
It's not cuz I like you!
Huh?! Huh?!
THOUGH IT CAN'T BE *STOLEN* FORCIBLY, IT *CAN* BE GIVEN TO AN UNWILLING RECIPIENT.
HYPOTHETICAL
*BOX: CHOCOLATE
IT'S A UNIQUE QUIRK, IN THAT SENSE...
...WITH A UNIQUE ORIGIN STORY.
BECAUSE ONE FOR ALL WAS ORIGINALLY DERIVED FROM A DIFFERENT QUIRK ALTOGETHER.

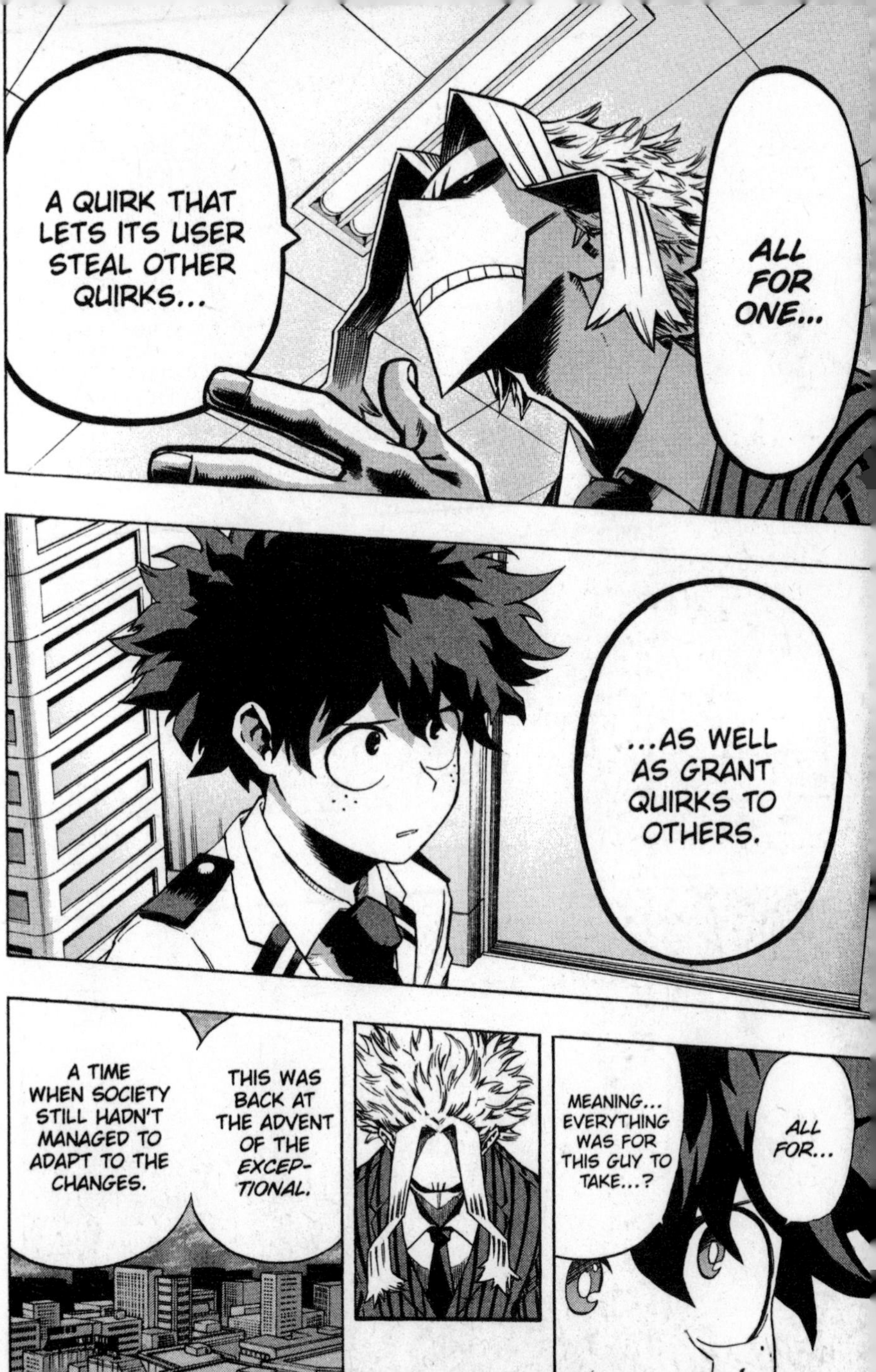
ALL FOR ONE...
A QUIRK THAT LETS ITS USER STEAL OTHER QUIRKS...
...AS WELL AS GRANT QUIRKS TO OTHERS.
ALL FOR...
MEANING... EVERYTHING WAS FOR THIS GUY TO TAKE...?
THIS WAS BACK AT THE ADVENT OF THE *EXCEPTIONAL*.
A TIME WHEN SOCIETY STILL HADN'T MANAGED TO ADAPT TO THE CHANGES.

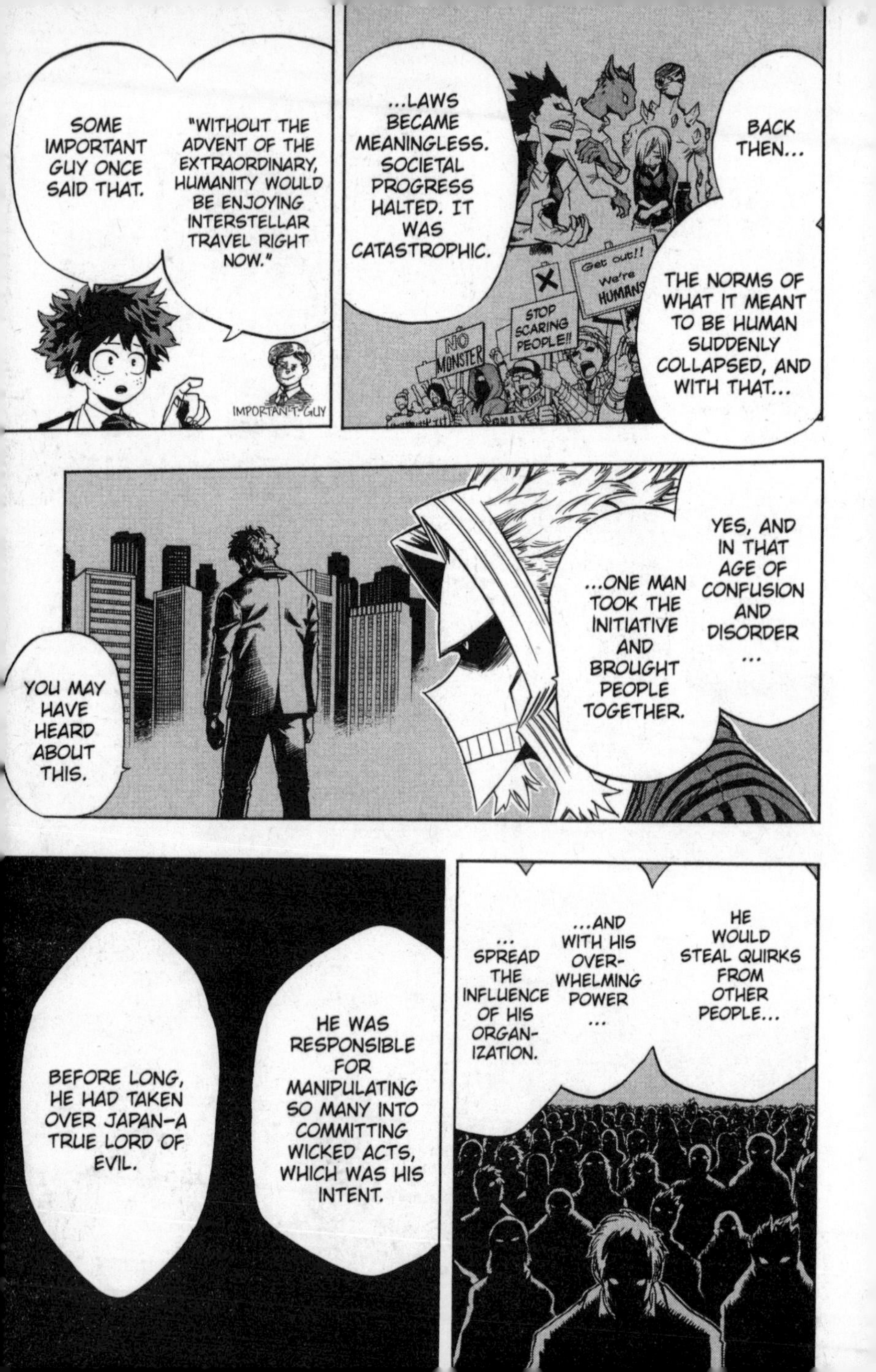
BACK THEN...
THE NORMS OF WHAT IT MEANT TO BE HUMAN SUDDENLY COLLAPSED, AND WITH THAT...
...LAWS BECAME MEANINGLESS. SOCIETAL PROGRESS HALTED. IT WAS CATASTROPHIC.
Get out!! We're HUMANS
STOP SCARING PEOPLE!!
NO MONSTER
"WITHOUT THE ADVENT OF THE EXTRAORDINARY, HUMANITY WOULD BE ENJOYING INTERSTELLAR TRAVEL RIGHT NOW."
SOME IMPORTANT GUY ONCE SAID THAT.
IMPORTANT GUY
YES, AND IN THAT AGE OF CONFUSION AND DISORDER...
...ONE MAN TOOK THE INITIATIVE AND BROUGHT PEOPLE TOGETHER.
YOU MAY HAVE HEARD ABOUT THIS.
HE WOULD STEAL QUIRKS FROM OTHER PEOPLE...
...AND WITH HIS OVER-WHELMING POWER...
...SPREAD THE INFLUENCE OF HIS ORGAN-IZATION.
HE WAS RESPONSIBLE FOR MANIPULATING SO MANY INTO COMMITTING WICKED ACTS, WHICH WAS HIS INTENT.
BEFORE LONG, HE HAD TAKEN OVER JAPAN—A TRUE LORD OF EVIL.

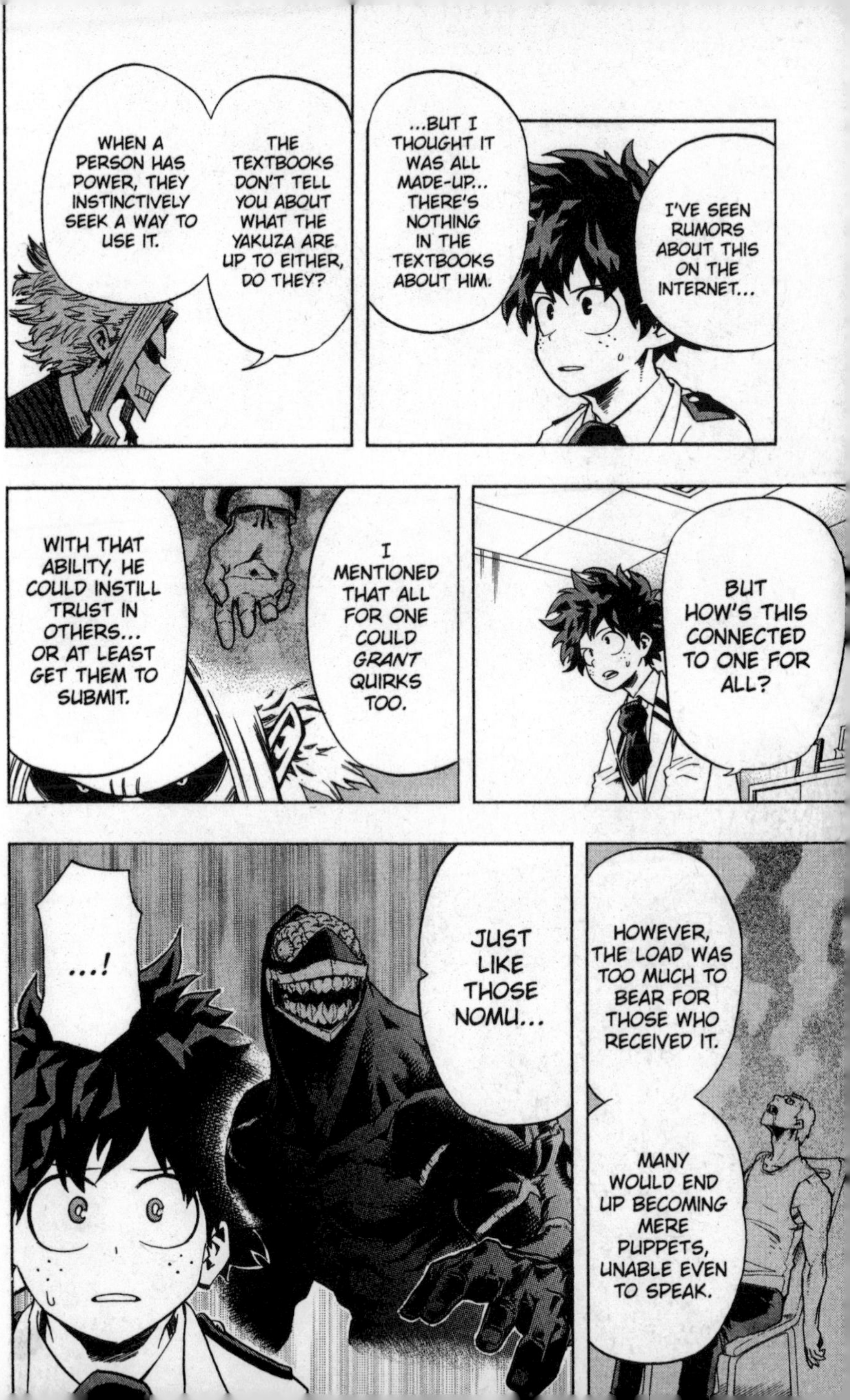
I'VE SEEN RUMORS ABOUT THIS ON THE INTERNET...
...BUT I THOUGHT IT WAS ALL MADE-UP... THERE'S NOTHING IN THE TEXTBOOKS ABOUT HIM.
THE TEXTBOOKS DON'T TELL YOU ABOUT WHAT THE YAKUZA ARE UP TO EITHER, DO THEY?
WHEN A PERSON HAS POWER, THEY INSTINCTIVELY SEEK A WAY TO USE IT.
BUT HOW'S THIS CONNECTED TO ONE FOR ALL?
I MENTIONED THAT ALL FOR ONE COULD *GRANT* QUIRKS TOO.
WITH THAT ABILITY, HE COULD INSTILL TRUST IN OTHERS... OR AT LEAST GET THEM TO SUBMIT.
HOWEVER, THE LOAD WAS TOO MUCH TO BEAR FOR THOSE WHO RECEIVED IT.
MANY WOULD END UP BECOMING MERE PUPPETS, UNABLE EVEN TO SPEAK.
JUST LIKE THOSE NOMU...
...!

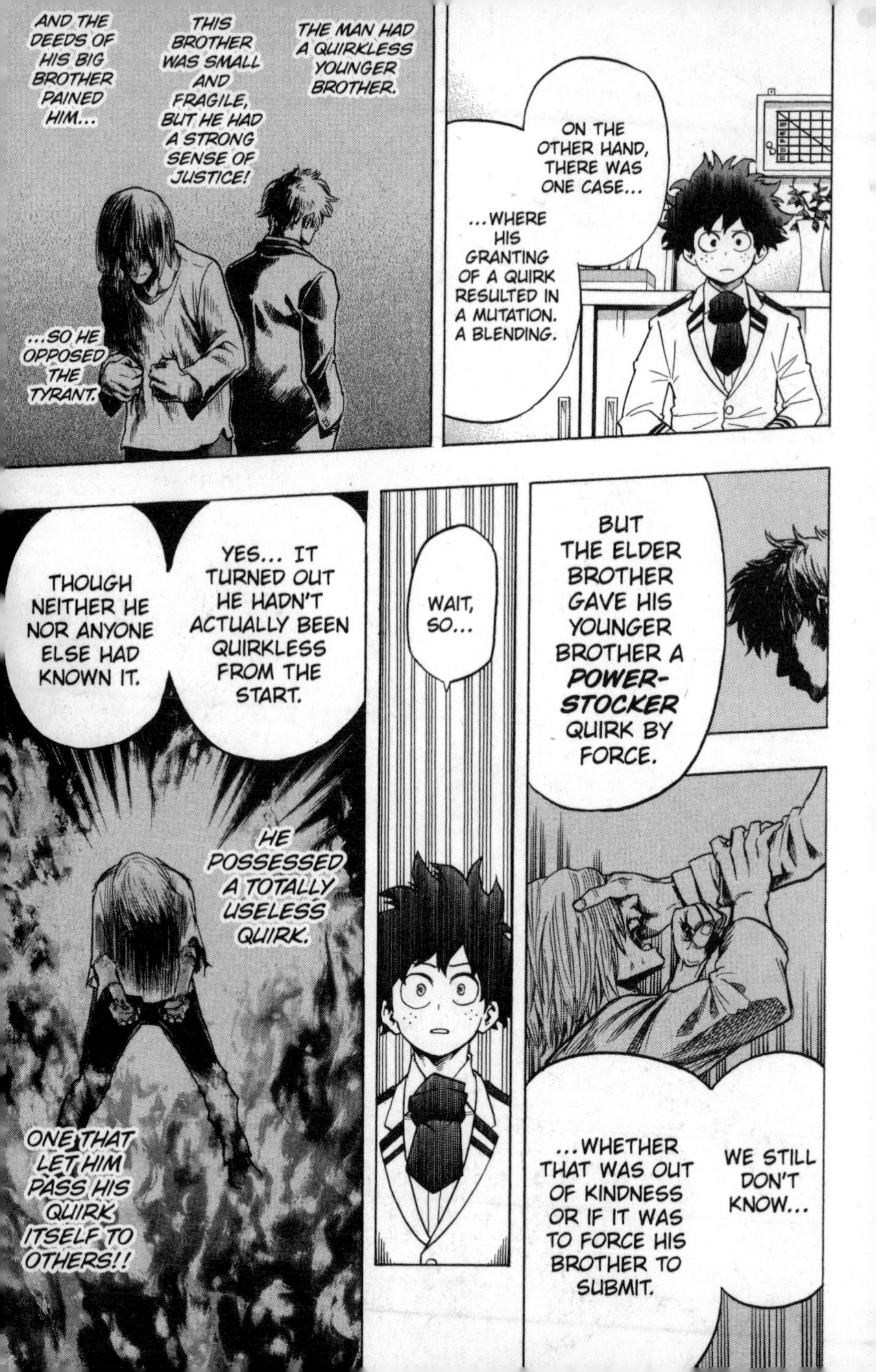
ON THE OTHER HAND, THERE WAS ONE CASE...
...WHERE HIS GRANTING OF A QUIRK RESULTED IN A MUTATION. A BLENDING.
THE MAN HAD A QUIRKLESS YOUNGER BROTHER.
THIS BROTHER WAS SMALL AND FRAGILE, BUT HE HAD A STRONG SENSE OF JUSTICE!
AND THE DEEDS OF HIS BIG BROTHER PAINED HIM...
...SO HE OPPOSED THE TYRANT.
BUT THE ELDER BROTHER GAVE HIS YOUNGER BROTHER A **POWER-STOCKER** QUIRK BY FORCE.
WE STILL DON'T KNOW...
...WHETHER THAT WAS OUT OF KINDNESS OR IF IT WAS TO FORCE HIS BROTHER TO SUBMIT.
WAIT, SO...
YES... IT TURNED OUT HE HADN'T ACTUALLY BEEN QUIRKLESS FROM THE START.
THOUGH NEITHER HE NOR ANYONE ELSE HAD KNOWN IT.
HE POSSESSED A TOTALLY USELESS QUIRK.
ONE THAT LET HIM PASS HIS QUIRK ITSELF TO OTHERS!!

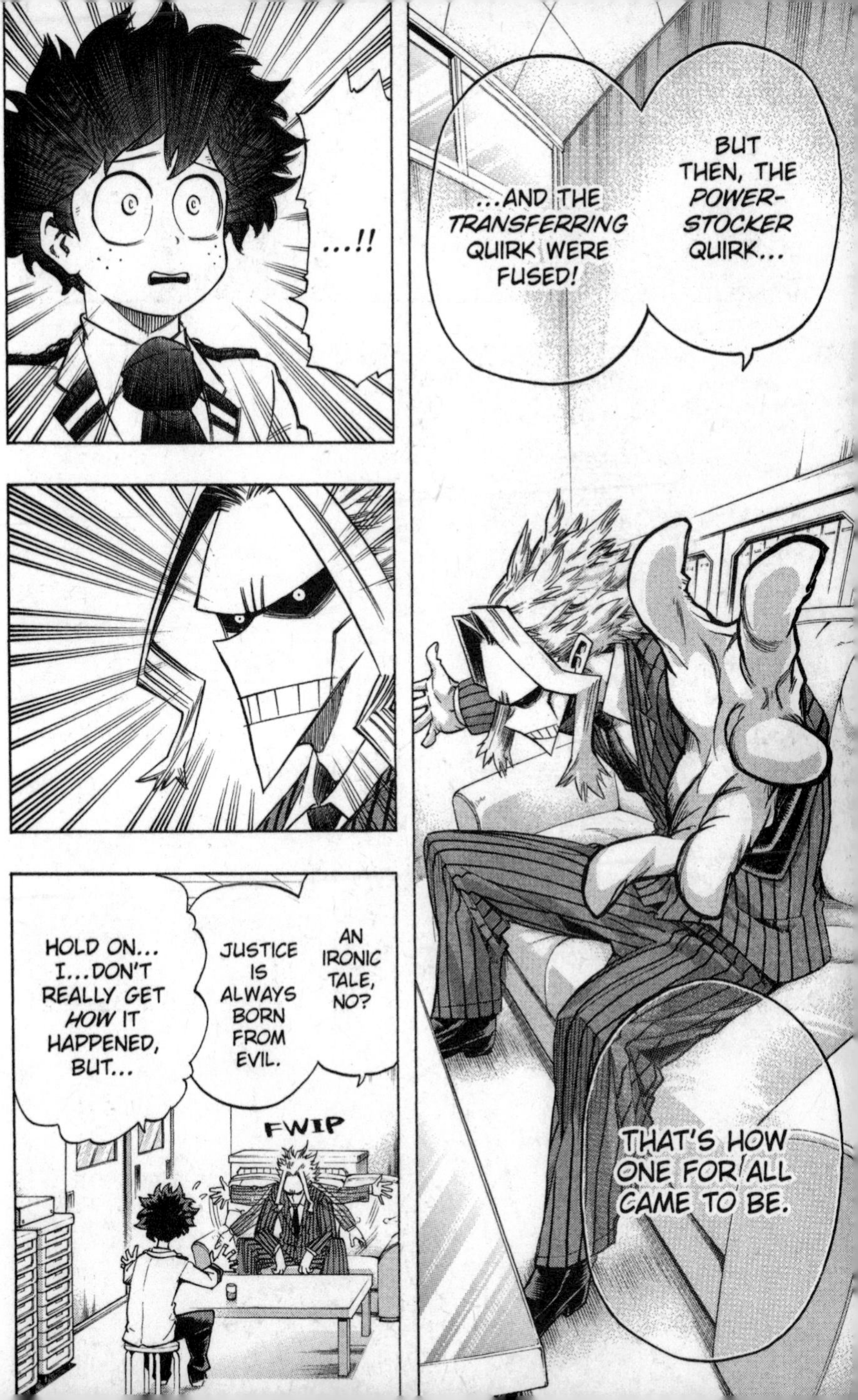
BUT THEN, THE POWER-STOCKER QUIRK...
...AND THE TRANSFERRING QUIRK WERE FUSED!
THAT'S HOW ONE FOR ALL CAME TO BE.
...!!
AN IRONIC TALE, NO?
JUSTICE IS ALWAYS BORN FROM EVIL.
HOLD ON... I...DON'T REALLY GET HOW IT HAPPENED, BUT...
FWIP

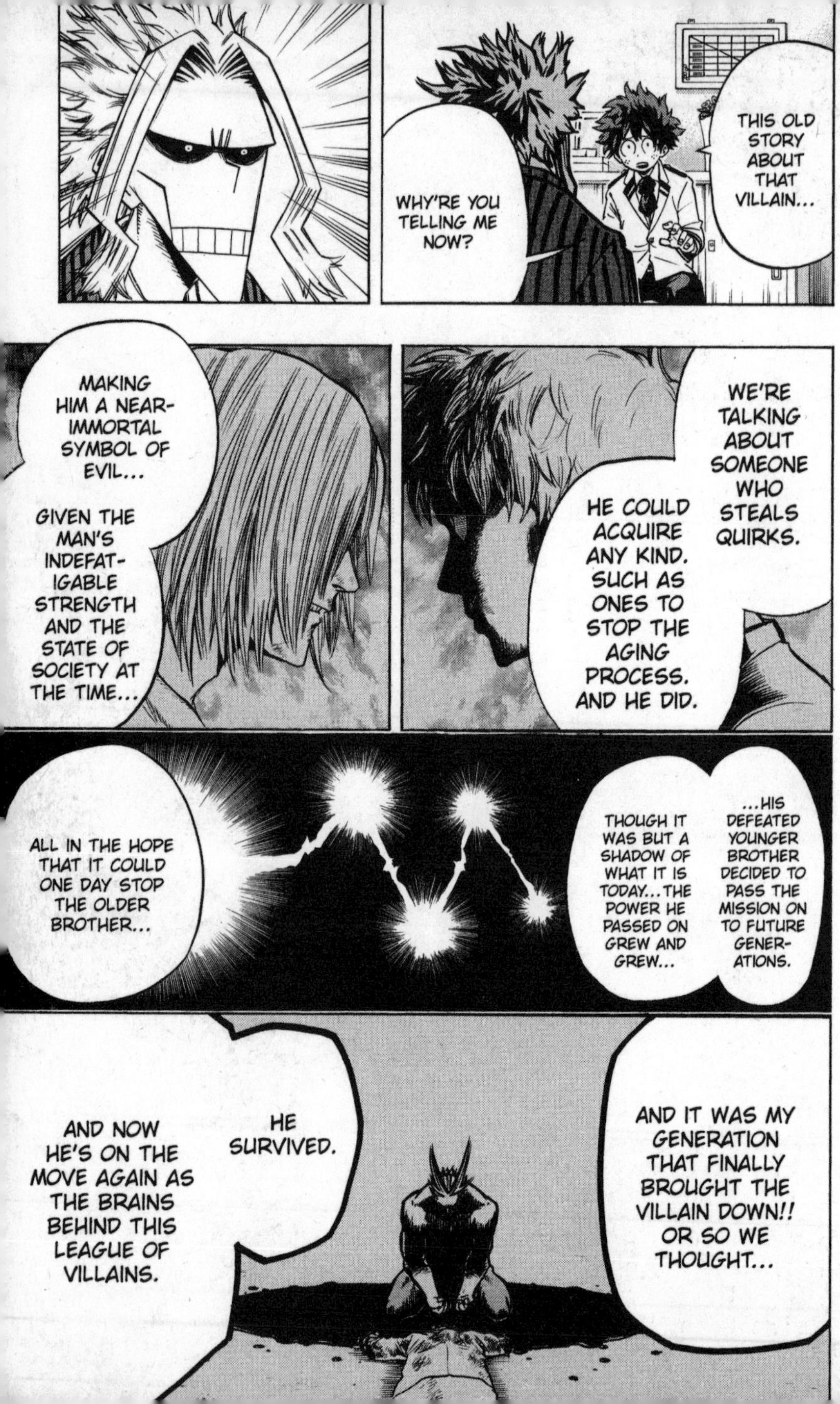
THIS OLD STORY ABOUT THAT VILLAIN...
WHY'RE YOU TELLING ME NOW?
WE'RE TALKING ABOUT SOMEONE WHO STEALS QUIRKS.
HE COULD ACQUIRE ANY KIND. SUCH AS ONES TO STOP THE AGING PROCESS. AND HE DID.
MAKING HIM A NEAR-IMMORTAL SYMBOL OF EVIL...
GIVEN THE MAN'S INDEFAT-IGABLE STRENGTH AND THE STATE OF SOCIETY AT THE TIME...
...HIS DEFEATED YOUNGER BROTHER DECIDED TO PASS THE MISSION ON TO FUTURE GENER-ATIONS.
THOUGH IT WAS BUT A SHADOW OF WHAT IT IS TODAY...THE POWER HE PASSED ON GREW AND GREW...
ALL IN THE HOPE THAT IT COULD ONE DAY STOP THE OLDER BROTHER...
AND IT WAS MY GENERATION THAT FINALLY BROUGHT THE VILLAIN DOWN!! OR SO WE THOUGHT...
HE SURVIVED.
AND NOW HE'S ON THE MOVE AGAIN AS THE BRAINS BEHIND THIS LEAGUE OF VILLAINS.

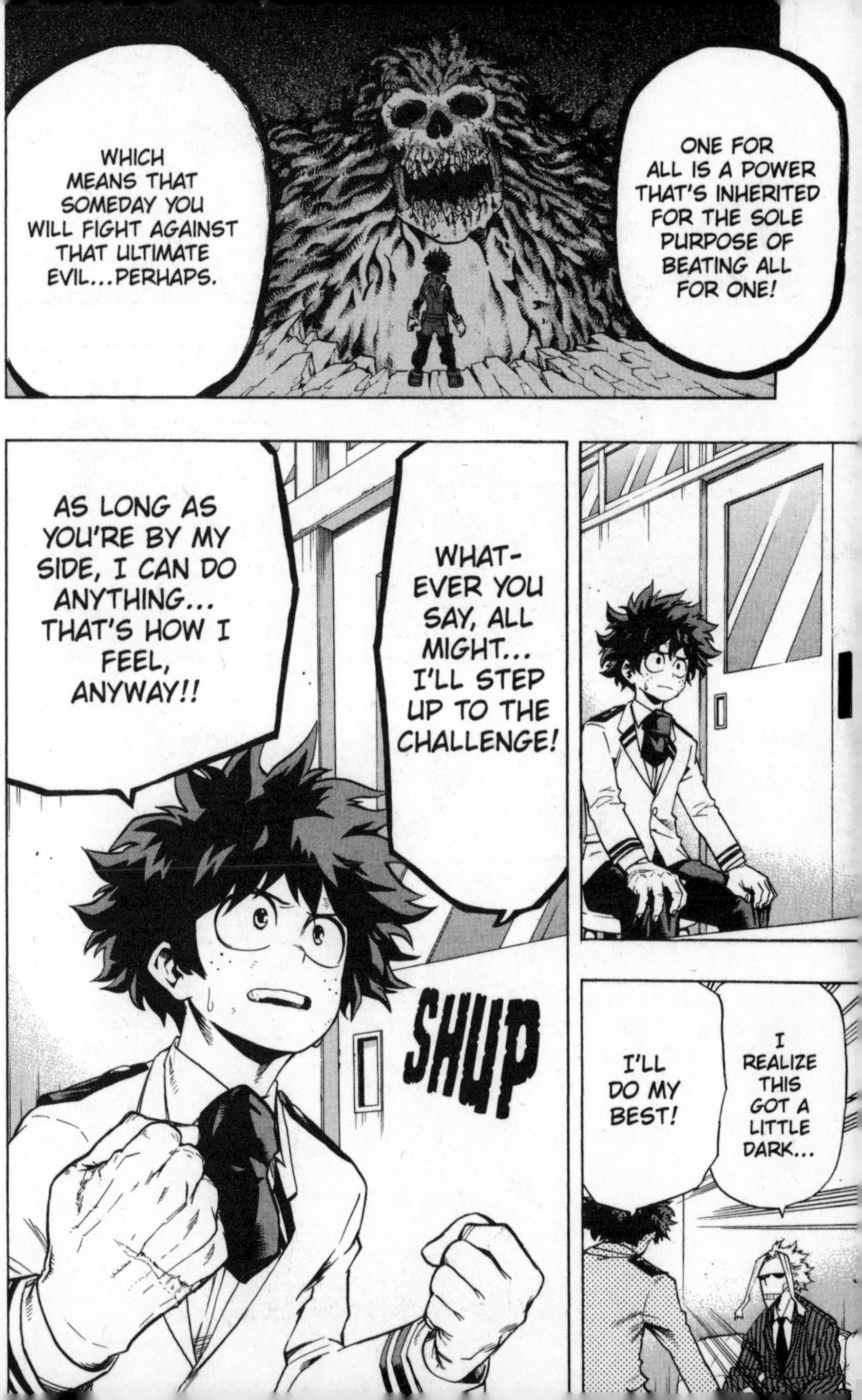
ONE FOR ALL IS A POWER THAT'S INHERITED FOR THE SOLE PURPOSE OF BEATING ALL FOR ONE!
WHICH MEANS THAT SOMEDAY YOU WILL FIGHT AGAINST THAT ULTIMATE EVIL...PERHAPS.
I REALIZE THIS GOT A LITTLE DARK...
I'LL DO MY BEST!
WHAT-EVER YOU SAY, ALL MIGHT... I'LL STEP UP TO THE CHALLENGE!
AS LONG AS YOU'RE BY MY SIDE, I CAN DO ANYTHING... THAT'S HOW I FEEL, ANYWAY!!
SHUP

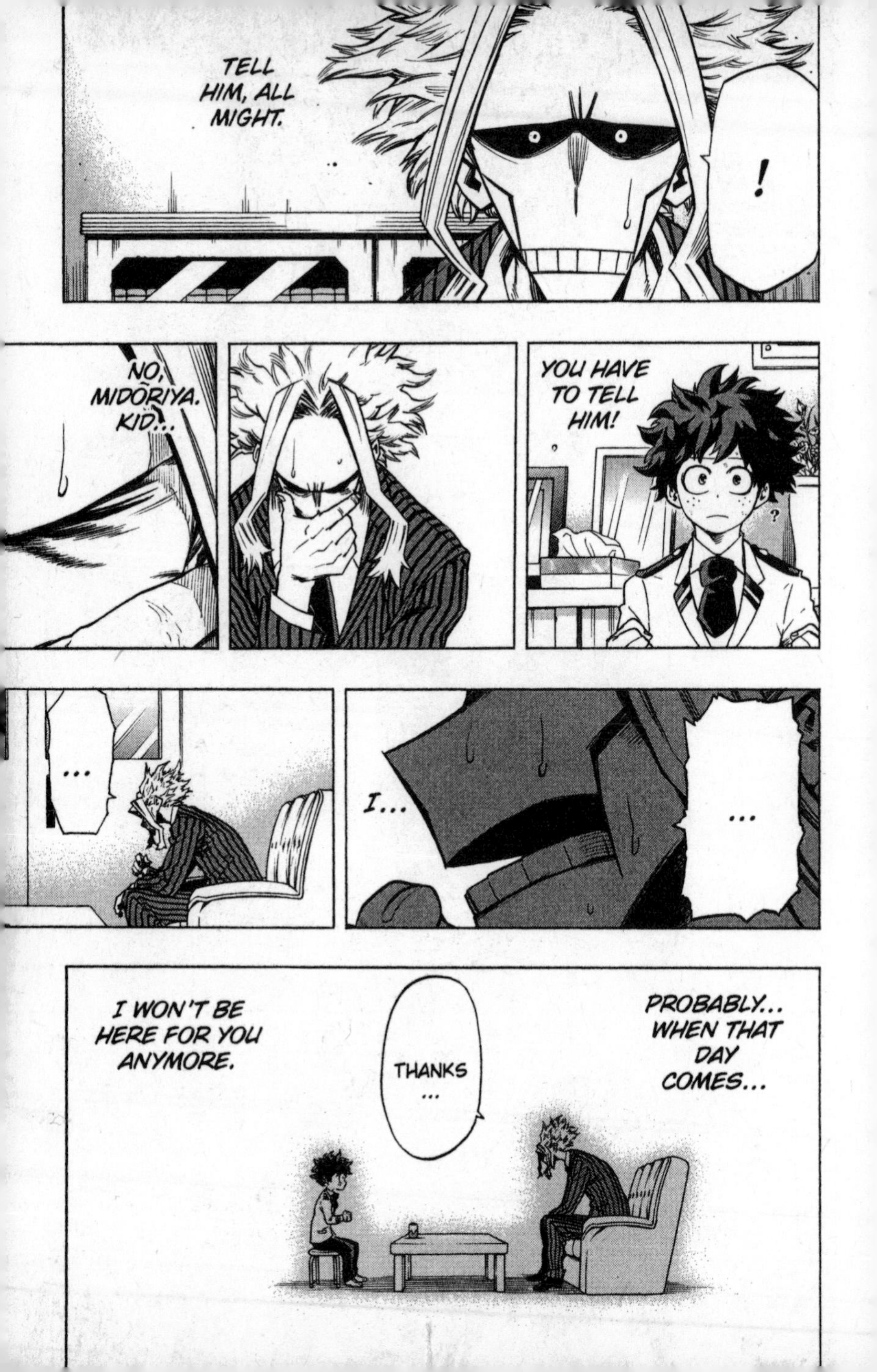
TELL HIM, ALL MIGHT.
!
YOU HAVE TO TELL HIM!
NO, MIDORIYA. KID...
...
I...
...
PROBABLY... WHEN THAT DAY COMES...
THANKS ...
I WON'T BE HERE FOR YOU ANYMORE.

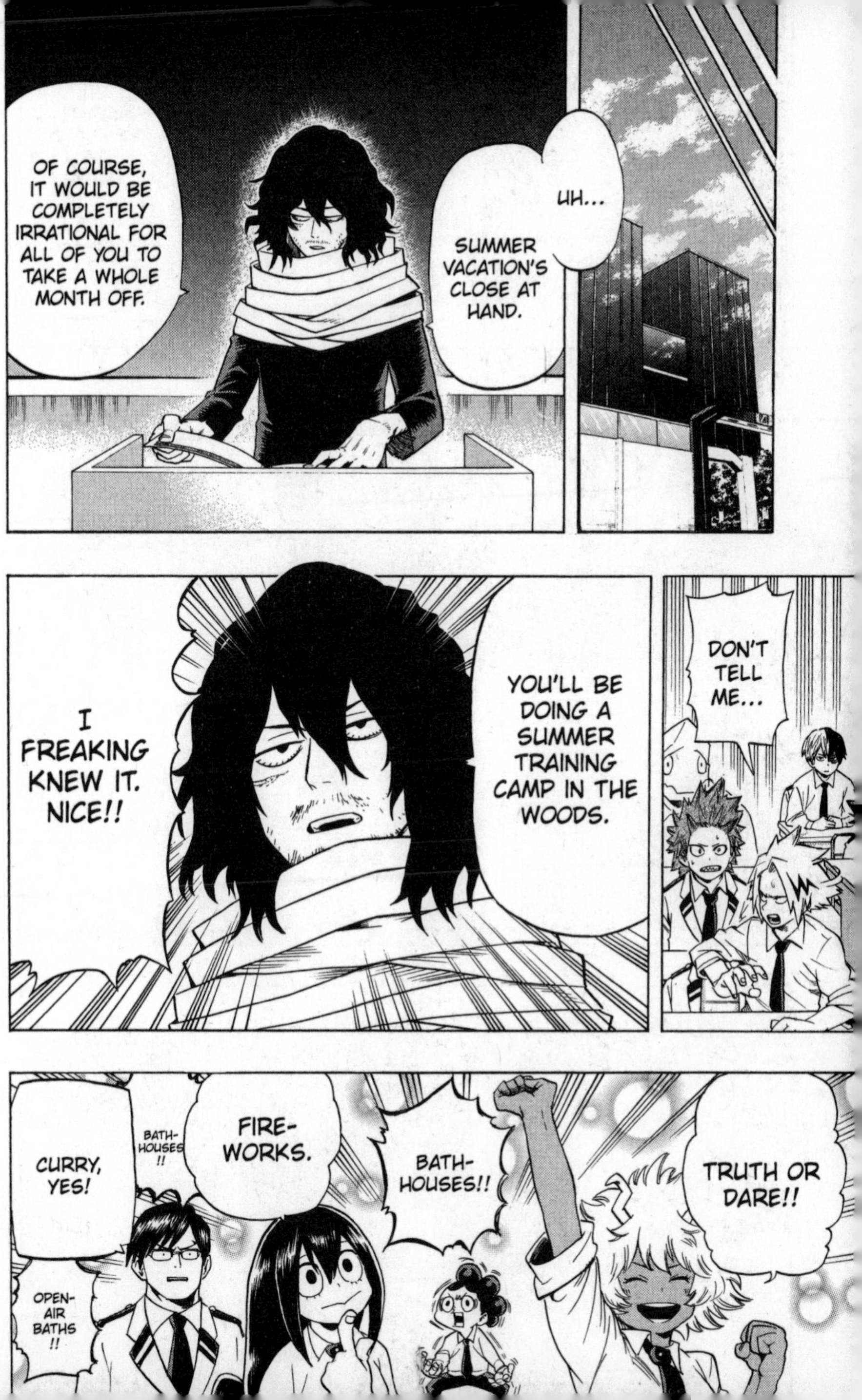
UH...
SUMMER VACATION'S CLOSE AT HAND.
OF COURSE, IT WOULD BE COMPLETELY IRRATIONAL FOR ALL OF YOU TO TAKE A WHOLE MONTH OFF.
DON'T TELL ME...
YOU'LL BE DOING A SUMMER TRAINING CAMP IN THE WOODS.
I FREAKING KNEW IT. NICE!!
TRUTH OR DARE!!
BATH-HOUSES!!
FIRE-WORKS.
BATH-HOUSES !!
CURRY, YES!
OPEN-AIR BATHS !!

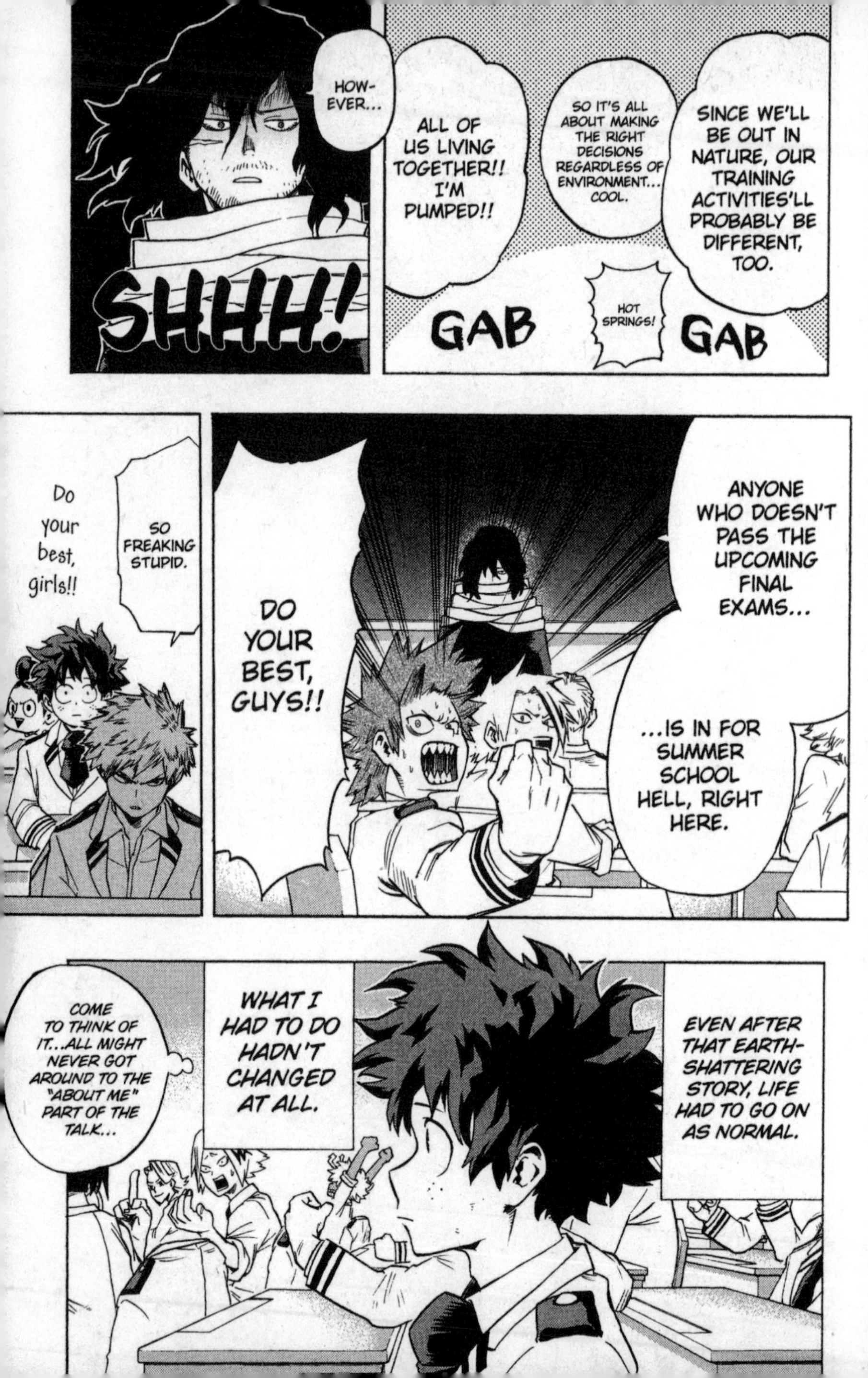
SINCE WE'LL BE OUT IN NATURE, OUR TRAINING ACTIVITIES'LL PROBABLY BE DIFFERENT, TOO.
SO IT'S ALL ABOUT MAKING THE RIGHT DECISIONS REGARDLESS OF ENVIRONMENT... COOL.
ALL OF US LIVING TOGETHER!! I'M PUMPED!!
GAB
HOT SPRINGS!
GAB
HOW-EVER...
SHHH!
ANYONE WHO DOESN'T PASS THE UPCOMING FINAL EXAMS...
...IS IN FOR SUMMER SCHOOL HELL, RIGHT HERE.
DO YOUR BEST, GUYS!!
SO FREAKING STUPID.
Do your best, girls!!
EVEN AFTER THAT EARTH-SHATTERING STORY, LIFE HAD TO GO ON AS NORMAL.
WHAT I HAD TO DO HADN'T CHANGED AT ALL.
COME TO THINK OF IT...ALL MIGHT NEVER GOT AROUND TO THE "ABOUT ME" PART OF THE TALK...

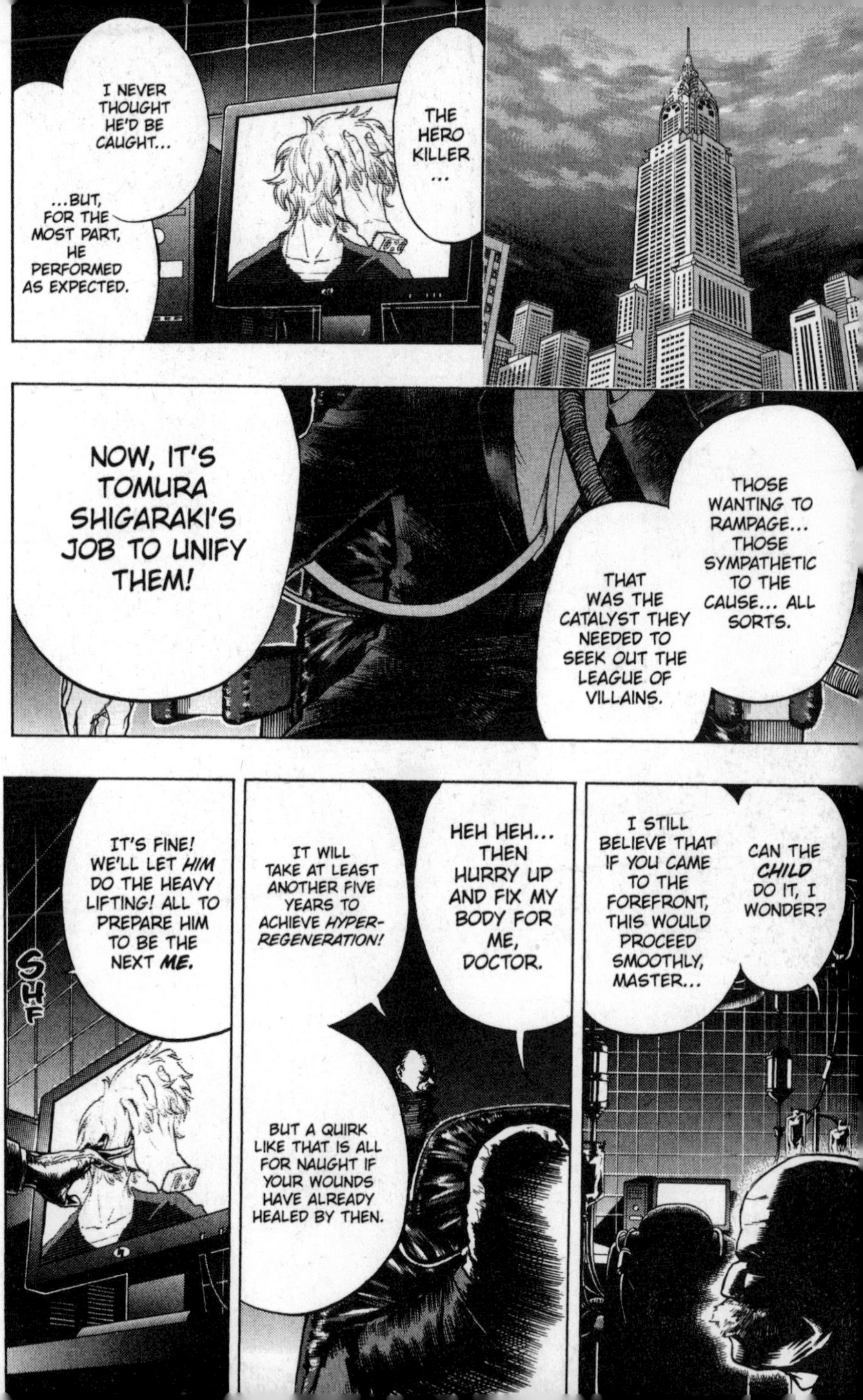
THE HERO KILLER ...
I NEVER THOUGHT HE'D BE CAUGHT...
...BUT, FOR THE MOST PART, HE PERFORMED AS EXPECTED.
THOSE WANTING TO RAMPAGE... THOSE SYMPATHETIC TO THE CAUSE... ALL SORTS.
THAT WAS THE CATALYST THEY NEEDED TO SEEK OUT THE LEAGUE OF VILLAINS.
NOW, IT'S TOMURA SHIGARAKI'S JOB TO UNIFY THEM!
CAN THE *CHILD* DO IT, I WONDER?
I STILL BELIEVE THAT IF YOU CAME TO THE FOREFRONT, THIS WOULD PROCEED SMOOTHLY, MASTER...
HEH HEH... THEN HURRY UP AND FIX MY BODY FOR ME, DOCTOR.
IT WILL TAKE AT LEAST ANOTHER FIVE YEARS TO ACHIEVE *HYPER-REGENERATION!*
BUT A QUIRK LIKE THAT IS ALL FOR NAUGHT IF YOUR WOUNDS HAVE ALREADY HEALED BY THEN.
IT'S FINE! WE'LL LET *HIM* DO THE HEAVY LIFTING! ALL TO PREPARE HIM TO BE THE NEXT ***ME.***
SHF

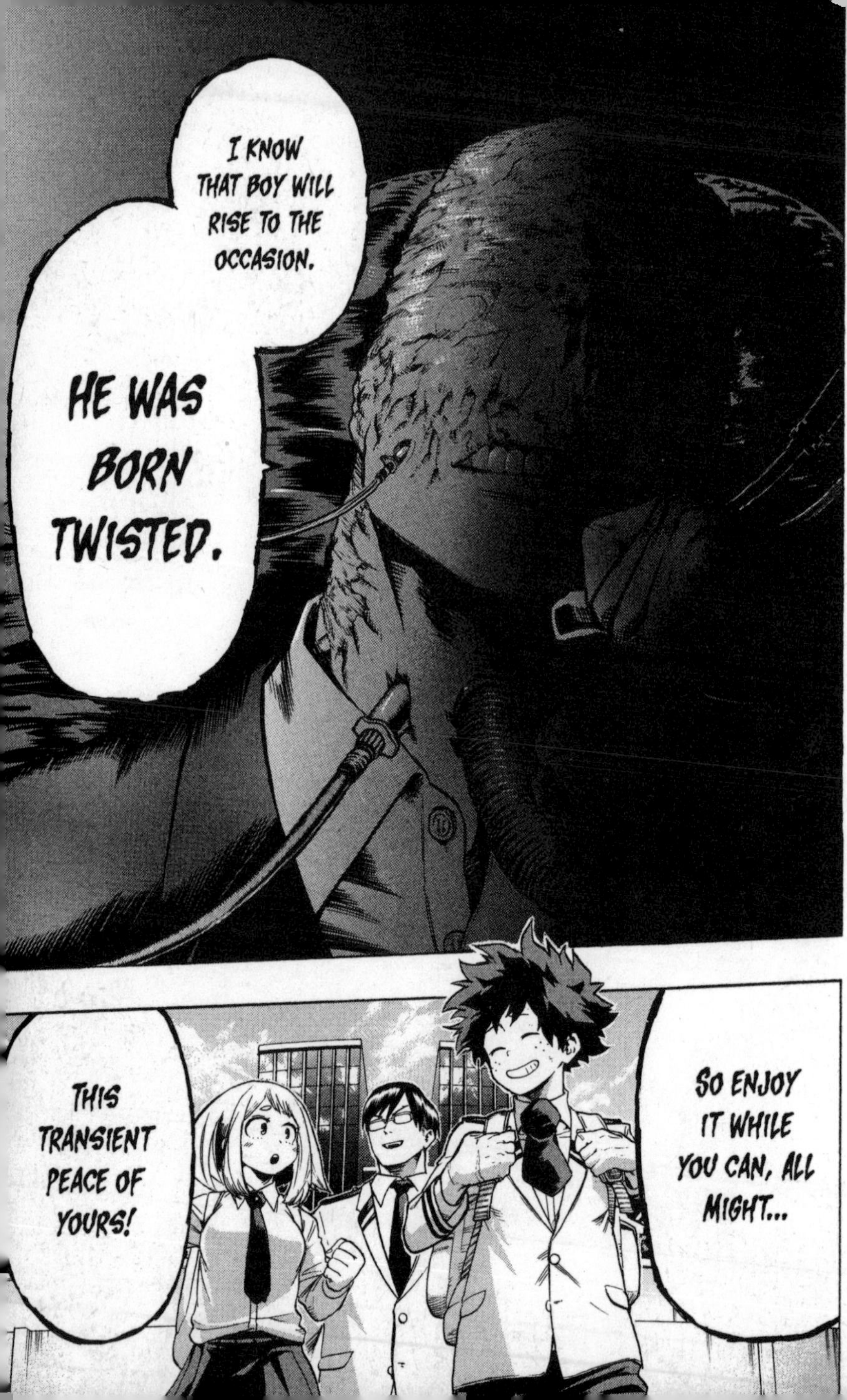
I KNOW THAT BOY WILL RISE TO THE OCCASION.
HE WAS BORN TWISTED.
SO ENJOY IT WHILE YOU CAN, ALL MIGHT...
THIS TRANSIENT PEACE OF YOURS!

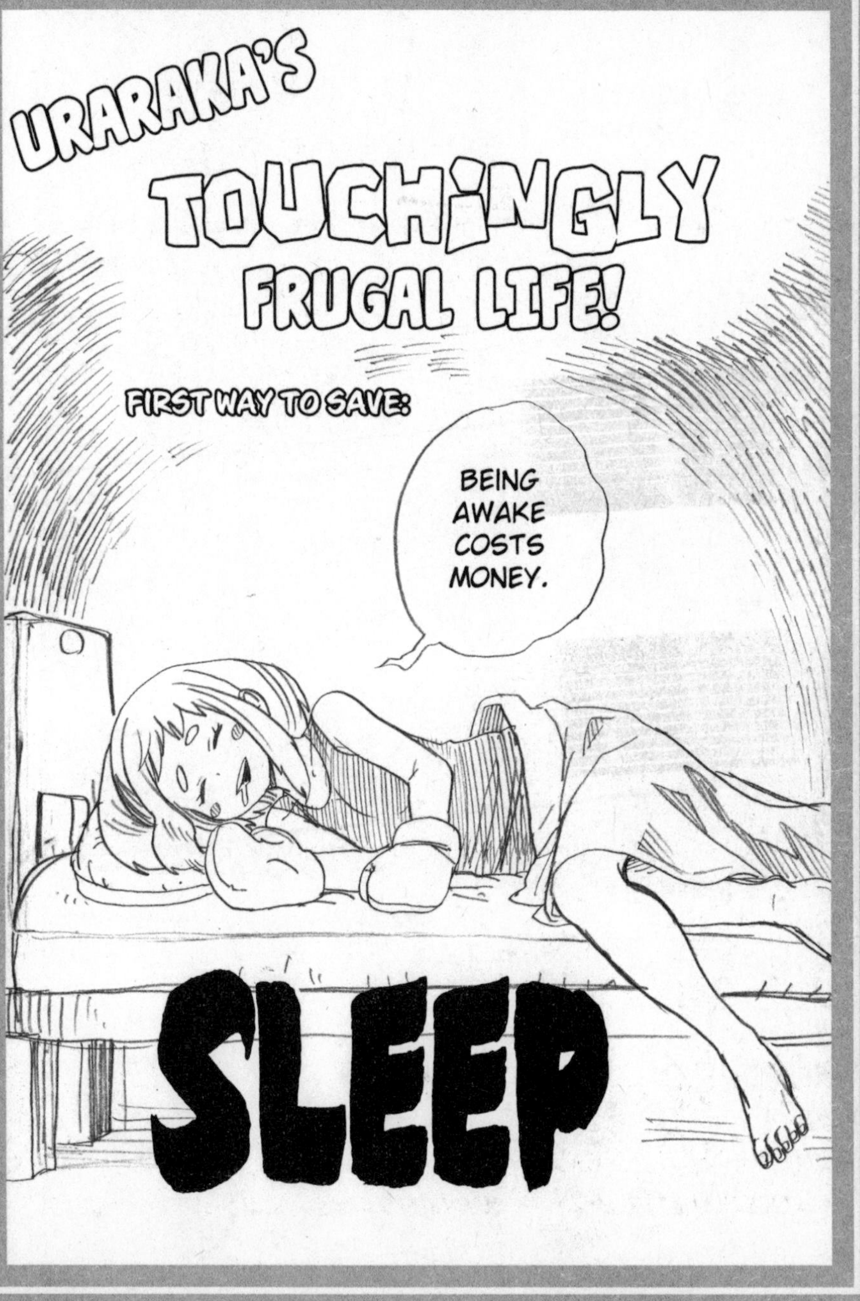
URARAKA'S
TOUCHINGLY
FRUGAL LIFE!
FIRST WAY TO SAVE:
BEING AWAKE COSTS MONEY.
SLEEP

NO. 60 - GEAR UP FOR FINAL EXAMS

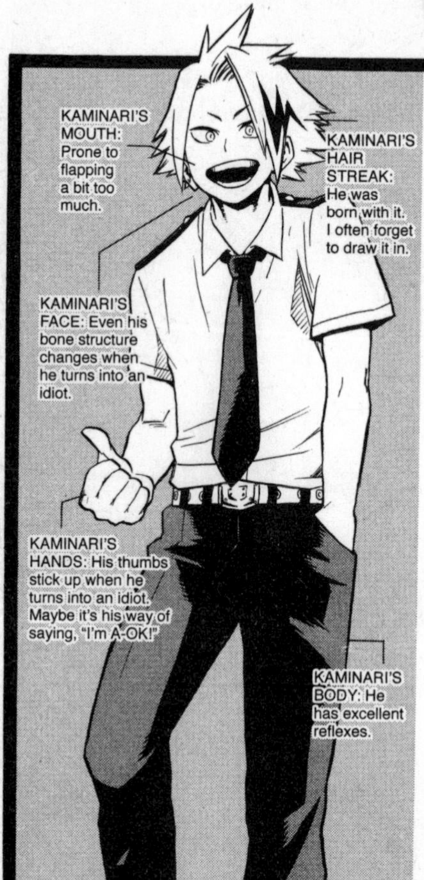
KAMINARI'S MOUTH: Prone to flapping a bit too much.
KAMINARI'S HAIR STREAK: He was born with it. I often forget to draw it in.
KAMINARI'S FACE: Even his bone structure changes when he turns into an idiot.
KAMINARI'S HANDS: His thumbs stick up when he turns into an idiot. Maybe it's his way of saying, "I'm A-OK!"
KAMINARI'S BODY: He has excellent reflexes.

U.A. FILE.09

CLASS No.07

DENKI KAMINARI

QUIRK

ELECTRIFICATION

His body can store up and discharge electricity!

But misuse and overuse of his ability results in him temporarily becoming an idiot! Naturally he tries to avoid that, but much to his own chagrin, he often loses his cool in battle! You need more training, Denki Kaminari!

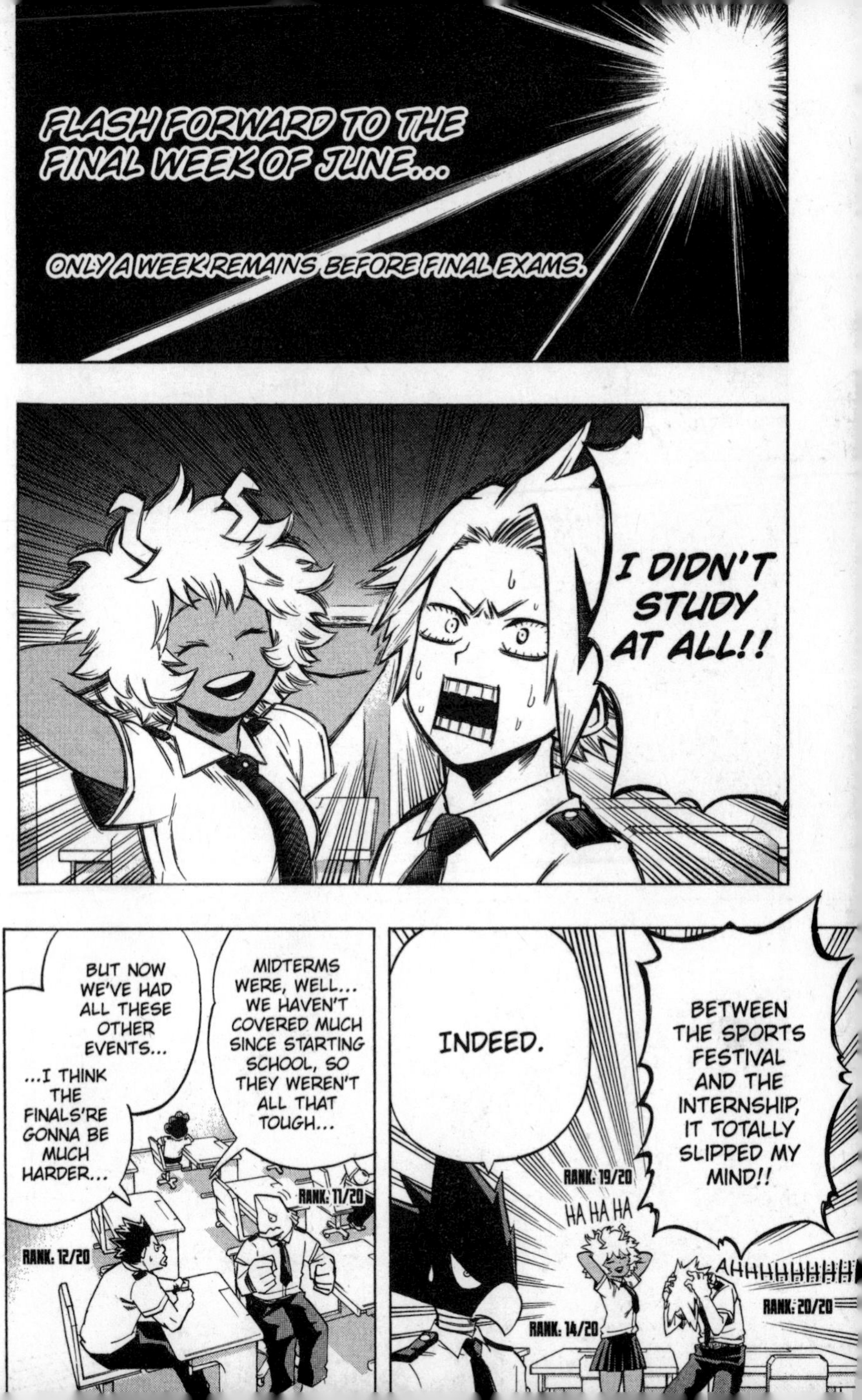
FLASH FORWARD TO THE FINAL WEEK OF JUNE...
ONLY A WEEK REMAINS BEFORE FINAL EXAMS.
I DIDN'T STUDY AT ALL!!
BETWEEN THE SPORTS FESTIVAL AND THE INTERNSHIP, IT TOTALLY SLIPPED MY MIND!!
INDEED.
RANK: 19/20
HA HA HA
AHHHHHHHHH
RANK: 20/20
RANK: 14/20
MIDTERMS WERE, WELL... WE HAVEN'T COVERED MUCH SINCE STARTING SCHOOL, SO THEY WEREN'T ALL THAT TOUGH...
BUT NOW WE'VE HAD ALL THESE OTHER EVENTS...
...I THINK THE FINALS'RE GONNA BE MUCH HARDER...
RANK: 11/20
RANK: 12/20

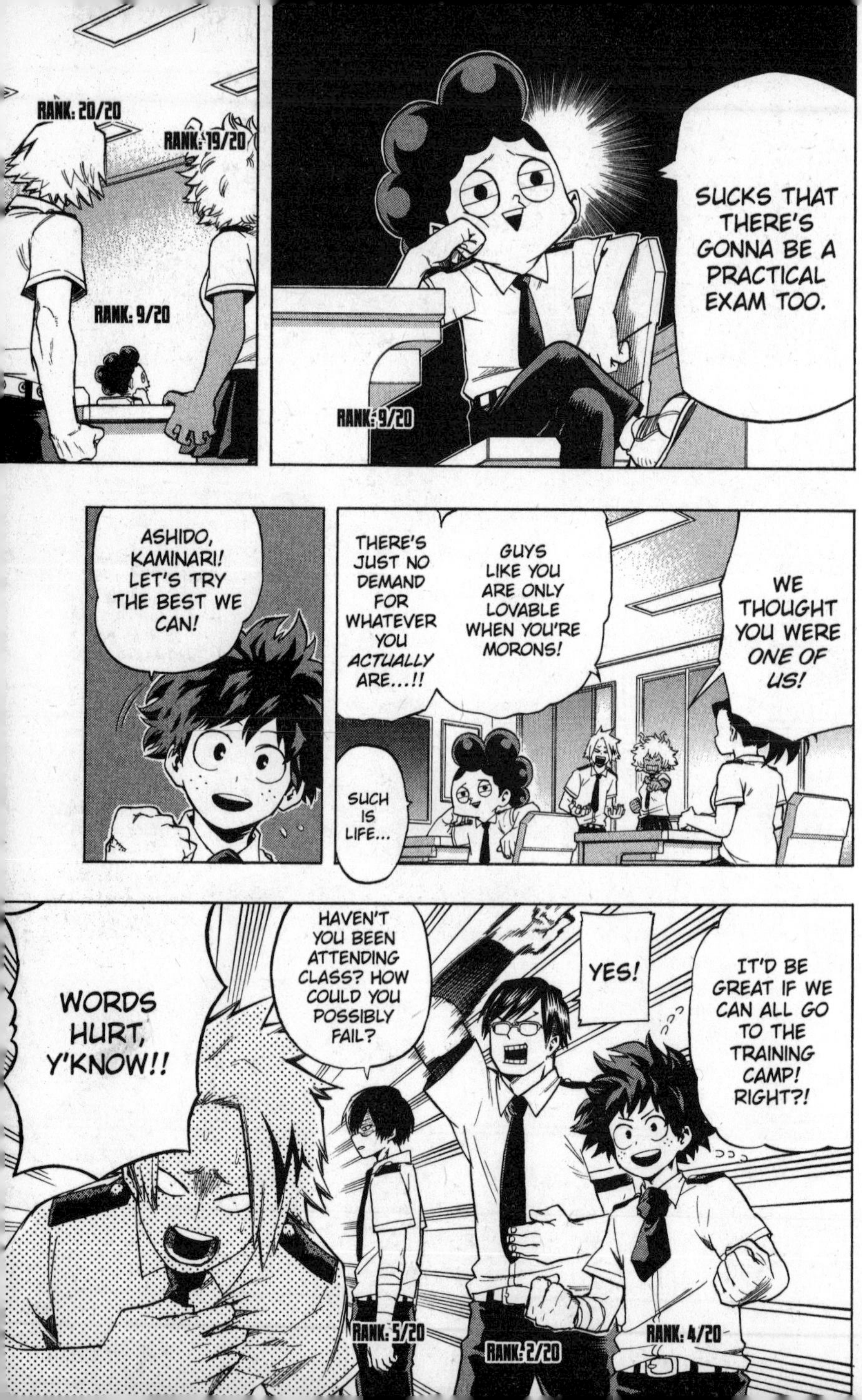
SUCKS THAT THERE'S GONNA BE A PRACTICAL EXAM TOO.
RANK: 9/20
RANK: 19/20
RANK: 20/20
RANK: 9/20
WE THOUGHT YOU WERE ONE OF US!
GUYS LIKE YOU ARE ONLY LOVABLE WHEN YOU'RE MORONS!
THERE'S JUST NO DEMAND FOR WHATEVER YOU ACTUALLY ARE...!!
SUCH IS LIFE...
ASHIDO, KAMINARI! LET'S TRY THE BEST WE CAN!
IT'D BE GREAT IF WE CAN ALL GO TO THE TRAINING CAMP! RIGHT?!
YES!
HAVEN'T YOU BEEN ATTENDING CLASS? HOW COULD YOU POSSIBLY FAIL?
WORDS HURT, Y'KNOW!!
RANK: 4/20
RANK: 2/20
RANK: 5/20

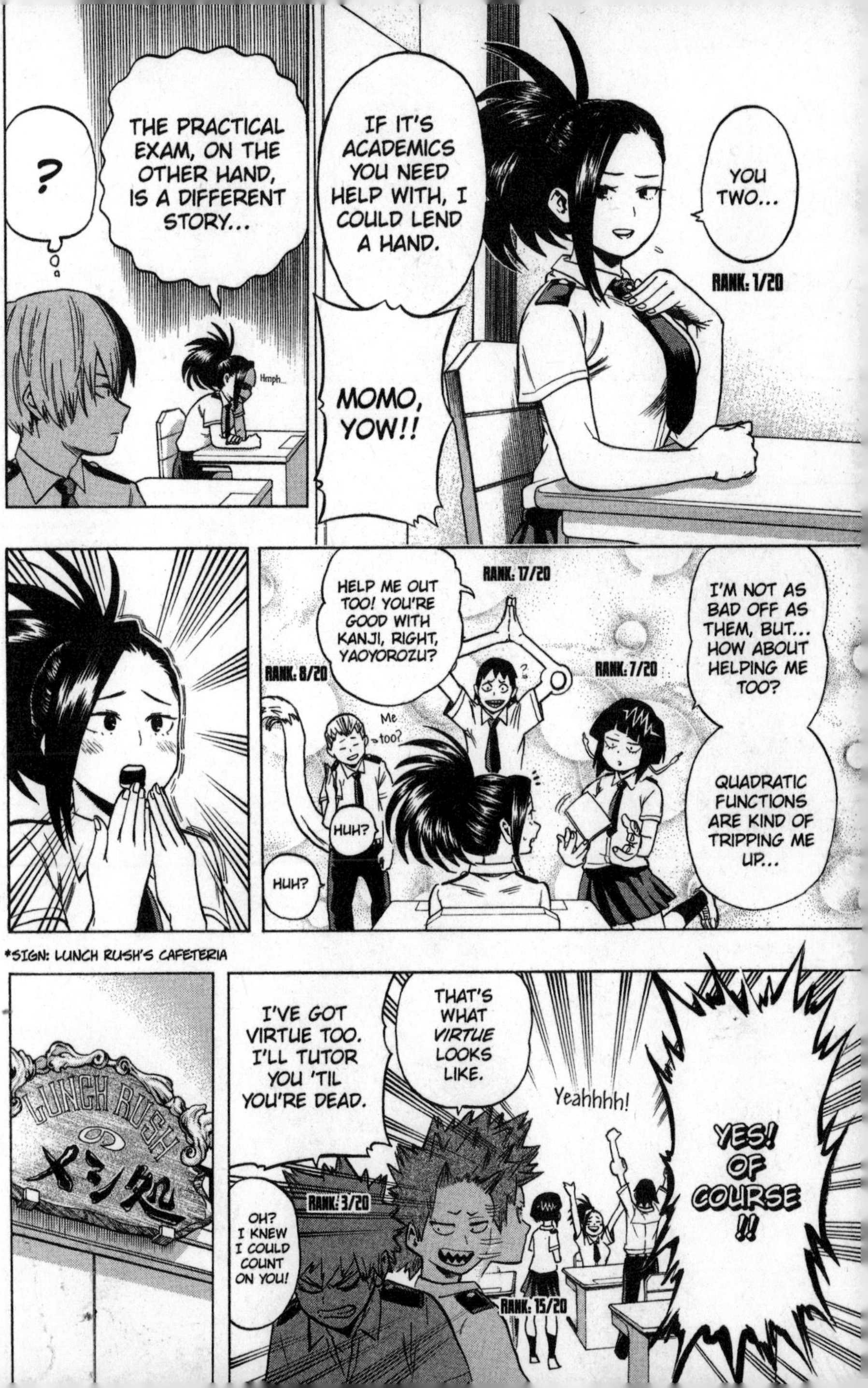
YOU TWO...
RANK: 1/20
IF IT'S ACADEMICS YOU NEED HELP WITH, I COULD LEND A HAND.
MOMO, YOW!!
THE PRACTICAL EXAM, ON THE OTHER HAND, IS A DIFFERENT STORY...
?
Hmph...
I'M NOT AS BAD OFF AS THEM, BUT... HOW ABOUT HELPING ME TOO?
QUADRATIC FUNCTIONS ARE KIND OF TRIPPING ME UP...
RANK: 7/20
RANK: 17/20
HELP ME OUT TOO! YOU'RE GOOD WITH KANJI, RIGHT, YAOYOROZU?
RANK: 8/20
Me too?
HUH?
HUH?
YES! OF COURSE!!
Yeahhhh!
THAT'S WHAT VIRTUE LOOKS LIKE.
I'VE GOT VIRTUE TOO. I'LL TUTOR YOU 'TIL YOU'RE DEAD.
RANK: 3/20
OH? I KNEW I COULD COUNT ON YOU!
RANK: 15/20
LUNCH RUSH

*SIGN: LUNCH RUSH'S CAFETERIA

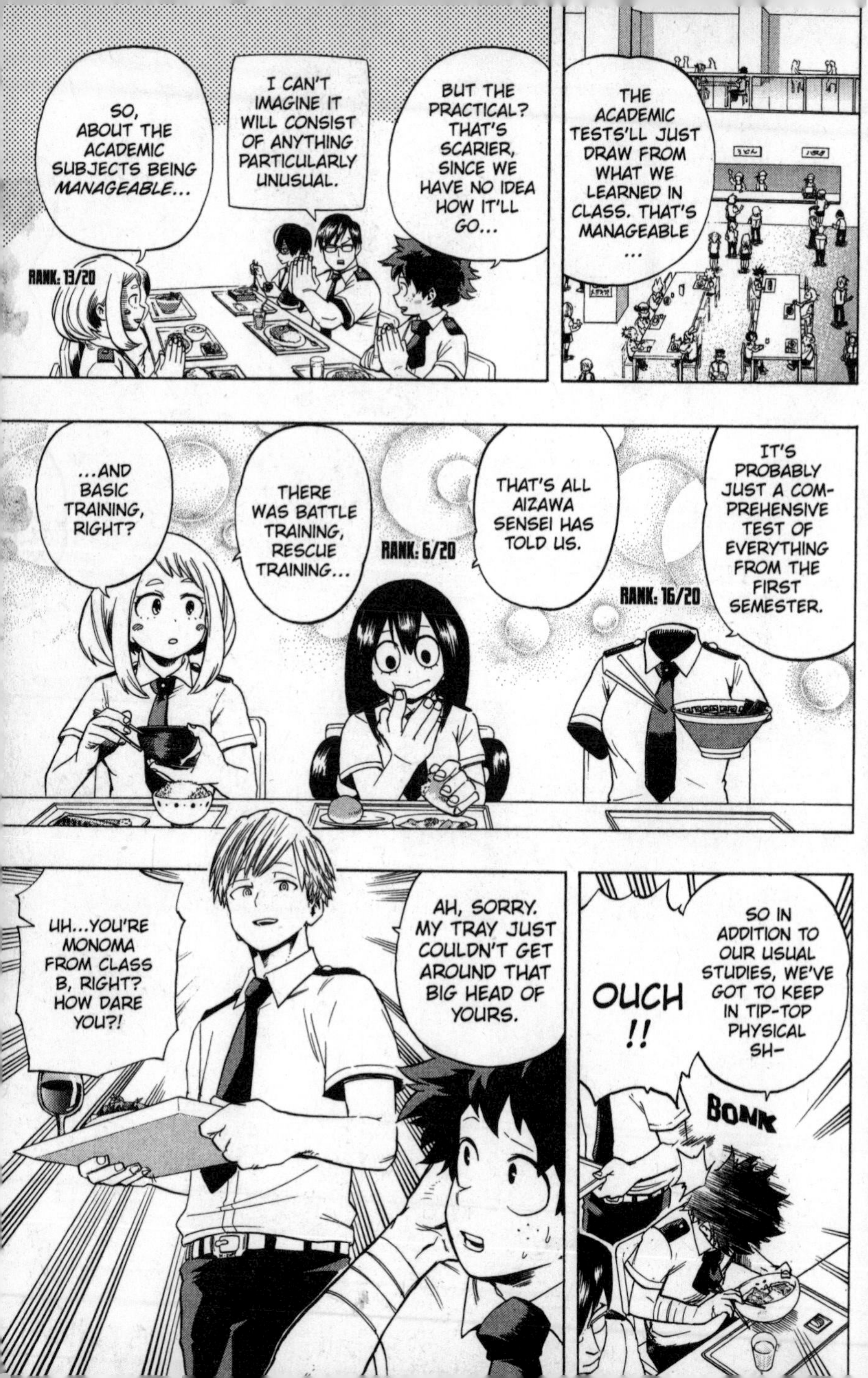
THE ACADEMIC TESTS'LL JUST DRAW FROM WHAT WE LEARNED IN CLASS. THAT'S MANAGEABLE...
BUT THE PRACTICAL? THAT'S SCARIER, SINCE WE HAVE NO IDEA HOW IT'LL GO...
I CAN'T IMAGINE IT WILL CONSIST OF ANYTHING PARTICULARLY UNUSUAL.
SO, ABOUT THE ACADEMIC SUBJECTS BEING *MANAGEABLE*...
RANK: 13/20
IT'S PROBABLY JUST A COM-PREHENSIVE TEST OF EVERYTHING FROM THE FIRST SEMESTER.
RANK: 16/20
THAT'S ALL AIZAWA SENSEI HAS TOLD US.
RANK: 6/20
THERE WAS BATTLE TRAINING, RESCUE TRAINING...
...AND BASIC TRAINING, RIGHT?
SO IN ADDITION TO OUR USUAL STUDIES, WE'VE GOT TO KEEP IN TIP-TOP PHYSICAL SH-
OUCH !!
BONK
AH, SORRY. MY TRAY JUST COULDN'T GET AROUND THAT BIG HEAD OF YOURS.
UH...YOU'RE MONOMA FROM CLASS B, RIGHT? HOW DARE YOU?!

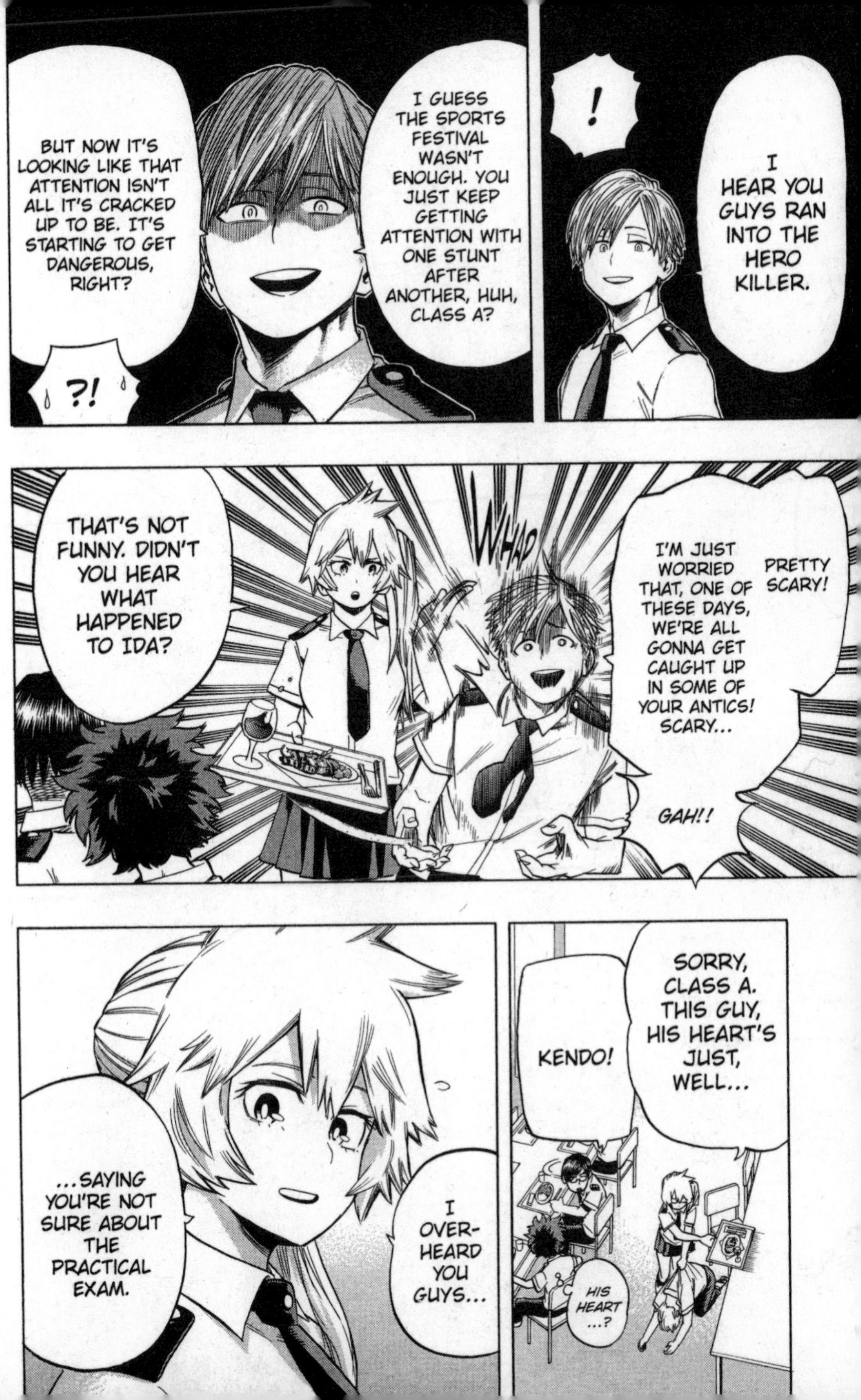
!
I HEAR YOU GUYS RAN INTO THE HERO KILLER.
I GUESS THE SPORTS FESTIVAL WASN'T ENOUGH. YOU JUST KEEP GETTING ATTENTION WITH ONE STUNT AFTER ANOTHER, HUH, CLASS A?
BUT NOW IT'S LOOKING LIKE THAT ATTENTION ISN'T ALL IT'S CRACKED UP TO BE. IT'S STARTING TO GET DANGEROUS, RIGHT?
?!
I'M JUST WORRIED THAT, ONE OF THESE DAYS, WE'RE ALL GONNA GET CAUGHT UP IN SOME OF YOUR ANTICS! SCARY... PRETTY SCARY!
GAH!!
WHAP
THAT'S NOT FUNNY. DIDN'T YOU HEAR WHAT HAPPENED TO IDA?
SORRY, CLASS A. THIS GUY, HIS HEART'S JUST, WELL...
KENDO!
HIS HEART ...?
I OVER-HEARD YOU GUYS...
...SAYING YOU'RE NOT SURE ABOUT THE PRACTICAL EXAM.

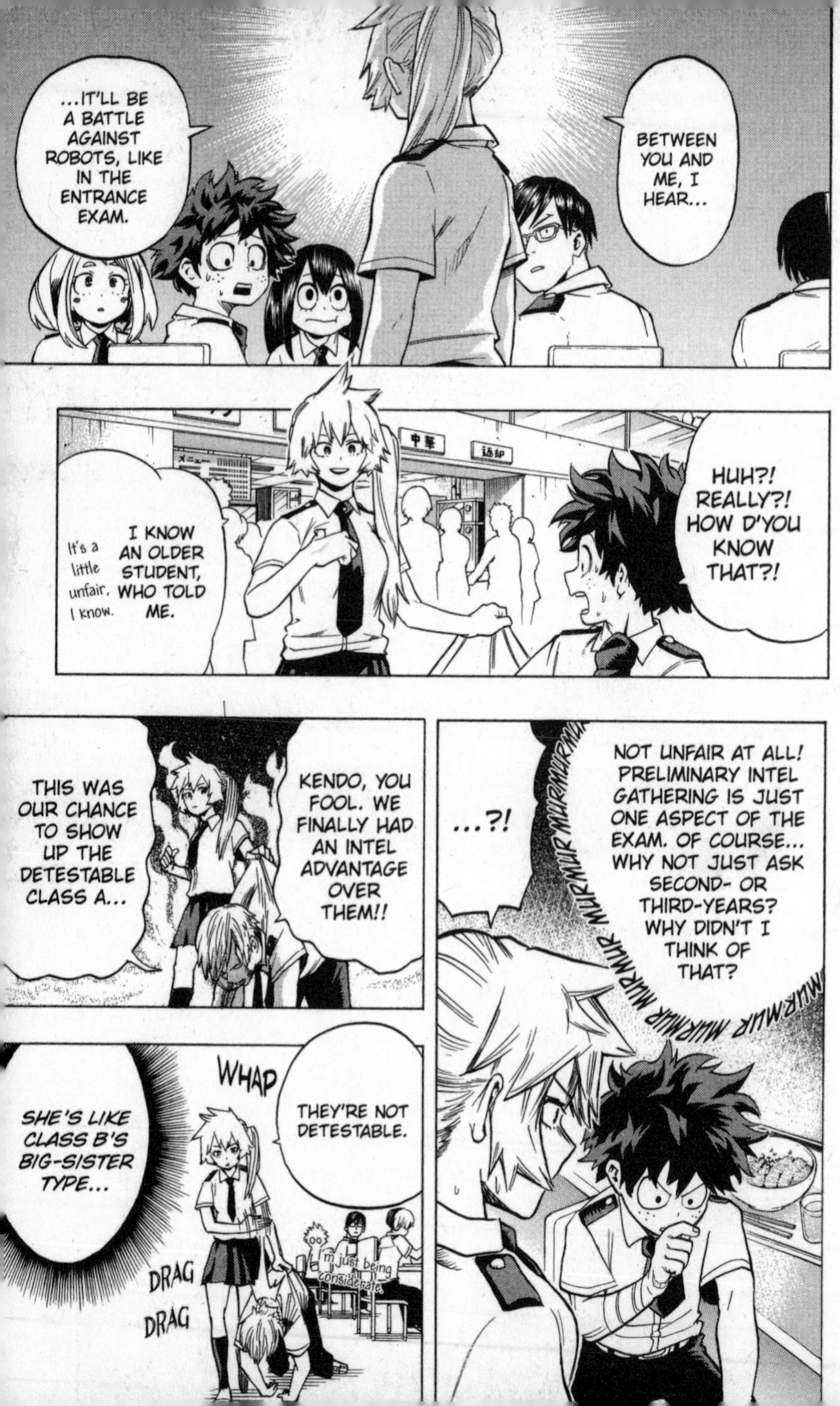
BETWEEN YOU AND ME, I HEAR...
...IT'LL BE A BATTLE AGAINST ROBOTS, LIKE IN THE ENTRANCE EXAM.
HUH?! REALLY?! HOW D'YOU KNOW THAT?!
I KNOW AN OLDER STUDENT, WHO TOLD ME.
It's a little unfair, I know.
NOT UNFAIR AT ALL! PRELIMINARY INTEL GATHERING IS JUST ONE ASPECT OF THE EXAM. OF COURSE... WHY NOT JUST ASK SECOND- OR THIRD-YEARS? WHY DIDN'T I THINK OF THAT?
MURMUR MURMUR MURMUR MURMUR MURMUR MURMUR MURMUR MURMUR
...?!
KENDO, YOU FOOL. WE FINALLY HAD AN INTEL ADVANTAGE OVER THEM!!
THIS WAS OUR CHANCE TO SHOW UP THE DETESTABLE CLASS A...
WHAP
THEY'RE NOT DETESTABLE.
SHE'S LIKE CLASS B'S BIG-SISTER TYPE...
I'm just being considerate.
DRAG
DRAG

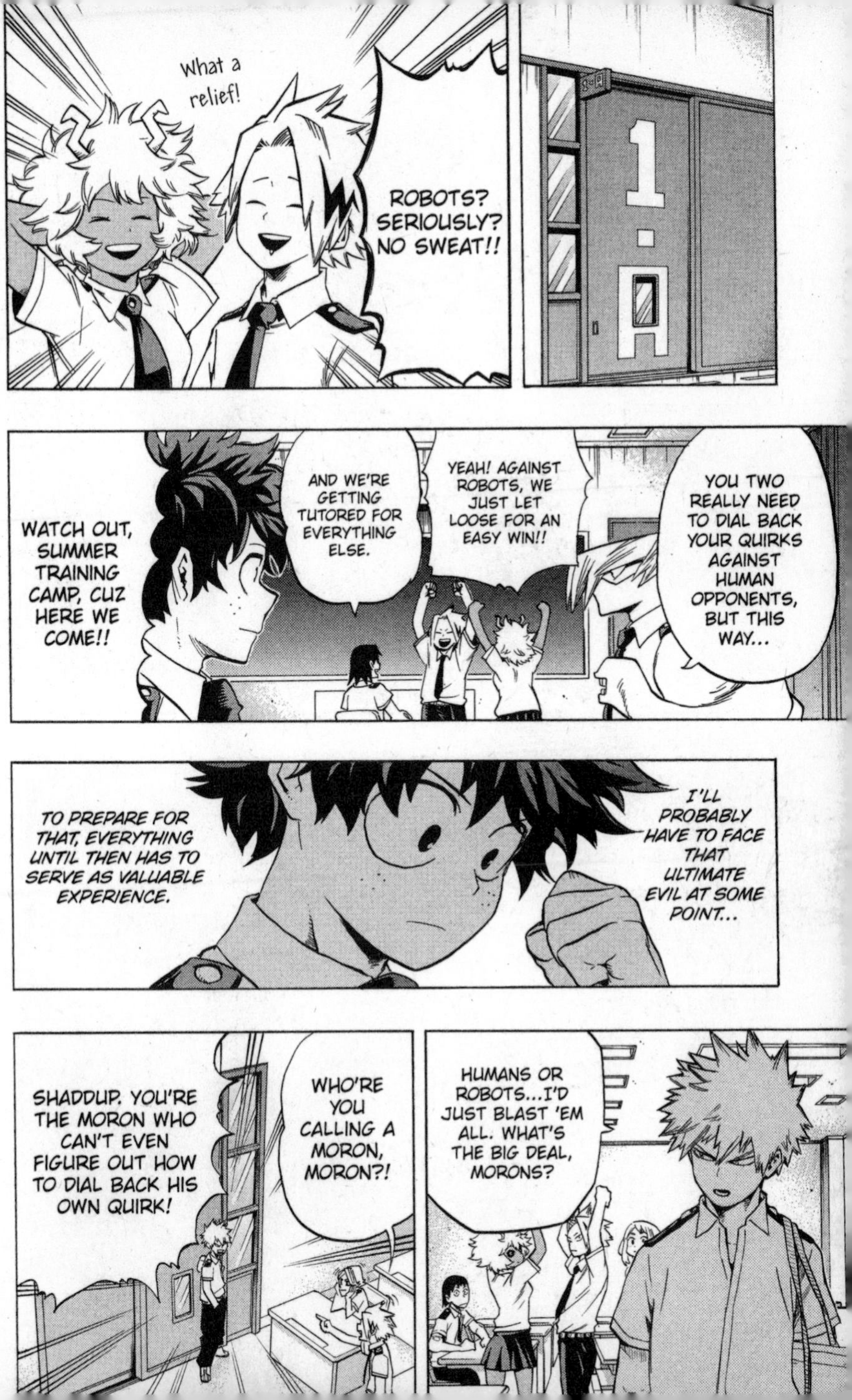
ROBOTS? SERIOUSLY? NO SWEAT!!
What a relief!
YOU TWO REALLY NEED TO DIAL BACK YOUR QUIRKS AGAINST HUMAN OPPONENTS, BUT THIS WAY...
YEAH! AGAINST ROBOTS, WE JUST LET LOOSE FOR AN EASY WIN!!
AND WE'RE GETTING TUTORED FOR EVERYTHING ELSE.
WATCH OUT, SUMMER TRAINING CAMP, CUZ HERE WE COME!!
I'LL PROBABLY HAVE TO FACE THAT ULTIMATE EVIL AT SOME POINT...
TO PREPARE FOR THAT, EVERYTHING UNTIL THEN HAS TO SERVE AS VALUABLE EXPERIENCE.
HUMANS OR ROBOTS...I'D JUST BLAST 'EM ALL. WHAT'S THE BIG DEAL, MORONS?
WHO'RE YOU CALLING A MORON, MORON?!
SHADDUP. YOU'RE THE MORON WHO CAN'T EVEN FIGURE OUT HOW TO DIAL BACK HIS OWN QUIRK!

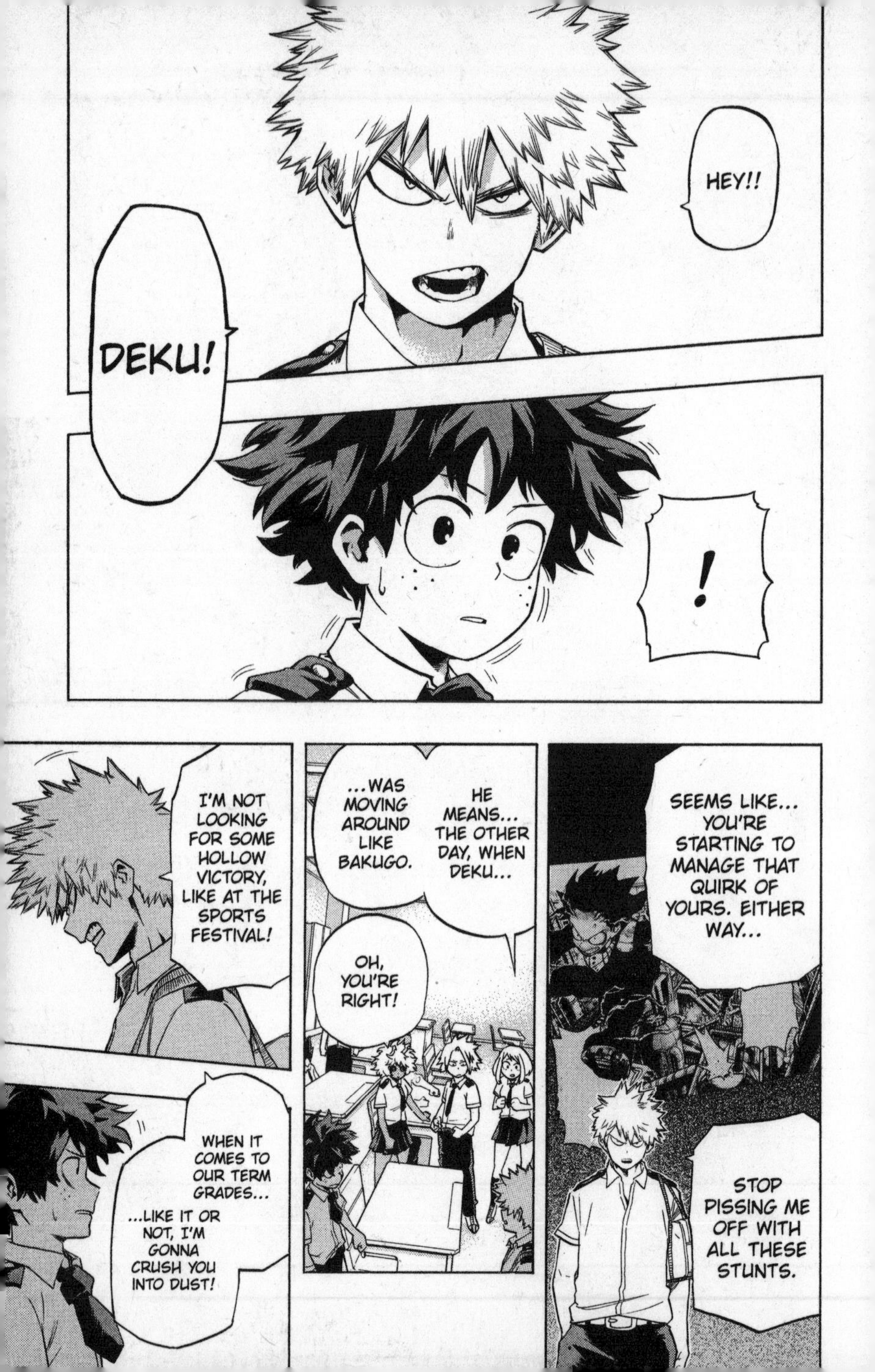
HEY!!
DEKU!
!
SEEMS LIKE... YOU'RE STARTING TO MANAGE THAT QUIRK OF YOURS. EITHER WAY...
STOP PISSING ME OFF WITH ALL THESE STUNTS.
HE MEANS... THE OTHER DAY, WHEN DEKU...
...WAS MOVING AROUND LIKE BAKUGO.
OH, YOU'RE RIGHT!
I'M NOT LOOKING FOR SOME HOLLOW VICTORY, LIKE AT THE SPORTS FESTIVAL!
WHEN IT COMES TO OUR TERM GRADES...
...LIKE IT OR NOT, I'M GONNA CRUSH YOU INTO DUST!

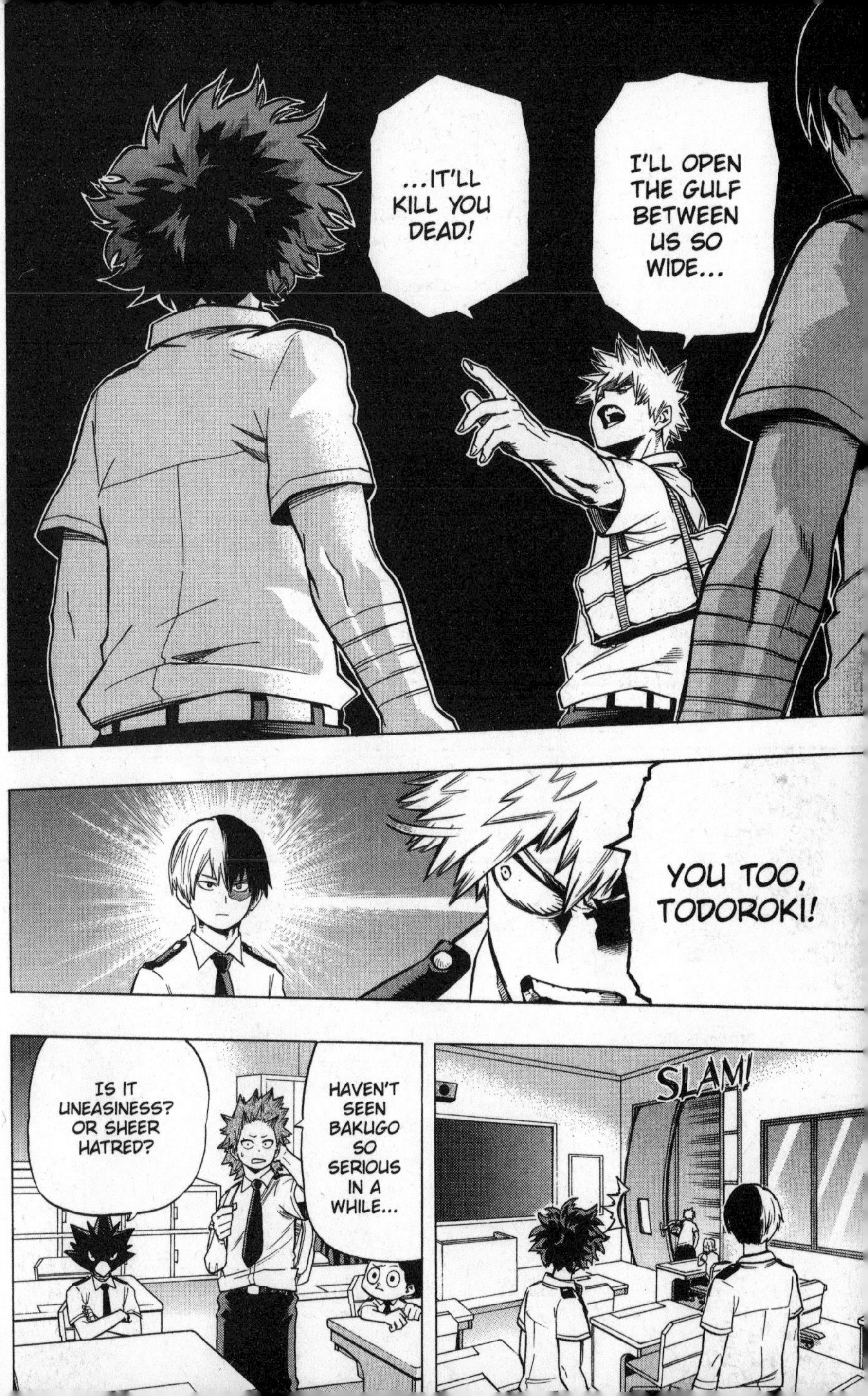
I'LL OPEN THE GULF BETWEEN US SO WIDE...
...IT'LL KILL YOU DEAD!
YOU TOO, TODOROKI!
SLAM!
HAVEN'T SEEN BAKUGO SO SERIOUS IN A WHILE...
IS IT UNEASINESS? OR SHEER HATRED?

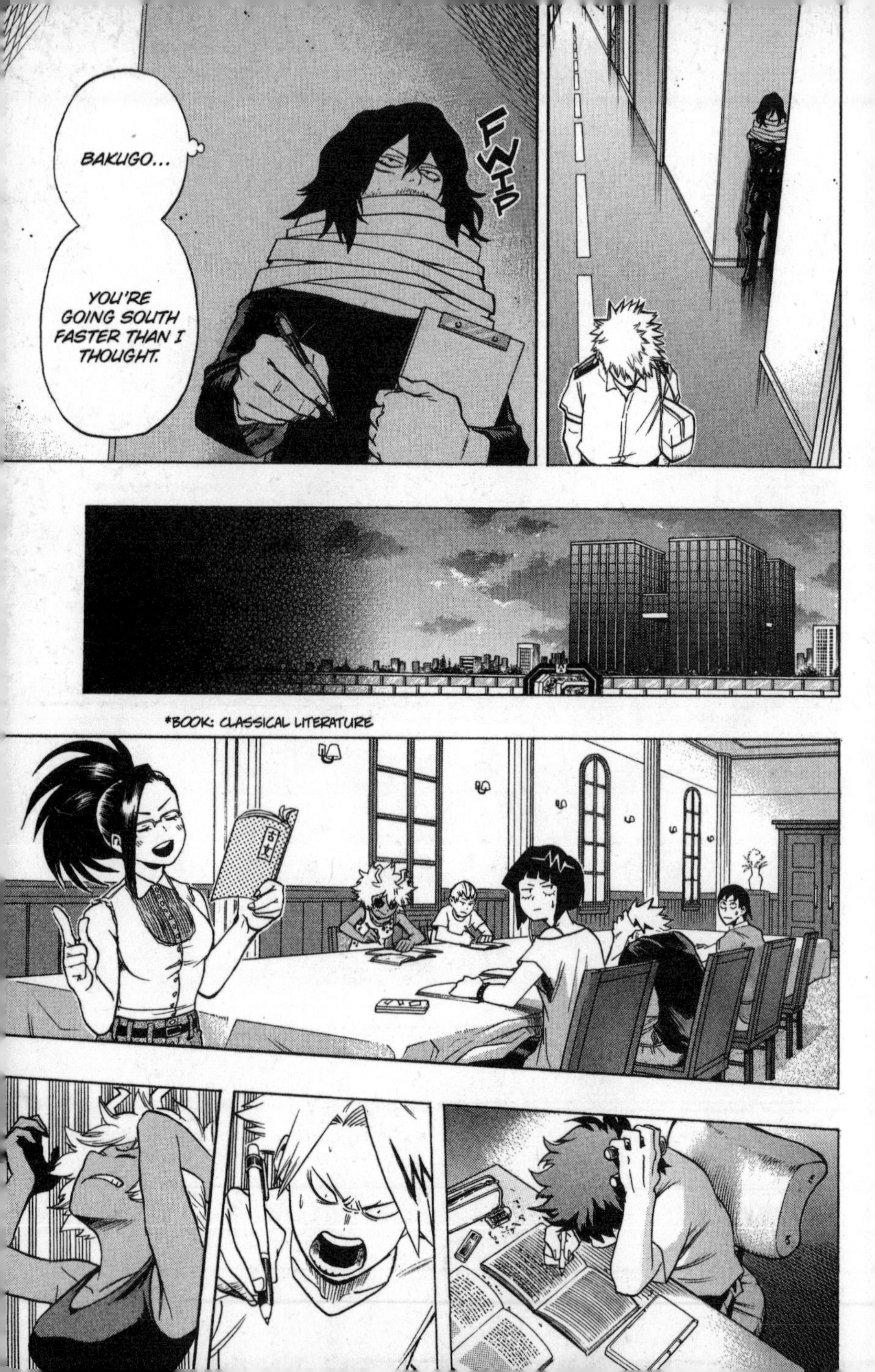
BAKUGO...
YOU'RE GOING SOUTH FASTER THAN I THOUGHT.
FWIP
*BOOK: CLASSICAL LITERATURE
古文

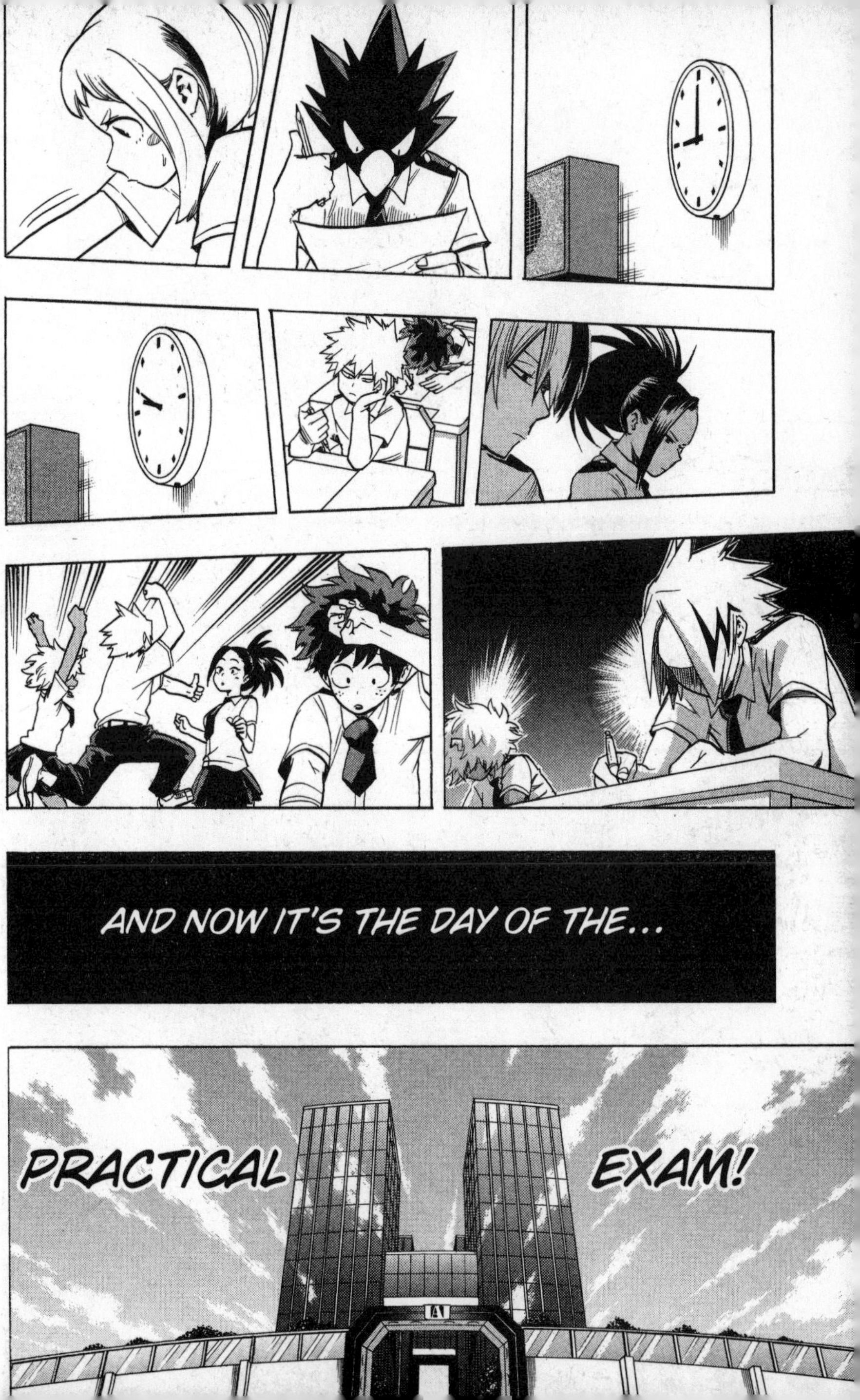
AND NOW IT'S THE DAY OF THE...
PRACTICAL EXAM!

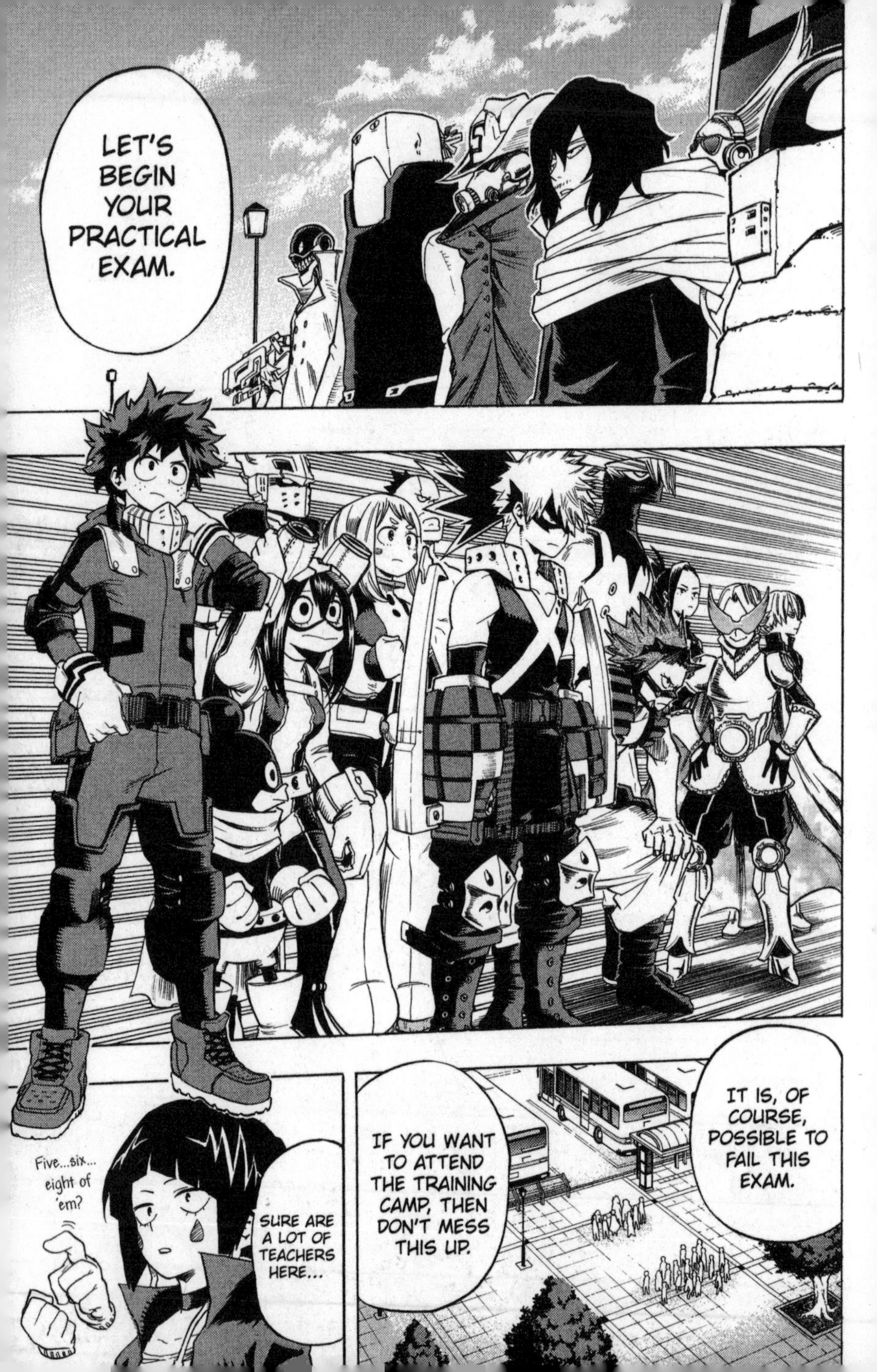
LET'S BEGIN YOUR PRACTICAL EXAM.
IT IS, OF COURSE, POSSIBLE TO FAIL THIS EXAM.
IF YOU WANT TO ATTEND THE TRAINING CAMP, THEN DON'T MESS THIS UP.
SURE ARE A LOT OF TEACHERS HERE...
Five...six... eight of 'em?

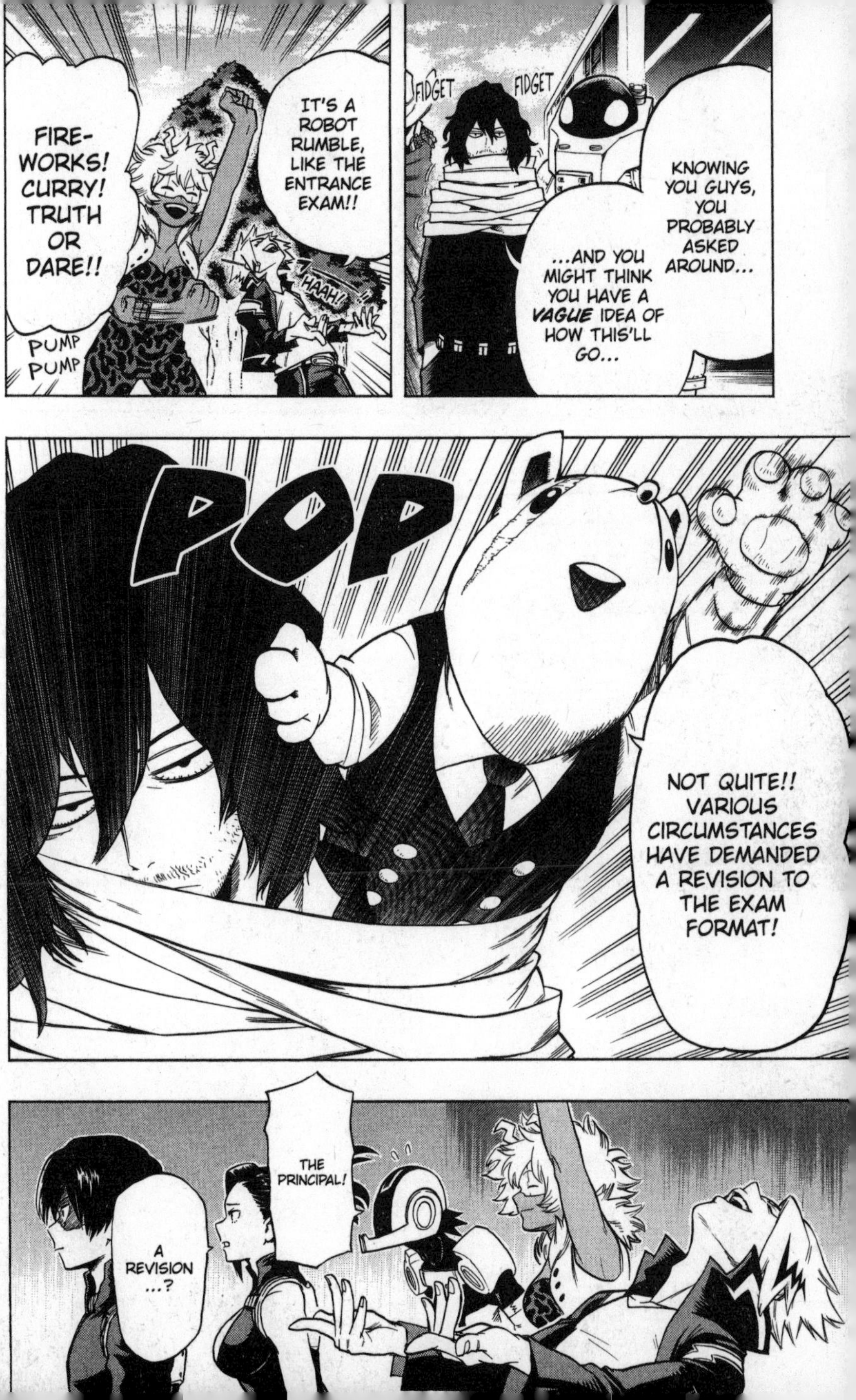
FIDGET
FIDGET
KNOWING YOU GUYS, YOU PROBABLY ASKED AROUND...
...AND YOU MIGHT THINK YOU HAVE A VAGUE IDEA OF HOW THIS'LL GO...
IT'S A ROBOT RUMBLE, LIKE THE ENTRANCE EXAM!!
HAAH!!
FIRE-WORKS! CURRY! TRUTH OR DARE!!
PUMP PUMP
POP
NOT QUITE!! VARIOUS CIRCUMSTANCES HAVE DEMANDED A REVISION TO THE EXAM FORMAT!
THE PRINCIPAL!
A REVISION ...?

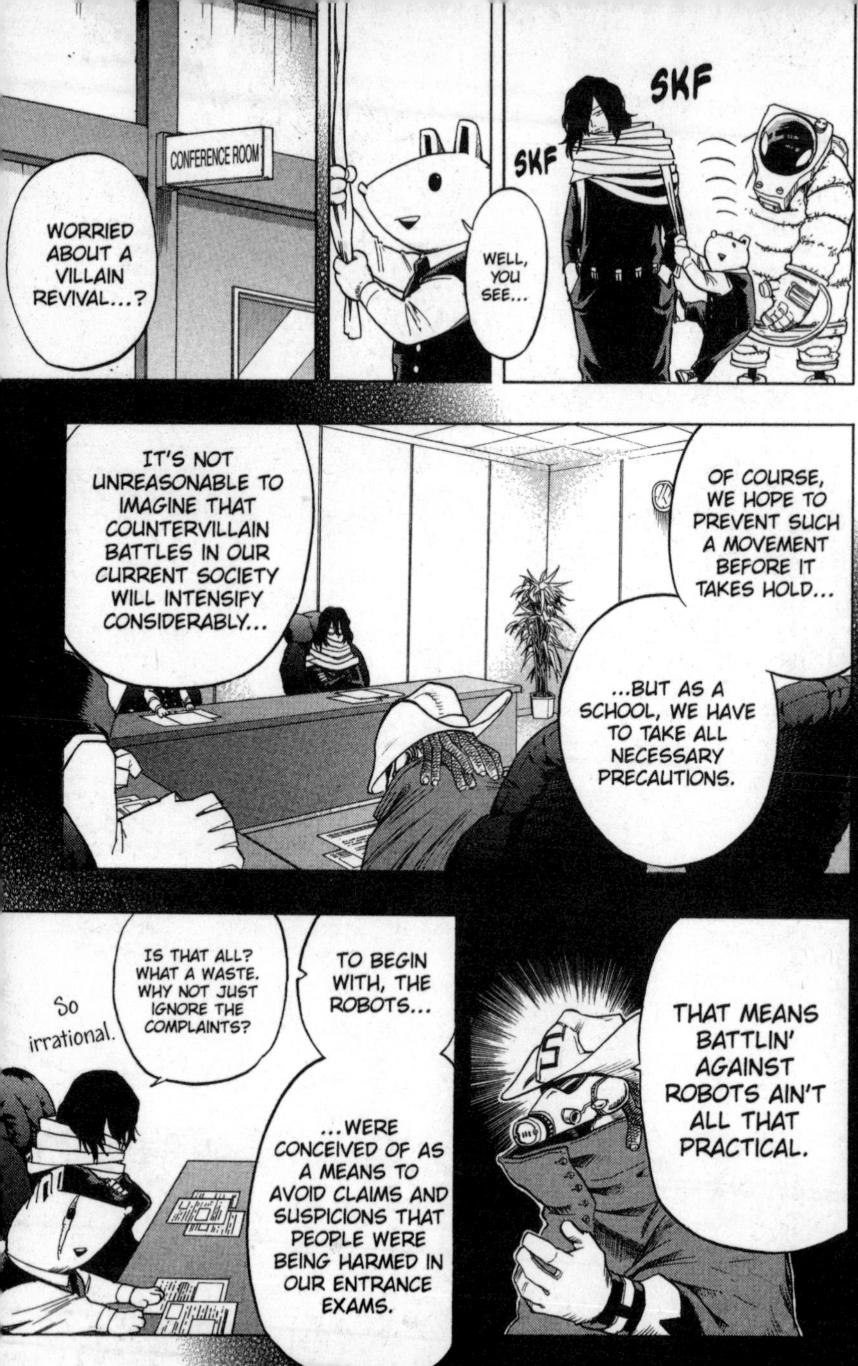
SKF
SKF
WELL, YOU SEE...
CONFERENCE ROOM
WORRIED ABOUT A VILLAIN REVIVAL...?
OF COURSE, WE HOPE TO PREVENT SUCH A MOVEMENT BEFORE IT TAKES HOLD...
...BUT AS A SCHOOL, WE HAVE TO TAKE ALL NECESSARY PRECAUTIONS.
IT'S NOT UNREASONABLE TO IMAGINE THAT COUNTERVILLAIN BATTLES IN OUR CURRENT SOCIETY WILL INTENSIFY CONSIDERABLY...
THAT MEANS BATTLIN' AGAINST ROBOTS AIN'T ALL THAT PRACTICAL.
TO BEGIN WITH, THE ROBOTS...
...WERE CONCEIVED OF AS A MEANS TO AVOID CLAIMS AND SUSPICIONS THAT PEOPLE WERE BEING HARMED IN OUR ENTRANCE EXAMS.
IS THAT ALL? WHAT A WASTE. WHY NOT JUST IGNORE THE COMPLAINTS?
So irrational.

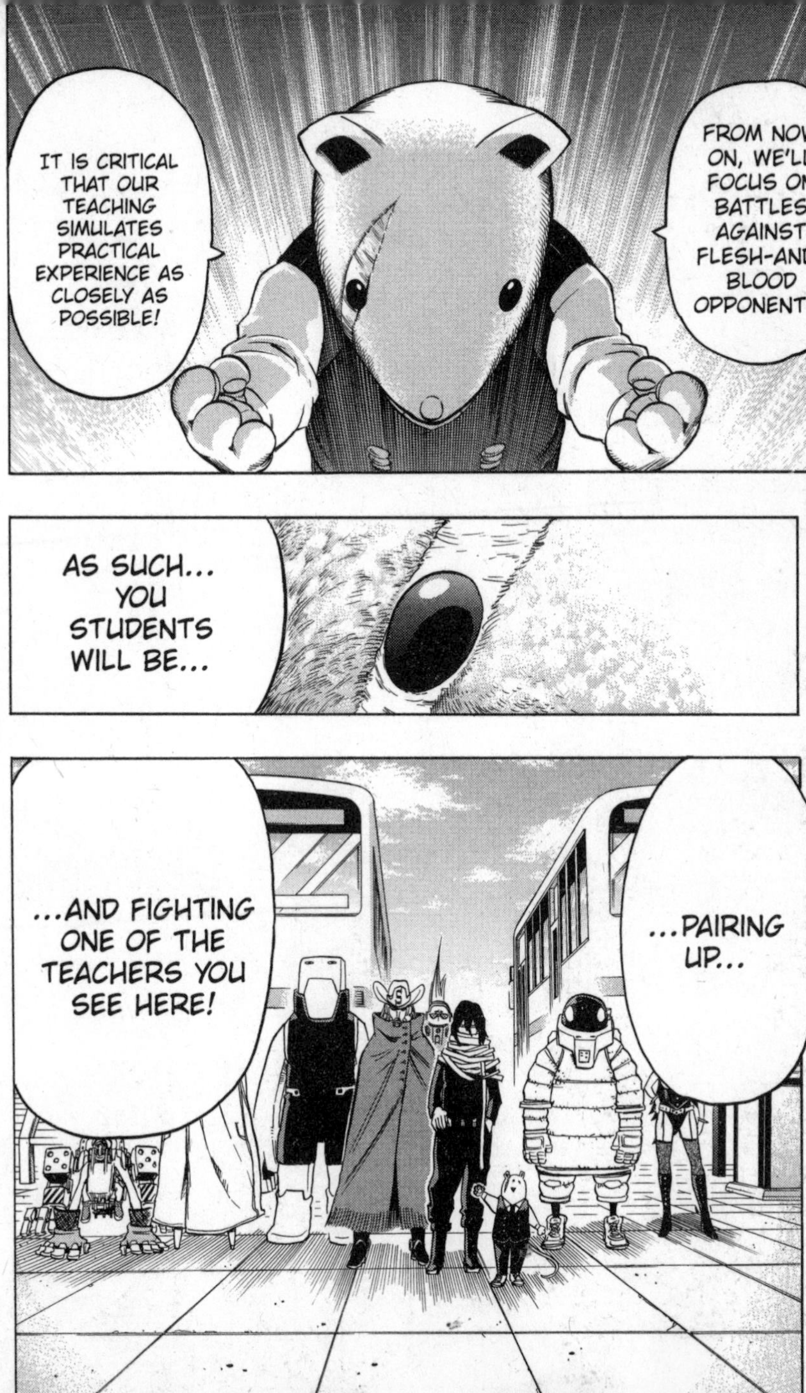
FROM NOW ON, WE'LL FOCUS ON BATTLES AGAINST FLESH-AND-BLOOD OPPONENTS.
IT IS CRITICAL THAT OUR TEACHING SIMULATES PRACTICAL EXPERIENCE AS CLOSELY AS POSSIBLE!
AS SUCH... YOU STUDENTS WILL BE...
...PAIRING UP...
...AND FIGHTING ONE OF THE TEACHERS YOU SEE HERE!

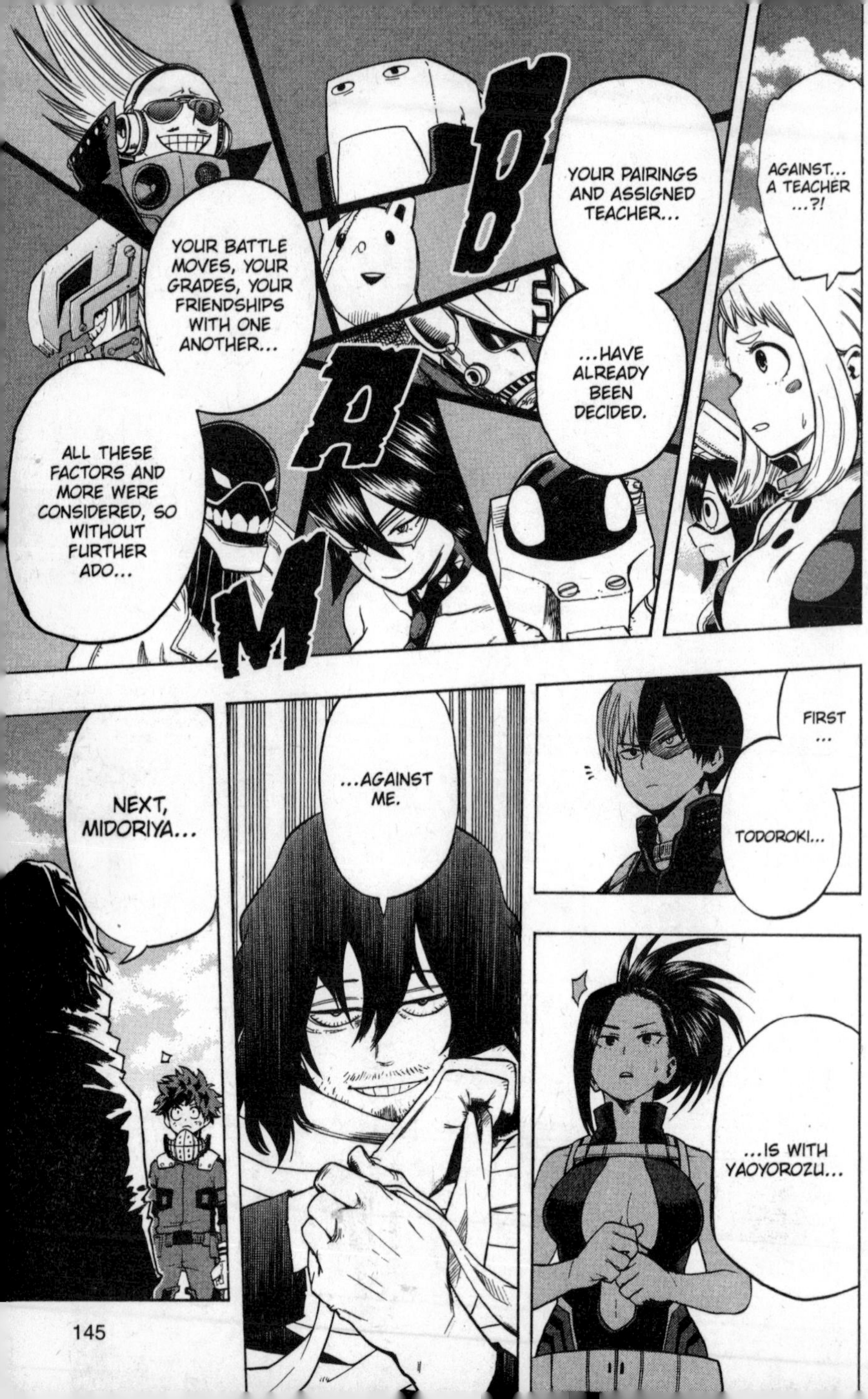
AGAINST... A TEACHER ...?!
YOUR PAIRINGS AND ASSIGNED TEACHER...
...HAVE ALREADY BEEN DECIDED.
YOUR BATTLE MOVES, YOUR GRADES, YOUR FRIENDSHIPS WITH ONE ANOTHER...
ALL THESE FACTORS AND MORE WERE CONSIDERED, SO WITHOUT FURTHER ADO...
BAM
FIRST ...
TODOROKI...
...IS WITH YAOYOROZU...
...AGAINST ME.
NEXT, MIDORIYA...

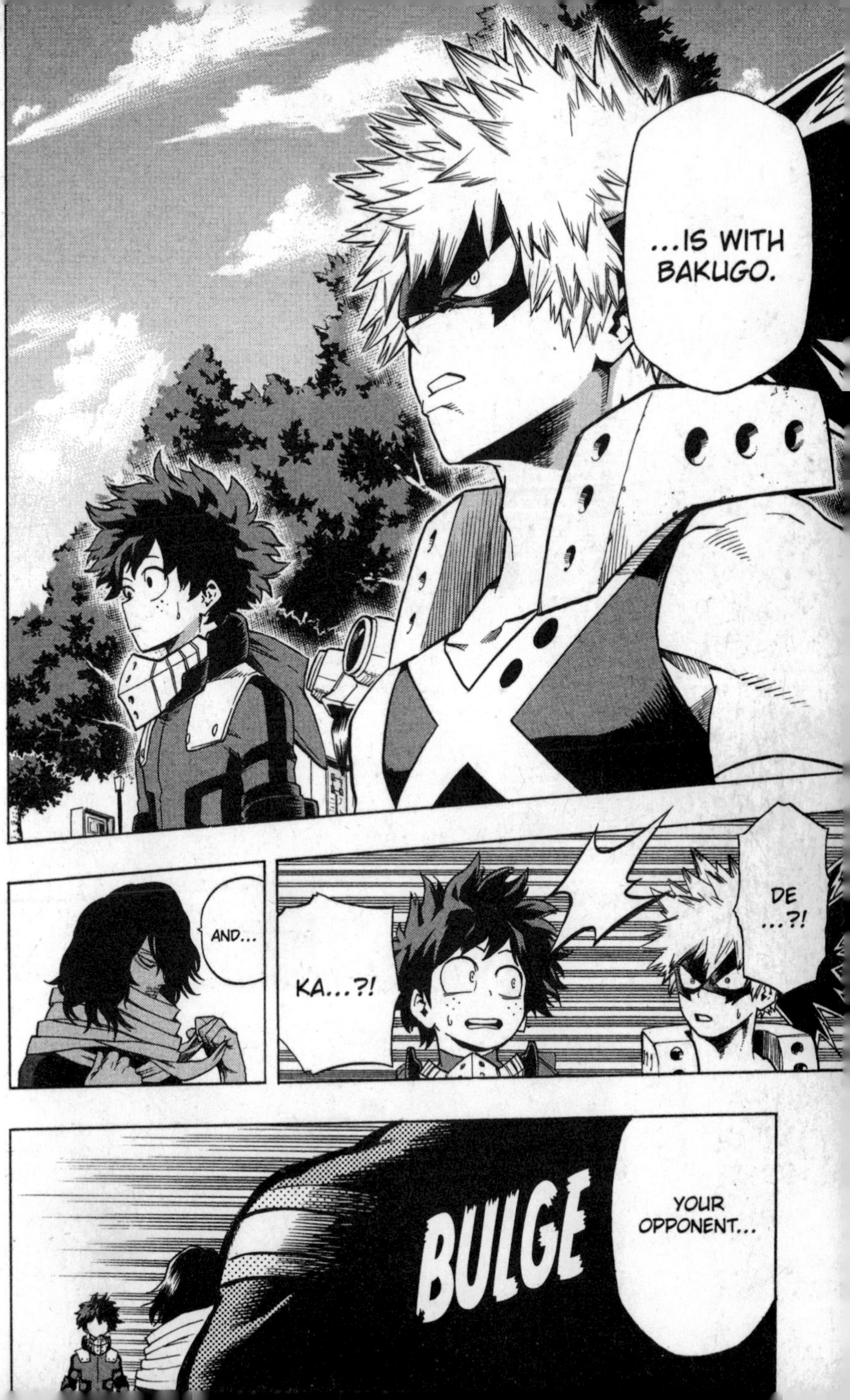
...IS WITH BAKUGO.
DE ...?!
KA...?!
AND...
YOUR OPPONENT...
BULGE

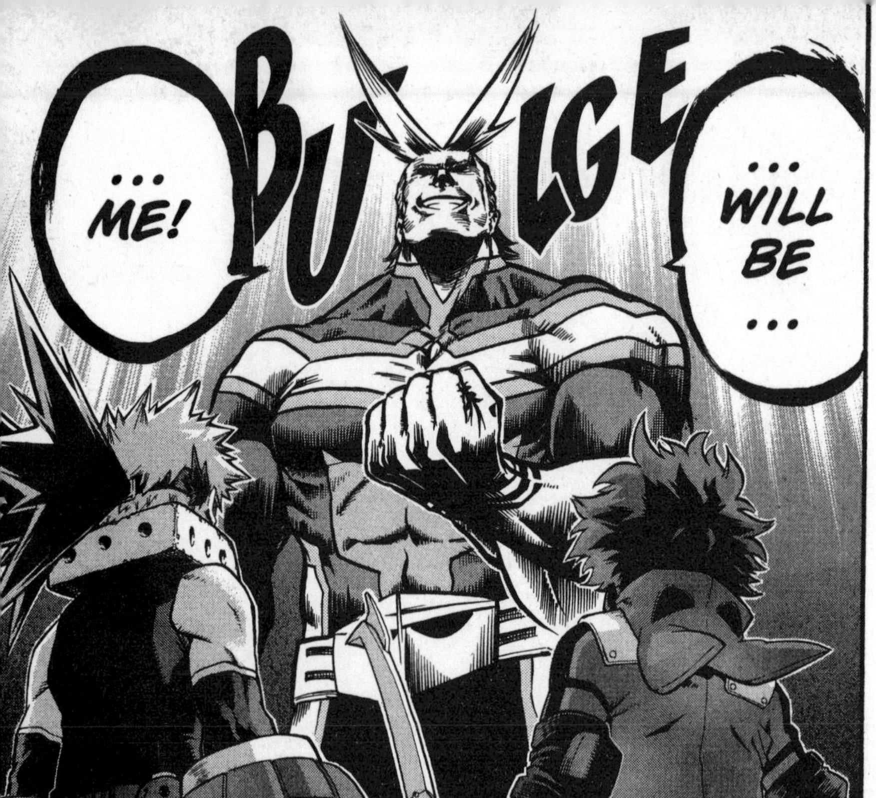
... WILL BE ...
BULGE
... ME!

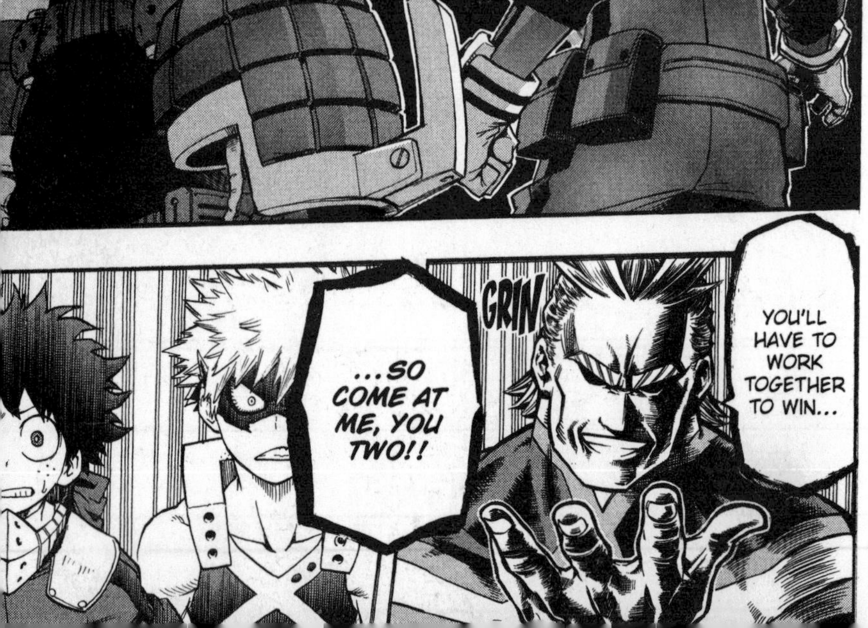
YOU'LL HAVE TO WORK TOGETHER TO WIN...
GRIN
...SO COME AT ME, YOU TWO!!

CONTINUING FROM PANEL 5 OF PAGE 132

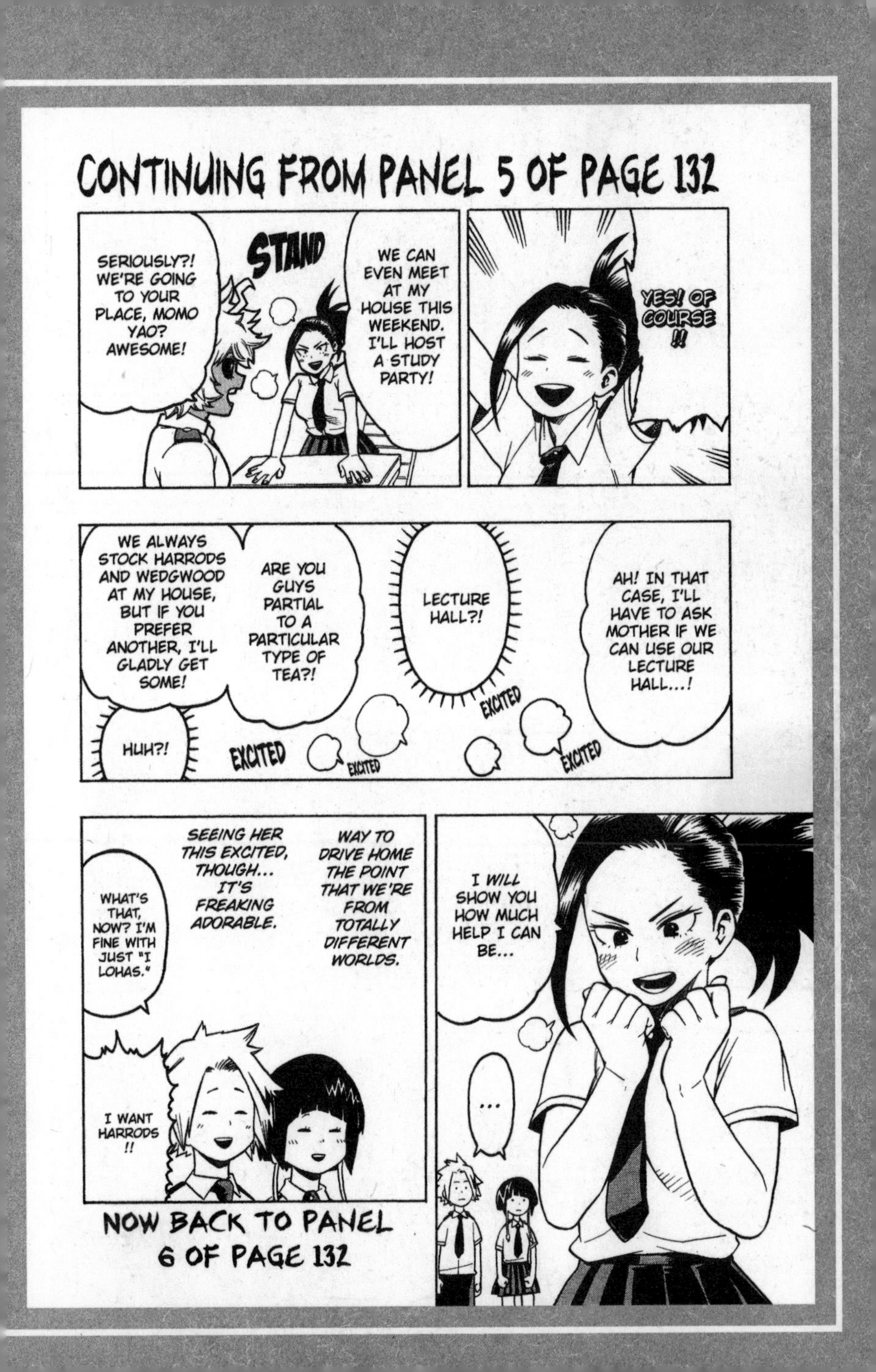

YES! OF COURSE!!
WE CAN EVEN MEET AT MY HOUSE THIS WEEKEND. I'LL HOST A STUDY PARTY!
STAND
SERIOUSLY?! WE'RE GOING TO YOUR PLACE, MOMO YAO? AWESOME!
AH! IN THAT CASE, I'LL HAVE TO ASK MOTHER IF WE CAN USE OUR LECTURE HALL...!
EXCITED
EXCITED
LECTURE HALL?!
ARE YOU GUYS PARTIAL TO A PARTICULAR TYPE OF TEA?!
WE ALWAYS STOCK HARRODS AND WEDGWOOD AT MY HOUSE, BUT IF YOU PREFER ANOTHER, I'LL GLADLY GET SOME!
EXCITED
EXCITED
HUH?!
I WILL SHOW YOU HOW MUCH HELP I CAN BE...
...
WAY TO DRIVE HOME THE POINT THAT WE'RE FROM TOTALLY DIFFERENT WORLDS.
SEEING HER THIS EXCITED, THOUGH... IT'S FREAKING ADORABLE.
WHAT'S THAT, NOW? I'M FINE WITH JUST "I LOHAS."
I WANT HARRODS!!

NOW BACK TO PANEL 6 OF PAGE 132

NO. 61 - THE WORST COMBO

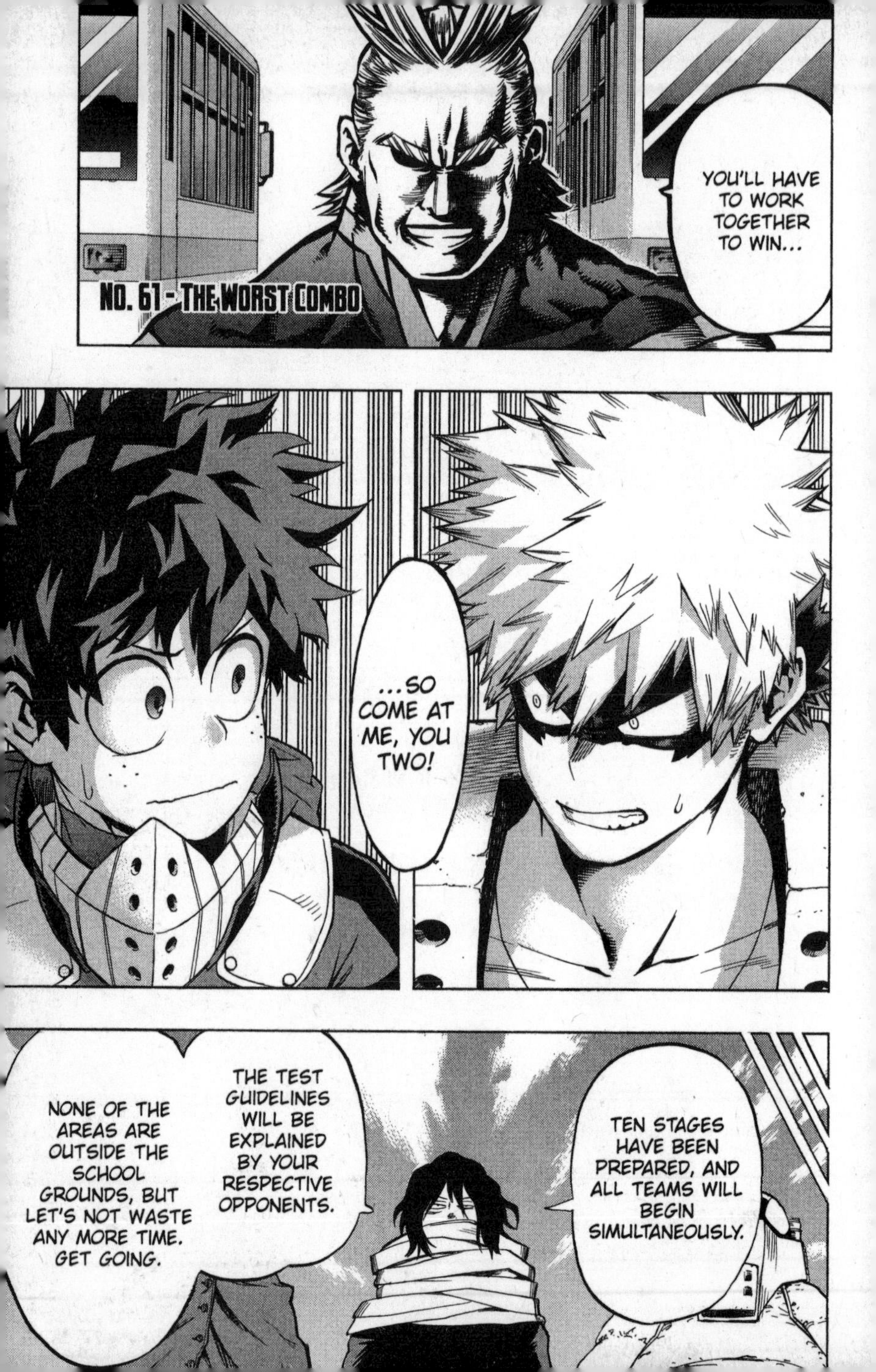
YOU'LL HAVE TO WORK TOGETHER TO WIN...
...SO COME AT ME, YOU TWO!
TEN STAGES HAVE BEEN PREPARED, AND ALL TEAMS WILL BEGIN SIMULTANEOUSLY.
THE TEST GUIDELINES WILL BE EXPLAINED BY YOUR RESPECTIVE OPPONENTS.
NONE OF THE AREAS ARE OUTSIDE THE SCHOOL GROUNDS, BUT LET'S NOT WASTE ANY MORE TIME. GET GOING.

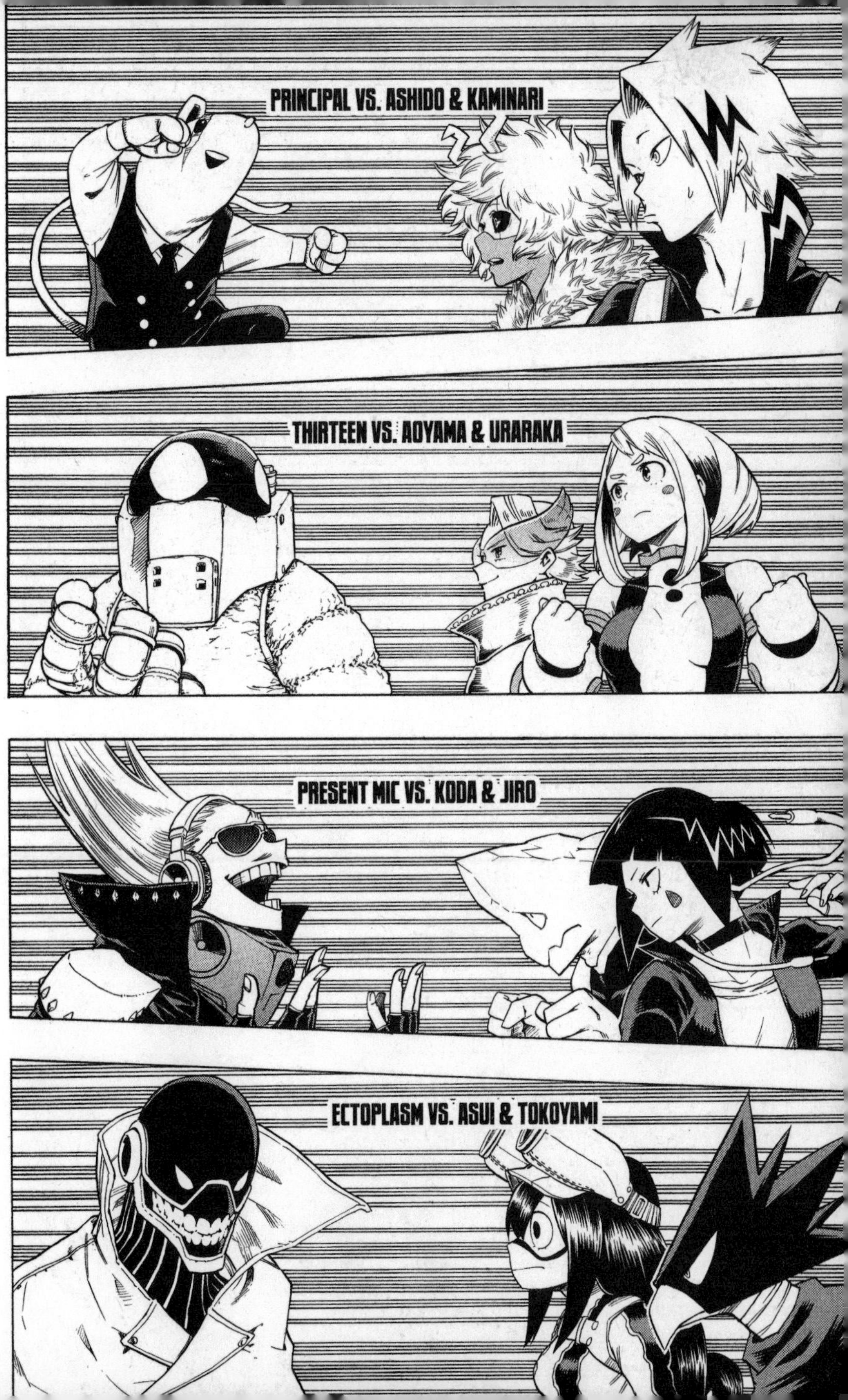
PRINCIPAL VS. ASHIDO & KAMINARI
THIRTEEN VS. AOYAMA & URARAKA
PRESENT MIC VS. KODA & JIRO
ECTOPLASM VS. ASUI & TOKOYAMI

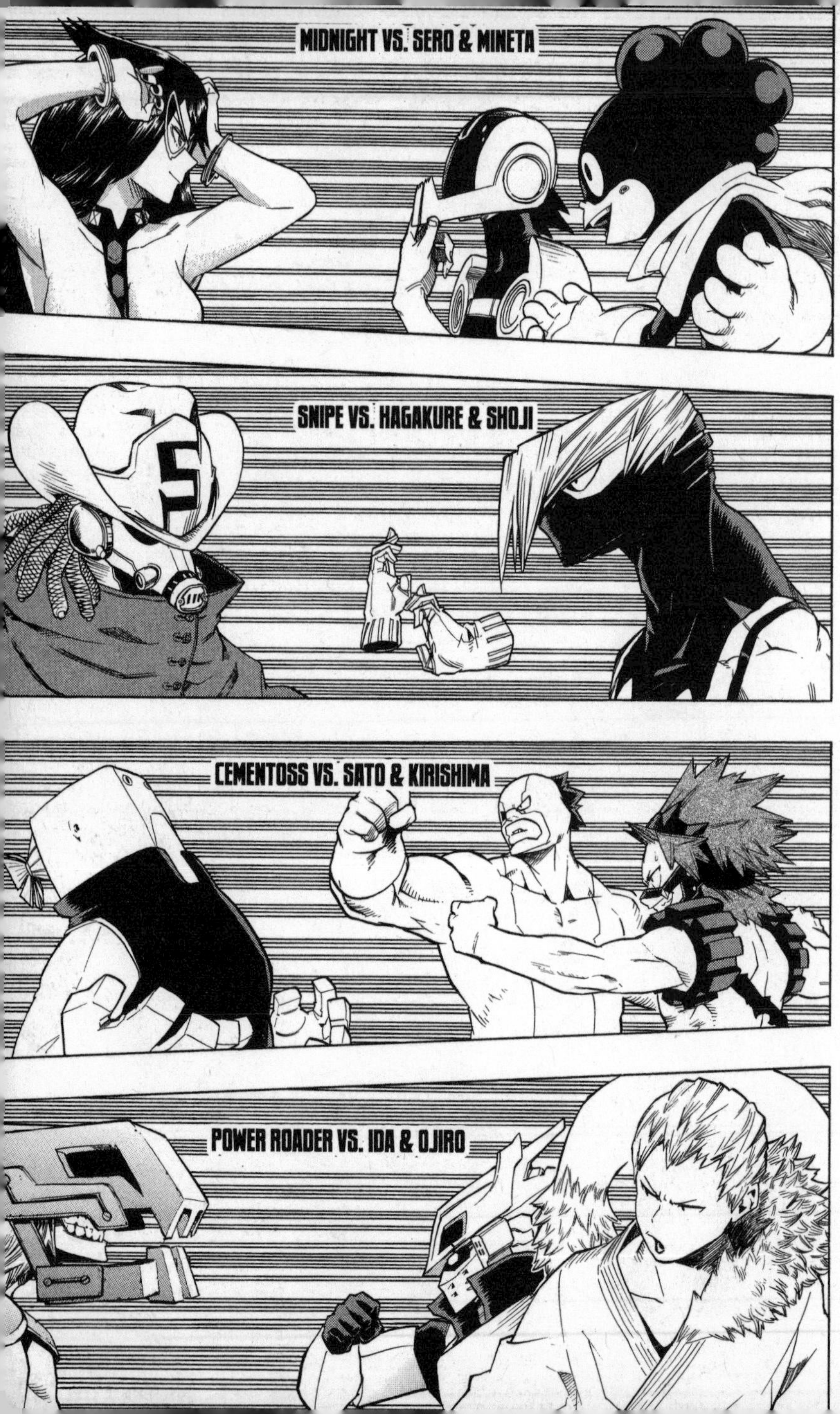
MIDNIGHT VS. SERO & MINETA
SNIPE VS. HAGAKURE & SHOJI
CEMENTOSS VS. SATO & KIRISHIMA
POWER ROADER VS. IDA & OJIRO

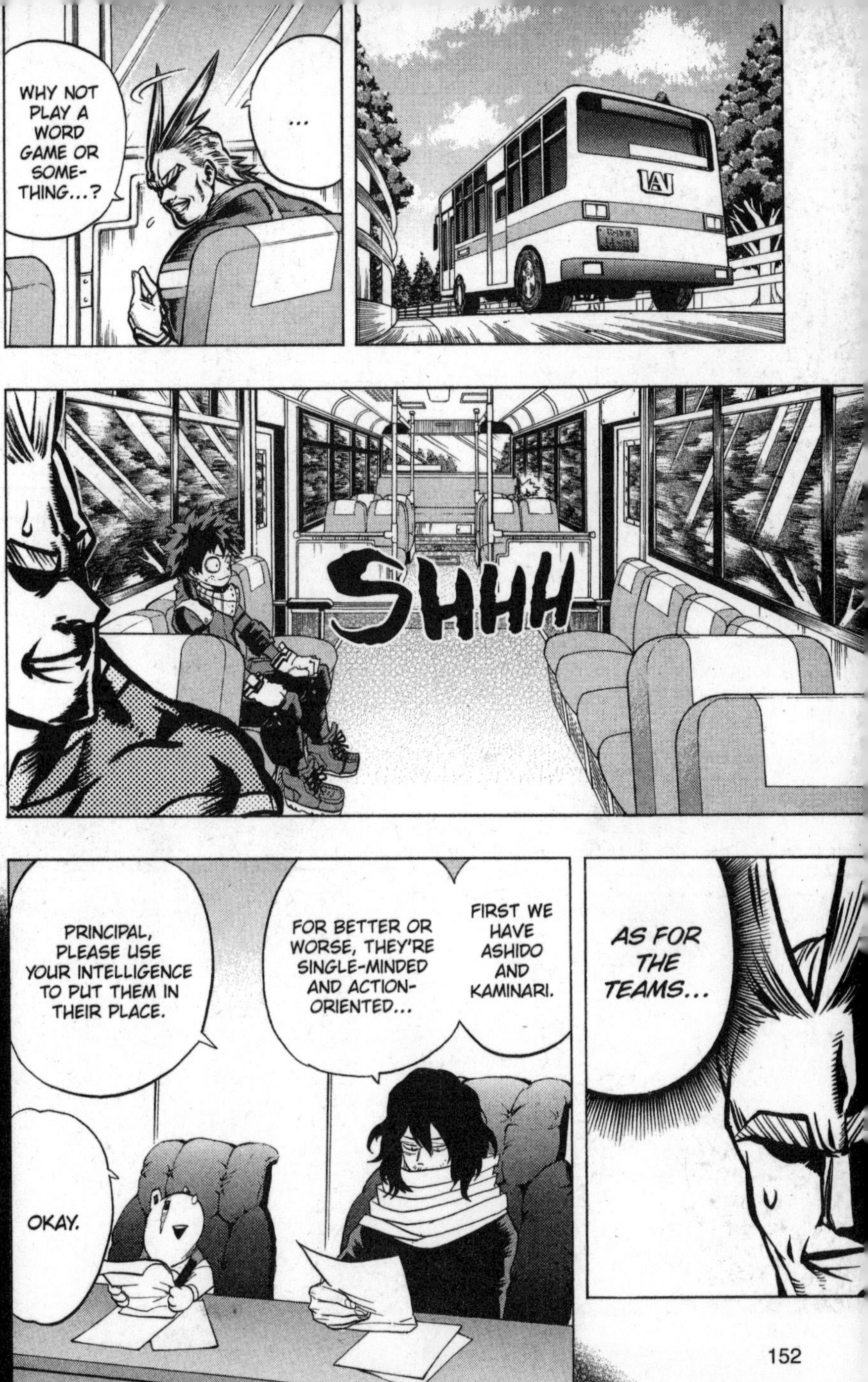
...
WHY NOT PLAY A WORD GAME OR SOME- THING...?
SHHH
AS FOR THE TEAMS...
FIRST WE HAVE ASHIDO AND KAMINARI.
FOR BETTER OR WORSE, THEY'RE SINGLE-MINDED AND ACTION-ORIENTED...
PRINCIPAL, PLEASE USE YOUR INTELLIGENCE TO PUT THEM IN THEIR PLACE.
OKAY.

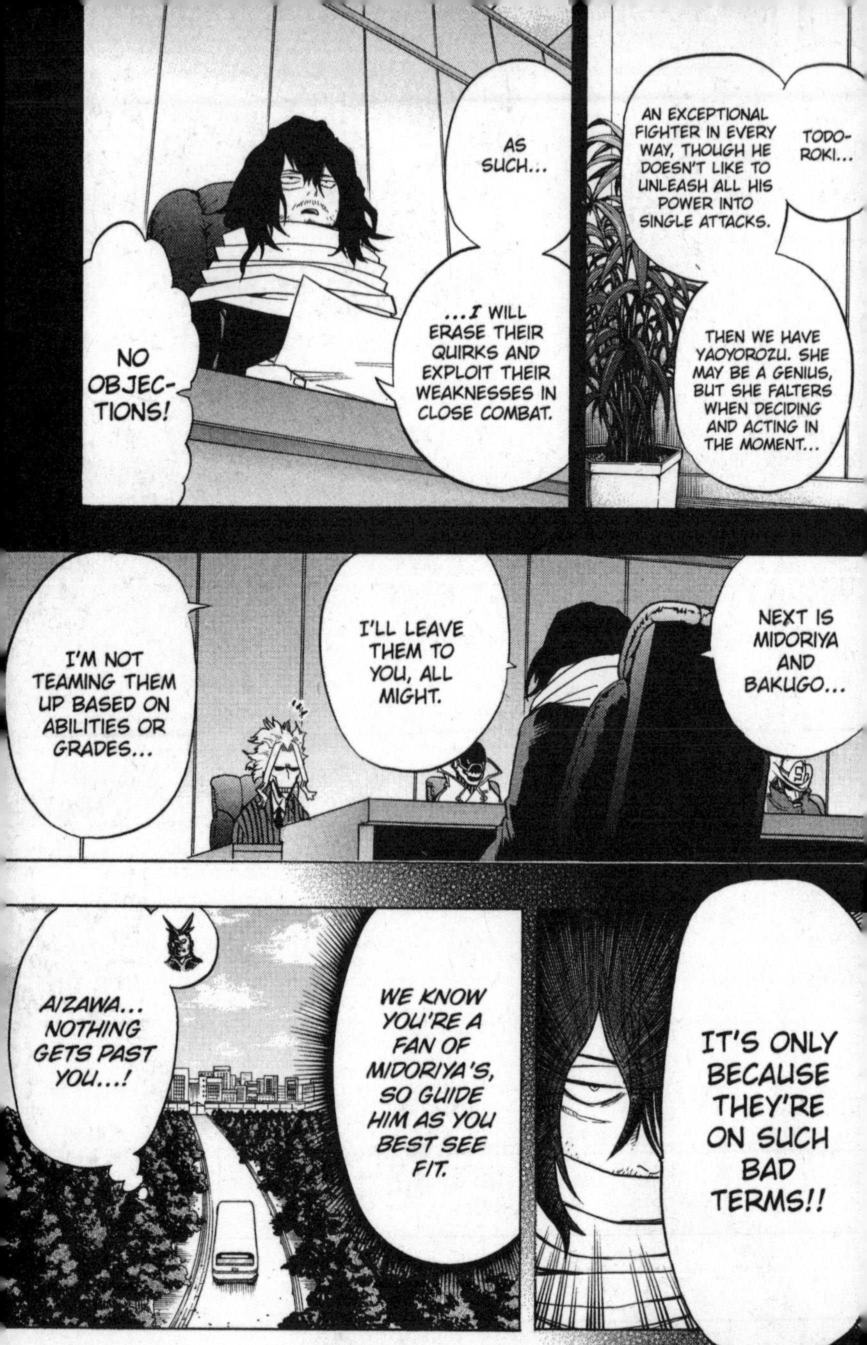
TODO-ROKI...
AN EXCEPTIONAL FIGHTER IN EVERY WAY, THOUGH HE DOESN'T LIKE TO UNLEASH ALL HIS POWER INTO SINGLE ATTACKS.
THEN WE HAVE YAOYOROZU. SHE MAY BE A GENIUS, BUT SHE FALTERS WHEN DECIDING AND ACTING IN THE MOMENT...
AS SUCH...
...I WILL ERASE THEIR QUIRKS AND EXPLOIT THEIR WEAKNESSES IN CLOSE COMBAT.
NO OBJEC-TIONS!
NEXT IS MIDORIYA AND BAKUGO...
I'LL LEAVE THEM TO YOU, ALL MIGHT.
I'M NOT TEAMING THEM UP BASED ON ABILITIES OR GRADES...
IT'S ONLY BECAUSE THEY'RE ON SUCH BAD TERMS!!
WE KNOW YOU'RE A FAN OF MIDORIYA'S, SO GUIDE HIM AS YOU BEST SEE FIT.
AIZAWA... NOTHING GETS PAST YOU...!

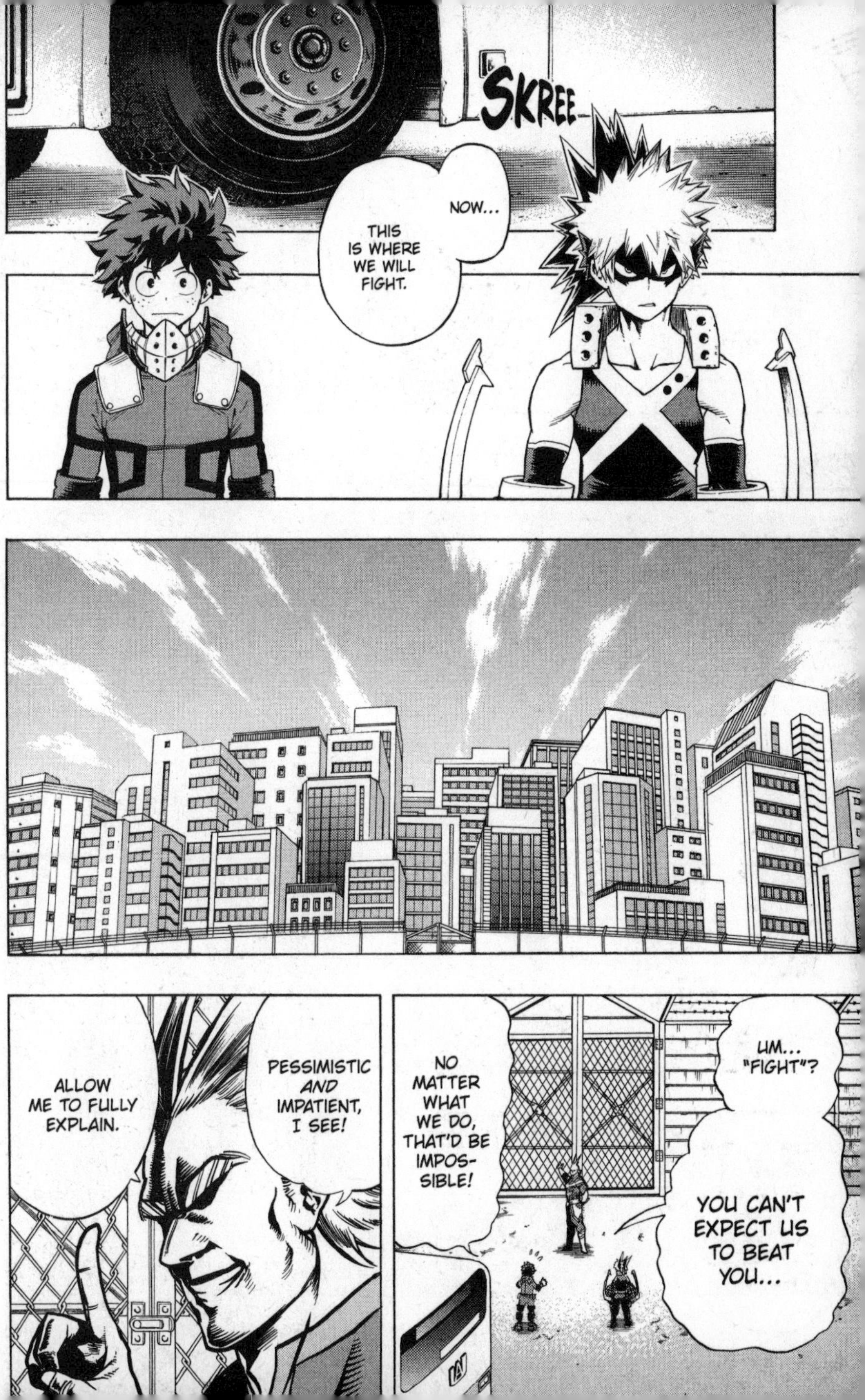
SKREE
NOW... THIS IS WHERE WE WILL FIGHT.
UM... "FIGHT"?
YOU CAN'T EXPECT US TO BEAT YOU...
NO MATTER WHAT WE DO, THAT'D BE IMPOSSIBLE!
PESSIMISTIC AND IMPATIENT, I SEE!
ALLOW ME TO FULLY EXPLAIN.

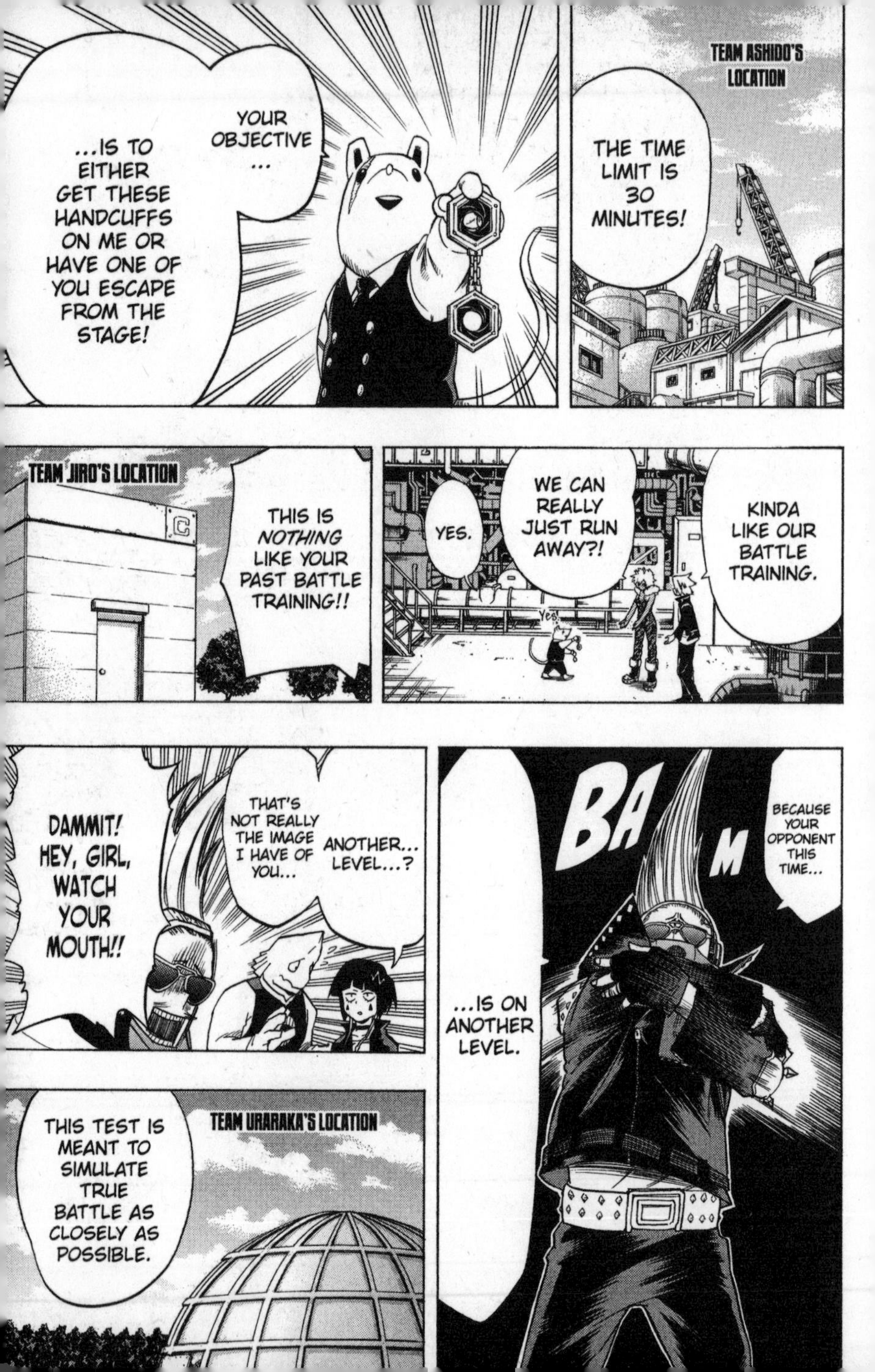
TEAM ASHIDO'S LOCATION
THE TIME LIMIT IS 30 MINUTES!
YOUR OBJECTIVE...
...IS TO EITHER GET THESE HANDCUFFS ON ME OR HAVE ONE OF YOU ESCAPE FROM THE STAGE!
KINDA LIKE OUR BATTLE TRAINING.
WE CAN REALLY JUST RUN AWAY?!
YES.
Yes!
TEAM JIRO'S LOCATION
THIS IS *NOTHING* LIKE YOUR PAST BATTLE TRAINING!!
BECAUSE YOUR OPPONENT THIS TIME...
BAM
...IS ON ANOTHER LEVEL.
ANOTHER... LEVEL...?
THAT'S NOT REALLY THE IMAGE I HAVE OF YOU...
DAMMIT! HEY, GIRL, WATCH YOUR MOUTH!!
TEAM URARAKA'S LOCATION
THIS TEST IS MEANT TO SIMULATE TRUE BATTLE AS CLOSELY AS POSSIBLE.

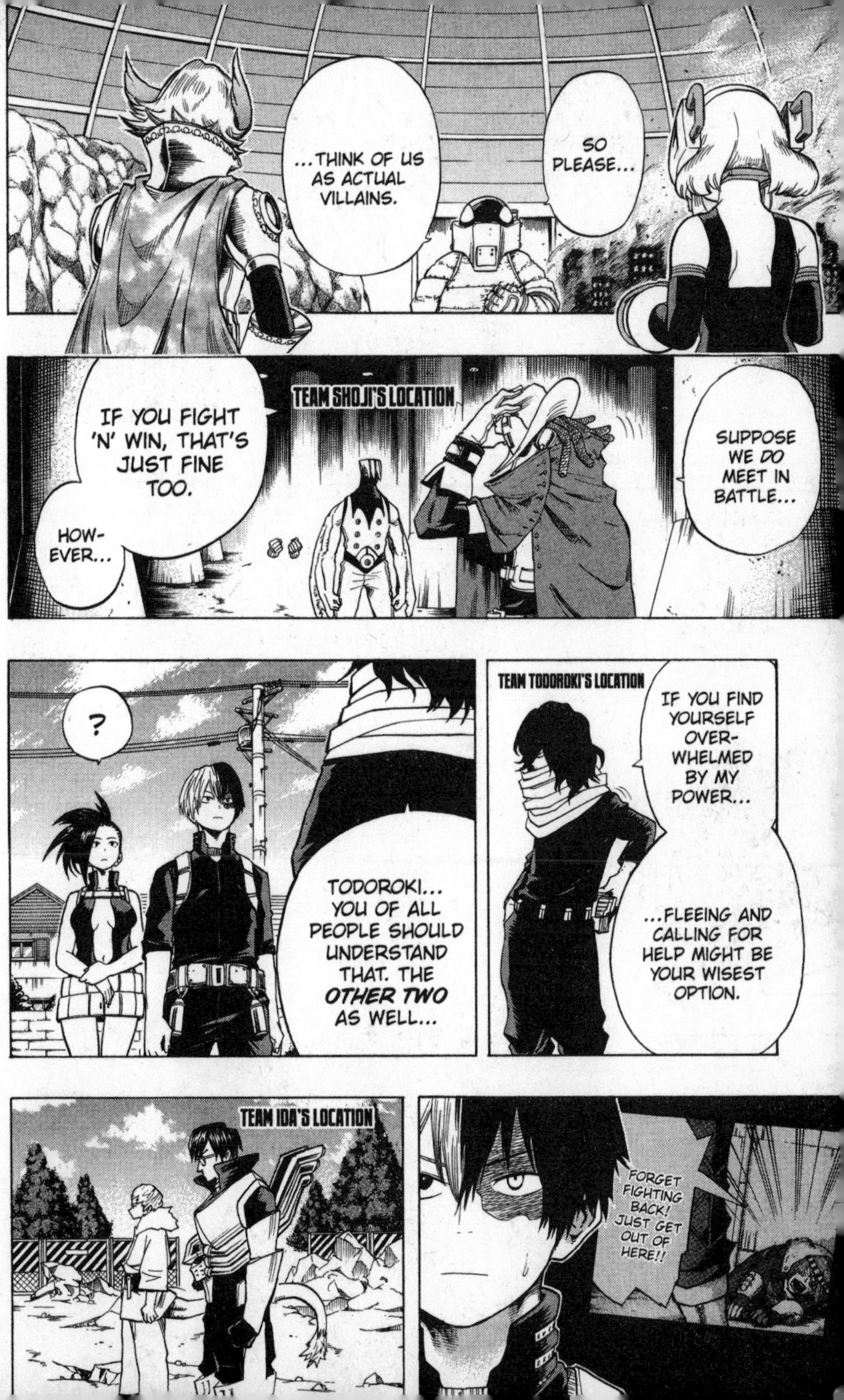
SO PLEASE...
...THINK OF US AS ACTUAL VILLAINS.
SUPPOSE WE *DO* MEET IN BATTLE...
TEAM SHOJI'S LOCATION
IF YOU FIGHT 'N' WIN, THAT'S JUST FINE TOO.
HOW-EVER...
TEAM TODOROKI'S LOCATION
IF YOU FIND YOURSELF OVER-WHELMED BY MY POWER...
...FLEEING AND CALLING FOR HELP MIGHT BE YOUR WISEST OPTION.
?
TODOROKI... YOU OF ALL PEOPLE SHOULD UNDERSTAND THAT. THE ***OTHER TWO*** AS WELL...
FORGET FIGHTING BACK! JUST GET OUT OF HERE!!
TEAM IDA'S LOCATION

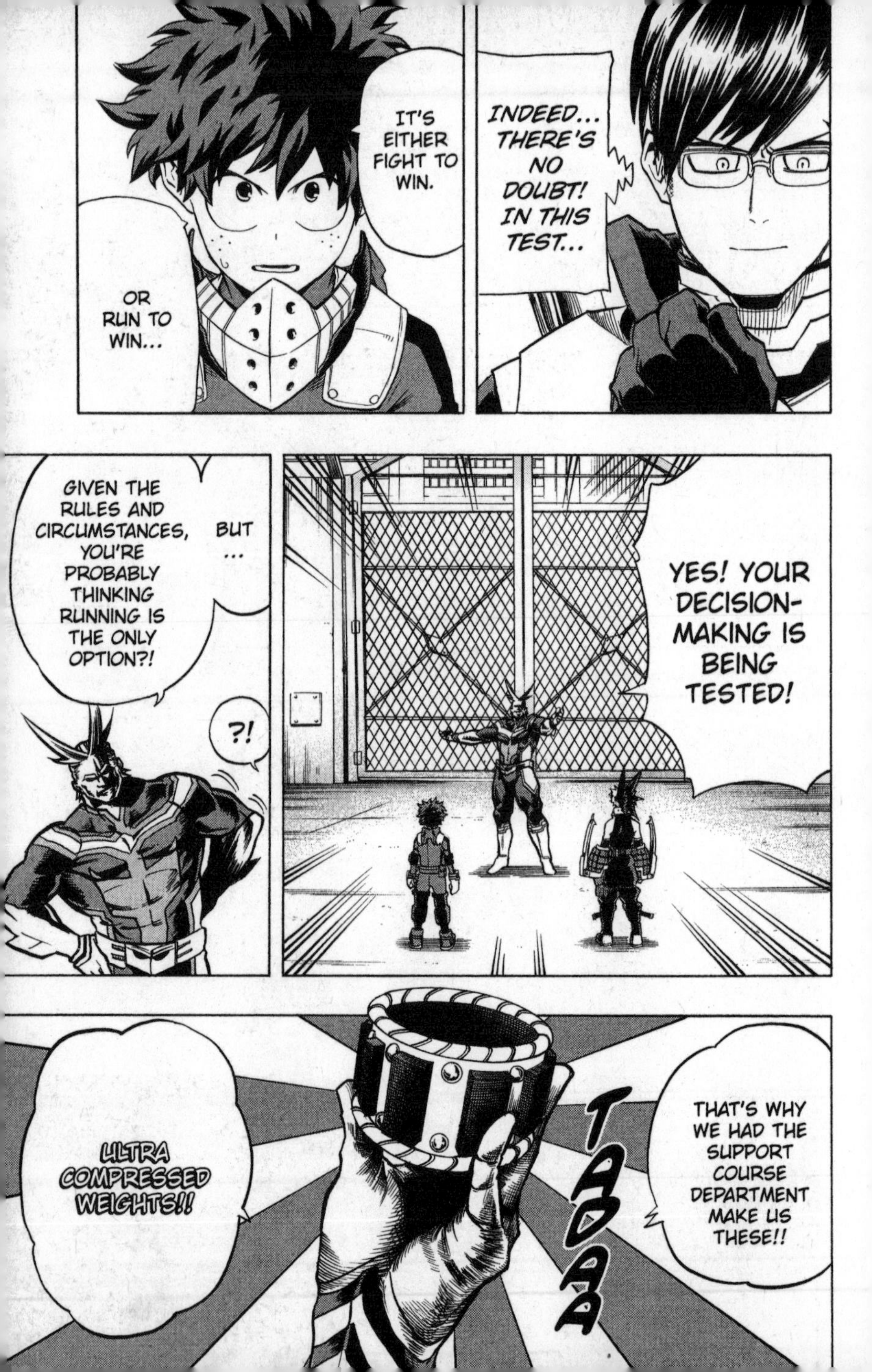
INDEED... THERE'S NO DOUBT! IN THIS TEST...
IT'S EITHER FIGHT TO WIN.
OR RUN TO WIN...
YES! YOUR DECISION-MAKING IS BEING TESTED!
BUT ...
GIVEN THE RULES AND CIRCUMSTANCES, YOU'RE PROBABLY THINKING RUNNING IS THE ONLY OPTION?!
?!
THAT'S WHY WE HAD THE SUPPORT COURSE DEPARTMENT MAKE US THESE!!
TADAA
ULTRA COMPRESSED WEIGHTS!!

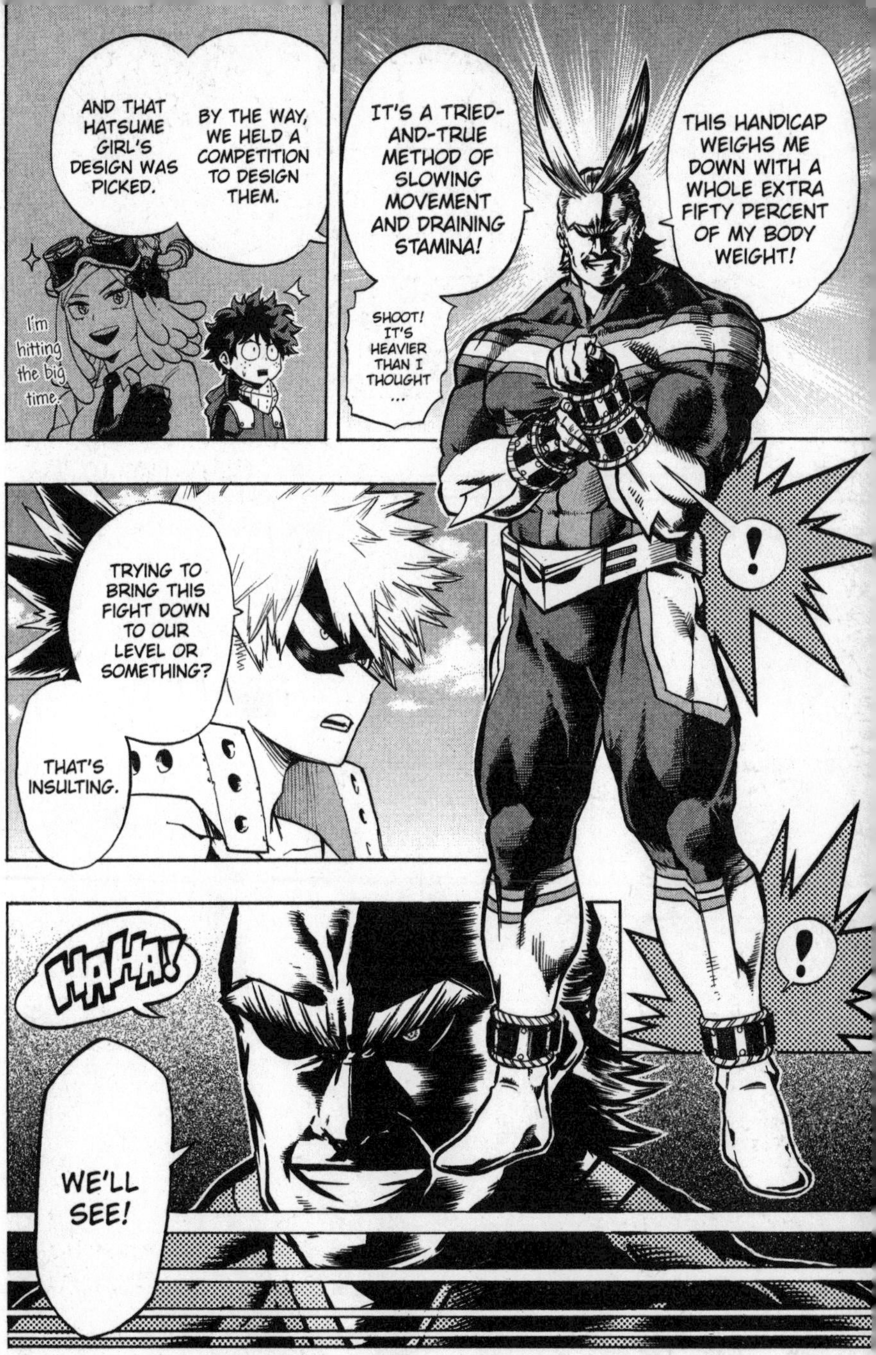
THIS HANDICAP WEIGHS ME DOWN WITH A WHOLE EXTRA FIFTY PERCENT OF MY BODY WEIGHT!
IT'S A TRIED-AND-TRUE METHOD OF SLOWING MOVEMENT AND DRAINING STAMINA!
SHOOT! IT'S HEAVIER THAN I THOUGHT...
BY THE WAY, WE HELD A COMPETITION TO DESIGN THEM.
AND THAT HATSUME GIRL'S DESIGN WAS PICKED.
I'm hitting the big time.
!
TRYING TO BRING THIS FIGHT DOWN TO OUR LEVEL OR SOMETHING?
THAT'S INSULTING.
!
HAHA!
WE'LL SEE!

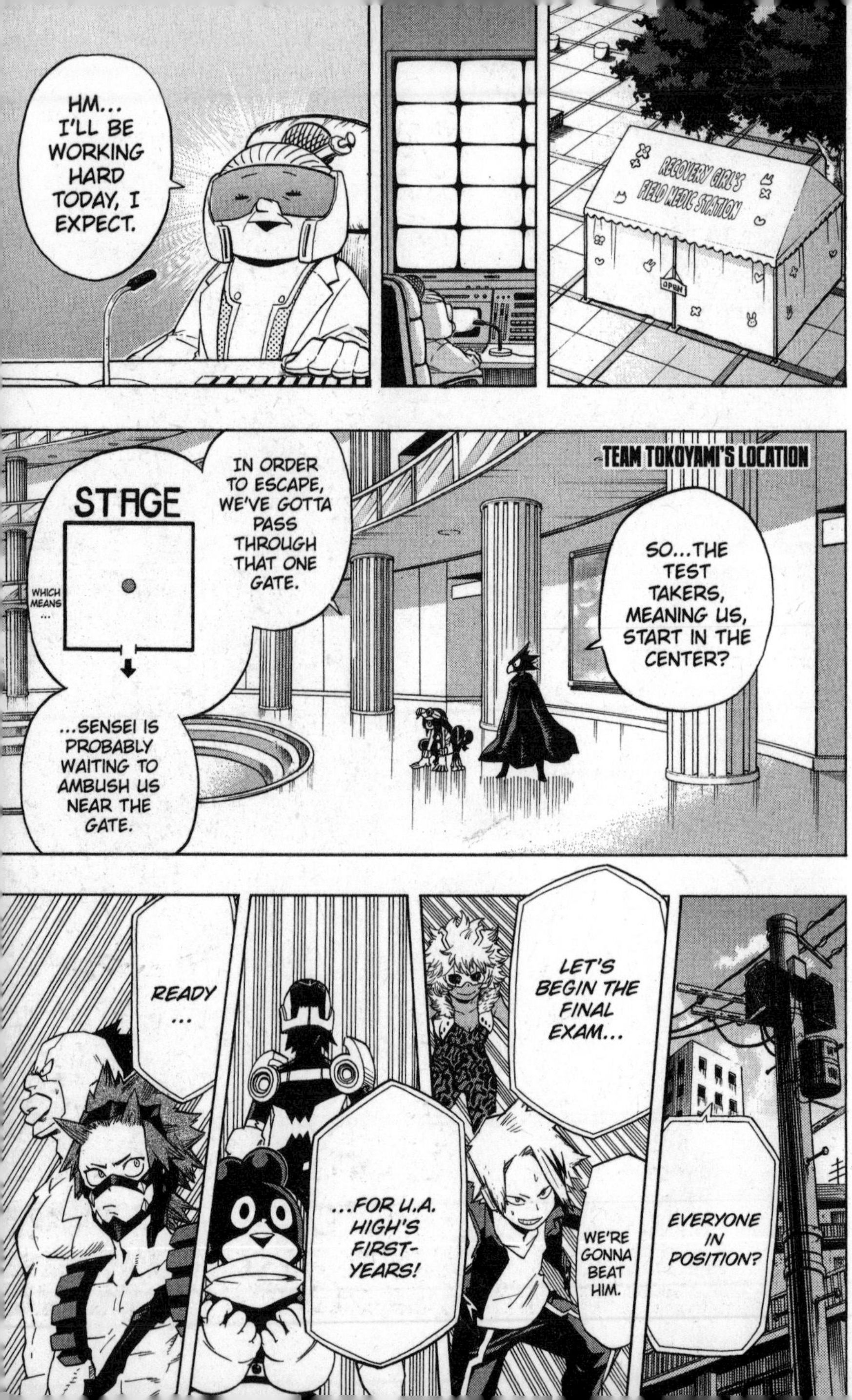
RECOVERY GIRL'S FIELD MEDIC STATION
OPEN
HM... I'LL BE WORKING HARD TODAY, I EXPECT.
TEAM TOKOYAMI'S LOCATION
SO...THE TEST TAKERS, MEANING US, START IN THE CENTER?
IN ORDER TO ESCAPE, WE'VE GOTTA PASS THROUGH THAT ONE GATE.
STAGE
WHICH MEANS...
...SENSEI IS PROBABLY WAITING TO AMBUSH US NEAR THE GATE.
EVERYONE IN POSITION?
WE'RE GONNA BEAT HIM.
LET'S BEGIN THE FINAL EXAM...
...FOR U.A. HIGH'S FIRST-YEARS!
READY...

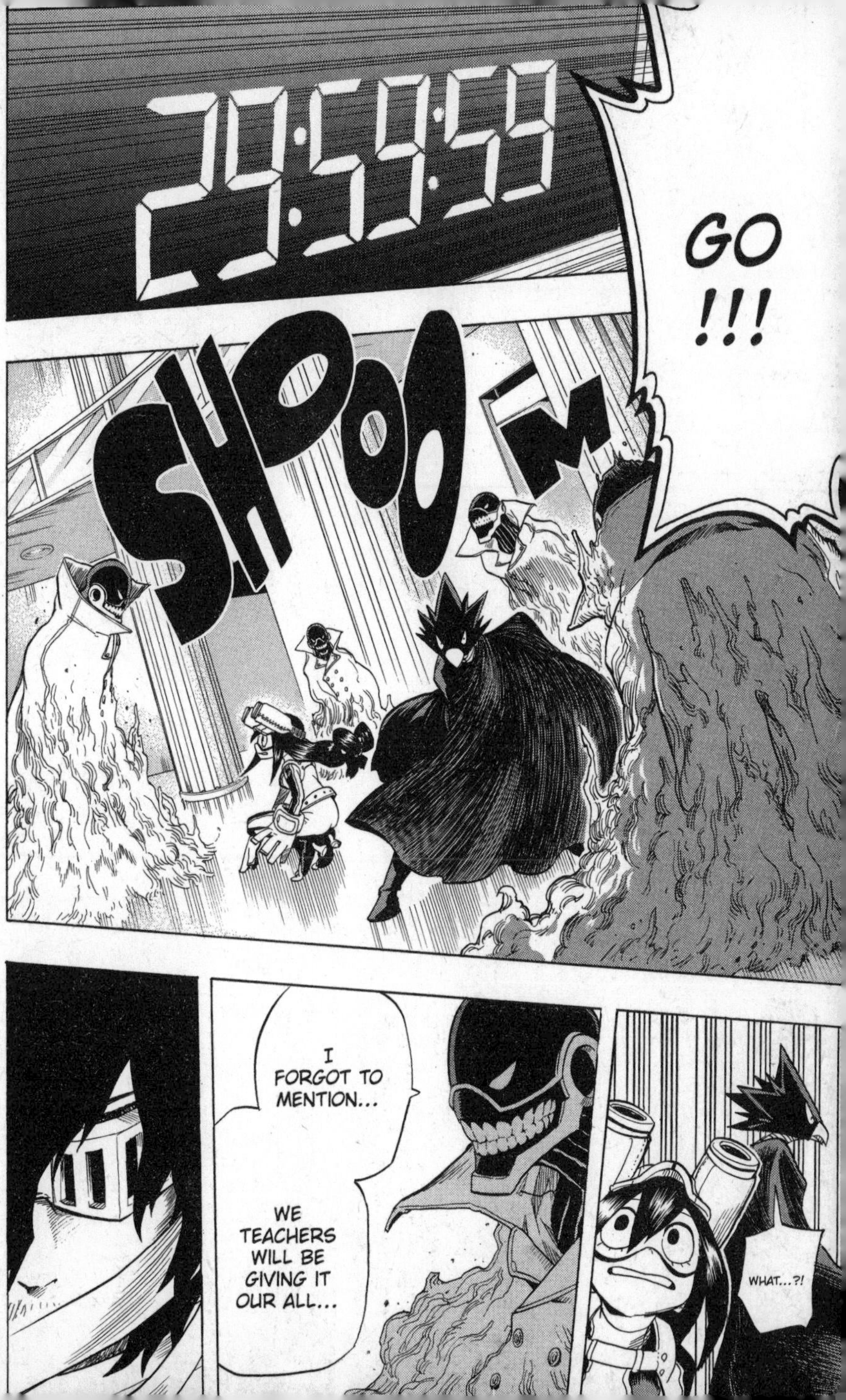
29:59:59
GO !!!
SHOOM
WHAT...?!
I FORGOT TO MENTION...
WE TEACHERS WILL BE GIVING IT OUR ALL...

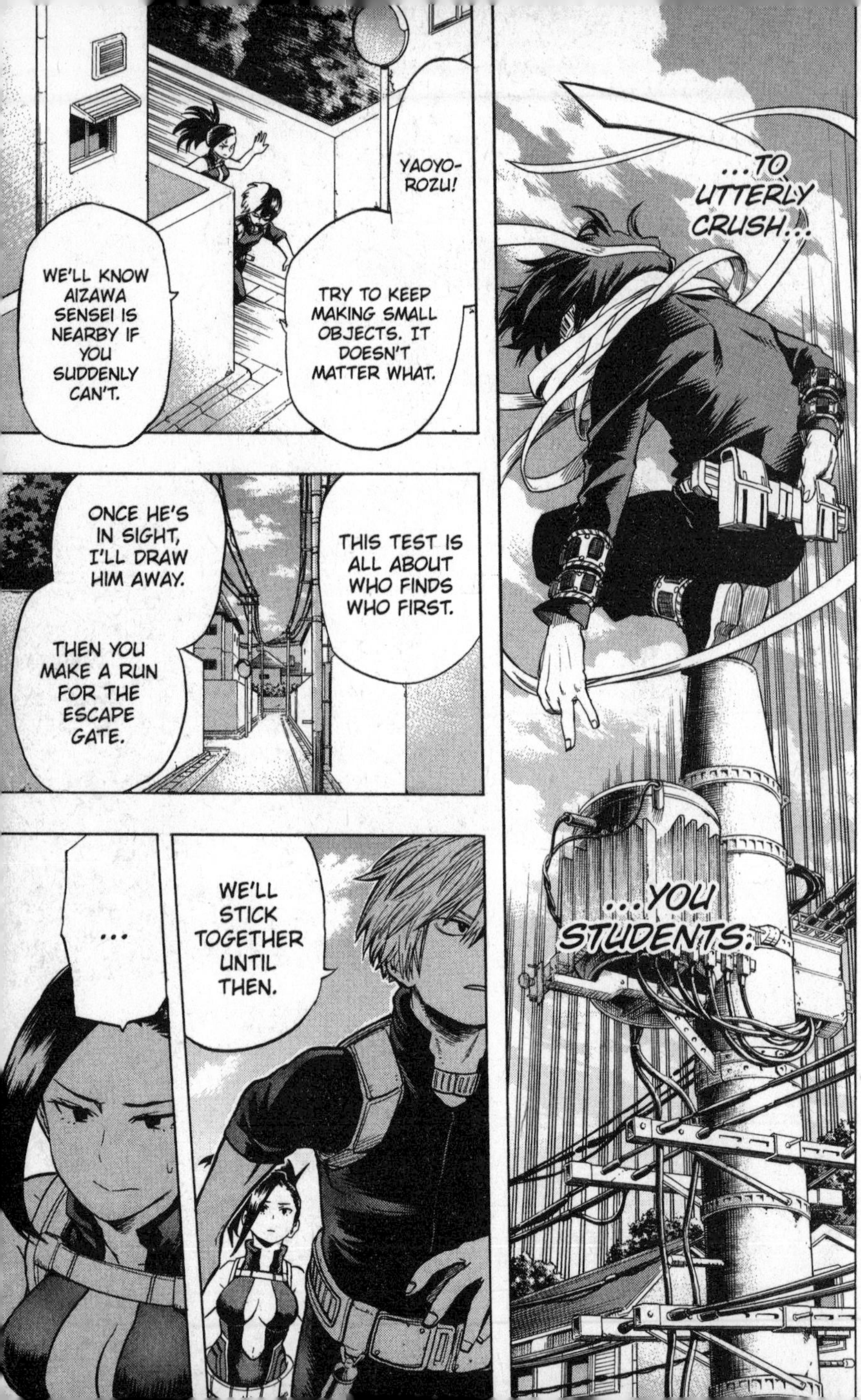
...TO UTTERLY CRUSH...
...YOU STUDENTS.
YAOYO-ROZU!
TRY TO KEEP MAKING SMALL OBJECTS. IT DOESN'T MATTER WHAT.
WE'LL KNOW AIZAWA SENSEI IS NEARBY IF YOU SUDDENLY CAN'T.
THIS TEST IS ALL ABOUT WHO FINDS WHO FIRST.
ONCE HE'S IN SIGHT, I'LL DRAW HIM AWAY.
THEN YOU MAKE A RUN FOR THE ESCAPE GATE.
WE'LL STICK TOGETHER UNTIL THEN.
...

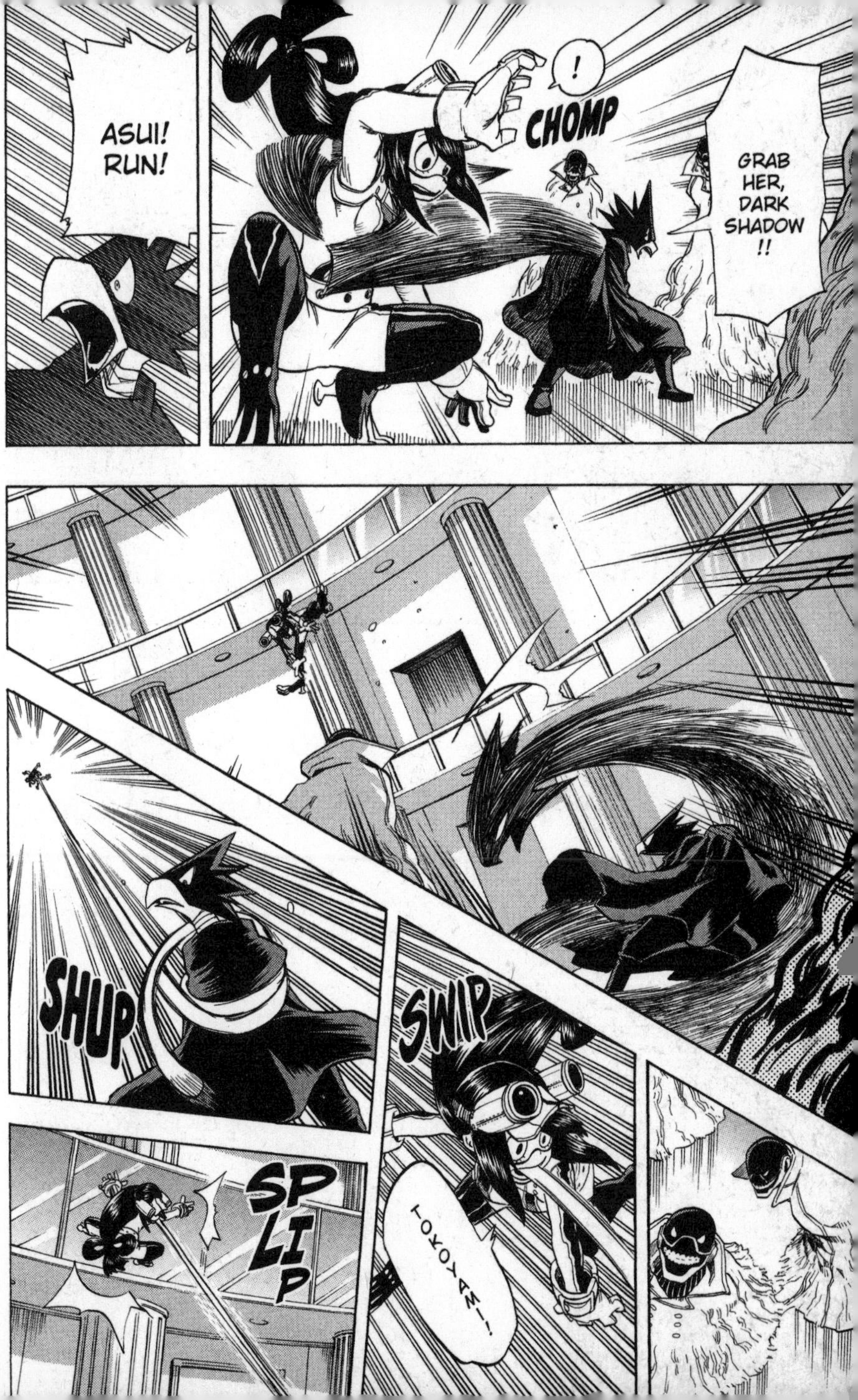
GRAB HER, DARK SHADOW !!
!
CHOMP
ASUI! RUN!
SHUP
SWIP
TOKOYAMI!!
SPLIP

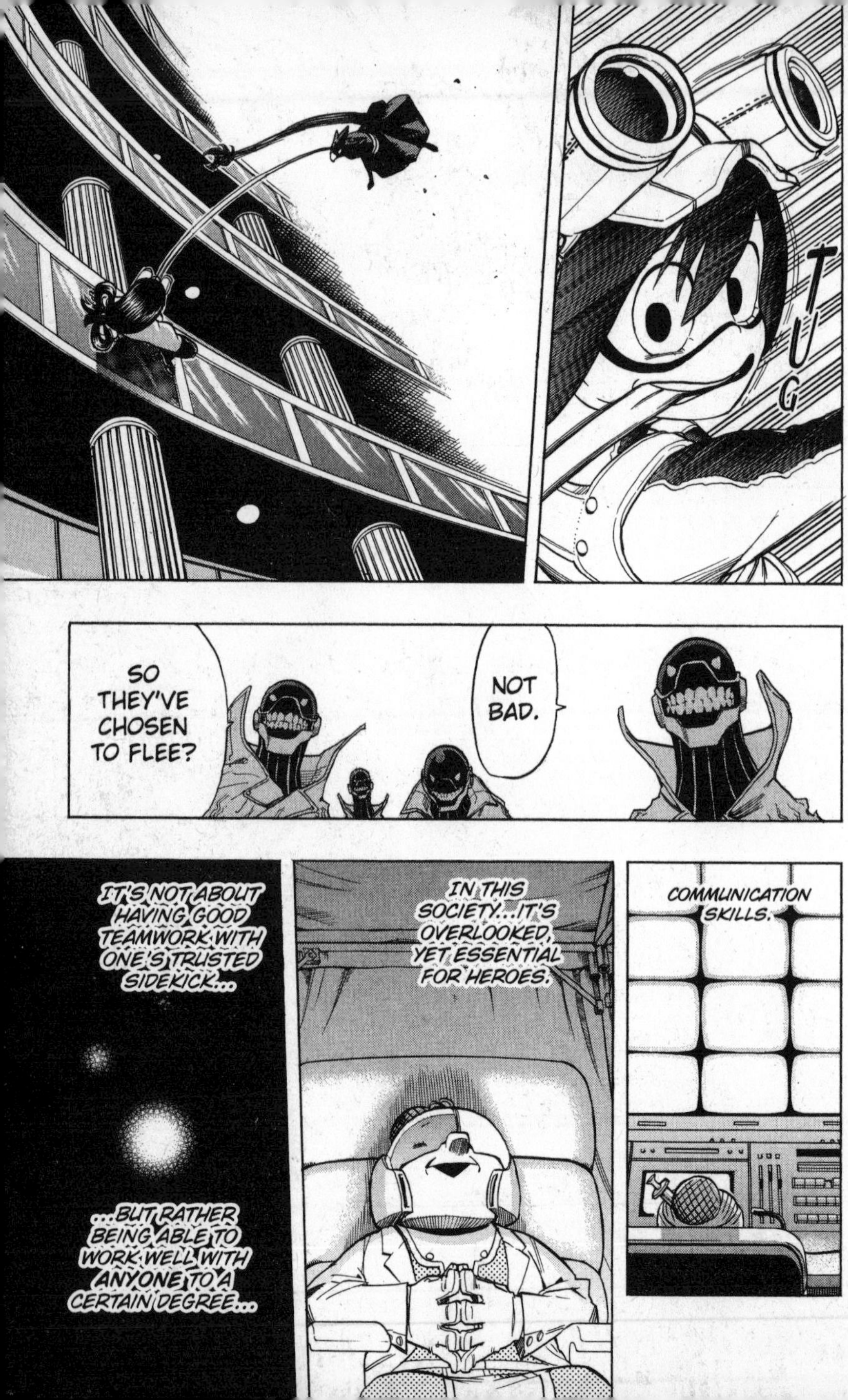
TUG
NOT BAD.
SO THEY'VE CHOSEN TO FLEE?
COMMUNICATION SKILLS.
IN THIS SOCIETY...IT'S OVERLOOKED, YET ESSENTIAL FOR HEROES.
IT'S NOT ABOUT HAVING GOOD TEAMWORK WITH ONE'S TRUSTED SIDEKICK...
...BUT RATHER BEING ABLE TO WORK WELL WITH ANYONE TO A CERTAIN DEGREE...

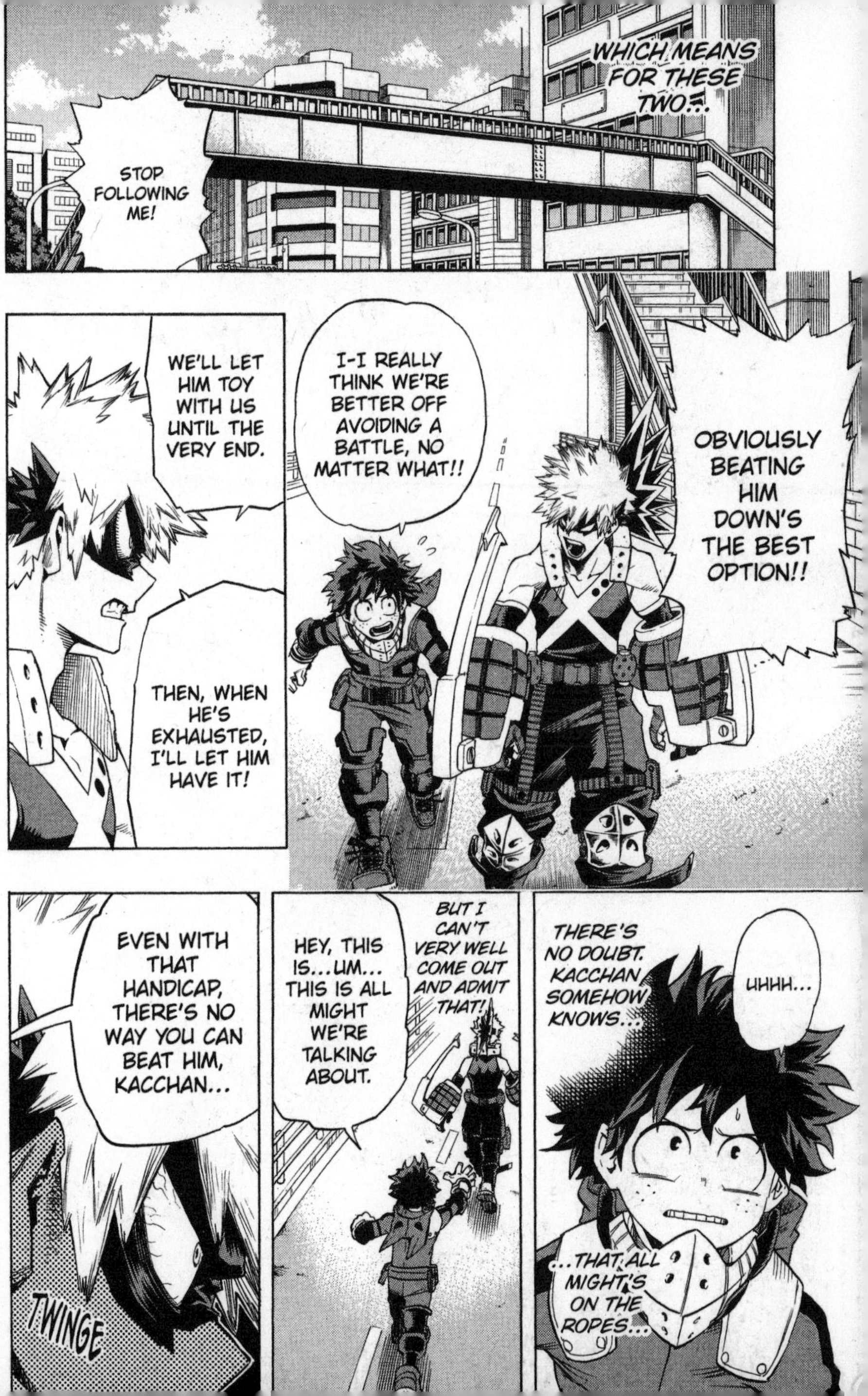
WHICH MEANS FOR THESE TWO...
STOP FOLLOWING ME!
OBVIOUSLY BEATING HIM DOWN'S THE BEST OPTION!!
I-I REALLY THINK WE'RE BETTER OFF AVOIDING A BATTLE, NO MATTER WHAT!!
WE'LL LET HIM TOY WITH US UNTIL THE VERY END.
THEN, WHEN HE'S EXHAUSTED, I'LL LET HIM HAVE IT!
UHHH...
THERE'S NO DOUBT. KACCHAN SOMEHOW KNOWS...
...THAT ALL MIGHT'S ON THE ROPES...
BUT I CAN'T VERY WELL COME OUT AND ADMIT THAT!
HEY, THIS IS...UM... THIS IS ALL MIGHT WE'RE TALKING ABOUT.
EVEN WITH THAT HANDICAP, THERE'S NO WAY YOU CAN BEAT HIM, KACCHAN...
TWINGE

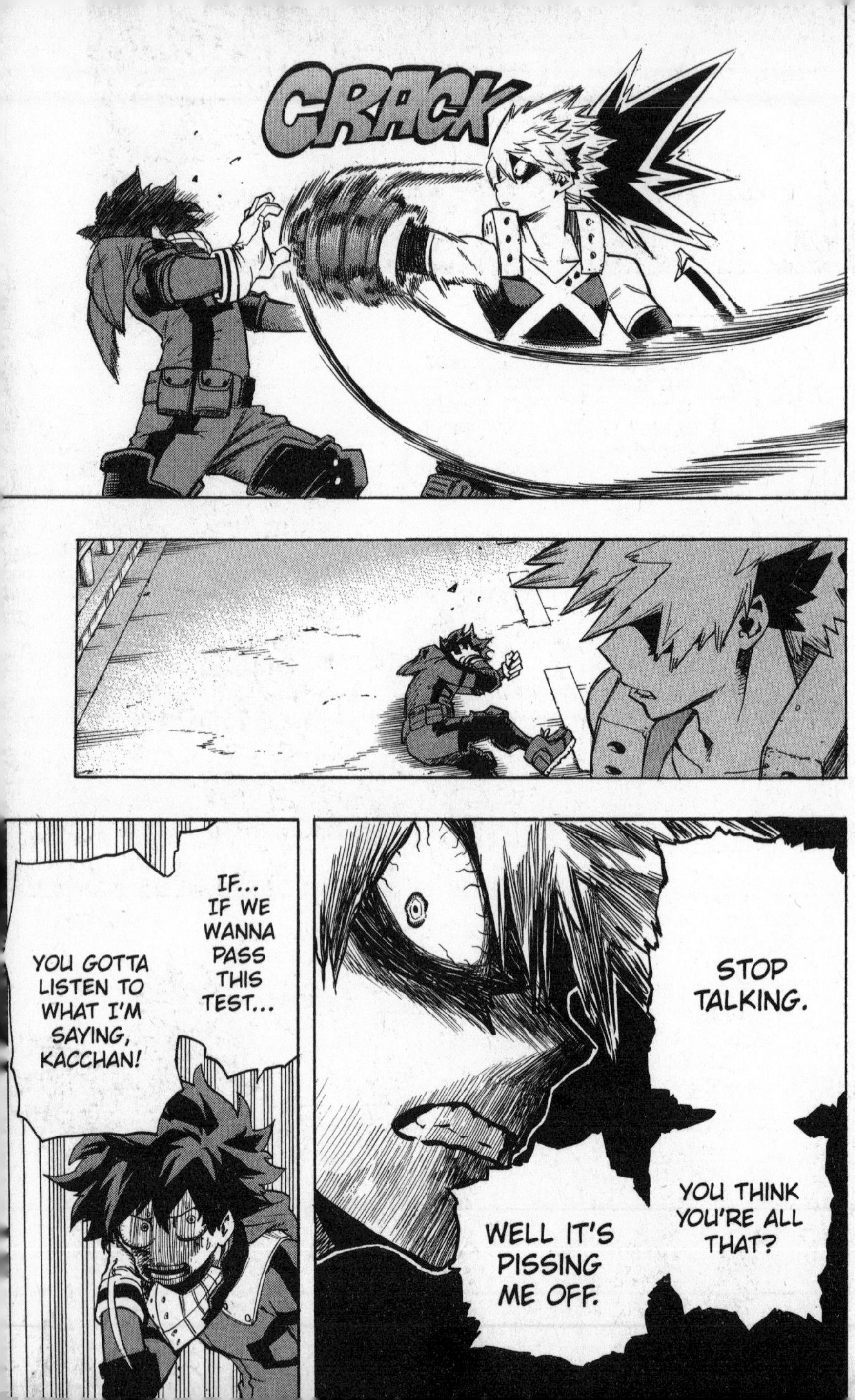
CRACK
STOP TALKING.
YOU THINK YOU'RE ALL THAT?
WELL IT'S PISSING ME OFF.
IF... IF WE WANNA PASS THIS TEST...
YOU GOTTA LISTEN TO WHAT I'M SAYING, KACCHAN!

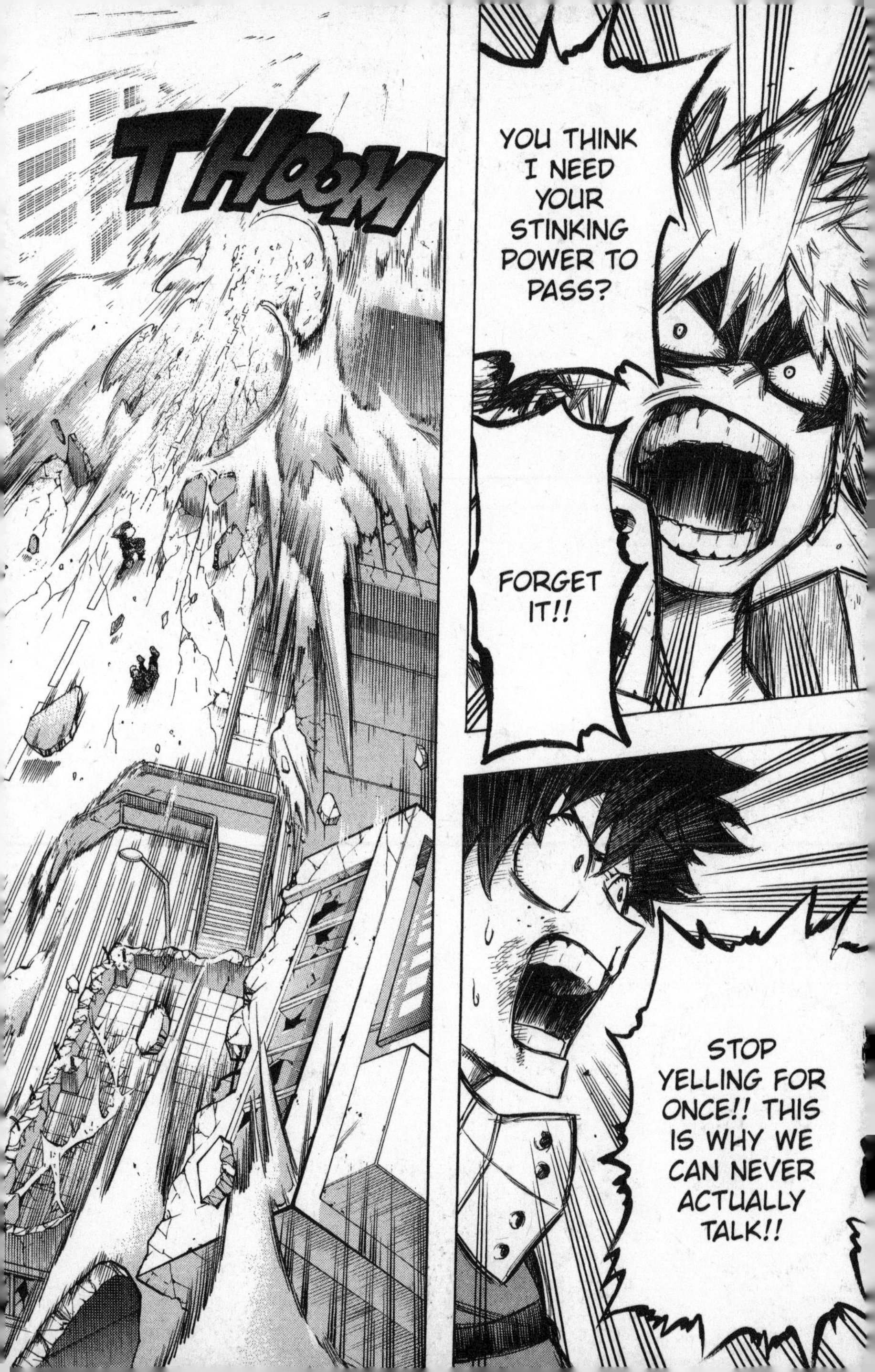
YOU THINK I NEED YOUR STINKING POWER TO PASS?
FORGET IT!!
STOP YELLING FOR ONCE!! THIS IS WHY WE CAN NEVER ACTUALLY TALK!!
THOOM

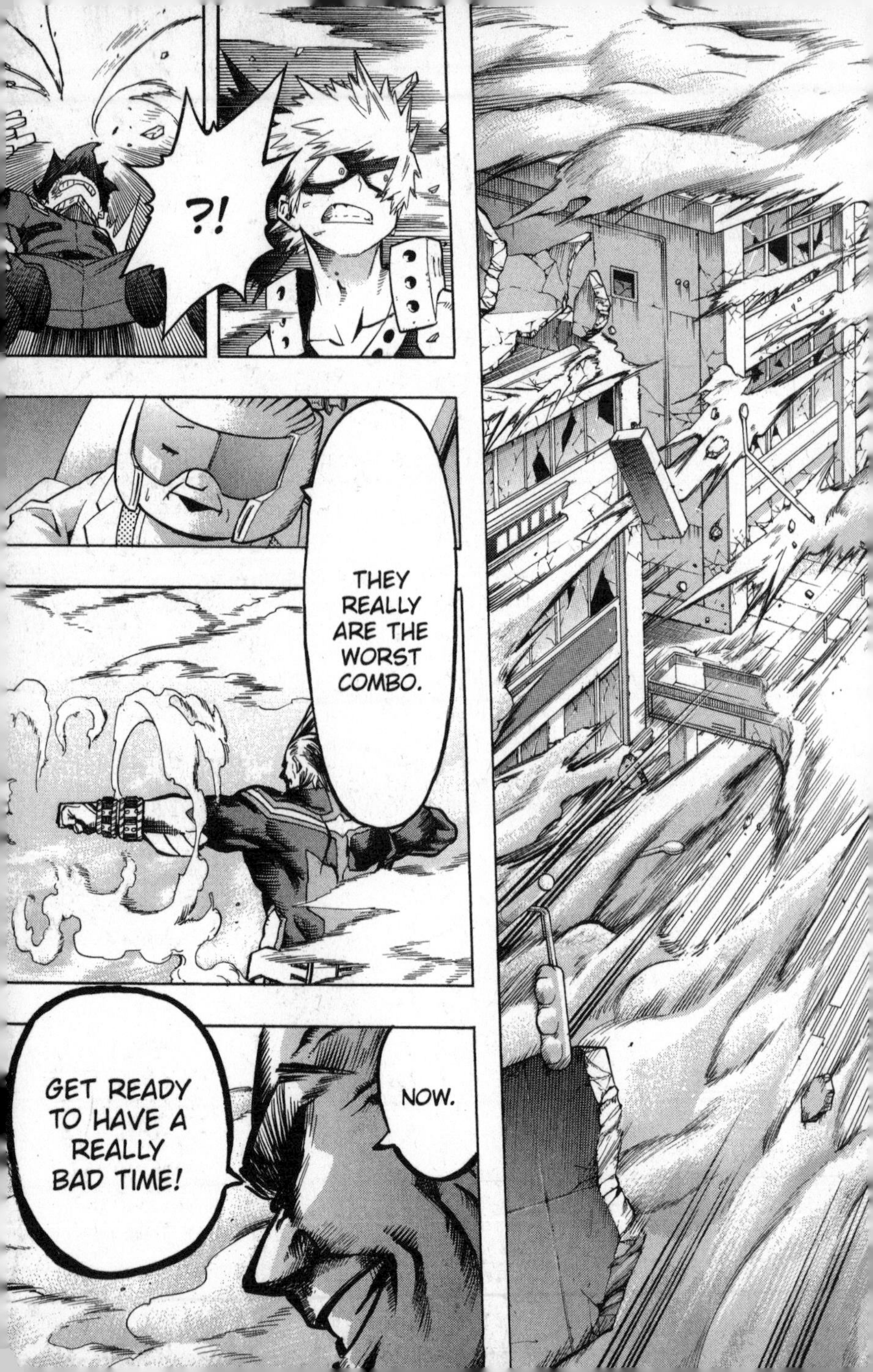
?!
THEY REALLY ARE THE WORST COMBO.
NOW.
GET READY TO HAVE A REALLY BAD TIME!

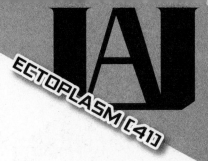

STREET CLOTHES

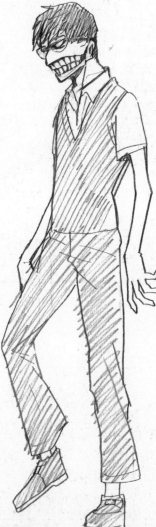

Birthday: 3/23
Height: 180 cm
Favorite Thing: Karaoke

THE SUPPLEMENT

A while back, he lost his legs to a certain villain.

In off-hours, he uses ordinary prosthetic legs, but while in costume, he uses special, light-weight ones meant for combat.

He may look scary, but after coming back from his loss with renewed persistence, this hero has received continued support.

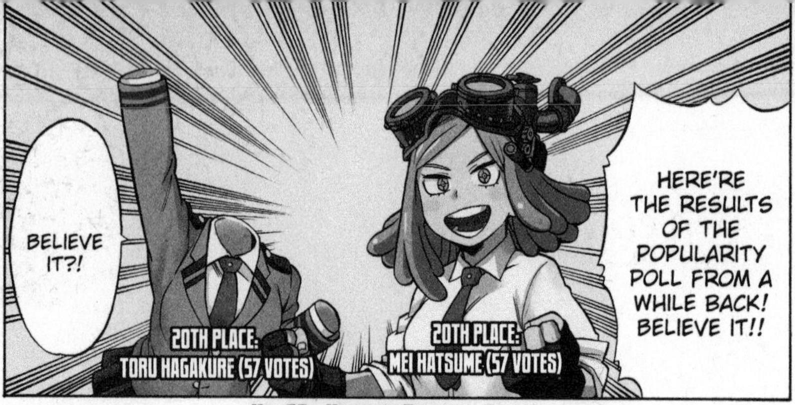
HERE'RE THE RESULTS OF THE POPULARITY POLL FROM A WHILE BACK! BELIEVE IT!!
20TH PLACE: MEI HATSUME (57 VOTES)
20TH PLACE: TORU HAGAKURE (57 VOTES)
BELIEVE IT?!

No. 62 - Katsuki Bakugo: Origin

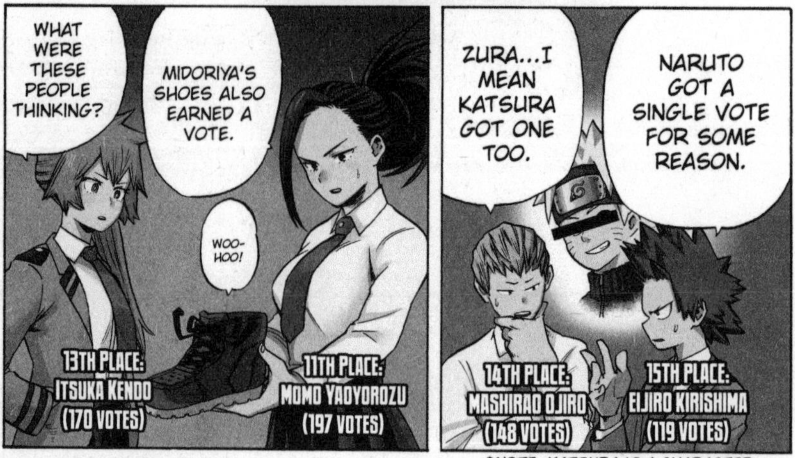
NARUTO GOT A SINGLE VOTE FOR SOME REASON.
ZURA...I MEAN KATSURA GOT ONE TOO.
15TH PLACE: EIJIRO KIRISHIMA (119 VOTES)
14TH PLACE: MASHIRAO OJIRO (148 VOTES)
MIDORIYA'S SHOES ALSO EARNED A VOTE.
WHAT WERE THESE PEOPLE THINKING?
WOO-HOO!
11TH PLACE: MOMO YAOYOROZU (197 VOTES)
13TH PLACE: ITSUKA KENDO (170 VOTES)

*NOTE: KATSURA IS A CHARACTER FROM THE SERIES GIN TAMA.

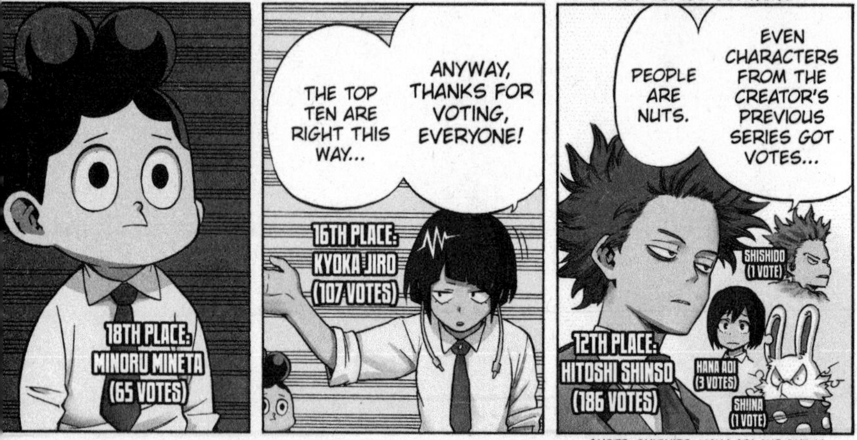
EVEN CHARACTERS FROM THE CREATOR'S PREVIOUS SERIES GOT VOTES...
PEOPLE ARE NUTS.
SHISHIDO (1 VOTE)
12TH PLACE: HITOSHI SHINSO (186 VOTES)
HANA AOI (3 VOTES)
SHIINA (1 VOTE)
ANYWAY, THANKS FOR VOTING, EVERYONE!
THE TOP TEN ARE RIGHT THIS WAY...
16TH PLACE: KYOKA JIRO (107 VOTES)
18TH PLACE: MINORU MINETA (65 VOTES)

*NOTE: SHISHIDO, HANA AOI AND SHIINA ARE CHARACTERS FROM HORIKOSHI SENSEI'S EARLIER WORK, OUMAGADOKI ZOO.

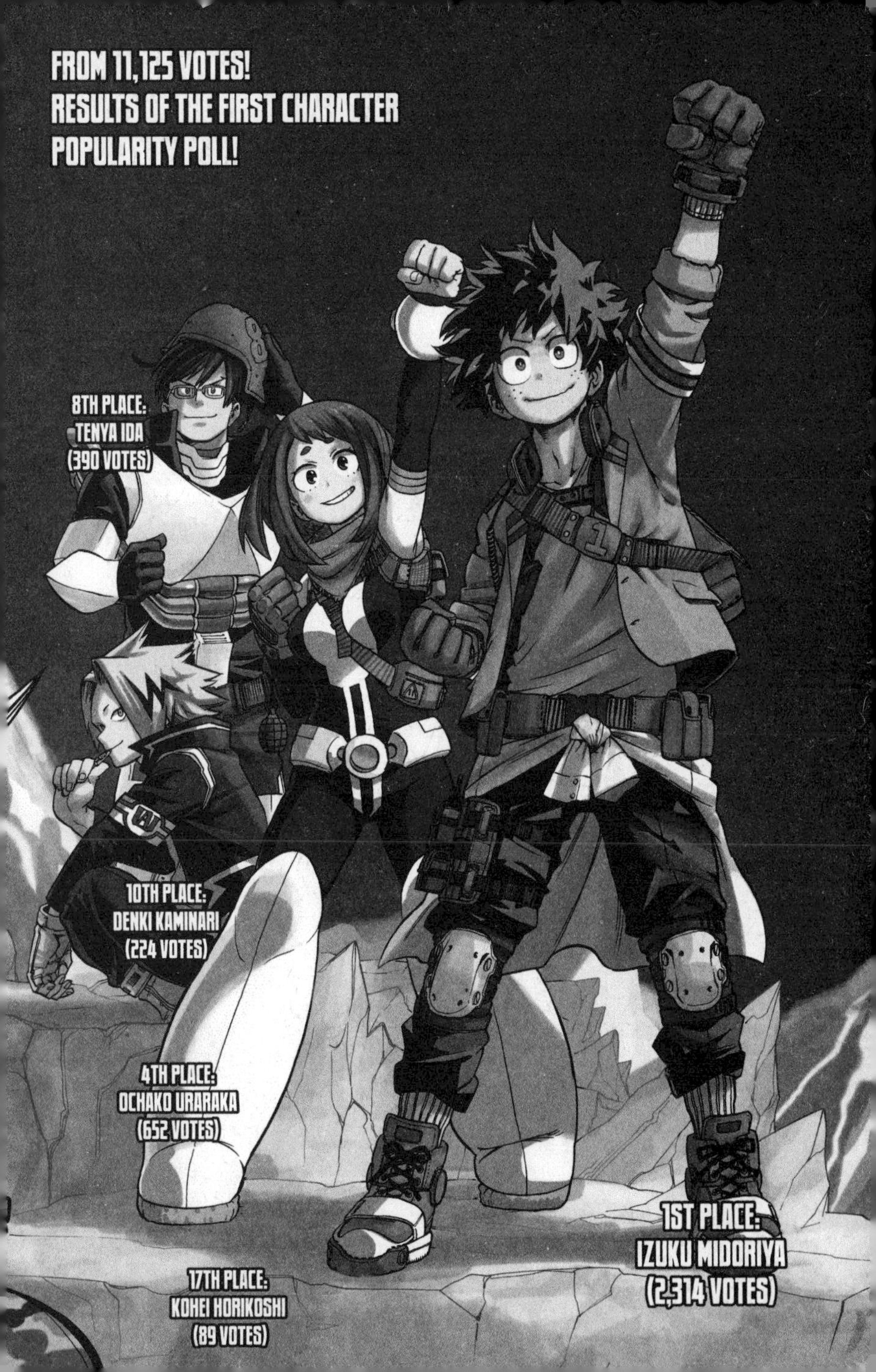
FROM 11,125 VOTES!
RESULTS OF THE FIRST CHARACTER
POPULARITY POLL!
8TH PLACE:
TENYA IDA
(390 VOTES)
10TH PLACE:
DENKI KAMINARI
(224 VOTES)
4TH PLACE:
OCHAKO URARAKA
(652 VOTES)
1ST PLACE:
IZUKU MIDORIYA
(2,314 VOTES)
17TH PLACE:
KOHEI HORIKOSHI
(89 VOTES)

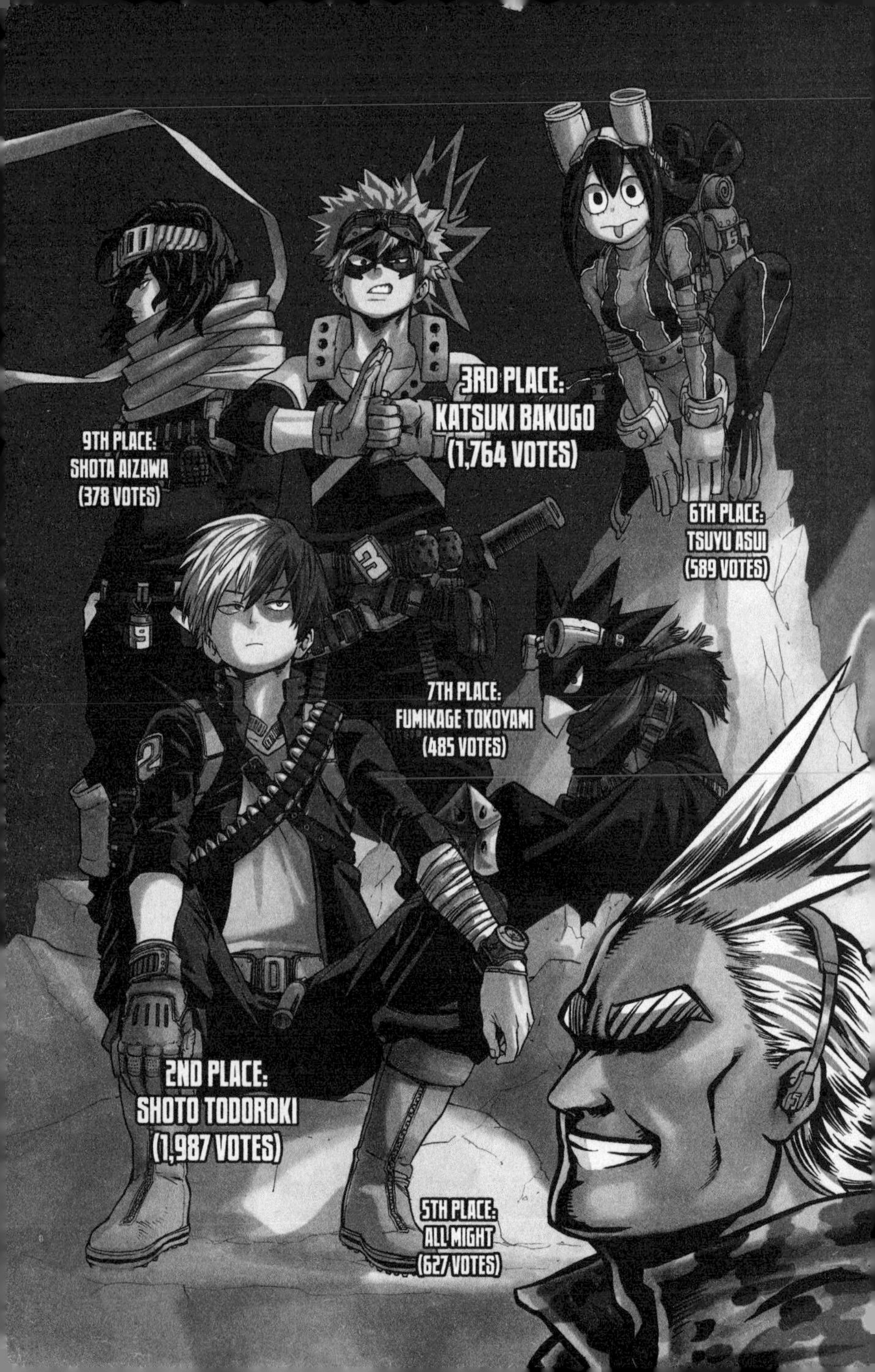
3RD PLACE:
KATSUKI BAKUGO
(1,764 VOTES)
6TH PLACE:
TSUYU ASUI
(589 VOTES)
9TH PLACE:
SHOTA AIZAWA
(378 VOTES)
7TH PLACE:
FUMIKAGE TOKOYAMI
(485 VOTES)
5TH PLACE:
ALL MIGHT
(627 VOTES)
2ND PLACE:
SHOTO TODOROKI
(1,987 VOTES)

MY HERO ACADEMIA

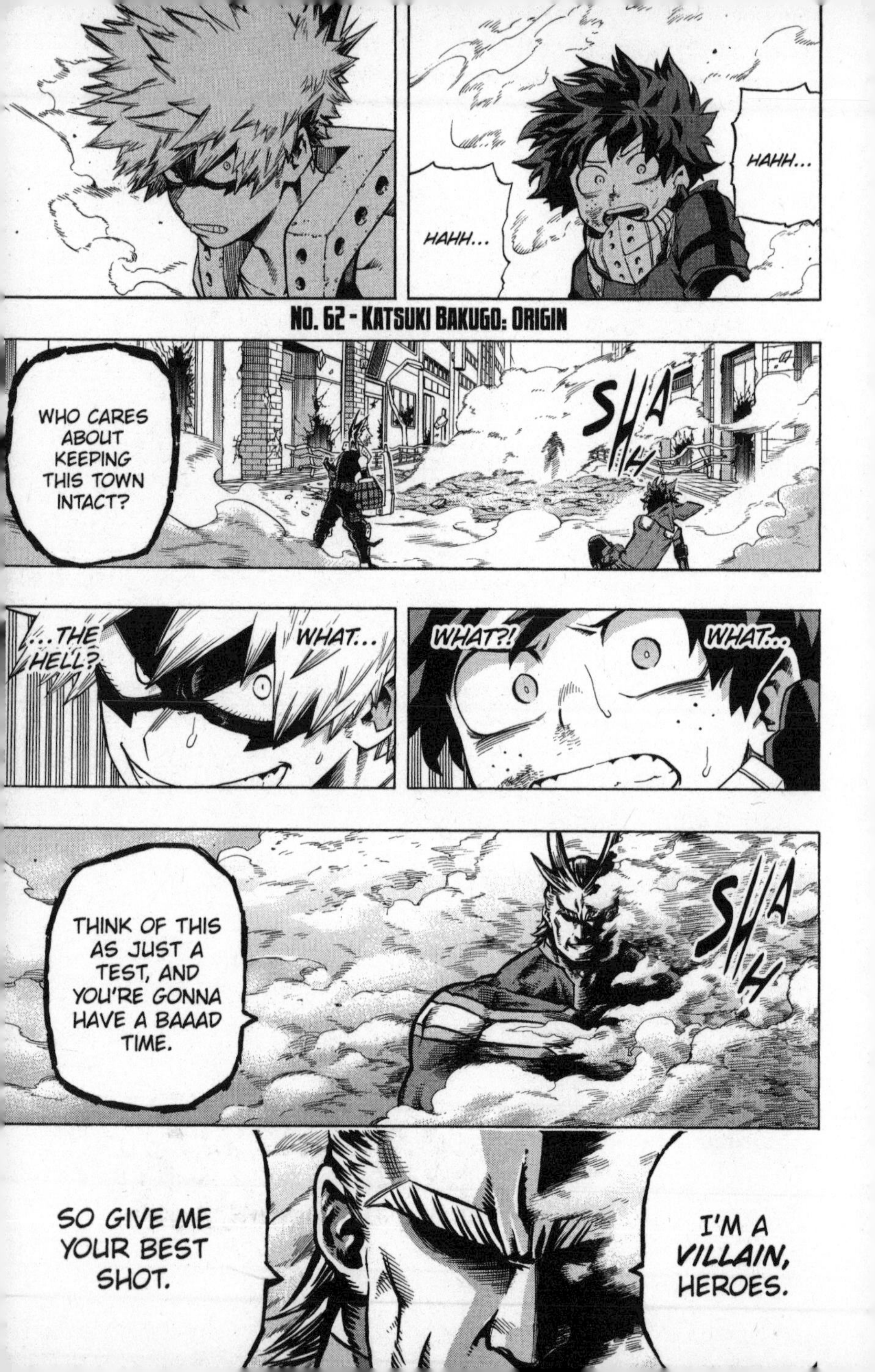
HAHH...
HAHH...
No. 62 - Katsuki Bakugo: Origin
WHO CARES ABOUT KEEPING THIS TOWN INTACT?
SHA
WHAT...
WHAT?!
WHAT...
...THE HELL?
SHA
THINK OF THIS AS JUST A TEST, AND YOU'RE GONNA HAVE A BAAAD TIME.
I'M A VILLAIN, HEROES.
SO GIVE ME YOUR BEST SHOT.

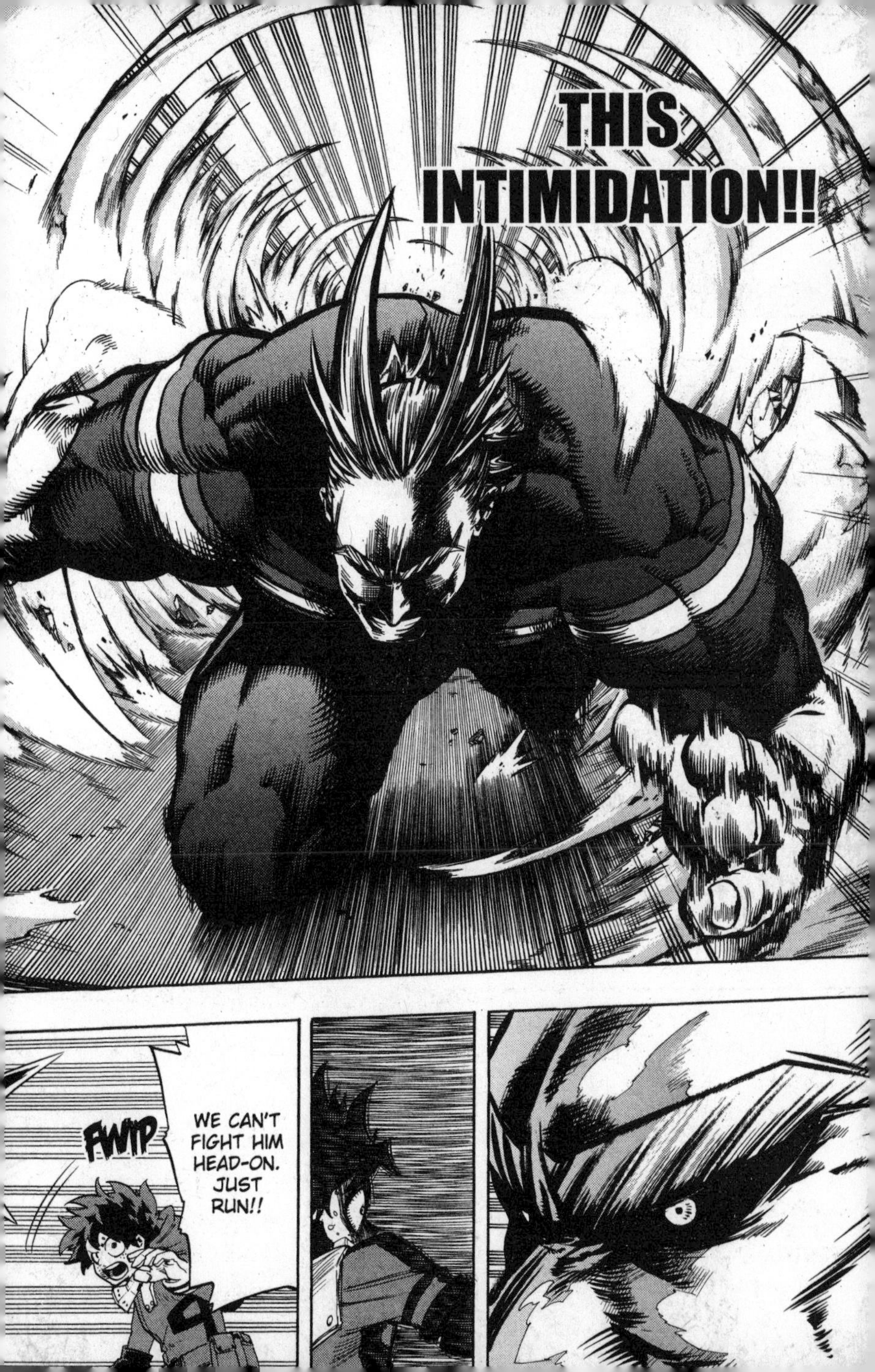
THIS INTIMIDATION!!
WE CAN'T FIGHT HIM HEAD-ON. JUST RUN!!
FWIP

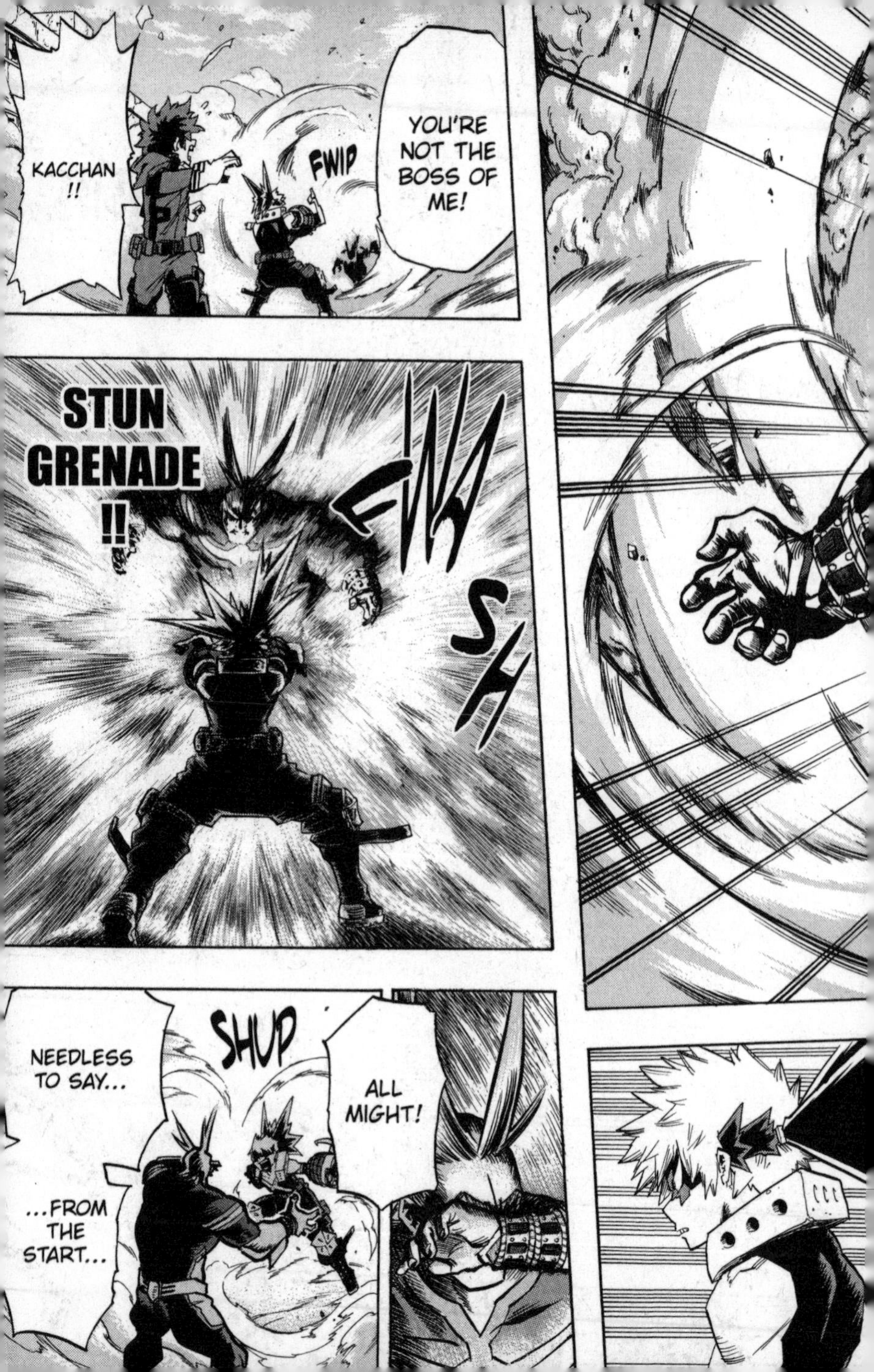

YOU'RE NOT THE BOSS OF ME!
FWIP
KACCHAN !!
FWASH
STUN GRENADE !!
ALL MIGHT!
SHUP
NEEDLESS TO SAY...
...FROM THE START...

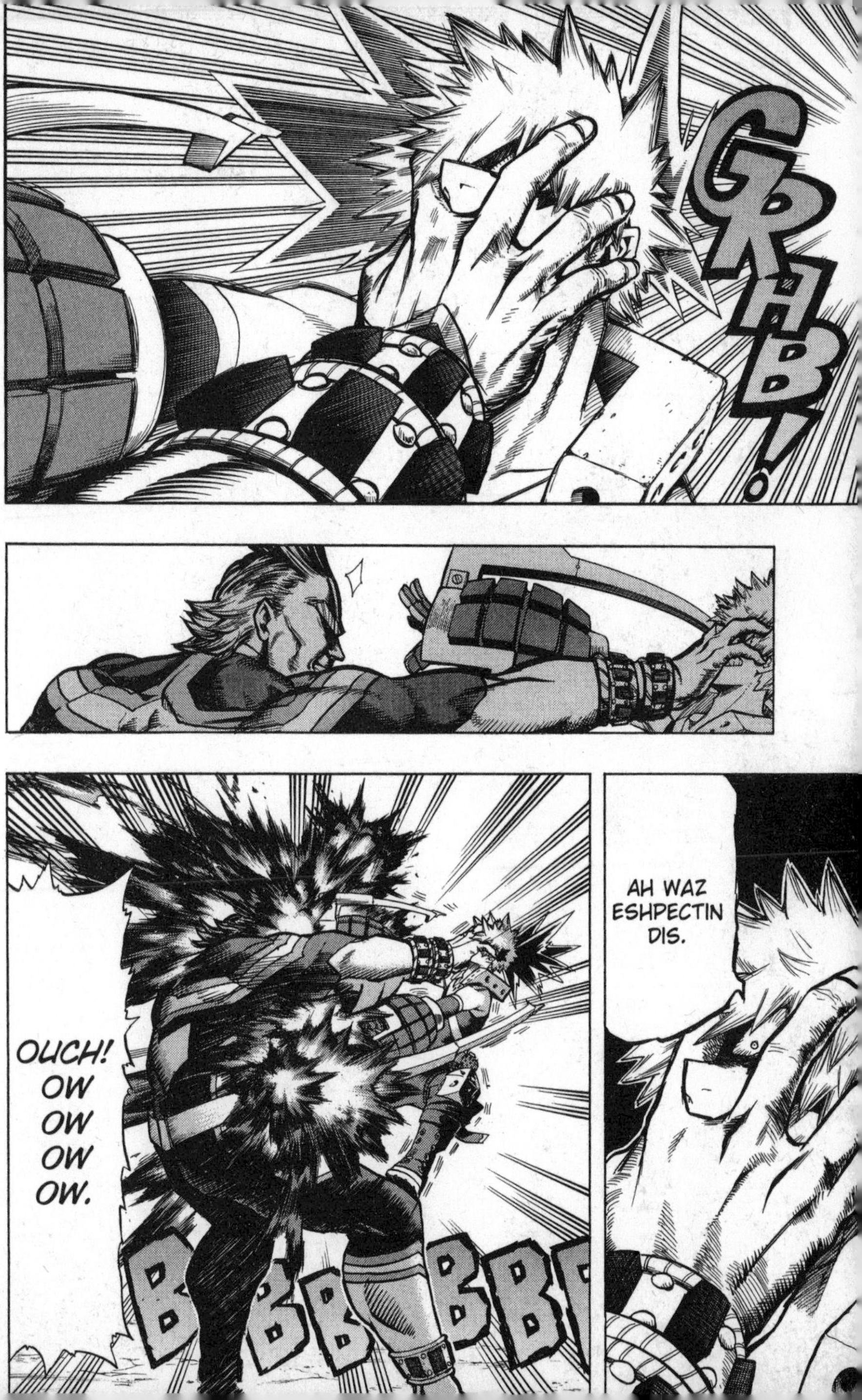
GRAB!
AH WAZ ESHPECTIN DIS.
OUCH! OW OW OW OW.
BBBBBBB

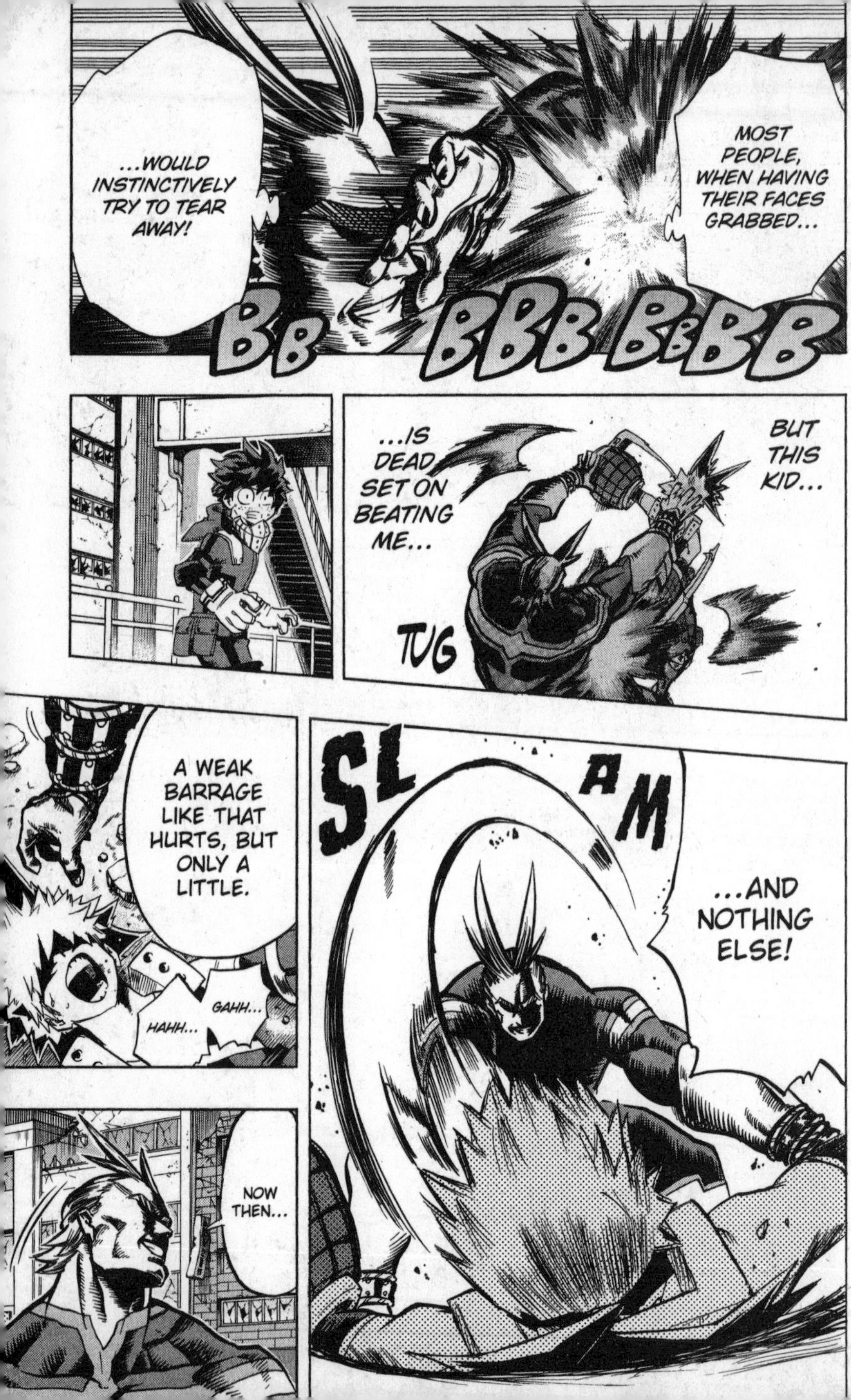
MOST PEOPLE, WHEN HAVING THEIR FACES GRABBED...
...WOULD INSTINCTIVELY TRY TO TEAR AWAY!
BB BBB BBBB
BUT THIS KID...
...IS DEAD SET ON BEATING ME...
TUG
SLAM
...AND NOTHING ELSE!
A WEAK BARRAGE LIKE THAT HURTS, BUT ONLY A LITTLE.
GAHH...
HAHH...
NOW THEN...

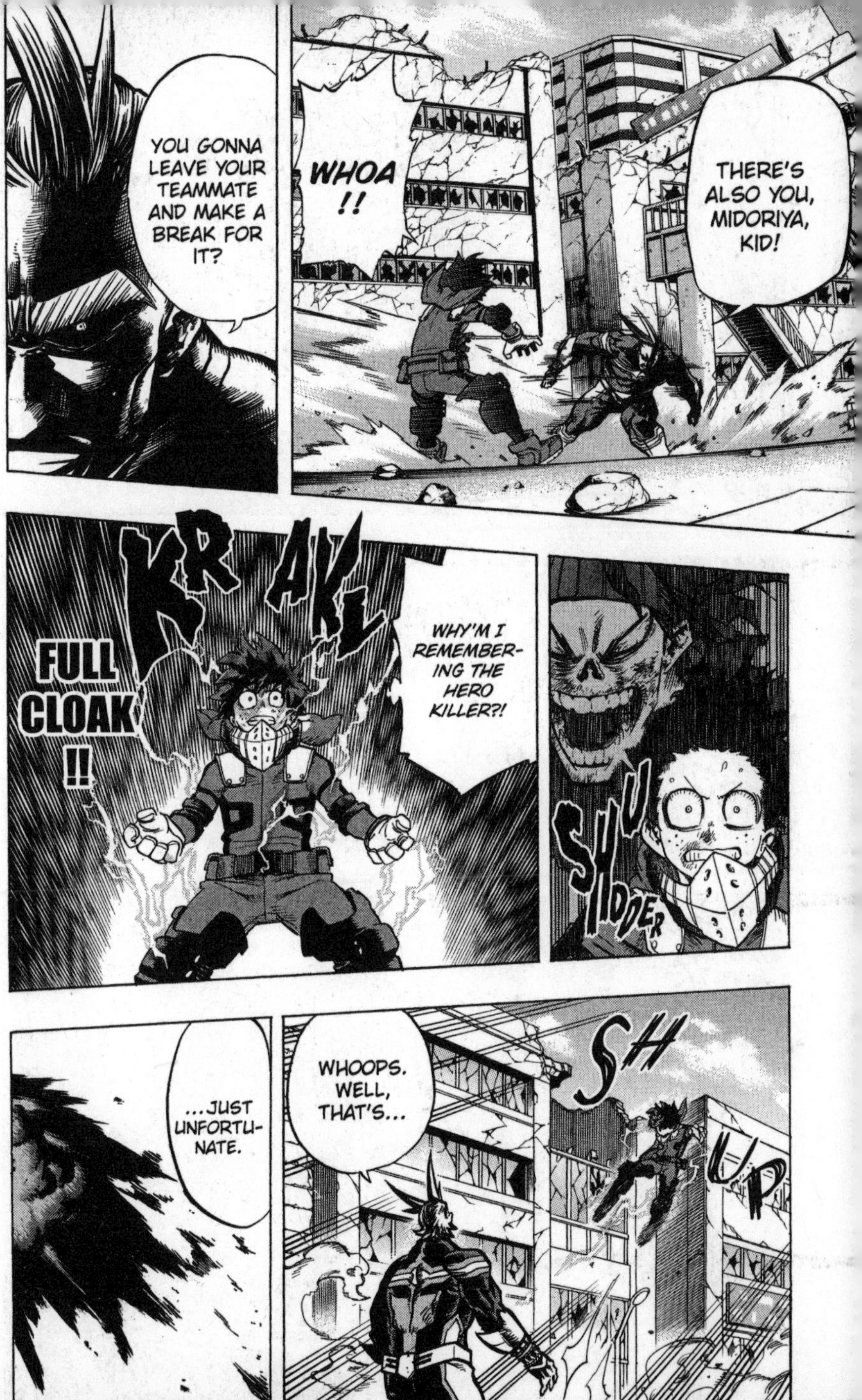
THERE'S ALSO YOU, MIDORIYA, KID!
WHOA!!
YOU GONNA LEAVE YOUR TEAMMATE AND MAKE A BREAK FOR IT?
SHUDDER
KRAKL
WHY'M I REMEMBERING THE HERO KILLER?!
FULL CLOAK!!
SHUP
WHOOPS. WELL, THAT'S...
...JUST UNFORTUNATE.

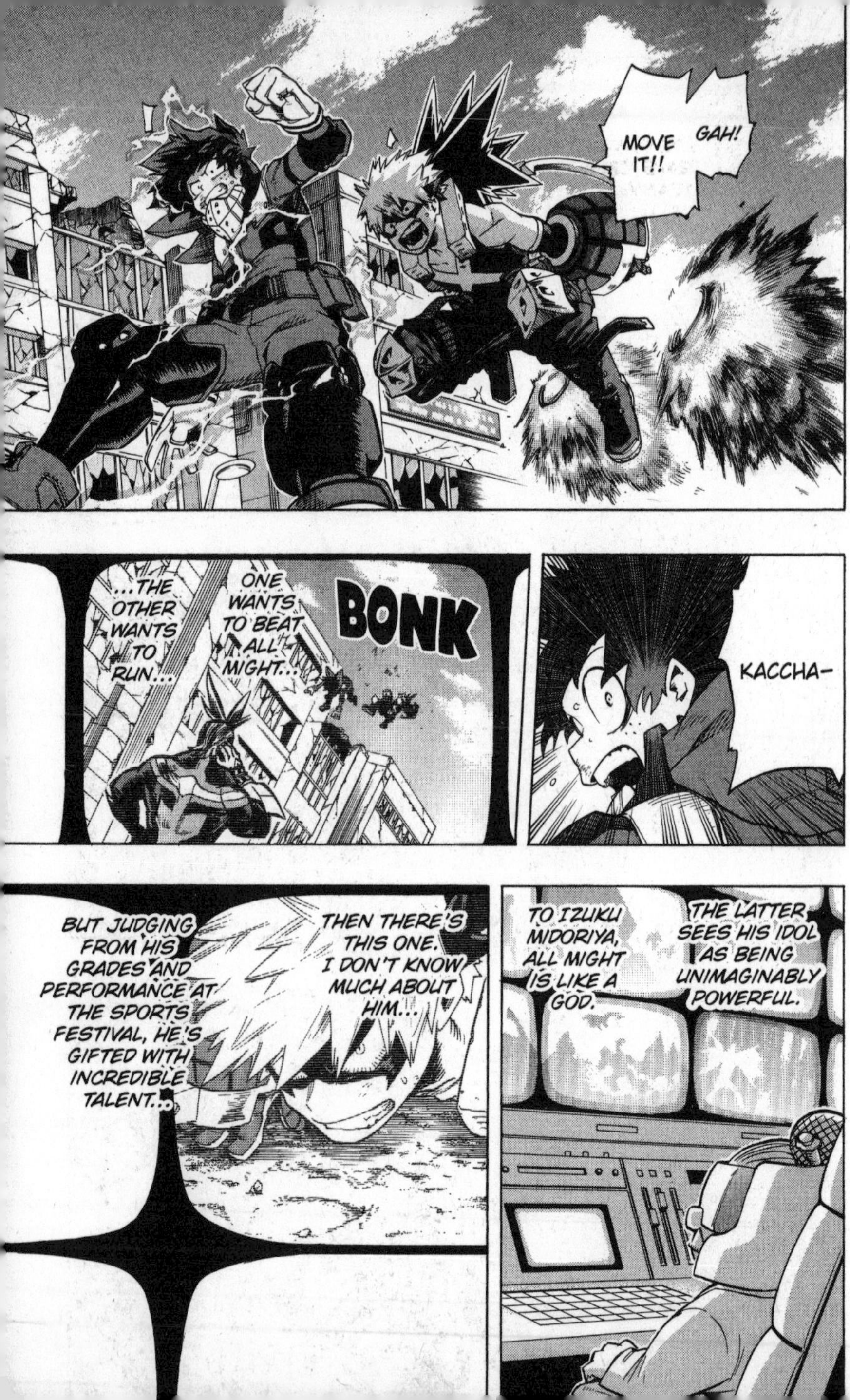
GAH!
MOVE IT!!
KACCHA-
BONK
ONE WANTS TO BEAT ALL MIGHT...
...THE OTHER WANTS TO RUN...
THE LATTER SEES HIS IDOL AS BEING UNIMAGINABLY POWERFUL.
TO IZUKU MIDORIYA, ALL MIGHT IS LIKE A GOD.
THEN THERE'S THIS ONE. I DON'T KNOW MUCH ABOUT HIM...
BUT JUDGING FROM HIS GRADES AND PERFORMANCE AT THE SPORTS FESTIVAL, HE'S GIFTED WITH INCREDIBLE TALENT...

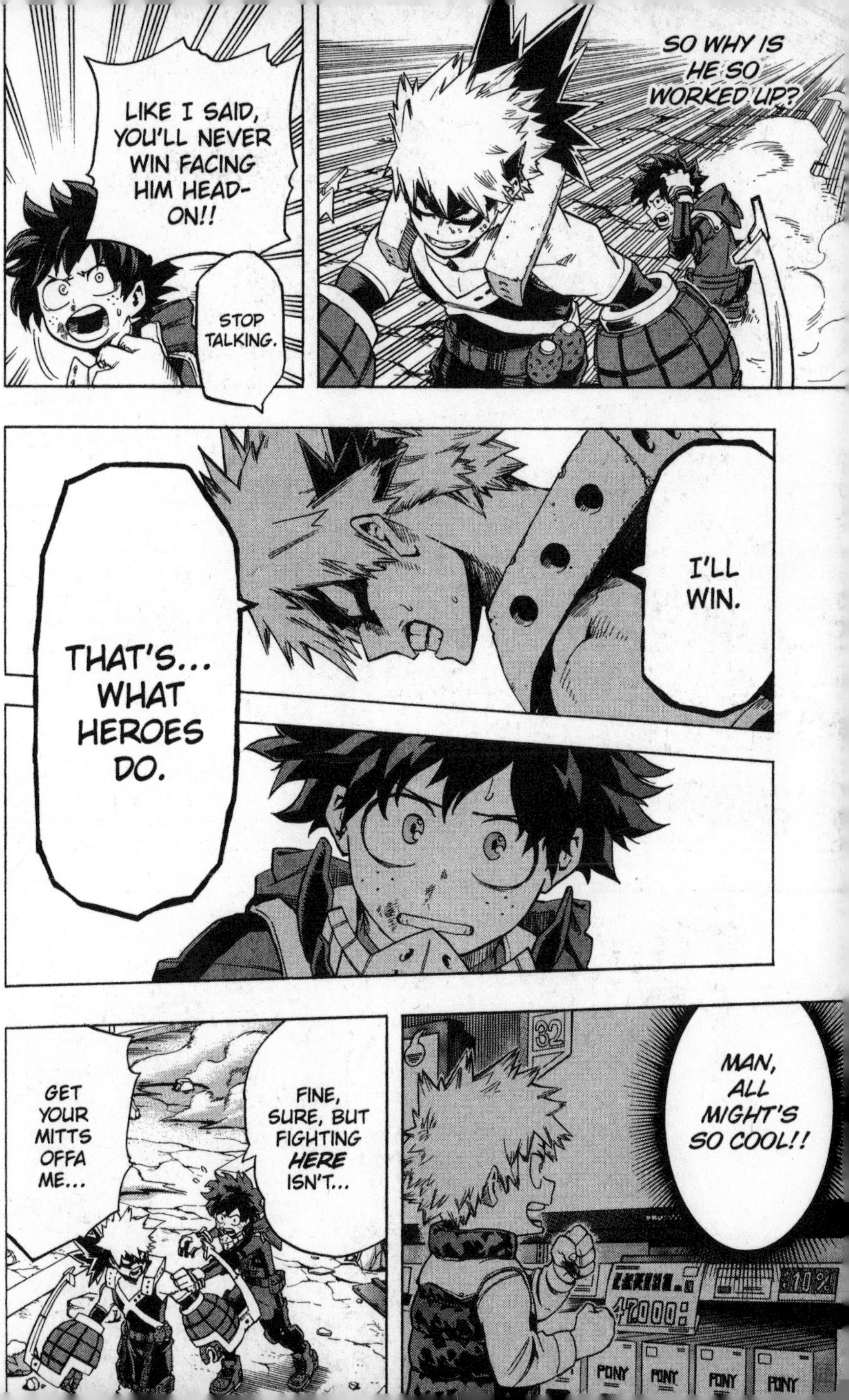
SO WHY IS HE SO WORKED UP?
LIKE I SAID, YOU'LL NEVER WIN FACING HIM HEAD-ON!!
STOP TALKING.
I'LL WIN.
THAT'S... WHAT HEROES DO.
MAN, ALL MIGHT'S SO COOL!!
FINE, SURE, BUT FIGHTING *HERE* ISN'T...
GET YOUR MITTS OFFA ME...

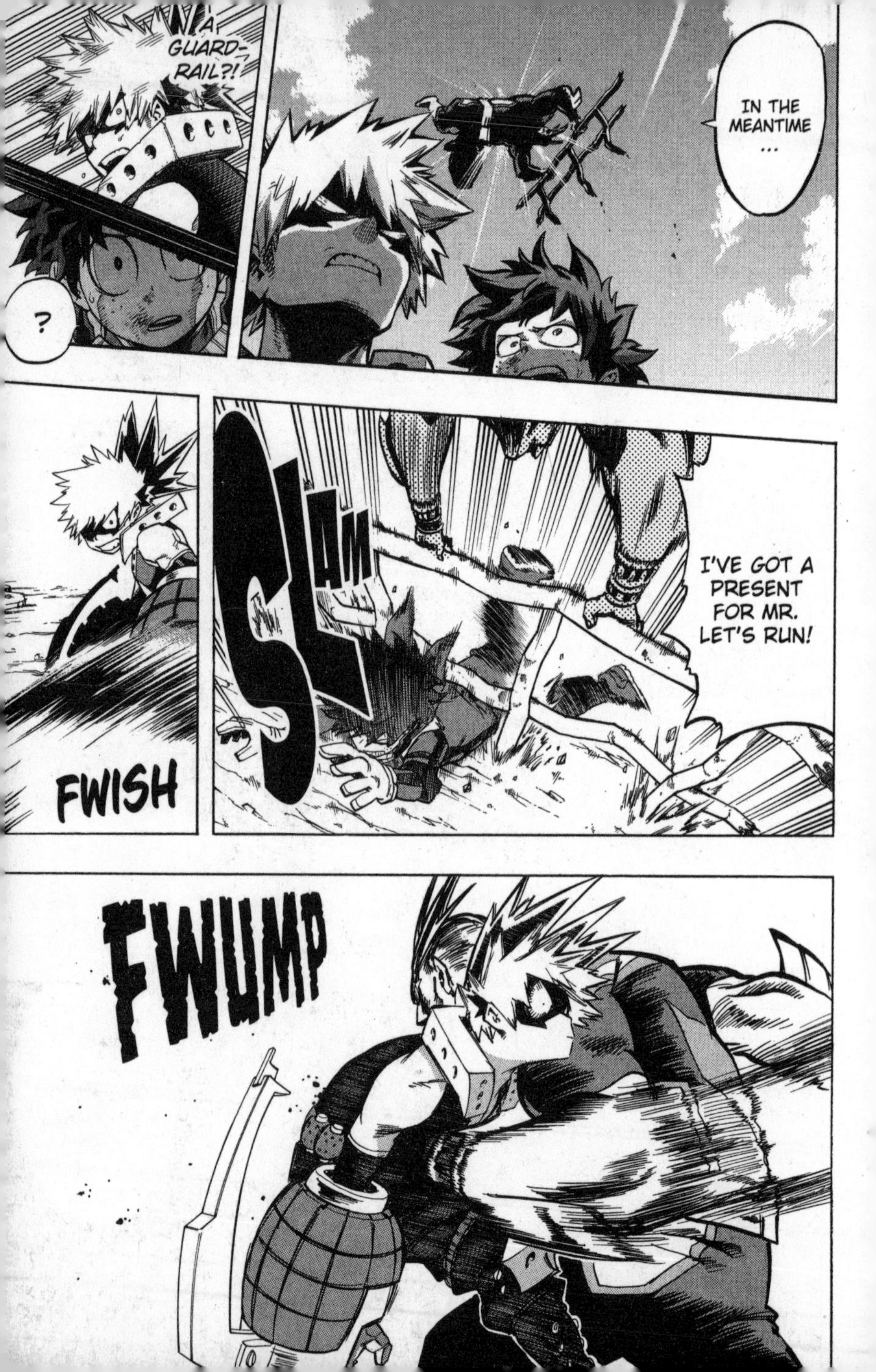
IN THE MEANTIME...
A GUARD-RAIL?!
?
I'VE GOT A PRESENT FOR MR. LET'S RUN!
SLAM
FWISH
FWUMP

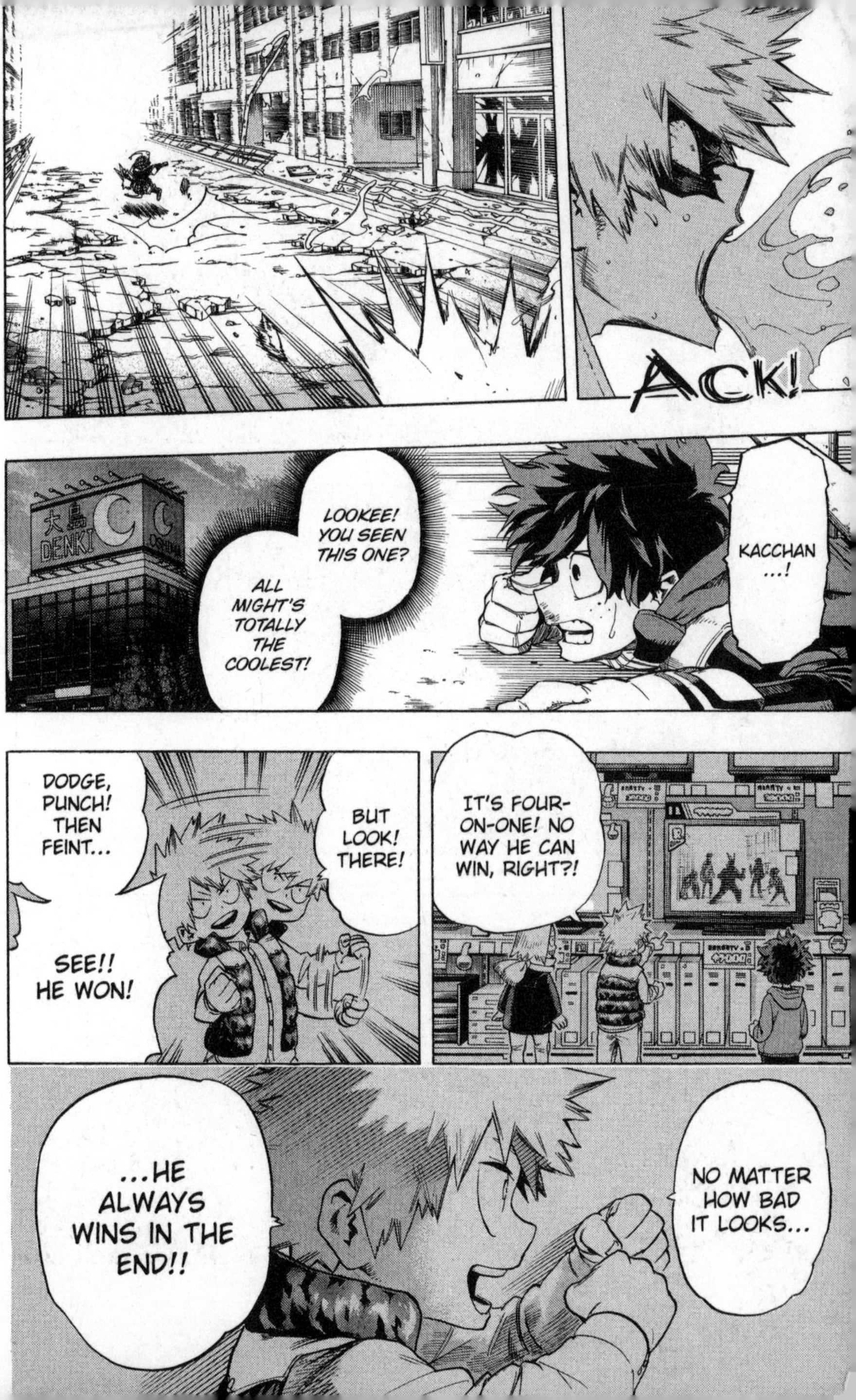
ACK!
KACCHAN ...!
LOOKEE! YOU SEEN THIS ONE?
ALL MIGHT'S TOTALLY THE COOLEST!
大島 DENKI
IT'S FOUR-ON-ONE! NO WAY HE CAN WIN, RIGHT?!
BUT LOOK! THERE!
DODGE, PUNCH! THEN FEINT...
SEE!! HE WON!
NO MATTER HOW BAD IT LOOKS...
...HE ALWAYS WINS IN THE END!!

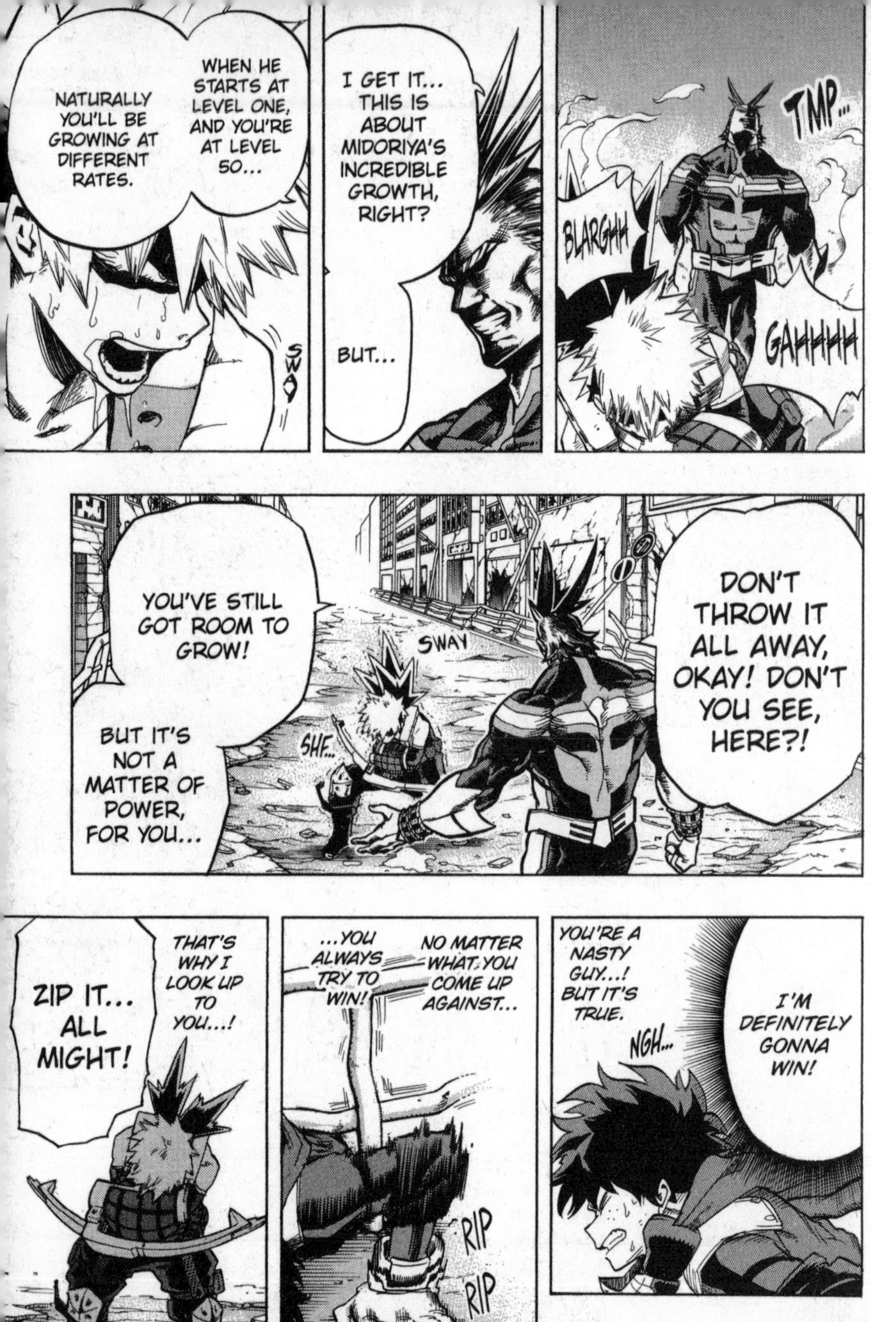
TMP...
BLARGHH
GAHHHHH
I GET IT... THIS IS ABOUT MIDORIYA'S INCREDIBLE GROWTH, RIGHT?
BUT...
WHEN HE STARTS AT LEVEL ONE, AND YOU'RE AT LEVEL 50...
NATURALLY YOU'LL BE GROWING AT DIFFERENT RATES.
SWAY
DON'T THROW IT ALL AWAY, OKAY! DON'T YOU SEE, HERE?!
SWAY
YOU'VE STILL GOT ROOM TO GROW!
BUT IT'S NOT A MATTER OF POWER, FOR YOU...
SHF...
I'M DEFINITELY GONNA WIN!
YOU'RE A NASTY GUY...! BUT IT'S TRUE.
NGH...
NO MATTER WHAT YOU COME UP AGAINST...
...YOU ALWAYS TRY TO WIN!
RIP
RIP
THAT'S WHY I LOOK UP TO YOU...!
ZIP IT... ALL MIGHT!

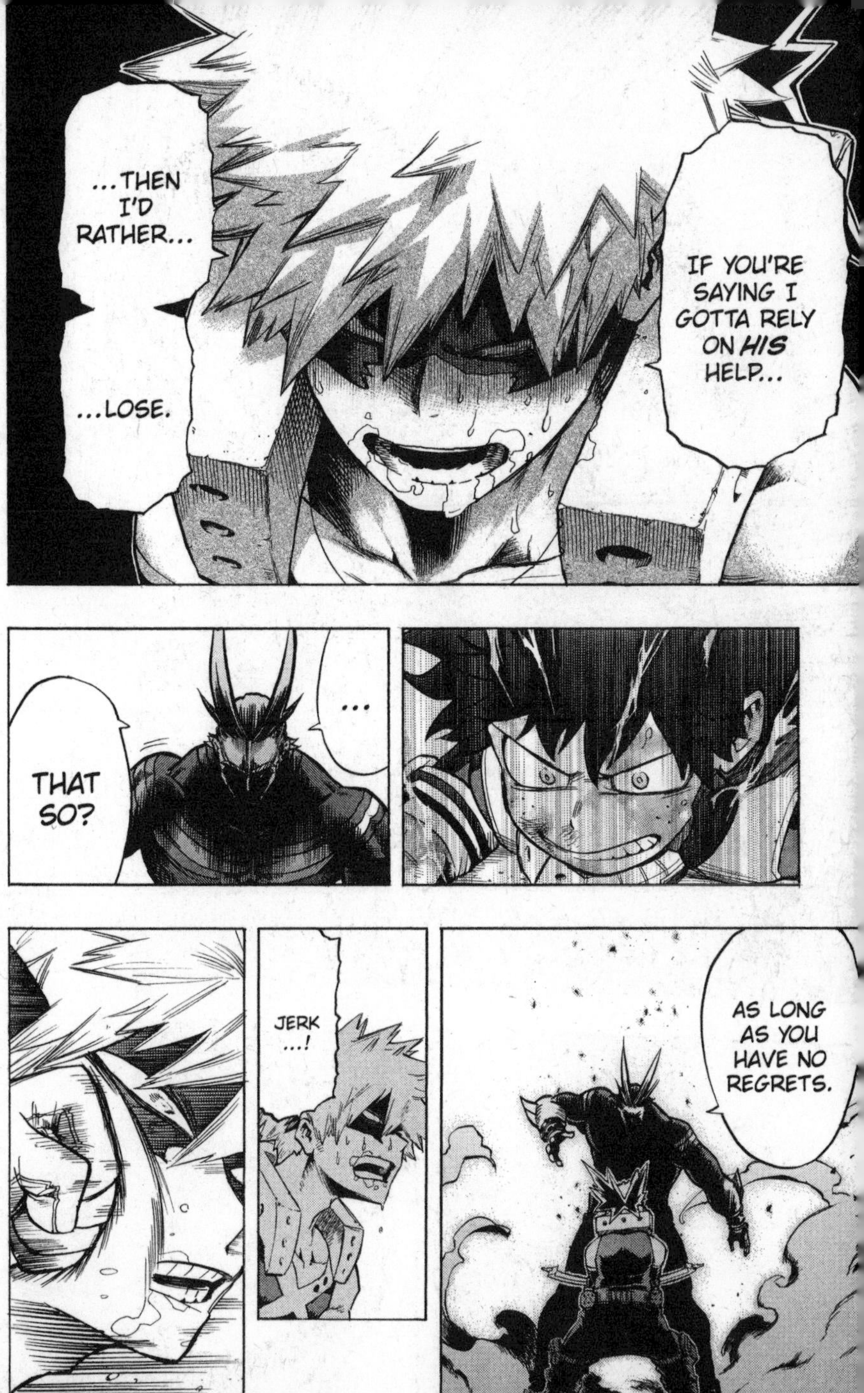
IF YOU'RE SAYING I GOTTA RELY ON *HIS* HELP...
...THEN I'D RATHER...
...LOSE.
...
THAT SO?
AS LONG AS YOU HAVE NO REGRETS.
JERK ...!

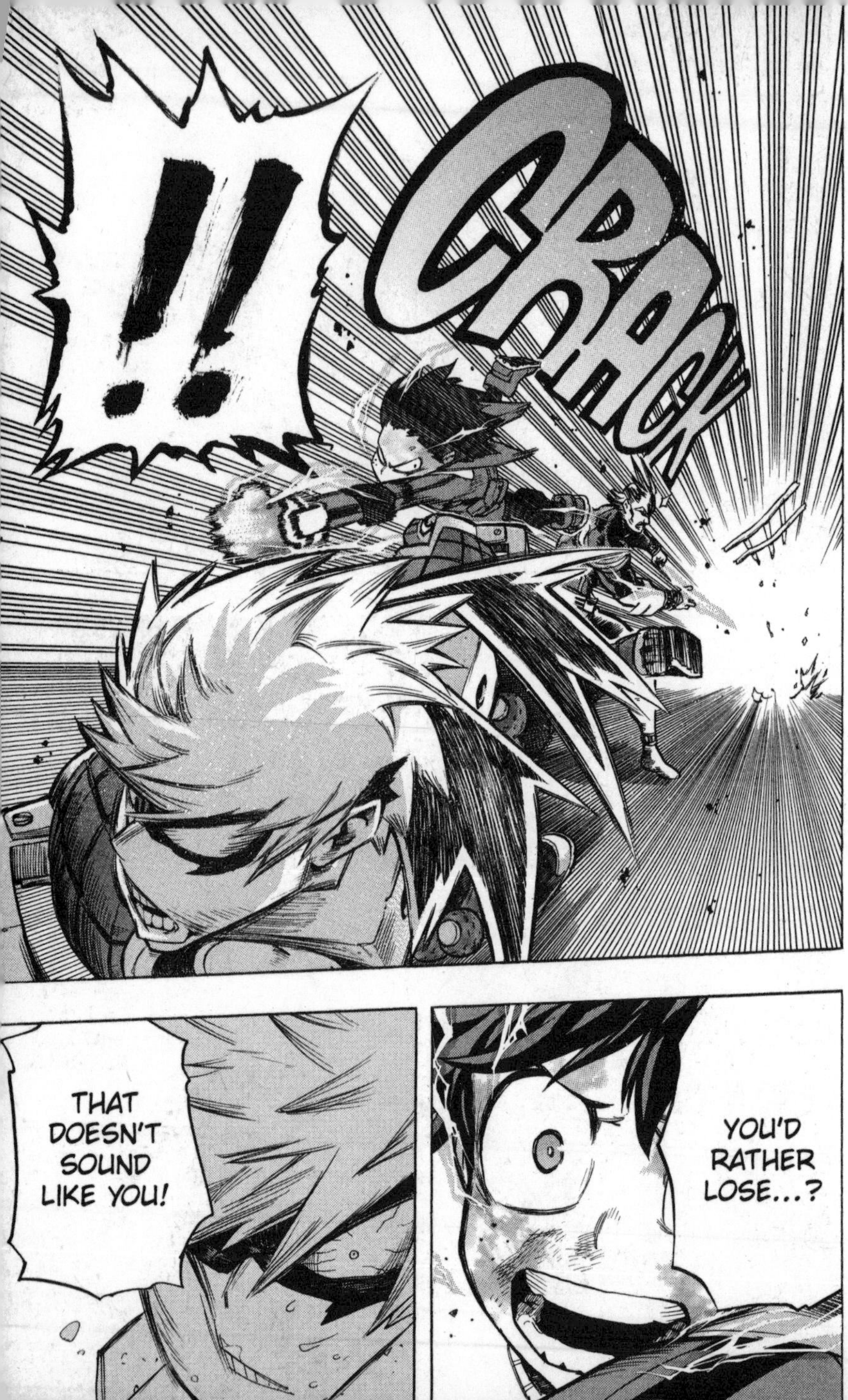
CRACK
!!
YOU'D RATHER LOSE...?
THAT DOESN'T SOUND LIKE YOU!

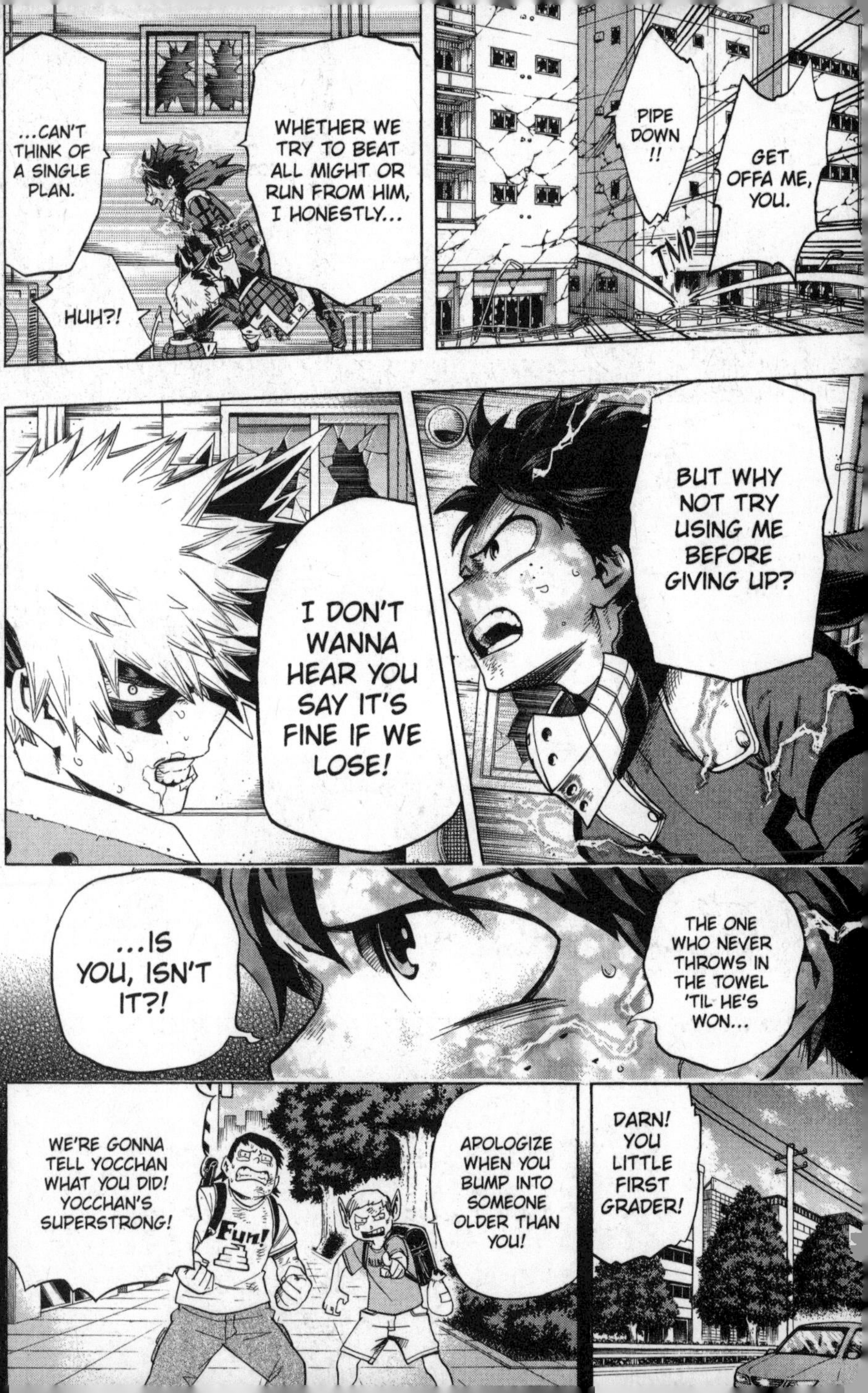
GET OFFA ME, YOU.
PIPE DOWN!!
TMP
WHETHER WE TRY TO BEAT ALL MIGHT OR RUN FROM HIM, I HONESTLY...
...CAN'T THINK OF A SINGLE PLAN.
HUH?!
BUT WHY NOT TRY USING ME BEFORE GIVING UP?
I DON'T WANNA HEAR YOU SAY IT'S FINE IF WE LOSE!
THE ONE WHO NEVER THROWS IN THE TOWEL 'TIL HE'S WON...
...IS YOU, ISN'T IT?!
DARN! YOU LITTLE FIRST GRADER!
APOLOGIZE WHEN YOU BUMP INTO SOMEONE OLDER THAN YOU!
WE'RE GONNA TELL YOCCHAN WHAT YOU DID! YOCCHAN'S SUPERSTRONG!
Fun!

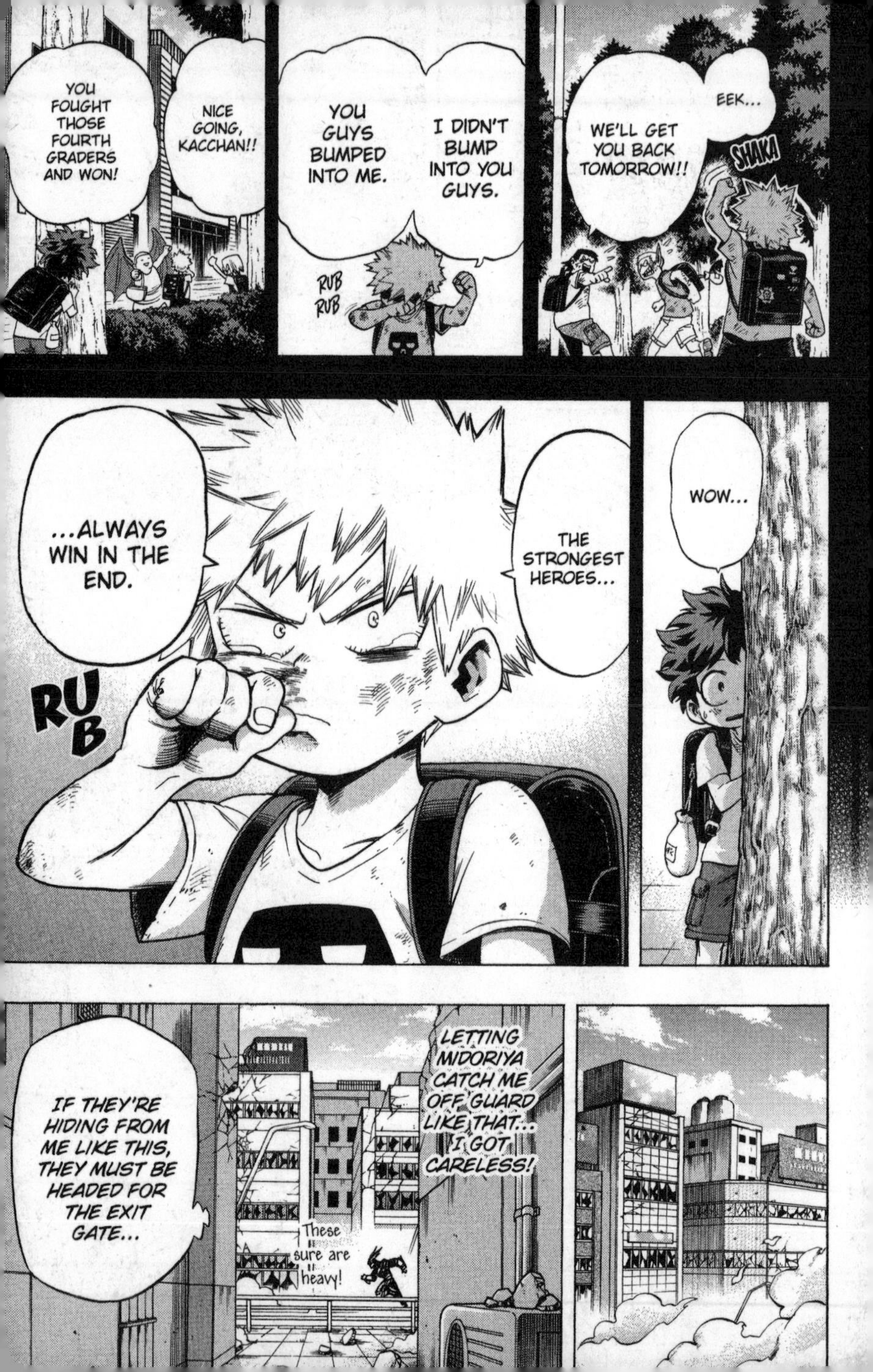
EEK...
WE'LL GET YOU BACK TOMORROW!!
SHAKA
I DIDN'T BUMP INTO YOU GUYS.
YOU GUYS BUMPED INTO ME.
RUB RUB
NICE GOING, KACCHAN!!
YOU FOUGHT THOSE FOURTH GRADERS AND WON!
WOW...
THE STRONGEST HEROES...
...ALWAYS WIN IN THE END.
RUB
LETTING MIDORIYA CATCH ME OFF GUARD LIKE THAT... I GOT CARELESS!
IF THEY'RE HIDING FROM ME LIKE THIS, THEY MUST BE HEADED FOR THE EXIT GATE...
These sure are heavy!

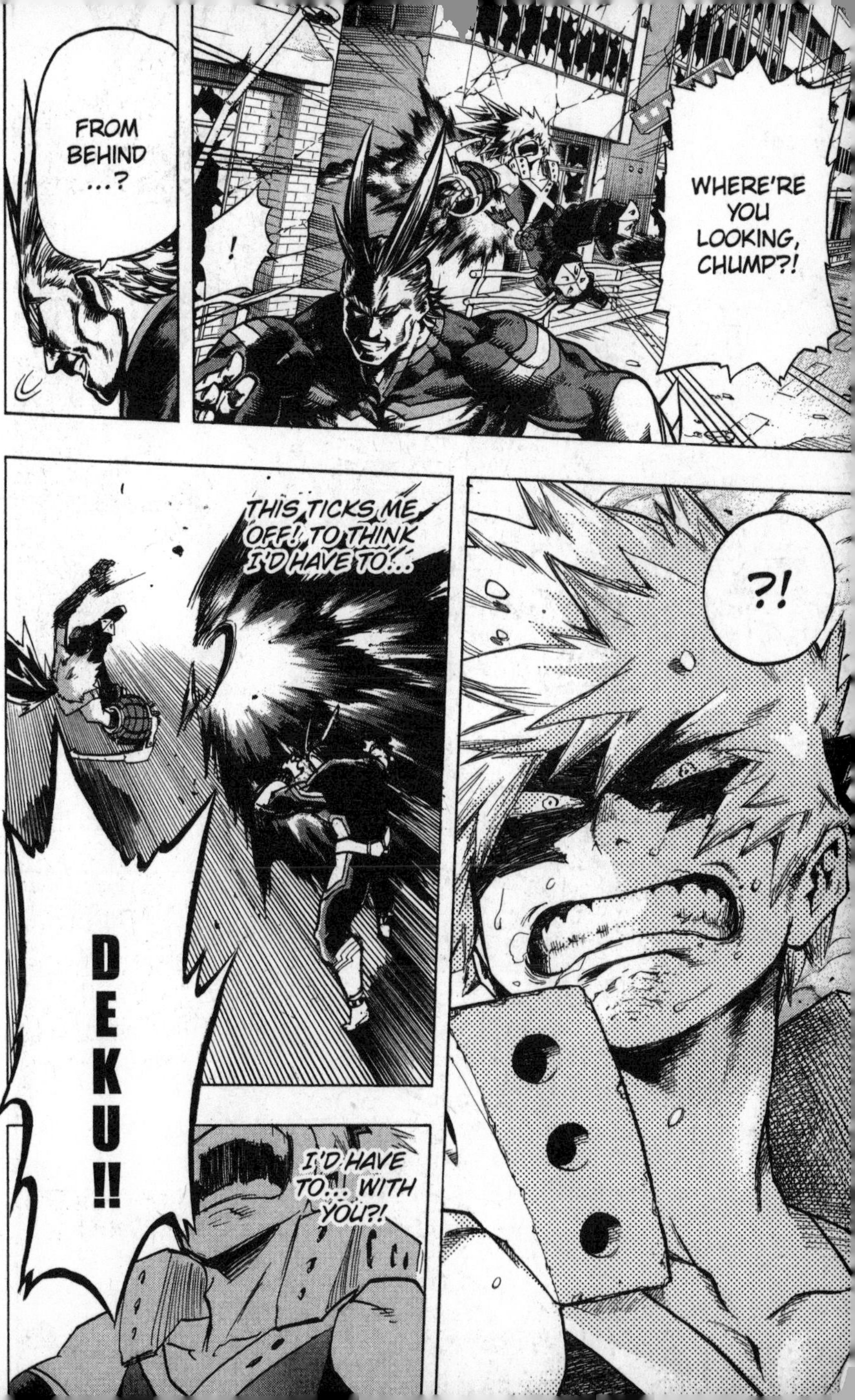
WHERE'RE YOU LOOKING, CHUMP?!
!
FROM BEHIND ...?
?!
THIS TICKS ME OFF! TO THINK I'D HAVE TO...
DEKU!!
I'D HAVE TO... WITH YOU?!

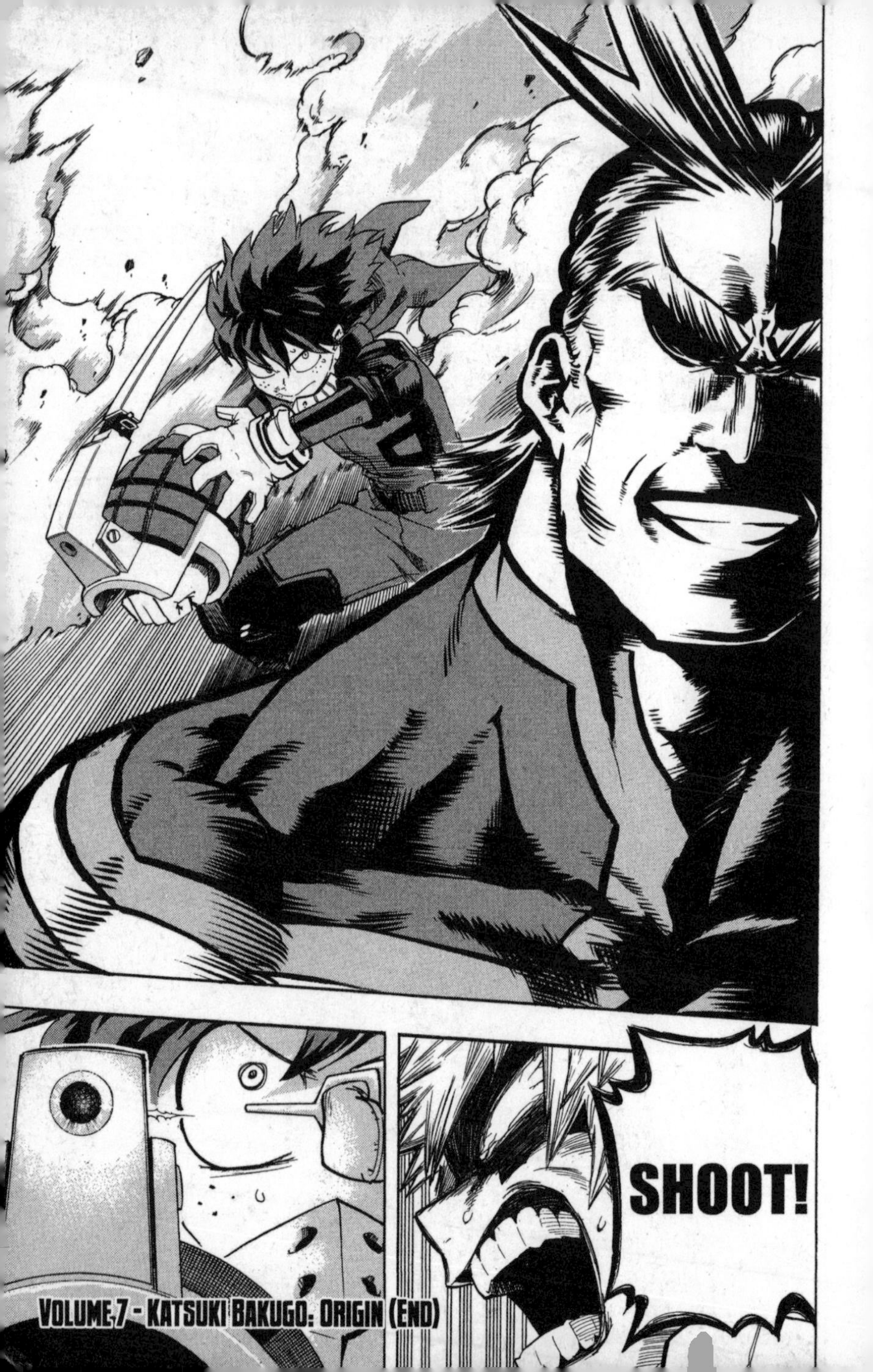
SHOOT!
VOLUME 7 - KATSUKI BAKUGO: ORIGIN (END)

THE FIRST CHARACTER POPULARITY POLL

FINAL TALLY (TOP 50)

1ST IZUKU MIDORIYA- 2,314 VOTES

2ND SHOTO TODOROKI- 1,987 VOTES

3RD KATSUKI BAKUGO- 1,764 VOTES

RANKING	NAME	VOTES
4th	Ochaco Uraraka	652
5th	All Might	627
6th	Tsuyu Asui	589
7th	Fumikage Tokoyami	485
8th	Tenya Ida	390
9th	Shota Aizawa	378
10th	Denki Kaminari	224
11th	Momo Yaoyorozu	197
12th	Hitoshi Shinso	186
13th	Itsuka Kendo	170
14th	Mashirao Ojiro	148
15th	Eijiro Kirishima	119
16th	Kyoka Jiro	107
17th	Kohei Horikoshi (the author)	89
18th	Minoru Mineta	65
19th	Tomura Shigaraki	62
20th	Toru Hagakura	57
	Mei Hatsume	
22nd	Stain	48
23rd	Midnight	45
24th	Mina Ashido	36
25th	Neito Monoma	31
26th	Mt. Lady	26
27th	Hanta Sero	24

RANKING	NAME	VOTES
28th	Endeavor	19
29th	Uwabami	17
30th	Mezo Shoji	16
31st	Yuga Aoyama	14
32nd	Nezu (Principal)	13
33rd	Mrs. Midoriya	10
	Gran Torino	
35th	Ibara Shiozaki	9
36th	Koji Koda	7
	Tetsutetsu Tetsutetsu	
	Present Mic	
	Cementoss	
	Toytoy	
41st	Fuyumi Todoroki	6
42nd	Thirteen	5
	Mrs. Todoroki	
44th	Sansa	4
	Yosetsu Awase	
46th	Kosei Tsuburaba	3
	Best Jeanist	
	Kamui Woods	
	Kurogiri	
	Nomu	

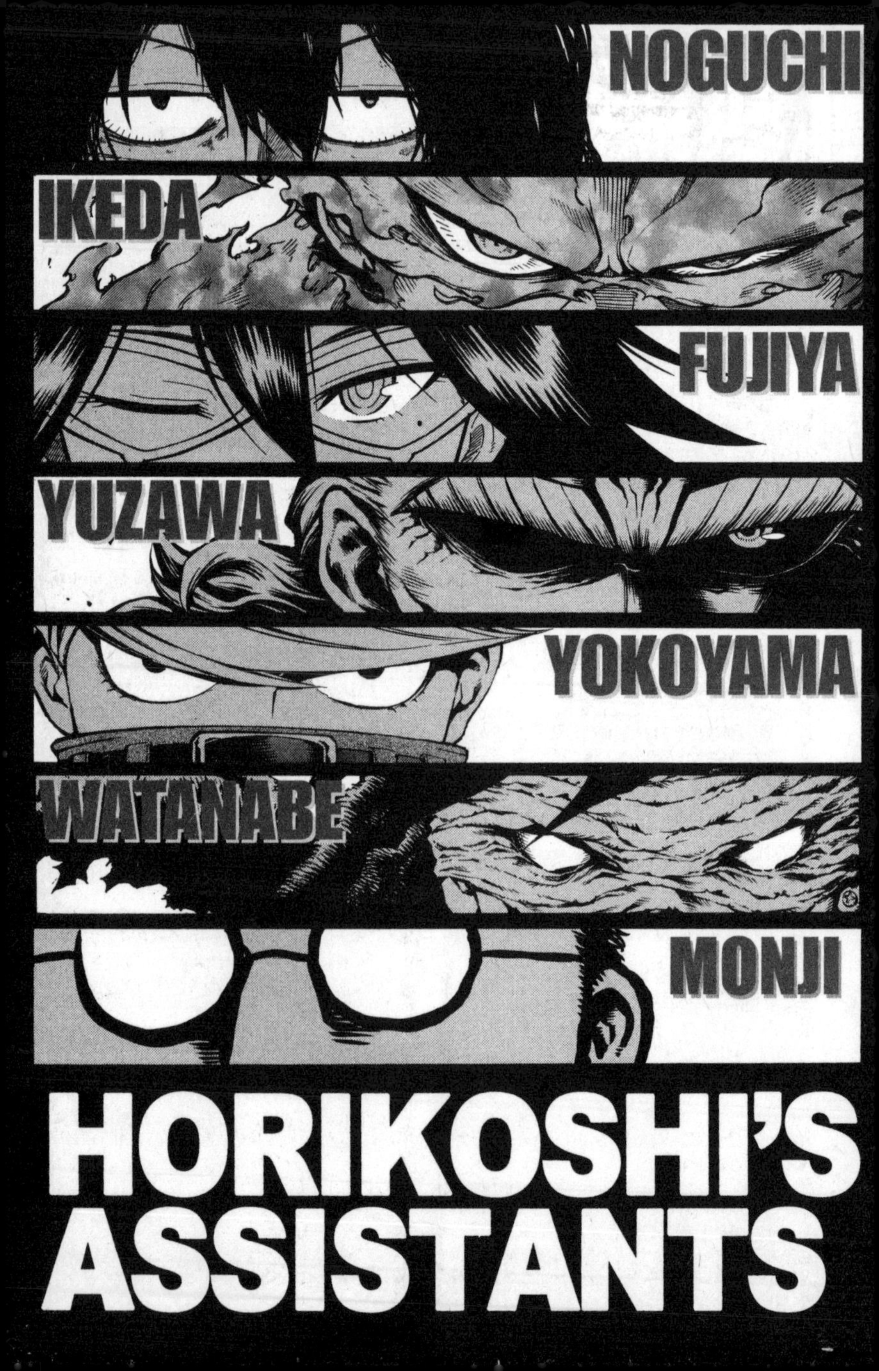
NOGUCHI
IKEDA
FUJIYA
YUZAWA
YOKOYAMA
WATANABE
MONJI

HORIKOSHI'S ASSISTANTS

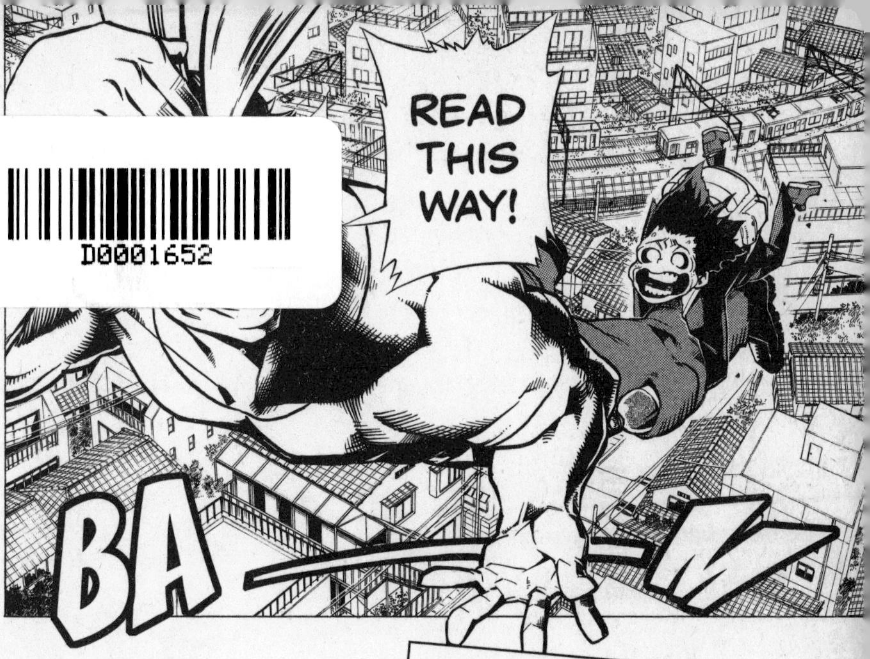
READ
THIS
WAY!
BA-M

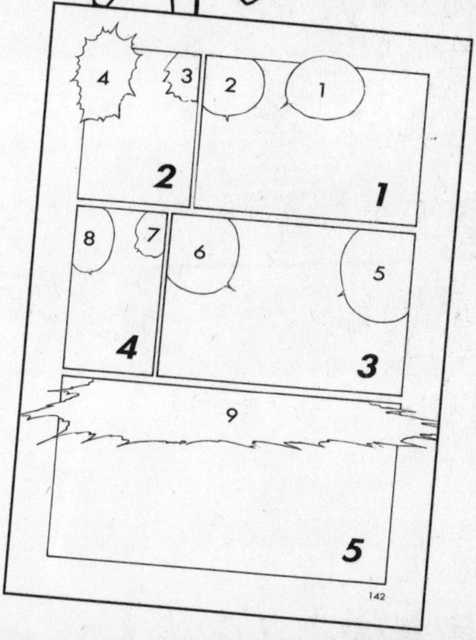
1
2
3
4
1
2
5
6
7
8
3
4
9
5
142

MY HERO ACADEMIA

reads from right to left, starting in the upper-right corner. Japanese is read from right to left, meaning that action, sound effects and word-balloon order are completely reversed from English order.